REVOLUTION PLANET EARTH

Paul Thor

REVOLUTION PLANET EARTH
Copyright © 2019 Paul Thor

All rights reserved. No part of this book may be used or reproduced by any means, graphic, electronic, or mechanical, including photocopying, recording, taping or by any information storage retrieval system without the written permission of the author except in the case of brief quotations embodied in critical articles and reviews.

Because of the dynamic nature of the Internet, any web addresses or links contained in this book may have changed since publication and may no longer be valid. The views expressed in this work are solely those of the author and do not necessarily reflect the views of the publisher, and the publisher hereby disclaims any responsibility for them.

Library of Congress Control Number: 2019920803
Paperback: 978-1-951822-51-4
Hardcover: 978-1-951822-52-1
eBook: 978-1-951822-53-8

30 Wall Street, 8th Floor
New York City, NY 10005
www.bookartpress.us

+1-800-351-3529

Contents

Introduction & Interface 5

What Is Man Anyway? 43

Governments 53

Earth's Taxes, Wages And Unemployment Fiascos 65

The EEC & The USA 105

Overview Of Global Economy 127

The Rich, The Working Class & The Poor 183

Slavery 195

Psychiatry/Psychology Vs Religious/Spiritual/Mental Freedom ... 207

Viruses, Cancers, Flues And Diseases 229

Science/Physics/Maths/Education/Experts 233

Drugs/Alcohol/Cigarettes/Sins/Crimes/Happiness 239

How One Should Live! 251

Money 257

The Banking/Finance/Loan Systems 275

Asylum Seekers/Illegal Immigrants 283

Class/Caste/Social Systems 293

Pollution 299

Nature 313

Art 325

Alternative Energy 331

The Theory Of All 347

Who Are The Powers-That-Be And Who Really Runs
This Planet? 353

Terrorism 411

The Truth 417

Appendix 1 455

Appendix 2 479

"An encyclopedia of information about the New World Order."

—Dean Henderson, Author of The Federal Reserve Cartel, The Grateful Unrich and Big Oil & Their Bankers https://www.amazon.co.uk/Dean-Henderson

"Paul Thor is on a crusade to change the world. Whether you agree with what he says, whether you believe him or not, there is much food for thought. Thor writes with a refreshing candour that often reads like a rant. He's plainly angry about the injustices and ills humanity suffers. But when you look over the plethora of statistics he offers, you can understand why. This is no erudite treatise. Thor places himself with the common man and his language is peppered with the lingo of everyday, and some profanity. Yet the power of his convictions shines through and draws you into his picture of the underbelly of the planet where puppet-masters pull the strings. Whatever one's views, Paul Thor provides a unique insight into his take on what is really going on in the world. He's persuasive, straightforward and intriguing. I recommend this book to anyone who is willing to examine a novel view of their environment. Also, to those who feel they have been pushed down as an underdog, because Thor's no-nonsense approach may give them hope."

—Elizabeth Bailey, author of historical romance and historical mystery www.elizabethbailey.co.uk

INTRODUCTION & INTERFACE

I thank you for taking the time to stop what you were doing, and to now enter my book - my world: The World of Truth! But it is not just my world but OUR world; or is it? Question is: Whose planet is this anyway and who is actually running it and where are we headed; going by past and current statistical, logical, historical and factual data and analysis?

I could have written a book which claims the truth that life is great and so wonderful (which it can be, don't get me wrong!) but for how many people can this be said to be true for, in this, our current economic age and climate? How many people have to hold down two or more jobs (sometimes including both parents) just to keep their heads just above the ever rising water? How many people have no jobs at all or little or no food (even though there is plenty of food and money to go round on this planet?) What actual future does Mankind have anyway and what could it be? What future do our children, teenagers and young graduates have? Why is the wealth and lands of planet Earth not being shared around instead of being hoarded by the few? Who really runs planet Earth, what are their names and how do they do it? What is Man anyway? Is money everything? Will we choke ourselves and our lovely planet to death by our own, ever-increasing pollution and greed? Why are taxes SO HIGH and why is everything going up and up in price, with inflation raging out of control like a newly discovered mutated epidemic virus or breed of wild animal? Taxes on this, rates on that,

VAT (value added tax) on everything we buy or sell: Council Tax/ Poll Tax, Fuel Tax, Phone Tax, Water rates (tax), gas tax, holiday/ airplane flight tax, Capital Gains Tax, Inheritance Tax, and just when we think there can be no more; another one is created: maybe a Pollution Tax or Air-Intake and Breathing tax: or a secret stealth tax – no-one knows about it except when it has already been passed by law and we have to pay it. Funny how we do not have votes and referendums on laws, taxes and other important issues any more (like leaving the Euro and the EEC and putting right a few important issues and matters). Oh, I'm sorry, maybe they have banned these and we were not informed about it – yes, that is very much probably 1000% the truth. We have Taxes on Taxes and taxes within taxes for frigging sakes!!!!! And how ironic is this – you work your whole life, paying your bills and taxes, hopefully being a good little citizen-slave-worker and then when you retire, can you believe this, they even tax your pension!? Is that not the Government sticking their dirty, filthy fingers up at you for being such a good, loyal and faithful servant to them and *THEIR* system (which WE allowed to come into existence and let it continue to exist and we do NOTHING effective about it!?) and for paying their wages? Yes, **WE** pay them (and vote them in!) to shaft us up the ass even more every year!!! I don't know about you, but I think it is time for **US**, the peoples of planet Earth to open our eyes, even if just a little bit, and even if we have to prop our eyelids open with some matchsticks; and have a REAL, HONEST-TO- GOODNESS look at what is really happening around us and in our lives on this beautiful little planet; which is spinning and revolving around that bright Sun of ours every day, and it has probably been doing so for many billions of years (despite what the scientists say). No wonder worry and stress are the number one mental ailments people suffer from around the world.

In this book, we are going to look at life from the highest level to the lowest, from the good, the bad and the very bad point of view and; actually and factually, we are going to look at how things really are and what factors and circumstances exist: NOT what we think or imagine they are; but what and how they actually and truly are in reality. It is SO IMPORTANT that you understand and believe what I say here (but muse it over, check it out and think for yourself too on the subjects and points I will bring up in my little big book. I request it. Why, because YOUR future, that of your family and friends and ALL mankind depend on it.) We are going to be honest and truthful with ourselves and we are going to take our blinkers off and look with our own true eyes.

Funny that, but lots of people have eyes and they look with them every day but they don't **see** fully what is to be seen or observe what is there and what is going on around them. Not really. Some do. But not many. And some just see what they want to see and even though they see other things and observe other facts, like people suffering, dying, etc., they just turn a blind eye. They just see what they want to see or what their bodies or mental machinery will allow them to see. Most people ONLY look or partially look at certain people and things and ignore or avoid the rest. Have you ever noticed that or maybe you have even done it yourself, huh? They just look at what they want to see or what they imagine they see or they are too afraid to see or whatever the case may be. But last time I checked, it costs us nothing to look and to observe and see what is there to be seen. That is how you know something or someone is there and that is how we learn, reason, invent, create and solve things – by looking, seeing and then analyzing, understanding and acting on what we see. Amazing that! Honestly, if we (all of Mankind) would only look and see what IS actually around us and see our true condition and circumstances, then so many things could be possible by just doing this one little simple action.

In fact, do it right now. I'm not joking. Just open your eyes (and even if they are open, REALLY open them and start looking around at the things, people or whatever there is around one right at this moment, and just **LOOK**, observe, perceive and **SEE** what is there. (You can look with your bodies' eyes; but best to look with your spiritual eyes, if you can!) NOT what you imagine or think is there: but just see/observe/ notice/put all your attention on what is actually and truly there! You can think thoughts, have mental pictures or analyze or do whatever you want to do while you are doing this, anything, just so long as you keep looking and seeing what _IS_ there. I don't even care if you talk to yourself. Do this for a while and you will see that nothing is going to happen to you for looking and seeing things and other people. You can look and see one thing, person, etc. as long as you want or as fast as you want; and you can look at as many things, people, etc. that you want – it is entirely your choice. The purpose of this is just to

REALLY look with and through your own eyes and just see exactly what IS there - that is all. You will also find that things will become more real to you and things or people will exist more for you. You are also communicating with them just by looking and seeing. Do this until you feel good or smile, then stop. This can all take a few minutes to a few hours or even days for certain people, depending on who is doing it. There is no pass or fail. Just do it until you feel good and ARE able to look and see what is there. That is all. We are all different and it is these essential qualities, characteristics, thoughts, etc. that make us who we are. When you feel and are certain that **YOU** are looking and seeing what is there – with your own eyes, then come back to this book again. Or if it is taking too long, just do it for half an hour to an hour every day until you can actually see/observe well and feel very good about it. Then stop. But continue to read my book.

Right, I am not going to hold anything back in this little big book. Honest! I don't care if you cry, get angry and want to smash the wall in or you want to run away and hide or even, dare I say it, you want to commit suicide: I am not sorry – and I don't care what you may do or go through while reading this book or after you have finished reading this book. You can do all these things now or later if you want, but I would prefer if you would wait (if you can) until after you have read my words and they have had time to sink in. (You might want to read this book twice and also get others to read it.) And doing any of the above actions will not actually help you in any way whatsoever but they may make you feel better: except committing suicide – which makes no-one feel any better and actually solves nothing. Why? Because the problems that Mankind faces today – and this includes each and every individual one of us - can NOT be run away from or avoided or shoved under the carpet, ignored or kept secret or locked up any more. They **MUST** be confronted and **NOW!!!!** before it is too late and there are no more chances left. THIS IS OUR LAST AND MAYBE ONLY CHANCE LEFT FOR REAL AND LASTING FREEDOM!!! Maybe you have heard all this before, many times, but you either did not believe it, did not know how to act or what to do about it or you were just too concerned about yourself or your own every-day-world and life's problems. But if we had of all united, joined and acted together EARLIER in mankind's history, in an organized and orderly manner, then maybe Mankind would not be in the sorry state he is in today? And if we had of known more about ourselves, this planet and more importantly who is covertly running it; then yes we could have acted sooner; but we didn't. But there is no time like the present and we have no time for regrets. Actually, all we ever have is the present. As the past is gone and only left recorded in our minds and the future has not happened: and it is only us who are going to create it, whether we know it or not. And if **WE** do not create our own future (the good future we really want) then someone else will. And I promise that it will not be a nice one! More on this later.

And how does one confront? One confronts by looking and seeing and by having the strong will and determination to do, change, create or cause something!!! Then anything is possible and then anything can be reasoned and solved. It's like magic.

It is my intention to cover all the relevant topics and subjects of why and how Man got into the state he is in today and, more importantly, what **_HE_** is going to do about it? One cannot blame God or others for how Mankind is today. And by '_HE_' I mean you and I and the rest of the good people who compose Mankind and who are able and aware enough to:

> Read and understand what I have written here and know it is true
> Be brave enough to do something _effective_ and sane about it
> Tell others about it and organize others and oneself into <u>effective</u> groups and organizations that can cause and make happen the necessary changes to put Mankind back on the <u>_RIGHT_</u> path and course to happiness and freedom (mental, spiritual, financial and whatever other forms freedom takes for one and all: It cannot be freedom just for the few; it must be freedom for all, even those with black, dark, nefarious souls; if they have any that is?)

What I will write about may not be funny and will not be pandering in to Man's general opinions of: 'What can be done about it all anyway? It's all pointless and hopeless! I am just one person, what can I do? It has nothing to do with me! It's a dog-eat-dog-world! Look after number one! I'm scared! ...' or whatever the common response is to taking more responsibility for the state and condition Mankind is in right now, at this point in time. We are at the crossroads of: this

9

way and Man will win and be in Nirvana, Eden, Heaven - FREE and HAPPY and in control of himself and his own destiny: Goodness will reign. The other way leads to complete and utter slavery, domination, control by the Powers-That-Be, their Technologists and those at the top: the Royal Families, the Super Rich and Wealthy Families with ulterior motives [sadly not good]). This road also leads to oblivion, sadness, pain, suffering, gloom, utter poverty and loss of Self or the mind, Spirit and Soul, and Evil (people, if one can call them people?) in total supreme power and control. To make a point: Did you ever see someone die or have someone die in front of your own eyes or in your arms; or see your child die or see your child have an accident or even have your pet die, well? How did you feel? You did not feel good at all did you? You felt terrible (the evil people on Earth would **NOT** feel bad about any of this by the way [even if they pretended to cry] – they would just laugh, smirk or feel good inside.) Well this is nothing compared to the future pain, misery and suffering Mankind could be forced to experience if he makes the VERY BIG MISTAKE of taking the wrong turn at the crossroads' junction – even if it is not signposted or he does not know the way to go. Fact!!!!!!

My intentions are good. Feel it in my words? As you read this book you may squirm or feel tired or go through some weird mental or spiritual stuff. This is normal and good. Just keep reading and you will come out the other end a different, hopefully better (sadly we are not all not of the same ilk or substance) person. Hopefully a newer, more moral, better, gooder one. It is my intention, through my words, to communicate to you what is really going on on Planet Earth, who is doing it, why and how; and by the end, to put forward to you and get you thinking of possible ethical, legal and moral solutions. Nothing in this book condones violence, crime, bad behavior, murder, racism, anarchy or anything else illegal or sinful; and the destruction and decay of the society we live in today. But on the other hand: change is necessary and vital at this time – but it must be constructive, positive and bring about: a better, fairer, saner world, with fair and good, just systems (that benefit and help everyone, not just *the* few!) and a better society than the one we currently have today. And it must be also be said that some laws and taxes on this planet are completely unjust, unfair, too high and are there not to help US but to help them and to further make us suffer and be their slaves, with more and more loss of freedom. To keep us down. Now what I have said above is where I am coming from and what I am all about: good and positive changes for all – and that includes changes in those who are doing us wrong!! But, however, if we have to fight or go to war to attain, keep and maintain our good lives, happiness and freedom, then so be it. This would be the last resort of course but one that must be kept in mind as an option and this option must ONLY be continued until we force those to give us what we want. No more.

I believe in simple, plain English that communicates to people and can be understood by them and everyone else. I am not writing a treatment or dissertation for some top professors or geniuses/savants. And I am not writing for the 'experts' and critics. I am not against any of these people either. Some do vital and important work. Others do not. No. I am writing this book for everyone so they can understand it and use it to good effect to help themselves, Mankind and this lovely planet that we live on today. I hope you enjoy and are with me on the adventure of knowledge within my book and on the future life and world we are going to create on this planet, as a result of my book and of us working together to make it happen!?

And please note, while you are reading this book, the Earth is spinning about its axis at about 1,000 mph; the Earth is orbiting the Sun at 70,000 mph and our entire solar system is orbiting the center of our Milky Way galaxy at approximately 515,000 mph! Enjoy your high speed read.

We all like statistics, so I thought I would give you some. Do not forget that the population of Earth today is 7 billion and growing! This in itself poses a lot of problems, which are in addition to the topics I will cover in this book.

Note: all stats, graphs, numbers and percentages in this book are approximate and can and do change at any time but they do give one a good indication of what is going on:

World Poverty Statistics

Statistic Verification
Source: Global Issues, The Human Development Report
Research Date: 7.8.2014

World Poverty Statistics	
Total Percentage of World Population that lives on less than $2.50 a day	50%
Total number of people that live on less than $2.50 a day	3 Billion
Total Percentage of People that live on less than $10 a day	80%
Total percent of World Populations that live where income differentials are widening	80%
Total Percentage of World Income the richest 20% account for	75%
Total Number of children that die each day due to Poverty	22,000
Total Number of People in Developing Countries with Inadequate Access to Water	1.1 billion
Total Number of School Days lost to Water Related Illness	443 million school days
Child World Poverty Statistics	
Number of children in the world	2.2 billion
Number of Children that live in Poverty	1 billion
Total Number of Children that live without adequate shelter	640 million (1 in 3)
Total Number of Children without access to safe water	400 million (1 in 5)
Total Number of Children with no access to Health Services	270 million (1 in 7)
Total Number of Children who die annually from lack of access to safe drinking water and adequate sanitation	1.4 million

Poverty to Wealthy Ratio Statistics	
Year	**Ratio of People at Poverty to Wealthy Level**
2013	88 to 1

1992	72 to 1
1973	44 to 1
1950	35 to 1
1913	11 to 1
1820	3 to 1

World Hunger Statistics

Statistic Verification
Source: Facing the Future, Think Quest, Hunger Relief Organizations
Research Date: 5.7.2013

World Hunger Statistics	
Total number of children that die every year from hunger	1.5 million
Percent of world population considered to be starving	33%
Time between deaths of people who die from hunger	3.6 seconds
Total number of people in the world who suffer from hunger and malnutrition	800 million
Total number of people who do not have enough to eat	936 million people
Total percentage who do not have enough to eat who live in developing countries	98%
Total percentage of world's hungry that live in 7 countries	65%
Number of people who died of hunger today	20,864
Total number of people who will die of hunger this year	7,615,360
Total percentage of U.S. households that are at risk of hunger	11%

Plastic Bag Statistics

Statistic Verification
Source: Smart Green Tips, Earth 911
Date Verified: 4.21.2012

Plastic Statistics	
Total number of plastic bags used worldwide annually	1 trillion
Total number of plastic bags China consumes everyday	3 billion
Total number of plastic bags used every minute	1 million
Total number of years it takes for a plastic bag to degrade	1,000 years
Total amount of plastic bags that were discarded in 2008	3.5 million tons
Total amount of plastic floating in every square mile of ocean	46,000 pieces
Average amount of plastic bags consumed per family in 4 trips to the grocery store	60
Percent of plastic made every year that will end up in the ocean	10%
Total amount of plastic bags used by U.S. citizens every year	100 billion
Average amount of plastic bottles a U.S. household will use each year	500 plastic bottles
Percent of household waste that is plastic	11%

Environmental Statistics

Statistic Verification
Source: Energy Information Administration, Environmental Defense
Research Date: August 1st, 2014

We know power plants have a heavy impact on the environment, but just how much pollution are we putting into the environment?

Environmental Statistics	Data
Metric tons of CO2 emitted each year by U.S. cars and trucks	314
Average number of ocean water oil spills each day	27
Number of cars and trucks on the road in the U.S.	250 Million
Number of acres of land paved annually	1.3 Million
Pounds of chemical pesticides used on residential lawns annually	80 Million
Tons of fertilizer used annually	70 Million
Percent of U.S. land that is forest area	33.08 %

Greenhouse Gas Emission (GHG) Statistics	Percent
Percent of GHG made up of CO2	95 %
Percent of GHG made up of methane	4 %
Percent of GHG made up of nitrous oxide and fluorinated gases	1 %

Facilities Producing Carbon Dioxide Equivalent mmtCO2e	Data
Tons of carbon dioxide equivalent (mmtCO2e) emitted by power plants annually	2,324
Tons of mmtCO2e emitted by petroleum refineries annually	183
Number of U.S. facilities with emissions over 7 mmtCO2e	100
U.S. Energy Usage Statistics	**Data**
Gigawatt hours of electricity used annually	3,771,908
Percent of electricy generated from Coal-Fired power plants	48%

Percent of electricy generated from Liquid Petroleum plants	6 %
Percent of electricy generated from Natural Gas energy producers	21%
Percent of electricy generated from Nuclear power plants	19
Percent of electricy generated from Conventional Hydroelectric turbines	5%
Percent of electricy generated from Solor, Wind, and Geo-Thermal energy	1%

Statistic Verification
Source: UK Guardian, World Book
Research Date: 9.5.2012
Deforestation has continued at an alarming rate since the early 1950s. Almost half of the original forest habitat has been cut down. The removal of trees without sufficient reforestation has resulted in damage to habitat, biodiversity loss and aridity. It has adverse impacts on biosequestration of atmospheric carbon dioxide.

Deforestation Statistics	Hectares Lost Per Year
Square miles of mature forest that originally covered the planet (pre 1947)	5.9 million
Square miles of mature forest that have been cut down	3 million

Top 10 Most Endangered Forests		
Endangered forest	Region	Remaining habitat
Indo-Burma	Asia-Pacific	5%
New Caledonia	Asia-Pacific	5%
Sundaland	Asia-Pacific	7%
Philippines	Asia-Pacific	7%
Atlantic Forest	South America	8%

Top 10 Most Endangered Forests		
Endangered forest	**Region**	**Remaining habitat**
Mountains of Southwest China	Asia-Pacific	8%
California Floristic Province	North America	10%
Coastal Forests of Eastern Africa	Africa	10%
Madagascar & Indian Ocean Islands	Africa	10%
Eastern Afromontane	Africa	11%

Countries with highest deforestation of natural forests 2000-2005		
	Country	**Hectares Lost Per Year**
1	Brazil	-3,466,000
2	Indonesia	-1,447,800
3	Russian Federation	-532,200
4	Mexico	-395,000
5	Papua New Guinea	-250,200
6	Peru	-224,600
7	United States of America	-215,200
8	Bolivia	-135,200
9	Sudan	-117,807
10	Nigeria	-82,000

Countries with the most forest cover		
	Country	**Hectares of Forest**
1	Russian Federation	808,790,000
2	Brazil	477,698,000
3	Canada	310,134,000
4	United States of America	303,089,000
5	China	197,290,000
6	Australia	163,678,000
7	Democratic Republic of the Congo	133,610,000
8	Indonesia	88,495,000

9	Peru	68,742,000
10	India	67,701,000
11	Sudan	67,546,000
12	Mexico	64,238,000
13	Colombia	60,728,000
14	Angola	59,104,000
15	Bolivia	58,740,000
16	Venezuela (Bolivarian Republic of)	47,713,000
17	Zambia	42,452,000
18	United Republic of Tanzania	35,257,000
19	Argentina	33,021,000
20	Myanmar	32,222,000

Price of Gasoline by Country
Category: Financial

Statistic Verification
Source: US Department of Energy
Date Verified: 12.26.2013
This table represents the relative price of gasoline by country. Italy ranks the highest at $2.49 per liter while Venezuela only pays $0.11 per liter. The United States falls below the global average at just $0.97 per liter. The price per liter is in US dollars.

Rank	Country	Price of Gasoline (1 liter)
1	Italy	$2.49
2	Norway	2.43
3	Greece	2.42
4	Netherlands	2.42
5	Finland	2.35
6	United Kingdom	2.30
7	Portugal	2.28
8	Monaco	2.28

9	Denmark	2.24
10	Ireland	2.23
11	Sweden	2.23
12	Turkey	2.22
13	Germany	2.21
14	Israel	2.21
15	Belgium	2.21
16	Hong Kong	2.19
17	Iceland	2.15
18	France	2.08
19	Slovenia	2.07
20	Slovakia	2.07
21	Switzerland	2.03
22	Palestinian Territory	2.01
23	Spain	2.00
24	Malta	2.00
25	Hungary	1.98
26	Guernsey	1.98
27	Albania	1.97
28	Austria	1.96
29	Lithuania	1.96
30	Croatia	1.95
31	Cyprus	1.94
32	Latvia	1.91
33	Montenegro	1.91
34	Poland	1.90
35	South Korea	1.90
36	Estonia	1.88
37	Luxembourg	1.87
38	Czech Republic	1.87
39	Macedonia	1.87
40	Serbia	1.87
41	Romania	1.86

42	Bulgaria	1.84
43	Uruguay	1.79
44	Mauritius	1.78
45	New Zealand	1.78
46	Bosnia And Herzegovina	1.73
47	Singapore	1.66
48	Papua New Guinea	1.57
49	Macao	1.55
50	Chile	1.53
51	Dominican Republic	1.53
52	Zimbabwe	1.50
53	Uganda	1.50
54	Costa Rica	1.44
55	Japan	1.43
56	Peru	1.43
57	Argentina	1.40
58	Ukraine	1.34
59	Jordan	1.34
60	Australia	1.34
61	Honduras	1.32
62	China	1.32
63	Tanzania	1.30
64	Moldova	1.30
65	Morocco	1.28
66	El Salvador	1.26
67	Georgia	1.26
68	Nepal	1.26
69	Bangladesh	1.25
70	Cambodia	1.25
71	Sri Lanka	1.24
72	Nicaragua	1.22
73	Canada	1.22
74	Thailand	1.22

75	India	1.21
76	Armenia	1.21
77	Brazil	1.21
78	Afghanistan	1.20
79	Lebanon	1.20
80	Jamaica	1.20
81	Colombia	1.19
82	South Africa	1.18
83	Guatemala	1.18
84	Philippines	1.17
85	Taiwan	1.17
86	Mongolia	1.15
87	Namibia	1.15
88	Vietnam	1.14
89	Ethiopia	1.13
90	Panama	1.11
91	Ghana	1.10
92	Botswana	1.08
93	Myanmar	1.00
94	Pakistan	1.00
95	United States	0.97
96	Puerto Rico	0.96
97	Tunisia	0.96
98	Russia	0.92
99	Belarus	0.90
100	Mexico	0.84
101	Azerbaijan	0.82
102	Uzbekistan	0.80
103	Syria	0.80
104	Kazakhstan	0.79
105	Malaysia	0.61
106	Nigeria	0.61
107	Bolivia	0.54

108	Indonesia	0.53
109	Sudan	0.51
110	Iraq	0.48
111	United Arab Emirates	0.47
112	Iran	0.40
113	Ecuador	0.39
114	Oman	0.31
115	Algeria	0.30
116	Bahrain	0.27
117	Egypt	0.27
118	Qatar	0.27
119	Kuwait	0.23
120	Saudi Arabia	0.13
121	Libya	0.12
122	Venezuela	0.11

ALL THE ABOVE FROM: Statisticbrain.com

WRITER: This is a **lot** of money for oil producing countries (OPEC); Oil Production Companies and a lot of income to governments in the form of Taxes!

Average Rise In Sea Level:

2mm: Average yearly rise in sea level since the 19th century, fastest rate of increase in 2,100 years

Number of cars in the World:

SOURCE: statisticbrain.com

Total Cars Produced In The World

Statistic Verification
Source: OICA

Research Date: 1.1.2014
The first practical automobile with a petrol engine was built by Karl Benz in 1885 in Mannheim, Germany. Around the world, there were about 806 million cars and light trucks on the road in 2007, consuming over 260 billion gallons of gasoline and diesel fuel yearly.

Year	Cars Produced
2013	65,140,268
2012	63,069,541
2011	59,929,016
2010	58,264,852
2009	47,772,598
2008	52,726,117
2007	53,201,346
2006	49,918,578
2005	46,862,978
2004	44,554,268
2003	41,968,666
2002	41,358,394
2001	39,825,888
2000	41,215,653
1999	39,759,847
*Numbers do not include commercial vehicles	

Rank	Country	2013	2012	2011
1	China	16,664,502	15,523,658	
2	Japan	7,859,320	8,554,219	7,158,525
3	Germany	5,438,155	5,388,456	5,871,918
5	U.S.A.	4,540,985	4,105,853	2,966,133
4	South Korea	4,160,596	4,167,089	4,221,617
6	India	3,212,988	3,285,496	3,053,871
7	Brazil	2,808,094	2,623,704	2,534,534

11	Spain	1,848,867	1,539,680	1,819,453
9	Mexico	1,822,525	1,810,007	1,657,080
8	Russia	1,801,014	1,968,789	1,738,163
10	France	1,488,100	1,682.814	1,931,030
13	U.K.	1,464,390	1,464,983	1,343,810
22	Thailand	1,092,101	945,100	549,770
14	Czech Republic	1,020,835	1,171,774	1,191,968
17	Slovakia	1,001,071	900,000	639,763
15	Canada	996,163	1,040,298	990,483
21	Indonesia	884,241	743,501	561,863
12	Iran	620,600	871,997	1,413,276
18	Turkey	606,783	576,660	639,734
23	Malaysia	528,487	509,621	496,440
19	Argentina	521,866	497,376	577,233
16	Poland	508,732	540,000	785,000
25	Romania	448,759	326,556	310,243
24	Italy	444,848	396,817	485,606
20	Belgium	324,700	507,204	562,386
21	South Africa	286,487	274,873	312,265
22	Taiwan	282,189	278,043	288,523
23	Hungary	186,400	215,440	211,218

How Many Cars Are There In The World Today?

As of 2012, there are 1.1 billion automobiles on the earth, which is a 57% increase from the 700 million automobiles that were on earth's roads just 8 years earlier in 2004.

In short, there are so many cars in the world today that the fuel burnt on the world's roads by this many cars emits 1.73 billion metric tons (equivalent to 3.81 trillion pounds) of carbon dioxide into the atmosphere every year.

That is equal to burning all of the coal in a fully-loaded coal train that stretches 304,000 miles, long enough to wrap 12 times around the earth at the equator. And that's just the pollution from the 1.1 billion automobiles in just one year!

The USA has over 250 million vehicles and China is expected to overtake USA as the largest automobile market on the planet within the next decade.

The 1.1 billion automobiles in 2012 already average a set of new tires about every 2 years, or 2.2 billion tires annually, and those 2.2 billion tires consume over half of the earth's rubber production, which of course burns even more fuel.

This will all rise as China, Brazil, Russia and India continue to develop, industrialize and expand. And this applies to other developing and third world countries too.

Note: all of the above data ONLY includes cars. It does not include airplanes, boats, cargo ships, tankers, cruise ships, trucks, motorbikes, vans, tractors, harvesters, transporters, generators and lorries. My god, this is staggering! A world full of Carbon (and nuclear waste too) cannot be good? One does not need to be a mathematician or physicist to work out the total cumulative bad effects and side effects caused by all of this gobal pollution!!!???

Trees Cut Down Each Year:

3 billion to 6 billion trees are cut down each year globally

Forest area is reduced by 60,000 square kilometers per year globally

Forests cover a third of our planet's land

Forest area decreased worldwide by 0.22% per year in the period 1990-2000 and 0.18% per year between 2000 and 2005

Water Statistics:

Statistic Verification
Source: UNICEF, The Water Project
Date Verified: 2.23.2012

Water Statistics	Data
Total Percent of Water used on Agriculture and Irrigation	70%

Total Percent of Water used for Domestic Purposes	10%
Total Percentage of All Water that is Salt Water	97.5%
Total Percent of Earth Surface that is Water	71%
Total Percent of Fresh Water / Water Locked in Glaciers	2.5%
Average household water use annually (including outdoor)	1 2 7 , 4 0 0 gallons
Average daily household water use (including outdoor)	350 gallons
Total Number of people who do not have access to safe water	884 million (1 in 8)

Water Use Statistics	
Daily indoor per capita water use is 69.3 gallons	**Note: Per Capita means: per person**

Use	Galls per Capita
Showers	11.6
Clothes Washers	15
Dishwashers	1
Toilets	18.5
Baths	1.2
Leaks	9.5
Faucets	10.9
Other Domestic Uses	1.6

Statistic Verification
Source: MSNBC, Kinsey Institute, Reuters
Date Verified: 8.10.2011

Number of Adult Films released yearly	11,000

Amount Paid by the California Adult Film Industry in Yearly Taxes	$36 Million
2006 Adult Film revenues	$13.3 Billion

Adult Film Industry Breakdown	In Billions
Video Sales / Rentals	$3.62
Internet	$2.84
Cable/PPV/In-Room/Phone Sex	$2.19
Exotic Dance Clubs	$2
Novelties	$1.73
Magazines	$0.95
2006 Total Sales	$13.3
2005 Total Sales	$12.62
Percent of Adult Films rentals in hotel rooms	55 %
Average viewing time of an Adult Film in a hotel room	12 Minutes
Percent of University Students who had sex over Webcams or Telephone	87 %
Percent of website visits that are sexual in nature	60 %
Percent of Adults who watched an Adult Film in the last year	25 %
Percent of Women who view Adult Films Regularly	17 %
Percent of female Adult site visitors	33%
Percent of Adults who believe looking at nude pictures in 'morally acceptable"	38 %
Number one internet search term	"sex"
Number of unique visits to adult websites per month	72 Million

Online Adult Site Visitor Demographics	
Percent Male	77 %
Average Age	41
Average Annual Income	$60,000

Percent Married	46 %
Number of Websites offering child pornography	100,000
Percent who say Porn has not lowered their sexual activity with their partner	66 %

Reasons Cited for Viewing Pornography	
Masturbation / Physical Release	72 %
Sexual Arousal of Self / Others	69 %
Curiosity	54 %
Fantasize things I would not necessarily want in real life	43 %
Distract Myself	38 %

Statistic Verification	
Source: Facing the Future, Think Quest, Hunger Relief Organizations	
Date Verified: 3.8.2012	

From: Statisticbrain.com

World Cancer Statistics:

Cases Per 100,000 People:
    Denmark – 326
    Ireland – 317
    Australia – 314
    New Zealand – 309
    Belgium – 307
    France – 300
    USA – 300
    Norway – 299
    Canada – 297

Czech Republic – 295
Israel – 288
The Netherlands – 287
Luxembourg – 284
Hungary – 283
Iceland – 282
Germany – 282
Uruguay – 280
Italy – 274
French Polynesia – 270
Switzerland – 269

Body Fat Statistics:

Statistic Verification
Source: Center for Disease Control and Prevention
Date Verified: 2.20.2012

Body Weight Statistics	Data
Percent of adult U.S. population that is overweight	68 %
Percent of adult U.S. population that is obese	34 %
Average amount of life years lost by being severely obese	9 years
Average increase in health care expenditure for an obese person	25 %

The following is the medically recommended ideal weight for an adult age 30

Height	Ideal Weight in lbs			
5'0"	97 – 128			
5'2"	104 – 137			
5'4"	111 – 146			
5'6"	118 – 155			
5'8"	125 – 164			

5'10"	132 – 174			
6'0"	140 – 184			
6'2"	148 – 195			
6'4"	156 – 205			

Adult BMI Statistics	Body Mass Index (BMI)	
Defining Term	Women	
Anorexic	< 17.5	
Underweight	<19.1	
Normal Range	19.1 – 25.8	
Marginally Overweight	25.8 – 27.3	
Overweight	27.3 – 32.3	
Very Overweight or Obese	> 32.3	
Severely Obese	40 – 50	
Morbidly Obese	40 – 50	
Super Obese	50 – 60	

	Top 10 Countries by Obesity Rate	Obesity Rate
1	United States	30.6 %
2	Mexico	24.2 %
3	United Kingdom	23 %
4	Slovakia	22.4 %
5	Greece	21.9 %
6	Australia	21.7 %
7	New Zealand	20.9 %
8	Hungary	18.8 %
9	Luxembourg	18.4 %
10	Czech Republic	14.8 %

From: Statisticbrain.com

Countries With The Highest Income Tax:

Average income tax percent 26.1%
- Denmark – 53.2%
- New Zealand – 42.3%
- Iceland – 38.6%
- Australia – 38.5%
- United States – 37.7%
- Canada – 35%
- Switzerland – 34.4%
- Belgium – 31.7%
- Finland – 31.2%
- Sweden – 30.4%
- United Kingdom – 29.8%
- Mexico – 28.9%
- Portugal – 27.6%
- Ireland – 26.2%
- Italy – 25.5%
- Germany – 25.1%
- Norway – 24.8%
- Poland – 22.9%
- Austria – 22.8%
- Hungary – 20.3%
- Spain – 19.4%
- Japan – 18.4%
- Netherlands – 18.3%
- Turkey – 17.6%
- France – 17.3%

World War I Statistics

http://commons.wikimedia.org/wiki/File:Royal_Irish_Rifles_ration_party_Somme_July_1916.jpg in public domain

Statistic Verification
Source: History Learnings, World War Three
Research Date: 3.20.2014

World War I Statistics (Stats are for all countries involved)	
Total number of men mobilized to fight in World War I	65 million
Percentage of men mobilized in World War I who died	57 %
Total number killed in World War I	8.5 million
Total number of casualities in World War I	37 million
Number of missing POW's from WWI	7.7 million
Number of wounded soldiers in WWI	19.7 million
Number of years of fighting that took place during WWI	4 years
Number of allied countris military casualities in WWI	5.7 million

Number of allied country civilian casualties from WWI	3.67 million
Number of allied countries wounded in WWI	12.8 million
Number of WWI Military casualities	9,720,450
Number of Civilian casualties in WWI	8,865,650
Total War Cost altogther of WWI	$186.3 billion

World War II Statistics

http://www.wwiiarchives.net/servlet/action/photo/202/0;jsessionid=B697A4A49C4F0500E5B7035C6EAA3413 in public domain

Statistic Verification
Source: Factmonsters, Factropolis, Air Warriors
Date Verified: 9.3.2013

World War II Statistics	
Number of Americans who served in World War II	16.1 million
Average amount of time each U.S. military serviceman served overseas during WWII	16 months
Number of people worldwide who served in WWII	1.9 billion

Number of of deaths sustained worldwide during WWII	72 million
Number of of European Jews killed during the holocaust	6 million
Number of U.S. troops engaged during WWII	16,112,566
Number of of American casualties during WWII	291,557
Number of of German Generals executed by Hitler	84
Number of bombs the allies dropped during WWII	3.4 million tons
Number of of U.S. soldiers that were wounded during WWII	671,846
Number of men who served on U-Boats	40,000
Number of men who served on U-Boats who never returned	30,000
Number of German planes that were destroyed on accidents	45%
Number of airplanes that US 8th Air Force shot down	6,098
Total average amount of bombs dropped by the allies each month during WWII	27,770 tons
Number of countries involved in WWII	61 countries

U.S. War Death Statistics

http://www.statisticbrain.com/u-s-war-death-statistics/

Statistic Verification
Source: Washington Post Database of U.S. Service-Member Casualties, McGavock Confederate Cemetery
Research Date: September 8th, 2014
This is a list of wars involving the United States of America during and since the American Revolutionary War, detailing all constituent military theatres and campaigns.

Major U.S. War Casualties	U . S . Deaths	Wounded	Date
Iraq War	4,800	31,965	2003 – Present
Afghanistan	2,344	19,675	2001 – Present
Gulf War	258	849	1990 – 1991
Vietnam War	58,209	153,303	1955 – 1975
Korean War	36,516	92,134	1950 – 1953
World War II	405,399	670,846	1941 – 1945
World War I	116,516	204,002	1917 – 1918
Civil War	625,000	281,881	1861 – 1865
American Revolutionary War	25,000	25,000	1775 – 1783
All U.S. Conflict Casualites	U.S Deaths	Wounded	Missing
Grand Total	1,343,812	1,529,230	38,159

US National Debt Statistics:

(**WRITER**: US debt is now about 17 trillion (and growing) and it is the US people who are paying it back! Surely such a rich country, with the highest number of wealthiest individuals in the world living in it, should have little or no debt? One has to ask WHO or WHAT COMPANIES/INDIVIDUALS received all this debt money and what was it spent on? And, to who is all this debt owed to or from where was all this money been borrowed from? I wonder?)

Statistic Verification
Source: US Treasury
Date Verified: 4.10.2012

US National Debt Statistics	National Debt	Debt Per Taxpayer
4.9.2011	$15,638,610,000,000	$137,000
2010	$13.6 Trillion	$121,000
2005	$9	$78,000
2000	$5.6	$53,000
1995	$5	$48,000
1990	$3.2	$32,000
1985	$1.9	$19,000
1980	$900 Billion	$9,183
1975	$600	$6,060
1970	$400	$4,123

OPEC Oil Revenue Statistics:

Statistic Verification
Source: Energy Information Administration

Date Verified: 2.14.2012

Year	Sales (Billions)	
2011	$810	
2010	$750	
2009	$510	
2008	$800	
2007	$620	
2006	$600	
2005	$510	
2004	$395	
2003	$220	
2002	$205	
2001	$200	
2000	$206	

1999	$190	

Wealthiest Country Statistics

(note: all of these indices and formulas for showing how wealthy a country is, do not give a real picture, as dividing the amount of wealth made or in a country by the number of people – does not give any indication who has the wealth and how it is shared out. For example a country may have 100 billionaires and 1,000 millionaires but they have most of the money for that country and the rest, as you go down, are earning far less and those at the bottom are earning 6 or 7 dollars, euros or pounds an hour. So it is not an even distribution):

Statistic Verification
Source: World Bank
Date Verified: 3.15.2012

	Country	GDP Per Capita
1	Liechtenstein	$118,000
2	Qatar	$101,000
3	Luxembourg	$85,000
4	Kuwait	$60,800
5	Norway	$57,500
6	Brunei	$54,100
7	Singapore	$52,900
8	United States	$48,000
9	Ireland	$47,800
10	San Marino	$46,100
11	Iceland	$42,600
12	Netherlands	$41,300
13	Switzerland	$40,900
14	United Arab Emirates	$40,400
15	Canada	$40,200
16	Austria	$39,600
17	Sweden	$39,600
18	Australia	$39,300
19	Denmark	$38,900
20	Andorra	$38,800

Statistic Verification
Source: World Bank
Date Verified: 3.14.2012

Year	Total World Population
2011	6,921,400,000
2010	6,840,500,000
2005	6,458,400,000
2000	6,079,800,000

1995	5,682,500,000
1990	5,272,400,000
1985	4,835,000,000
1980	4,434,000,000
1975	4,062,600,000
1970	3,685,100,000
1965	3,322,600,000
1960	3,027,200,000

ALL STATS ABOVE FROM: Statisticbrain.com

The World Resources Institute states that in 2011 CO_2 emissions were 150 times higher than they were in 1850. In 2011 it was approx 32274 metric tonnes and in 1850 it was approx 198 metric tonnes.

Statistica.com says that in 2014 the following countries had the following percentage of total world CO_2 emissions:

China 23.43%
US 14.69%
India 5.7%
Russia 4.87%
Brazil 4.17%
Japn 3.61%
Indonesia 2.31%
Germany 2.23%
Korea 1.75%
Canada 1.57%
Iran 1.57%

SOURCE: http://en.wikipedia.org/wiki/List_of_countries_by_carbon_dioxide_emissions

List of countries by 2013 emissions estimates

EDGAR (database created by European Commission and Netherlands Environmental Assessment Agency) released 2013 estimates. The following table lists the 2013 annual CO_2 emissions estimates (in thousands of CO_2 tonnes) along with a list of emissions per capita (in tonnes of CO_2 per year) from same source.

Country	CO_2 emissions (kt) [12]	Emission per capita (t) [12]
World	35,270,000	-
China	10,330,000	7.4
United States	5,300,000	16.6
European Union	3,740,000	7.3
India	2,070,000	1.7
Russia	1,800,000	12.6
Japan	1,360,000	10.7
International transport	1,070,000	-
Germany	840,000	10.2
South Korea	630,000	12.7
Canada	550,000	15.7
Indonesia	510,000	2.6
Saudi Arabia	490,000	16.6
Brazil	480,000	2.0
United Kingdom	480,000	7.5
Mexico	470,000	3.9
Iran	410,000	5.3
Australia	390,000	16.9
Italy	390,000	6.4
France	370,000	5.7
South Africa	330,000	6.2
Poland	320,000	8.5

This chart shows countries and territories ranked on perceived public sector corruption in 2014.

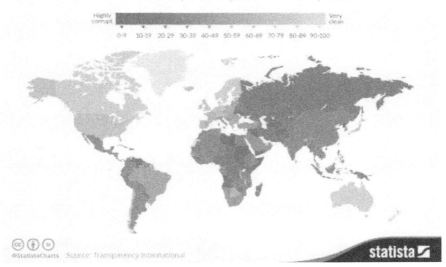

Source: http://www.statista.com/chart/3878/corruption-across-the-world-visualised/

According to the people who live there, Lithuania is the world's most corrupt nation. Gallup polled people in nearly 40 countries and the Baltic state is perceived to have the most government corruption. 75 percent of Americans said "yes" when asked if their government is corrupt, along with nearly half of Britons. Read more in the Independent.

This chart shows responses to the question: "is corruption widespread throughout the government in this country, or not?" (%)

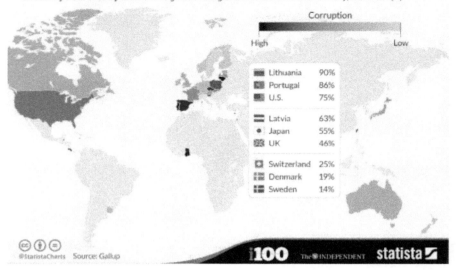

Source: http://www.statista.com/chart/3839/nearly-half-of-britons-think-the-government-is-corrupt/

If, after reading the above statistics, there has been very little or no impact on you; then you may as well close up shop, stop reading this book and go home. As only a callous, nefarious or stupid person would not have been emoted or affected by these.

OK, so let's take a short break from statistics and discuss something much more interesting: Human Beings - US ☺

WHAT IS MAN ANYWAY?

Down through the ages, Man has been searching and looking for answers to some vital questions: What or who am I? What can I do? What are my abilities? What can I achieve? Where did I come from? Who or what made me? What is me? Who or what made the Physical Universe? What is the purpose of it all and where are we headed? The list goes on and on; and – to be honest – Man is still pretty much confused about all of this or misinformed or intentionally kept in the dark about it. And it is true that some religions like Buddhism, Hindu, Muslim and Christianity, etc., have helped bring Spiritual enlightenment and moral fibre to the world but none except one that I know off, has managed to solve pretty much all the puzzles and provide the answers and remain out-of-the-control of the Powers-That-Be: more of this later. But I hope I can clarify some of this confusion, and supply some missing data and facts. But I do not and cannot force you or anyone else to believe what I say or what other great people have said down through the ages and history of Mankind. No. But I ask you, in a new unit of time, to consider or re-consider what I put to you here. This is all I can ask. We will get somewhere with all of this and it will hopefully dovetail to something special at the end ... trust me!

All the great men, geniuses, leaders; philosophers and savants, religious leaders and mystics have all sought, down through the ages and right up to modern times, the answers to very burning questions;

and some did provide some of them and bring man forward, little-by-little, to where he is now. But others did not and are taking us back in the direction of us all being animals, sub-animal or sub-human, namely Psychiatry and Psychology, which the politicians and Powers-That-be support. I wonder why that is? More on this later but suffice it to say ALL evil people or beings support evil or bad things, and that IS a fact. They attack what is good and those who are doing good. But the bad and evil activities they do do, they think are right and are actually helping us – when in fact they are not. That is because they are insane and nuts. That is how you know them. And, conversely, that is how one knows good people. You can take that as a law or a truth.

In so many ways, we have so much potential to do anything that Mankind can imagine and make it a reality: bring Science Fiction and Fantasy to complete reality! WOW! That would be nice. But then, in other ways, Mankind has everything at his fingertips to be inexorably trapped, enslaved or even wiped out forever: gone - no more. Complete oblivion! Complete opposites in intention! One good; one bad - insane and evil. The endless war of good against evil is always present on Earth and in this broad Universe (not just on Earth!). Sometimes good wins and sometimes evil wins. The battles and wars have been waging on Earth for at least 10,000 years – probably more like 50,000 to 100,000, maybe even more. Since WW I & WW II failed, WW III is and has been taking place on paper and secretly behind heavily guarded closed doors; since the end of WW II. This IS a fact - not fiction. The mother-fuckers I am talking about, will stop at nothing to achieve their dirty evil ends and goals. And I do not apologise for using these words as that is exactly what they are: Inhuman, sub-human scum. They know it. I know it. And now you do too.

Man is NOT an animal! He never has been and never will be; no matter how hard the Powers-That-Be and their minions (Politicians, Psychiatrists, Psychologists, certain leaders, certain Scientists, geniuses and business leaders/owners) try to tell us otherwise! Darwin was right about his theories about Evolution of the Species and Natural Selection: BUT, this only applies to our bodies, animal bodies and plants (Watson and Crick (DNA) said they had discovered the source of life. Well they hadn't. DNA is made of matter and elements. You put some in some liquid compound and it does not come alive. DNA is the internal code or instructions (the blueprint for the structure of the body or Life Form), which cells can read/follow and then know how to proceed and what to turn themselves into. DNA has nothing to do with the mind or intelligence. The Cells of our bodies are alive, each one of them and they communicate with each other. Cells and all living organisms are made of matter (various elements and compounds, which are animated by pure Life Force Energy, which is an animating, thinking, sentient energy that is different than Physical Universe Energy. One has to include in all life the Spiritual Plane of existence too, which most people avoid and know very little about and this includes the mind. DNA is purely to do with bodies. One can repair DNA or change it to make faster, better or more beautiful, better bodies, maybe even with super abilities and faster and better brains [your mind is not your brain but your mind does depend on the brain (if one has a body that is) to send it perception data to record from the senses] but the driver that is sitting in the driving seat is the Life Force Energy Plus its mind(in terms of animals and plants, this would be an animal mind which is not the same as a human mind but it is similar), and the Soul or Spirit (in terms of Human Beings). Cells are great examples of this. A cell knows what each element, compound, protein is and what to do with them. They talk to each other so they know what injury a body has, etc. and they know where every other cell in the body is and what it is doing. Call it telepathy and/or electrical communication: but they are aware, conscious and thinking. And, obviously, if one has bad or damaged DNA or cells, this could adversely affect one physically in some way, which could then affect the mind and soul, as if you have a body, they are all linked.)

Darwin's theories ONLY apply to our **physical side** of life and nature. If Mankind's bodies we not occupied by US - Spiritual Beings, then yes, the bodies we have right now would behave just like animals and the bodies we have right now are factually animals but under our control, and this control is assumed at birth (or just before or after). However; man has two other parts: his mind (not his brain which is part of the body. Our minds are not part of the body or brain but it can affect them and vice versa) and the MOST important component which makes up Man is, as I mentioned above, the Spiritual Being or the Soul or all those other names it has been called over thousands of years. It does exist and it is YOU right now reading this book and living your life on this planet. We are either in the body, normally in the head or we are outside, with or without perception (far less common, normally with no exterior perception except via the bodies' sense/perception channels.[The Spirit (US) gets data via its mind and it gets data, perceptions and sense messages from the body via the brain.]) There are some people on this planet right now who can spiritually (not astral body projection!) leave their bodies at will and be able to see their own bodies and everything else around them, from where they are spiritually located exterior. There are many records of people having outer body or near-death experiences (usually painful and upsetting) and they could see and recall everything that was going on with the doctors or emergency people standing around them: but from outside or above their bodies. Do not take my word for this and other facts I claim to be actually true in this book: you are very welcome to check the evidence and testimonies yourself and I would very much prefer that you do, honestly!

Films like 'Limitless' and 'Lucy', which are very good films by the way, give a clear message that certain drugs can make you super or give one unlimited intelligence and mind power. I do **NOT** think this is the case. They may help to enhance or alter one's body or brain, or repair one's body or brain; give one a chemical rush or improve electrical or signal flows or increase perception: but they have bad side-effects (mental and physical) and they do not address the mind directly but only address the brain and/or body. That is all they are good for. They may exteriorise oneself as a Soul or Spirit, like LSD has been known to do (with many bad side-effects) or repair or heal the body or brain - but that is about all one can do with them. To improve one's mind one addresses the mind directly via the Soul or Spirit (which is you right now reading this book!) and to improve the Soul or Spirit one deals with it directly. And Mind, Soul and Body can all affect one another, in good or bad ways. This is a fact. So do not buy or accept what the Scientists, Psychologists and Psychiatrists tell you, as it is false and incorrect data. It is important you understand that. I think most of Mankind aspires to or would like to have super powers and abilities like the X-men or Thor or be able do magic like Harry Potter or even be a god. So would I ☺

Actually, is it not time that <u>YOU</u> begin to think and reason for yourself and not be a slave to the knowledge, facts and data that is feed to us via our 'great' educational system, various books and magazines and our wonderful newspapers, media and TV? We are feed so much crap, lies and false data since the time of our birth (including from our parents [depends what parents you have – some are good, some bad, some are insane, some are just somewhat lost like the rest of us and looking for answers], that is a wonder we can walk and function at all. I do not think anyone really knows how far from the TRUTH Mankind really has gone and how close he has been (and still is) to total annihilation or total enslavement, never again (until someone comes along who awakens and becomes enlightened and who can free us again) to be free or happy or to know who or what he REALLY is. I really wish I could impart mentally and spiritually to you this NUMBER ONE point and fact. I cannot stress it enough:

YOU ARE A SPIRITUAL BEING AND YOU ARE IMMORTAL AND YOU DO NOT NEED TO HAVE A BODY TO EXIST AND YOU CAN STILL HAVE A BODY AND STILL BE ABLE TO FULLY PERCEIVE, REASON AND SENSE FROM OUTSIDE OF IT EXTERIOR; AND YOU SHOULD ALSO BE ABLE TO GO IN AND OUT OF THE BODY AT WILL. YOU ARE MADE OF SPIRITUAL ENERGY WHICH IS NOT PHYSICAL ENERGY AND YOU CAN CREATE AND CAUSE ANYTHING TO HAPPEN EITHER BY THE POWER OF THOUGHT OR BY HARNESSING AND CONTROLLING ALL FORMS OF MATTER, ENERGY, FORCE, SPACE AND TIME; AND INDEED, ONE CAN ACTUALLY MAKE ONE'S OWN. TRULY AND FACTUALLY THERE IS NOTHING WE CAN NOT DO, ACHIEVE, IMAGINE, CAUSE OR CREATE. OUR POWERS AND ABILITIES HAVE NO LIMITS. FACT! AND THE FACT THAT WE CANNOT EXERCISE THESE RIGHT NOW DOES NOT MEAN THAT WE ARE NOT CAPABLE OF THEM AND THAT ONE DAY WE _WILL_ REACH OUR FULL, UNLIMITED POTENTIAL AGAIN AS SPIRITUAL BEINGS (IF WE ARE ALLOWED TO) NOTE: I SAID '_AGAIN!?_'

This is possible and this IS a fact – one million percent the most important and ultimate truth you will ever want to know ever. And just because you are or may not be aware of it or cannot be in this state right now does not mean that it is not possible or that it cannot be attained. It CAN be attained! And in ONE lifetime without dying. And it is what mankind (the good ones of us anyway) have been trying to attain since we arrived or come to be on planet Earth at the beginning of our history or when we were created or whatever you believe in this.

So what does all this tell us? What does our knowledge of ghosts tell us? (I don't know why people are scared of or shun away from ghosts. They are just Spirits without bodies!!!! Usually they are confused, lost or stuck in the past.) It tells us that MANKIND IS not a body but is actually and correctly (despite what the experts say or try to make us think (to deny us the real TRUTH of who and what we are so we can be controlled and kept enslaved) a **Spiritual Being** and, he has a mind (used to think with, recall pictures and memories of things that have happened to us and/or to imagine anything we wish or to resolve problems or make decisions, etc. We can do anything with our minds that we wish. There is no limit! The same, but even more so, applies to us as Spiritual Being!!!!!!!!!!!! I must emphasize this as much as I can because it is vitally important that you understand this. Numero Uno! I say 'Being' because that is what you are right now - reading this book, and what you would also be if you were outside of your body reading this book, except you would be more you, without the limitations, feelings, constraints, etc., the body has. And it is nothing to be scared of. YOU is YOU and you are immortal and capable of ANYTHING and EVERYTHING, without limit!!!!! Just because we, as Spiritual Beings are not displaying and showing our full potential, still does mean it is not true or possible. **YOU ARE AMAZING!!!!!** And despite what has happened to us (pain, loss, suffering, ad infinitum), we still exist and keep going on and on. Mankind is amazing, seriously. I am NOT joking, jesting or selling you short. We are!!! And we are FAR more capable than what we currently have achieved (and that is saying a lot), if, we were only allowed to progress in the direction we should be going, without being fed false, wrong and misleading information and given a certain pre-planned type of education, which makes us confused and unable to think for ourselves, and if certain data was revealed to us and certain inventions and technologies we given back to us (instead of being locked up in some huge vaults somewhere), then Mankind could be free and could achieve all the dreams set forth in Science Fiction and Fantasy, and he could go to the stars and he could be fully, 1000% spiritually aware and free as a being, with his body still alive and be in or out of the body, as he chooses. Now that is freedom, and I don't mean freedom to kill and destroy and do whatever one wants: as that would also end up in no freedom for all. One needs some laws, some rules and things one can and cannot do but within reason. So we could then have another Golden Age, a Super Golden Age and not another even darker Dark Age.

Every major religion that has ever existed on this planet, has believed man to be a Spiritual Being. This is a fact. [However (and this is not to put you off religions, as they are not all bad) most of them (their leaders at the top or the politicians/rulers who have controlled and steered them in the direction that they wanted) have been used to control people, keep them as slaves, tell them lies and half-truths, and get money from him; and they have tricked people and misused their Holy positions (Popes, Bishops, Priests, Holy Emperors) and standings.] You can check it out yourself but I know, that you know this is true – a REAL TRUTH?! But some religions have also, despite how these religions have been abused and misused us, have also brought us some good ideas, beliefs and moral codes and some philosophy – which luckily **HAS** helped mankind move forward to a more civilized state. So it is not all bad. But I do think they should reveal their secrets and not keep us in the dark anymore?

You may have forgotten it or have become confused or lost. Can I also interject an important point here: I do believe in past lives and I do have actual recall of some of my own past lives. Others do too but not many. They ARE real! It is hard to explain the reason we do not remember all of our past existences but they are there. Trust me on this. It seems that at some very distant point in the past, that all of Mankind had his memories totally wiped out and replaced with other false ones. And then just after death and before birth, we also seem to automatically forget the life we just had and end up in a body again, remembering usually nothing (or if we went to Heaven, as most believe, then we should still be able to remember the life we just had... Strange this? And what a waste. Imagine how clever we would all be if we remembered everything we ever learnt and sensed/perceived from all our past lives and existences. Wow! One day I believe we will all be able to do this and we will have to if we are going to go to the Stars and beyond. But let's get back to my previous subject: look deep within yourself and you will know it to be true, what I have just said above. But the problem with this is manifold. We are born with bodies, and most of us begin to think we are bodies because we are sensing through them all the time from birth. We are also usually in bodies – normally in the head, and our minds too (in and around the head). We also get fed tons of false data (not by accident I may add but on purpose by the media: TV, radio, magazines, newspapers, certain books and our lovely school education. We also get some false information, sometimes, from our parents, aunts and uncles. And we also get it from the 'experts', who some, claim to know it all and even if they don't they pretend they do, they cannot admit they might be wrong; or they are paid by Governments to say so and so and support their policies, even though they may be harmful, destructive or insane. The Powers-That-Be and their wonderful minions [who have sold their souls to these Devils for some temporary and transient power, success, money or fame] own and/or control most, if not all of the media and media companies on Planet Earth today. More on this later…) every day that we are just bodies, and DNA and everything is all in our genes and the Brain is NO. 1. Or we are just 'MUD'. What a load of rubbish!!!!!! You are a Spiritual Being regardless if you agree with it or not or even if you do not understand it. Many people do believe this but it is just a belief and one will only truly know oneself by being spiritually exterior of one's own body and perceiving directly as a Being. People can tell you about this and you can think about it and read about it. But until you can actually do it oneself, without drugs or hypnosis, etc. then one will not truly know for oneself who one truly is and what you can do. And, you are also immortal. And there is _nothing_ you cannot do. These are amazing facts and one should take a few minutes to think about what I have just said. Because these words are worth more than all the money and material wealth in this world and the entire Physical Universe!

When Man really and truly discovers his true nature and identity - if he is allowed to, that is, and if **WE** make it happen too - and that means each and every one of us; and then on that glorious day, Man will be so amazed and in awe, and maybe so angry too, that, well, I don't know what might happen or how he would feel or what he might do? The truth of this will be revealed very soon but only if we take the actions to guarantee and allow it to happen. I know this seems all esoteric and pie in the sky. And some will scoff and laugh at this. And these same people may never discover the ultimate truth of this planet and Mankind or they will be the last to. But that does not mean it is not true. And this does not go against other religions. No. It merely completes what they started and fulfills the true goal of all religions: FULL SPIRITUAL FREEDOM AND KNOWLEDGE; WITH THE RETURN OF ALL POWERS AND ABILITIES!

Now on to a subject so dear to my heart – not!:

GOVERNMENTS

Last time I checked in my dictionary (**important note**: most people fail in their education or in learning something or a new profession [or anything actually] because they do not know what the actual and correct definitions or meanings of the words and/or symbols of what they are studying are. This applies to anything and everything. And no matter how long it takes to get defined those words and/or symbols in a dictionary, it will be time well spent and it will open so many doors for you and it also handles stupidity and the inability to learn, and a host of other factors and problems. This is a fact. Get a simple dictionary or google anything you do not understand. It works like magic! Try it and see?!) it said: A Government is *for* (that's a joke!) the people and *by* the people. It is *meant* to be a political system that **serves** and **helps** the people, their country, their work, culture, their children and their everyday lives, plus it is meant to handle the economics, defence, wealth and finances of the country as a whole, and protect, refine, educate and improve it. Not just for the few, but for the good of ALL its inhabitants. This is what it is meant to do by definition – but we know it doesn't do this. A government is meant to serve US, not us serve them. It exists to help us, not suppress us and keep us down as slaves to its taxes and systems. Now is that not a new definition or the original intended definition of 'government'?

Are any governments really doing this today?

Have *WE* (that includes all of us by-the-way!) been asleep for the last one hundred years or more while the G6, G8 and now the G20 & G60 countries (these lovely rich countries who believe they control and rule the world, and right now, they pretty much do; but there are some super powerful families even above them, who they take their orders from: more on this later) that have been shafting us up the ***? (Note: G means 'Group' and it was formed over Oil and has progressed beyond this now, with even the President of the European Commission - representing every country in Europe - now a member (how nice of him to represent us, huh? He and his cronies have our best interests at heart, not!!!) These G20 countries now attend their yearly meetings, at which they discuss what? And lest you think otherwise or erroneously: all of these rich G20 countries (and the number of countries in this Group is sadly now growing in membership to include other countries around the world) are ALL now being controlled behind the scenes by the Powers-That-Be and their minions in our lovely Governments. Where have our wonderful Governments, their leaders and their systems taken us? THEY caused the Recession we are in right now and if you read Jim Marrs' book 'Rule By Secrecy' you will get the full facts on them, on who the real powers-that-be are. There are also many other good books out there on the topics I have covered and will be covering in this book: Dean Henderson; Fritz springmeier and of course Jim Marrs, who I have already mentioned.

And get this: WE have allowed them to do it and WE have paid them to do it!!!! And WE voted them in. And we stupidly keep voting the assholes back in and having faith and trust in them. And they just keep kicking us in the nuts and putting taxes up; putting new taxes on this, taxes on that and making our hard-earned money disappear before we can even get to spend it, and then when we spend it, it buys very little than to what it used to do. And they create more stupid laws: as if we haven't got enough. No wonder lawyers get paid so much and have to specialize as there is just so much legal crap they have to wade through. And then one has rules, policies, procedures and red tape on top of all this. No wonder it takes so long to get something done.

And as long as we are not harmed or punished for being good, hard-working sheep, sorry I mean citizens, and we have a car and house to live in, some food to eat and some money in the bank, we do nothing about it. Now is that not the biggest joke and mistake of all or what??!!!

What needs to change is the political and governmental systems that each country employs around the world. Whether you have a President, Prime Minister, Sultan, Sheik, King, Queen, Dictator or a Supreme Ruler, one will still need some sort of Government and a Governmental system to run things, and a political system too. So what has to happen across the entire planet is the changing of the political systems that countries now employ. Capitalism, Colonialism, Imperialism, Communism and the current Socialism and all the other rubbish we now have, have all failed us but helped those at the top, as always, and don't think otherwise. None of these systems have worked, as they only help the few to get all the wealth and power and keep the rest of us down and slaves to them and their systems. And the new system/s we bring in should allow for and have a procedure for the immediate (after a vote, independent investigation, legal adjudication, or referendum, etc.) dismissal of one, a number or all of the entire Government, including the Head of the Government or state, if they do not perform as promised and how they were expected to: that is they should be helping us to lead happier, better lives; not taxing us into the ground and giving our tax money to people who do not want to work. You cannot have a system which allows the leader or its members to stay in power for 4 or 5 years or indefinitely if they are unjust, unfair, not doing what they promised in their manifesto or just messing up the country and economy and not doing their jobs correctly. One also has to have full transparency in a Government so its people know what is going on, including laws, taxes and finances (not all hidden, adjusted or altered/fixed to impress or mislead, etc.). Obviously a Government cannot disclose everything as some facts need to be kept secret from other countries in case of attack or enemies, etc., i.e. military stuff and all that.

One cannot have Governments (and its associated political parties) be allowed to run independently, with complete autonomy to pretty much do what they want. We cannot just let them be there and we are here and we do not know what they are up too and they do what they please. They serve us and we pay their wages and perks and grant them their privileges and powers: we can take them away too! So we need to know all the time what is going on and what they are up to, yes? And sadly, a lot of them are conniving, thieving, lying mother fuckers, who are insane psychotics and criminals (Clinton, Bush, Tony Blair, et c. And the recent Jimmy Saville saga and sex scandals in the UK confirms this and how high up it all goes, who knows?) And all they do is blabber on about nothing: empty talk and rhetoric. You know and judge people be their actions and their production and statistics. Not by what they say or who they know or if they smile or not! They should, most of them, all be in jail or in insane asylums. And they ALL should be tried for treason and high treason against their countries and for committing crimes against Mankind and the planet. And don't think THEY do not know what they are doing. They do! Believe me. And how they can keep smiling and continuing to do what they are doing, and sleep at night, is beyond me. But then, this is also proof of how bad they are.

We should be able to overturn, alter and change any laws and cancel, change, lower or get rid of any taxes that **WE** want to too, if they are unjust, too high or unfair. This should be easy and simple to do and we should be fully informed on how to do it, not kept in the dark. And if we can't do it, we need to find out why, who is stopping us from doing it and remedy the situation and get it changed, sorted out. Everything should not be set in stone. Independent people should be in there reporting and monitoring the Government and its leaders and staff, and that includes the Houses of Parliament, House of Lords, House of Representatives, Senate, Congress, or whatever the case may be. We cannot just allow Governments and Leaders to pretty much do whatever they please and go to war when they wish and spend/squander funds and taxpayer's money – OUR MONEY - as they wish. NO, this cannot be allowed to happen anymore!!! That is why I say the SYSTEMS used in and by Governments around the world must be changed for the betterment of that country and its people and for the betterment of all Mankind as a whole, not just to line the pockets of the few with more and more money and give them more and more power to make us more and more slaves to them and their evil will. (I must also add in here that the pay rates and systems used by businesses, business leaders and their owners must also be changed so everyone including the cleaner and those at or near the bottom of the working ladder, ALSO have a get a good decent wage, in which they too can buy a house and have one or two nice holidays a year and not have to scrimp and scrounge to survive and have to rent all the time because he and the rest of the working class gets paid minimum or such low wages. Yes a business needs to make profit and a business owner needs to make money but so does everyone else and it should be at the expense of the rest of us. There are far too many millionaires and billionaires now and this is NOT right when there are billions of poor, working class and starving people on this planet, with little or no money and not enough money to lead a good life and provide a good life for their children. This HAS to change too and people at and near the top and those with money and power need to stop thinking about only themselves and their immediate family and friends and start thinking about the harm and unjustness they are party too and allowing to happen by not paying their workers a good enough wage. There is too much avarice and greed in the world today and not enough fairness, equality and kindness. Stop just thinking about oneself for god's sake. There exist and there are OTHER people out there and alive on this planet too, and they need your help and they deserve to be treated better.)

We now have an EEC and US and god-knows how many other countries, who pretty much do what they want; tax us to the hilt and swamp us with some many 'helpful [being sarcastic]' laws. In Brussels, we don't even know what they do anymore and what laws they are passing and what power they are taking away from our *own* supposed countries. MEPs (Members of the European Parliament) do what and are paid for what? What laws do they pass? Do we, the citizens of this wonderful EEC, get a booklet that informs us of what is *REALLY* going on, the laws and taxes we have to abide by and pay, AND the rights and freedoms we have just lost? No we do not. And they do not want us to know what secret plots and schemes they are planning and working up to help US: the peoples of planet Earth. Oh, they are so kind and helpful to us, are they not?

Those of us that work, pay more and more taxes and not just on our wages. But on other hidden and additional taxes on services and products like fuel, alcohol, cigarettes, holidays, gas, phone, electricity, flights – the list goes on and on and keeps growing. And then some of the tax we have paid, goes to people who do not work and do not want to work. It makes one wonder why we are working at all and why should we want to earn more? If we earn more, then we pay more taxes. And now, in Europe, we have all these new poor Eastern European countries, like Hungary, Poland, etc. They pay little or no unemployment benefits over there. If you have no job, you get no money. So they have little jobs over there, so they all come here to the richer countries in the EEC. And if they do not have enough money to pay for their rent (some come over and have children or bring their children over with them – they are clever but they are legally allowed to do this by the wonderful people in our European Commission in Brussels). Then, the Council has to help them pay for their rent, if they have no job or do not earn enough money. So part of our hard-earned money is going to people who do not work and to people who were not even born in the country they are now living/working in; but they have legal benefits and rights, because Brussels has said so. Why don't we all go to Poland or Hungary (and all those other Eastern European countries and those countries outside of the EEC) and claim benefits or get lots of good paid jobs? Well you won't get many or any, which is why they come here to the UK, Germany and other countries with jobs they can take. Their own countries are a mess, with criminal politicians in power and doing what they are told by above and doing deals with big businesses and vested interests. And I have nothing against these poorer Eastern European countries or their peoples. Brussels dangles the carrot to these poorer countries with large hand-outs to get them to join the EEC. They use propaganda in the media to convince their citizens to join. They when they join, within 2 or 3 years, they see how wrong they were to join the EEC and in particular in joining the Euro. Then the leaders say how wonderful it is and look at all the benefits we are getting and free trade. What rubbish! All these countries that joined the Euro are slowly or quickly doing worse and worse. And the richer countries in Europe are paying more and more money to the poorer countries to do nothing and for nothing. And then Brussels pays the farmers to leave the fields empty.

And Brussels insists on Human Rights for the new Eastern European workers so the richer countries have to pay them benefits (I am not against Human Rights but this is not the issue here, is it? And Human Rights should be applied correctly and fairly and not misused or not ignored whenever one feels like it.)

I am just saying that things like this are going on and even worse than this is happening that we do not know about. And businesses and the richer countries of Europe are taking advantage of it too by paying low and crappy wages. And countries like China, Brazil, Russia and India, who now have many millionaires and billionaires yet most of their peoples are on low wages and living shit lives, barely surviving, working like dogs and being slaves. How can this be? Can anyone explain this injustice and why the money is not being shared around fairly? I think countries, businesses and governments, should be helping their own peoples, businesses and countries first, before they help others. People should not have to leave their own country to go to another country because there is no work or low paid work or high taxes. And really, they should stay and join together in changing the Government and in particular the governmental systems which are used in their own countries and put them right, rather than leaving to work in other richer countries. Their country will still be in a mess or even worse state, when they return back to their country after working abroad.

All of these weird and illogical activities that Brussels and the richer countries in Europe are doing, are actually completely messing up their own countries and economies and those of the poorer countries too that they give the hand-outs too (under a conditional contract of course: you do what 'WE' say or else!) and it is just turning it all into a Super Welfare Unfair State, with cheap slave labour (a large proportion of businesses today do not want workers that think for themselves. NO. They just want workers that do what they are told, stand all day on their feet [even though they could sit down on chairs and one must always look busy or appear to be doing something even if ones production is up or one, as a worker, has done ones work for the day] and more and more taxes, rates, restrictive laws and inflation, less and less money in our pockets to spend and we, the hard-working people, are getting our money being given to those who don't work and to those who were not even born in this country. And it gets even worse. Because, now, with this recession and everything being imported or being made in China or India (China and India are a mess too, with about 5 percent of the population at the top, earning all the money and rest are eking out a meagre existence on pittance. This is the pattern over pretty much the entire planet today and the people at the top and those who work with the people at the top, all want to keep it that way!!!!) and other such countries, there are less jobs available to those who do want to work. And some of the jobs they do get are paying 6-8 dollars/euros/pounds an hour. WOW! That is such great money. They will never be able to get anywhere in life with that, will they? But hey, this has all been planned out years ago. This is not all just suddenly happening by accident. Does that shock you? Well I hope so, because it is about time the good, honest and working productive peoples of Earth realize what is going on, how their money is being misspent and mismanaged and who is doing it. We are a not all bad and criminals like the Psychologists and Psychiatrists say we are. About 80% of us are good, sane and honest people. It is the rest of the real bad apples that should be rounded up and put in jail or put into the insane asylums and segregated from the rest of us, as THEY, not us, are the ones sending Mankind down the wrong road to slavery and self-destruction. We sort out these few evil people and Mankind will flourish and prosper, be free and be able to achieve all those good and great ideals and purposes that he has dreamed about for thousands of years.

But you see, the secret hidden agenda, that is going on in Europe and around the world right now, is supporting and creating the situation and laws that allow all this to occur. In the Western World, they heavily tax those who work - and if you earn more pay (or get a pay rise or get promoted), you pay even more tax – so where is the incentive to work harder and earn more money? And then they give it to those who do not to work or who earn little or are poor (housing benefits, etc.). And of course, they use our tax money to finance wars and when they borrow money from those wonderful people in the IMF and World Bank, then they raise the taxes even more and get **us** to pay back their loans, not ours. Funny that. I thought rich countries would be self-sufficient and would not have to borrow money? And their taxes would be very low? And rich countries should be able to help all their peoples buy cheap, affordable houses, flats and apartments or rent them very cheaply. And we should be earning enough so we do not have to take out a mortgage from Banks that are our owned by the Powers-That-Be. Why does all our money have to be paid into THEIR banks, and that includes business money? You are depositing your money into the dirty hands of our enemies! And going to University should be free (just pay for the books). No. Rich countries make the rich richer, the working classes (and even now the Middle-Income earners) poorer and the elite/ruling classes get even more powerful and wealthy. And they make it harder for businesses and those rich people (those who are good, as not all rich people are bad by the way. Some are very nice and do a lot to help people and pay a good wage to those they employ. I am talking about those who do not!) to make big or good money by imposing all these laws, rules and Health & Safety procedures, even higher rates of taxes and all the rest. This forces the businesses and the rich to take their business/money elsewhere or to pay their workers lower wages or to get their products made in China or India.

There is a law about all this and it is: If people are earning lower wages and being taxed more and more, then people have less money in their pockets to buy the products produced by businesses and therefore the businesses earn less, pay less taxes to the Governments, and so these governments and their economies do not prosper and do not recover from the recessions (or their hugs debts), which is currently happening now. And these wonderful, highly educated politicians do not know this? Rubbish, they know. And if they don't, they should. What are they being paid for and more importantly who are they working for?

Less money in people's pockets (especially the working classes, who are in fact the majority of the entire population of Earth) means less money made by businesses, means less taxes for Governments. Simple. If not enough money is going around and in circulation with the majority of the peoples, the Masses: those people who work; then the economy collapses. Why is the money not being shared around and why is it being hoarded by the few, who then lend it to other countries, businesses and individuals at high interest rates? These super rich people and banks, finance houses, etc. do not really produce anything. They just live of the interest they get on their loans to individuals, business and countries. They get others to do the work, you know, people like you and I, and they sit on their asses in their huge houses or on their islands or big estates, and contemplate how they make or lend even more money (while people are starving, struggling and farmers are paid to leave their fields empty) and increase the taxes more and more taxes and get more and more countries, businesses and people under their thumb and control. And we end up paying for it all: us the workers, and that includes the working classes and the Middle Classes (even though they do not like the working class and think they are above them – more on this later for a full delineation and separation between Middle Income earners and the wonderful Middle Class). And we all end up being suppressed and kept down and wondering: 'What the hell am I working for?????' 'And what chance or future do our children have?' 'What do I live for and where am I going?'

Very recently (Nov 2017) we had 13 million leaked tax documents called the Paradise Papers (strange - how did that happen?), which reveal the tax avoidance antics of rich and powerful people and companies around the world. The Queen, Prince Charles, Google, and many others are mentioned in these papers. I am in two minds about all this. Firstly, my tax is taken off of me before I even get paid, by my employer and is given to Tax Office. So there is nothing I can do about how much I pay. Self-employed people can claim this and that and some fiddle their books. Companies and accountants can and do find ways to avoid or lessen the taxes they pay. But there is one factor in all of this, which needs to be addressed: Why are taxes so high, both for employees and employers/companies? And how can large multi-national corporations get away with paying so little tax on such huge profits? If I have to pay my taxes, then so should they, especially since they have billions in their bank accounts and off-shore accounts? And, once again, they would not have to do this if their corporate taxes were lower. And why do employers, companies and multi-nationals get away with paying such low wages (all to make a profit and push share prices up). And they also do sordid backhander deals with many countries and political leaders to secure their contracts, cheap labour, raw materials and deals. They only get fined and/or go to jail if found out. Scandals. This is why, for example, Africa is and stays in the state it is in. It is not happening by chance or accident, I tell you that! And, by-the-way, I can't understand why people are so greedy and yet generally they do not seem(by their actions) to give a damn about anyone else in this, our wonderful now modern age?

Governments, taxes, minimum wages and international tax laws need to change for the betterment of all!

EARTH'S TAXES, WAGES AND UNEMPLOYMENT FIASCOS

I sometimes wonder in what direction Earth and mankind is heading? 'Money' seems to be worshipped more than anything, even God and Love. It is the number one means of buying and exchanging goods and services; the number one desire for man. And how Governments and Banks manipulate it at the expense of us but for the gain of the small few; is really a matter ethics, morals and criminal investigation on a global scale, as it has it all wrong and totally gone out of all proportions. Too much emphasis is put on money and work today. They are important. True. But life should be fun and enjoyable too. I think there needs to be a total shift of attention from fixation on money (and also fixation on mobile phones, computers, TV, computer games) to a more balanced life, where Human Beings are more important and where verbal and face-to-face communication and being fair, pleasant and treating others well; with respect, with proper, decent conversations and relationships count. And where people can get to do the jobs they really want to do and enjoy them and not just be a number or slave to someone else's system (not ours) or to line the pockets of or fill the bank account of someone else. Living and working just for money is actually quite low on the grand scale of life, spirituality and livingness!

If world leaders and our so-called experts ran our countries like any other business, and if they ran them like they should be: legally and ethically; then world debt, taxes, wages, inflation, laws, money flows and values, would all be fairly balanced out and working out good for all. But when you have a few people behind the scenes manipulating everything for THEIR own gain and profit and for their own evil ends, then one has problems for everyone. This has to change and Man needs to learn how to manage, run and do things right.

Some more facts, stats and data:

For Better Planning, Watch Global Demographic Trends
Certainty of demographic trends counters economic uncertainty
Joseph Chamie YaleGlobal, 12 December 2012

...First, at an estimated 7 billion, the world's population is growing at 1.1 percent annually, or 78 million people, half the peak level of 2.1 percent in the late 1960s. Although the world's demographic growth rate is continuing to slow due to declining birthrates, the 8 billion world population mark will likely be reached by 2025. This growth will increase the world's working age population, 15 to 64 years, by 610 million and those aged 65 years and older by 290 million, increases of 13 and 52 percent, respectively.

Second, nearly all of the world's annual demographic growth – close to 95 percent – is occurring in less developed regions. Top seven contributing nations are India, 22 percent; China, 9 percent; Nigeria, 5 percent; Pakistan, 4 percent; Indonesia, 3 percent; Brazil, 2 percent; and Ethiopia, 2 percent (see Figure 1). Due to its much higher growth, the juggernaut population of India – currently larger than all the developed regions combined – is expected to overtake China in a decade, when the Indian population is projected to reach 1.4 billion. Among more developed regions, the nation contributing most to world population growth is the United States at 3 percent, and the growth of the next six nations, including Spain, Italy, Australia, the

United Kingdom, France and Canada, ranges from 0.7 to 0.5 percent.

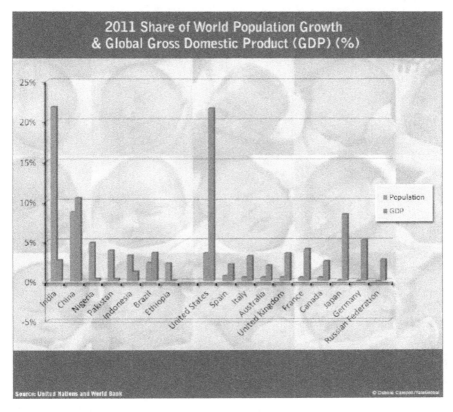

Figure 1. Uneven growth: Near 95 percent of the world's annual demographic growth takes place in less developed regions; yet more than half the world's GDP is center in the more developed economies. Source: United Nations and World Bank

Though nearly all of the world's demographic growth is occurring in less developed regions, **54 percent of the world's GDP is carried out by the 10 largest national economies of the more developed countries** (Figure 1). Collectively, these more developed countries – led by the United States, Japan and Germany – represent 14 percent of world population, expected to decline to 11 percent by midcentury...

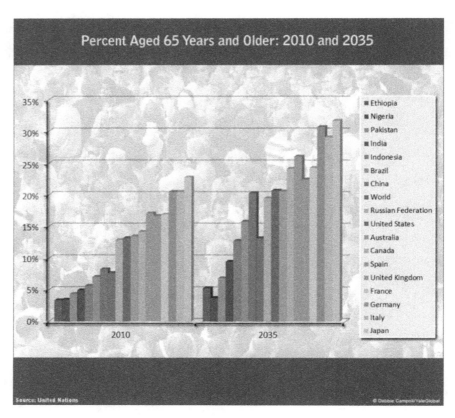

Figure 2. Old world: All countries can anticipate population aging, a consequence of declining birthrates and increasing life expectancies. Source: United Nations

...Some countries such as Germany, Italy and Japan have 20 percent or more of their populations aged 65 years and older (Figure 2). Although the proportions of elderly are lower, the pace of population aging among less developed countries is more rapid; Brazil, China and Indonesia are expected to see elderly proportions double within 25 years...

Over the next 25 years, the numbers of the oldest, of which nearly two-thirds are women, are expected to increase from 105 million to 246 million, reaching 3 percent of world population, or double today's proportion. Among developed countries, the proportions of oldest by 2035 will set record highs: 14 percent for Japan, near 10 percent for Germany and Italy. Also, in countries such as China, Indonesia and

South Korea, the proportion aged 80 years and older are expected to triple over the next 25 years.

Population aging and increased longevity are of mounting significance for policymakers in both more developed and less developed countries. Population aging, in particular, raises serious concerns about the financial viability of pensions and healthcare systems for the elderly. With the number of workers declining relative to those in the retirement category and growing numbers surviving to advanced ages, especially women, nations will face unavoidable fiscal challenges requiring thorny and unpopular economic decisions.

Seventh, as a result of differences in population growth and age-structures as well as in living standards between the more and less developed countries, powerful push-pull factors continue to produce large streams of international migrants. On the one hand, relative declines in the labor force and increases in the retired elderly present many wealthier nations with a difficult choice of more immigrants or fewer and older citizens. On the other hand, the populations of many developing nations, including India, Nigeria, Pakistan and the Philippines, continue to grow rapidly with many of their young men and women seeking opportunities in the urban centers of wealthier countries....

Joseph Chamie, former director of the United Nations Population Division, recently stepped down as research director at the Center for Migration Studies.

Rights: Copyright © 2012 Yale Center for the Study of Globalization

SOURCE: WORLDWATCH INSTITUTE – Vision for a Sustainable World

May, 2013

Writer: This article says that Worldwide, the amount spent on goods and services at the household level was about $20 trillion in 2000. In 2002, 1.12 billion households—about three quarters of humanity—owned at least one television set.

China

Every day in 2003, some 11,000 more cars merged onto Chinese roads—4 million new private cars during the year. Auto sales increased by 60 % in 2002 and by more than 80 % in the first half of 2003. If growth continues apace, 150 million cars could jam China's streets by 2015—18 million more than were driven on U.S. streets and highways in 1999.

The Poor

As many as 2.8 billion people on the planet struggle to survive on less than $2 a day, and more than one billion people lack reasonable access to safe drinking water.

The U.N. reports that 825 million people are still undernourished; the average person in the industrial world took in 10 percent more calories daily in 1961 than the average person in the developing world consumes today.

The U.S. Consumer

The United States, with less than 5 % of the global population, uses about a quarter of the world's fossil fuel resources—burning up nearly 25 % of the coal, 26 % of the oil, and 27 % of the world's natural gas.

As of 2003, the U.S. had more private cars than licensed drivers, and gas-guzzling sport utility vehicles were among the best-selling vehicles.

New houses in the U.S. were 38 % bigger in 2002 than in 1975, despite having fewer people per household on average.

> **Environmental Impacts of Consumption**
>
> **Calculations show that the planet has available 1.9 hectares of biologically productive land per person to supply resources and absorb wastes—yet the average person on Earth already uses 2.3 hectares worth. These "ecological footprints" range from the 9.7 hectares claimed by the average American to the 0.47 hectares used by the average Mozambican.**

> **Social Impacts of Consumption in the U.S.**
>
> **An estimated 65 % of U.S. adults are overweight or obese, leading to an annual loss of 300,000 lives and at least $117 billion in health care costs in 1999.**
>
> **In 2002, 61 % of U.S. credit card users carried a monthly balance, averaging $12,000 at 16 % interest. This amounts to about $1,900 a year in finance charges—more than the average per capita income in at least 35 countries (in purchasing power parity).**

The Rich Get Richer, the Poor Get Poorer, While the Middle Class Gets Decimated

U.S. Working Poor Population Grows, As Families Struggle To Pay The Bills

Reuters Posted:01/14/2013 11:00 pm EST Updated:03/20/2013 3:38 pm EDT

By Susan Heavey

In this article it gives the following data:

200,000 more low-income families in the U.S.

47.5 million Americans now live near poverty, which is earning $22,811 for a family of four.

More parents are being forced to work as cashiers, maids, waiters, etc. just to survive. And these jobs pay the minimum wage of $7.25.

How can people live on this? And it is the same in Europe and other parts of the world. I would like to see world leaders and politicians live on this? They wouldn't! So why don't they increase the minimum wage all over the world then? No, because they want to keep them down. That is why!

20% of Americans received 48% of all income; while the bottom 20% received only 5%.

As of 2011, about 37% of U.S. children lived in working class poverty.

WRITER: This is a joke for the richest country in the world! Why do the rich not share the money around? Why does the US Government and Obama not increase the minimum wage to at least $10 an hour?

Map of countries by unemployment rate

For a list of countries by unemployment rate go to: http://en.wikipedia.org/wiki/List_of_countries_by_unemployment_rate
From Wikipedia, the free encyclopaedia AUTHOR: Altes

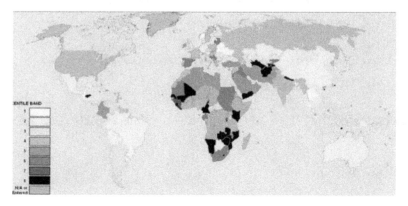

Map of world unemployment rates, 2010.

'Developing world's middle class is growing – but so is its 'near poor' SOURCE: ILO

ILO's (International Labour Organization) first global and regional estimates of developing world workforce across five economic classes promise new insights

This details that the working middle class, who are those living on at least $4 a day, now comprise more than 40% of the developing world's workforce.

The ILO estimates that 397 million workers are living in extreme poverty (defined as living on less than $1.25 a day) and another 472 million are living on $1.25 to $2 a day!

My god!!!!! How can this be and how can this be allowed?????

And more from the International Labour Organization (there is a wealth of more data on their website! www.ilo.org)

"On average, more than 40 % of jobseekers in advanced economies have been without work for more than a year."

At 19.8 % of GDP in 2010, global investment remains 3.1 percentage points lower than the historical average, with a more pronounced downward trend in advanced economies."

Employment rates have increased in only 6 of 36 advanced economies (Austria, Germany, Israel, Luxembourg, Malta and Poland) since 2007."

Youth unemployment rates have increased in about 80 % of advanced countries and in 66 % of developing countries."

Poverty rates have increased in half of developed economies and in one third of developing economies."

Involuntary part-time employment has increased in two-thirds of advanced economies."

The share of informal employment stands at more than 40 % in two-thirds of emerging and developing countries."

International Institute for Labour Studies
Unemployment in the EU remains high and rising in a majority of countries...
As of the fourth quarter of 2011, the EU-27 unemployment rate stood at 9.9 percent (figure 1) and thus remains 3 percentage points above the pre-crisis rate of the fourth quarter of 2007.

In most EU countries, unemployment has been increasing since the fourth quarter of 2010, with many struggling with rates well above 10 per cent. Only 10 out of 27 EU countries witnessed declines in unemployment rates.

The unemployment rate of people aged 15-24 is roughly twice as high as those of other age groups and has reached historical peaks in Southern European countries. Only Germany and Luxembourg managed to reduce youth unemployment since 2007 (figure 2).

...and new jobs created tend to be relatively precarious...

There are 42 million part-time workers in the EU of which around 20 per cent would like to work longer hours. In Greece and Spain the incidence of involuntary part-time work reaches 58 and 49 per cent, respectively.

Atypical forms of employment, such as temporary and agency work as well as informal employment have expanded in Central and Eastern European countries. A decline of atypical employment since the onset of the crisis has been registered only in a few Western European Countries.

...and raising the risk of poverty and social unrest.

In 2010 16.4 percent of the population in the EU had been at risk of poverty. The figure is even higher for young people aged 18-24 at 21.2 per cent. These trends are on the rise.

The IILS social unrest index has increased between 2010 and 2011 for

11 out of 24 EU countries (for which data are available). Between 2006 and 2011 the index increased for 17 out of 24 EU countries.

Austerity measures have had a negative impact on labour markets and business investment

Evidence presented in the *World of Work 2012 report* shows that the pace and content of fiscal consolidation measures are important if countries are to foster fiscal stability while simultaneously boosting employment growth. The current path of consolidation will lead to weak employment growth and a worsening of the fiscal position in the medium-term—owing to weakening of aggregate demand.

Countries faced with the twin challenge of low employment growth and limited fiscal space have turned increasingly towards labour market reform as a tool for reassuring financial markets and in the hope of boosting economic growth. This has led a number of EU member states to introduce lower employment protection regulations and decentralized collective bargaining, among them Estonia, France, Greece, Hungary, Italy, Latvia, Lithuania, Romania, Slovakia, and Spain.

Investment activity in the European Union is still weak with an investment/GDP ratio about 16 per cent below its historical average and only slightly above its all-time low. The *World of Work 2012* shows that higher investment growth is an integral part of any recovery as job growth is highly dependent on investment (figure 3).

Large businesses have built-up unprecedented large cash stocks since 2008. Between 2007 and 2011, the 50 European companies on the benchmark Euro Stoxx 50 Index increased their cash holdings by 77 per cent and the increase was 32 per cent between 2010 and 2011.

World of Work 2012: Better jobs for a better economy is available at (www.ilo.org/INST). For further comment, journalists are invited to contact Daniel Samaan (tel: +41 22 799 7539, email: samaan@ilo. org); or Raymond Torres (tel: +41 22 799 7908, email: torresr@ilo.org), Director of the ILO's International Institute for Labour Studies.

Here is an overview of some countries around the world, from the ILO:

World of Work 2012
Snapshot of the United States

Employment growth has weakened and remains well below crisis levels...

In March 2012, the unemployment rate stood at 8.2 per cent, a 2 percentage point decline from March 2010. Robust job growth (over 200 thousand per month) was registered from December 2011 through February 2012 (figure 1). However, in March 2012, the economy added only 120 thousand jobs (which is the same as the average monthly new entrants to the labour force), thus employment growth remains a concern and is still below crisis levels.

The United States economy still needs to create close to 4 million jobs to return to pre-crisis employment levels. This ignores the fact that the number of people looking for employment is growing by roughly 1.5 million per year over the next 5 years.

Meanwhile, 42.5 per cent of the unemployed are long-term unemployed (jobless for 27 weeks and over).

...while corporate profits have gone back to pre-crisis levels while business investment remains low

Corporate profits have gone back to pre-crisis levels (figure 2). This is mainly due to the fact that US firms streamlined their production following the global crisis, reducing overall production costs, which allowed for profits to increase.

However, investment has not responded much. Business investment as a per cent of GDP remains below its pre-crisis average of around 20 per cent. Since the second half of 2011, there are signs of weak recovery.

...this is partly due to increased cash holdings among firms, which stems from economic uncertainty

Firms' reluctance to take on additional investment risk is evidenced by their sizeable liquid asset holdings, which have reached unprecedented global levels. This is mainly due to economic uncertainty and constrained access to external finance.

The share of cash holdings in total assets in medium-sized firms in the US increased from around 5.2 per cent to around 6.2 per cent after the crisis; while in larger firms it rose from about 4.2 per cent in 2006 to 5.3 per cent in 2010 (Figure 3). This is evidence of the more aggravated situation for smaller firms and lends support to the argument that smaller firms, which finance more of their investment out of cash holdings and have more limited access to external financing tend to hold more cash as a share of total assets. Nevertheless, large firms, which tend to have better access to external finance, have also increased their cash holdings.

Moreover, there is an inverse relationship between investment and cash holdings, with the increase in cash holdings impacting investment more severely in the case of smaller firms than in larger firms.

The path to recovery lies in moving to a comprehensive job plan

There is a need to incentivize investment by reducing economic uncertainty facing businesses, chief among which is the financing condition for small and medium sized enterprises. Furthermore, well-designed public investment could "crowd-in" private investment and support more and better jobs. In this regard, the government could continue to improve investments in information and communication technology.

More generally, a comprehensive job plan is needed. In that respect, the American Jobs Act announced by the government in Sept. 2011 is a welcome step forward as some elements of the Bill have passed the US Congress. However, there are several major elements that remain stalled in the US Congress and a concerted effort from all respective stake holders is important in tackling the high unemployment.

Enhancing social protection is vital in supporting jobseekers and keeping people from falling into poverty, which has already become a growing problem in the United States. In a report released at the end of last year, the US Census Bureau indicated that close to 50 million

Americans were poor and the ranks of those just above poverty are larger than previously believed. A weak economy and job-less recovery calls for a further strengthening of antipoverty programmes.

World of Work 2012 is available at (www.ilo.org/INST). For further comment, journalists are invited to contact Sameer Khatiwada (tel +41 22 799 6308; email: khatiwada@ilo.org) or Raymond Torres (tel: +41 22 799 7908; email: torresr@ilo.org), Director of the ILO's International Institute for Labour Studies.

ILO World of Work Report 2013
Posted on April 3, 2013 by Florence Franks

The International Labour Organization have released their World of Work Report for 2013. The Report Includes an 'EU Snapshot' which addresses youth unemployment and the youth guarantee, it also gives a very good macro-level insight into the crisis. Some statements from the report below.

Firstly, **there are over 10 million more unemployed people in the EU in 2013 than in 2008.** Unemployment has been increasing consistently since the onset of the crisis, but has increased at an alarming rate over the past year. A core reason for this is that austerity measures are having a very negative impact on employment. Or to put it another way, we are currently experiencing the social after effects of the 2008 economic shock.

The Snapshot also points to a further polarisation of Europe. **Only 5 EU countries are currently experiencing employment levels higher than pre-crisis level**, these are: Austria, Germany, Hungary, Luxembourg and Malta. In some countries (Cyprus, Greece, Portugal, and Spain) employment rates have decreased by over 3%.

Austerity measures have reduced national debt at the expense of employment. As a result there is an increase in long-term unemployment. At the end of 2012 there were 11 million people unemployed for 12 months or more in the EU. In most EU countries over 40% of unemployed people are long-term unemployed. The largest increases in long-term unemployment have been recorded in Estonia. Ireland, Lithuania and Spain.

Youth unemployment stands at 23.5%. The only country that has experienced a decline in youth unemployment since 2008 is Germany. **Almost 30% of youth in the EU were at risk of poverty or social inclusion in the EU in 2011**. The rate has most likely increased even further since then.

Less people are working in stable, full time employment as temporary and part-time employment has increased in the majority of EU countries.

Amazingly **the EU has experienced the sharpest increase in the risk of social unrest** internationally between 2006 and 2012, with an increase of over 10%. As a point of contrast the likelihood of social unrest increased by just under 6% in the Middle East and North Africa and less than 2% in Sub-Saharan Africa. **The countries that experienced the sharpest increase of social unrest between 2010 and 2012 were Cyprus, the Czech Republic, Greece, Italy, Portugal, Slovenia and Spain**. The risk of social unrest declined in Belgium, Germany, Finland and Sweden.

The ILO is calling for a stronger emphasis on pro-employment programmes, a commitment to effective welfare entitlements, and for increased efforts to be made in reducing wasteful spending and fighting tax evasion. It is also calling for increased cooperation between public employment services in Europe.

This entry was posted in Home, News by Florence Franks. Bookmark the permalink.

World of Work 2012 Snapshot of Germany

Employment growth remains strong owing to strong export demand from non-Euro countries ...

Economic growth was 3 per cent in 2011. As of February 2012, the unemployment rate (ILO definition) was 5.4 per cent –even less than half the rate of 2005 (figure 1). The ratio of vacancies to registered unemployed in March 2012 reached 0.16, higher than in March 2011 (0.14).

These positive trends reflect strong manufacturing exports to high-growth countries, notably China. Non-Euro countries have gained in importance for exports (figure 2) since exports to Euro area countries are hampered by low growth.

... but a slowdown is likely in the near future ...

It is expected that the growth slowdown in high-growth non-Euro countries, the continuing Euro crisis and the diminished rebounding effect after the financial crisis will reduce growth in 2012. GDP already contracted in the fourth quarter of 2011 and is starting to affect job prospects.

The business sentiment index (IFO Geschäftsklimaindex) predicts a positive-stable environment (+12.1 in April 2012), despite the once again uncertain future of the Euro. In contrast, the manufacturing purchasing managers' index (PMI) already predicts a contraction (46.3 in April).

The uncertain environment could restrain investment (and thereby employment growth) which despite strong investment growth in 2010 and 2011 is still below its pre-crisis (2001-2007) average (as a ratio of GDP).

... necessitating further reinforcing domestic demand as a driver of growth.

Further strengthening domestic demand would not only allow employment growth to be less reliant on export performance, but could lead to stronger investment, rebalanced external trade and positively impacted intra-EU balances.

The key challenge is to improve the quality of atypical employment and ensure that wages catch up with productivity gains. Some improvement in this respect has been achieved as the share of part-time employment in total employment decreased, but more can be done:

Real wage growth was positive in 2010 and 2011. However, not all employees experienced real wage growth. In the low-wage sector in Germany the incidence of low pay increased by 4 per cent between 1995-2000 and 2007-2009.

The incidence of atypical employment in total employment, at 25 per cent, is relatively high. Atypical employment includes limited-term contracts, part-time employment, "mini-jobs" and temporary employment. Hourly wages in this type of employment are one third lower than is the case for standard employment.

Most recently adopted collective agreements seem to indicate further real wage increases in 2012 and 2013. Such outcomes are a major positive step. And real wage increases should also apply to groups of workers in the low paid sector and those that are not covered by collective agreements or a minimum wage.

World of Work 2012: Better jobs for a better economy is available at (www.ilo.org/INST). For further comment, journalists are invited to contact Stefan Kühn (tel: +41 22 799 6867), Daniel Samaan (tel: +41 22 799 7539) or Raymond Torres (tel: +41 22 799 7908; email: torresr@ ilo.org), Director of the ILO's International Institute for Labour Studies.

World of Work 2012
Snapshot of Japan

The labour market remains weak

The disaster which hit Japan in March 2011, had significant consequences on an already fragile recovery from the global crisis. All quarterly GDP figures for 2011 showed a decline compared to the same quarters in the previous year.

Japan's unemployment rate, which was below 4 per cent prior to 2007, increased to over 5 per cent in 2010. But, throughout 2011 unemployment decreased steadily and stabilized at 4.5 per cent by the end of the year. However, this stems from the fact that workers dropped out of the labour market, so the inactivity rate increased (from 40.1 per cent to 40.7 per cent between 2009 and 2011) rather than an improvement in employment.

Indeed, as the *World of Work report 2012* shows, employment has been declining in Japan in the recent years. In the third quarter of 2011 the employment to population ratio was only 56.6 per cent, while it was as high as 58.3 per cent in the same quarter in 2007 (see Figure 1).

The report also finds a decrease in Japan's non-standard employment (temporary or part-time jobs) in 2010. The share of those who were working with such contracts had been steadily increasing in recent years and reached one third of all workers in 2009. However, such a fall seems to be linked to the global crisis rather than an improvement in the quality of jobs—as initially the most precarious jobs were the first to be lost.

Addressing fiscal imbalances while meeting employment goals is possible

In order to cope with its debt problem (Figure 2), Japan is planning to introduce austerity measures similar to many other advanced countries, by cutting public spending especially that of social benefits. However, in the context of an increasing need for public investment after the disaster combined with an aging population, cuts in public spending might have significant negative social impacts.

The current economic situation in Japan makes public spending indispensable for reviving the economy. Therefore, budget consolidation should rely more on the revenue side through an increase in tax revenue instead of the expenditure side via spending cuts. There is a need to expand tax revenue by considering more innovative options such as environmental taxes. Even though this might seem difficult in the context of the energy bottleneck after the March disaster, in the longer term such taxes may contribute to revenue and the better use of natural resources.

Additionally, as the *World of Work report 2012* points out, public investment in the form of infrastructure "crowds in" private investment and increases employment. In Japan, where total investment has significantly decreased since the beginning of the crisis from 23.7 to 20.2 per cent of GDP, and employment is weak, cuts in such spending can hamper the growth prospects in 2012. Besides infrastructure investment, public spending on education in Japan, which is the lowest of all OECD countries (less than 3 per cent) can be increased.

Increases in tax revenue (on income, wealth, production and import taxes) are also planned in 2012. The VAT rate, which is relatively low in

Japan (5 per cent) will be increased progressively to 10 per cent. Even though the VAT is a regressive tax, such an increase seems to be one of the best options for the short term. Any increase should, however be accompanied by measures to support the disposable income of poorer households.

World of Work 2012: Better jobs for a better economy (www.ilo.org/ INST). For further comment, journalists are invited to contact Marva Corley (tel +41 22 799 7873; email: corley@ilo.org) or Raymond Torres (tel: +41 22 799 7908; email: torresr@ilo.org), Director of the ILO's International Institute for Labour Studies.

World of Work 2012
Snapshot of Italy

The labour market continues to deteriorate...

Labour market performance has continued to deteriorate throughout 2011. At 56.9 per cent in the 4ᵗʰ quarter of the year, the employment rate is still below pre-crisis levels. At the same time, the unemployment rate at 9.7 per cent has increased by 1.9 per cent compared to the preceding quarter, reaching its peak since 2001 (Figure 1). However, this unemployment rate can be underestimated. Indeed, in addition to almost 2.1 million unemployed, there are currently 250,000 workers under Short-Term Working Scheme (STWS).

Particularly hard hit are youth and long-term unemployed. Youth unemployment rate, which stood at 32.6 per cent in the 4ᵗʰ quarter of 2011 has increased by more than one half since the beginning of 2008. Similarly, the share of long-term unemployment over total unemployment has increased by as much as 51.1 per cent in the last quarter of 2011 (Figure 2). Furthermore, people are exiting the labour market altogether: the rate of discouraged workers has increased in the last year, reaching 5 per cent of the labour force. The number of youth NEET ("Not in Employment Education or Training") has currently reached the worrying level of 1.5 million.

There are also serious issues with regards to the quality of the jobs created. The shares of both temporary and part-time employment

83

have increased since the beginning of the crisis, reaching 13.4 and 15.2 per cent of total employment respectively. Moreover, 50 per cent of part-time and 68 per cent of temporary employment is involuntary.

...and fiscal austerity hampers economic recovery.

Italy has entered the second recession since the beginning of the global crisis. The recovery is being hampered by the contraction in private consumption, driven by the widening gap between inflation and wages. Furthermore, the investment rate has declined since 2010 and the growth in external demand has slowed. On top of this, government expenditures as a percentage of GDP have decreased by 2 per cent from 2009 to 2011, with a direct negative effect on public investments.

Public debt skyrocketed from 103 per cent in 2007 to 120 percent in 2011, increasing the country's borrowing costs and posing doubts on the sustainability of public finances. In order to reduce the government deficit, the tax burden has been increased, and it is estimated to reach 45 percent in 2012. Such austerity measures risk having a pro-cyclical effect on the recession, postponing economic recovery and fiscal consolidation.

The economic slowdown is also related to restrictions in the access to credit. Despite major liquidity injections from the European Central Bank (ECB), there has been a marked deterioration in the availability of bank loans and an increase in lending rates for most SMEs, together with traditional problems related to heavy administrative burdens. Limited access to credit, combined with high uncertainty in the European market can further decrease private investments, with additional negative effects on labour market recovery.

Thus, finding a sustainable balance between fiscal consolidation and employment recovery is paramount...

Reducing public debt without endangering economic growth: Italy presents the second highest public debt in the European Union and some fiscal consolidation is warranted. However, the *World of Work Report 2012* shows that public investments are important to stimulate domestic demand and counter-balance the negative effects of the austerity measures. Moreover, the gap between inflation, productivity and wages should be reduced, so that a shift in income distribution would lead to higher social cohesion and investment growth. Social dialogue and collective agreement are fundamental in order to guarantee an automatic stabilizer for sustaining wages.

Investment growth for employment creation: Small and medium enterprises represent the bulk of employment and it is necessary to provide them with sufficient financing options. Thus, it is important to ensure that liquidity injections from the ECB are translated into higher loans. Moreover, administrative burdens and the delay in payments from the public administration should be reduced.

Labour market reforms for better employment outcomes: Italy has recently modified the collective bargaining system, extending the scope of company level bargaining. Moreover, the country is currently modifying the legislation over unemployment benefits and employment protection. Finally, there is the promotion of apprenticeship as an entry contract into the labour market.

World of Work 2012: Better jobs for a better economy is available at (www.ilo.org/INST). For further comment, journalists are invited to contact Raymond Torres (tel: +41 22 799 7908; email: torresr@ilo.org), Director of the ILO's International Institute for Labour Studies.

World of Work 2012
Snapshot of Latin America

Employment in Latin America has grown remarkably fast...

The region as a whole has already recovered from the global crisis that erupted in 2008 (Figure 1). The employment rate, at 61.5 per cent in 2011 is 0.6 percentage points above its pre-crisis level. This is the second largest increase – after Central and South-Eastern Europe – of all regions during the crisis period. Important cross-country disparities can be observed:

Colombia and Uruguay show the highest increases in employment rates – 5 and 3.7 percentage points, respectively, between the third quarters of 2007 and 2011. Although to a lesser extent, employment rates also increased in Brazil, Peru and Argentina.

On the contrary, Caribbean countries as well as Ecuador, Venezuela and Mexico have seen a decrease in their rates of employment since the onset of the crisis.

... but there is concern about the quality of the jobs created...
The strong employment growth masks two important considerations. First, job quality remains of concern. The share of informal employment remains high in the region – close to 50 per cent on average – and has increased in over one-third of the countries for which data are available. Despite this fact, the region as a whole has seen a slight decrease in informal employment. Second, the crisis has led to an increase in income inequalities in one third of the countries analysed. There are, however, some exceptions to these general patterns. In particular, Argentina, Brazil, Peru and Uruguay increased their employment rates without compromising on job quality nor increasing inequalities.

... and there is a risk of a pronounced slowdown in growth and job creation.

Economic growth in the region reached 4.5 per cent in 2011, compared to 6.2 per cent in 2010, and is estimated to retrench to 3.7 per cent in 2012. Many of the countries have been affected by volatile capital inflows. This has contributed to the volatility of real investment in the region, thereby affecting the predictability of the production and employment horizon.

Investment as a share of GDP, at 22.3 per cent of GDP in average in 2011, has stagnated during the last decade. In fact, in half of the countries of the region the investment share fell during the crisis.

Yet, there are a number of positive developments, which, if properly supported could lay the foundations for a sustained recovery...
First of all, as Chapter 1 of the *Report* shows, in about three-quarters of the developing economies there was a decline in national poverty rates

between 2007 and 2010, which was most marked in the Latin American region followed by the Asian countries. Indeed, in Latin America and the Caribbean region the majority of countries with available information experienced a decrease in poverty rates. Uruguay and Paraguay are the Latin American countries where poverty decreased the most – 9.6 and 6.1 percentage points, respectively.

In addition, in the region, not only do a large majority of people perceive that their standards of living to have improved, but despite the crisis, the percentage has fallen only slightly over the last years (Figure 2). More importantly, this perception has increased by close to 1 percentage point between 2010 and 2011. Likewise, the region has seen an increase in confidence in national governments, which usually serves as an indicator of people's satisfaction towards the status quo.

As a result, the *Report's* score for the risk of social unrest in the region has declined between 2010 and 2011, despite a general tendency in the world towards an increase in the risk of unrest. This shows a general optimism towards the future in the region.

... and this can be accelerated through a coherent policy strategy with focus on the domestic sources of growth.

Progress can be accelerated through a coherent policy strategy with focus on further regional economic integration and domestic sources of growth – especially important given the weakening in advanced economies. Regional integration could contribute to industrial development and to diversify the economic base, often dominated by the exploitation of natural resources.

Strengthening labour market institutions and boosting public investment and social protection floors could help as well. Indeed, as the *Report* shows, an increase in public investment has positive effects on productivity and, if well targeted, may also "crowd in" private investment. Likewise, social policies, if well designed, have shown success in addressing poverty and inequalities while boosting aggregate demand and opening up new business opportunities.

World of Work 2012: Better jobs for a better economy is available at (www.ilo.org/INST). For further comment, journalists are invited to contact Verónica Escudero (tel +41 22 799 6913; email: escudero@ilo.org) or Raymond Torres (tel: +41 22 799 7908; email: torresr@ilo.org), Director of the ILO's International Institute for Labour Studies.

World of Work 2012
Snapshot of Spain

Spain's unemployment has continued to increase...

The impact of the global crisis on the labour market in Spain has been much stronger than in most other EU countries. In the fourth quarter of 2011, the unemployment rate stood at 22.8 per cent, which is 2.5 percentage points more than one year ago and over 14 percentage points more than in 2007 (figure 1).

Unemployment has been particularly widespread among vulnerable groups, especially youth and long-term unemployed. The youth unemployment rate escalated to 48.6 per cent in the fourth quarter of 2011, increasing by 30 percentage points since 2007 (figure 2). And more than 43 per cent of the unemployed have been without work for over one year –a very high figure by international comparison.

Spain continues to have the highest proportion of temporary employment in Europe (25.4 per cent), despite huge losses of temporary jobs during the crisis. Furthermore, more than 90 per cent of temporary employment in Spain is involuntary.

The social impact of the current economic crisis has been multi-fold as rising unemployment and falling incomes further worsens inequality. As consequence, the crisis has led to an increase in the Gini index by 2.6 percentage points between 2007 and 2010.

... and fiscal austerity measures have delayed labour market recovery.

Since the public deficit reached its peak in 2009 at 11.2 per cent of GDP, Spain has adopted fiscal consolidation measures with important implications for employment and social conditions. In fact, fiscal spending as a percentage of GDP decreased by 3 percentage points between the third quarters of 2009 and 2011 – with important cuts to public wages and investment, while the share of revenues in GDP increased by 0.6 percentage points during the same period. Indirect taxes as a per cent of GDP increased by 2.8 percentage points. Budget plans are for a further reduction in public spending relative to GDP by 0.9 percentages points in 2012, with social benefits being part of this policy.

Austerity measures have affected growth and employment in the short term. So far, they have not translated into a significant reduction in the fiscal deficit. Moreover, exports and investment growth have not compensated for the negative impact of austerity measures on household demand. Exports, which had grown at an annual rate of over 15 per cent in 2010, have grown at 5 per cent in 2011, reflecting the economic slowdown in other European countries. Investment has decreased, caused by the fall in public investment and depressed private investment due to the strong credit constraints. So the challenge is to reduce the medium-term deficit without endangering the labour market recovery...

Fostering fiscal stability while promoting jobs: Getting public finances under control is of critical importance. Yet, fiscal stability should not be an end goal in itself but the means for achieving a quicker and more equitable economic and labour market recovery.

World of Work 2012: Better jobs for a better economy is available at (www.ilo.org/INST). For further comment, journalists are invited to contact Raymond Torres (tel: +41 22 799 7908; email: torresr@ilo. org), Director of the ILO's International Institute for Labour Studies.

WRITER: Yes, all the above is basically saying let's have more job cuts, job losses and more unemployed and let's take more and more austerity measures both in Europe, the USA and across the world (which means HIGHER taxes and rates!); and let's join together even more in this terrible time of crisis and give more and more power, in every way, to the wonderful experts in Brussels and our expert world governments, who do actually know who caused this current and past recessions and booms. They - who know everything, right? Well, they talk like they do. The banks and their owners **INTENTIONALLY** caused this recession and the Governments (who lost money investing in some of these banks too) then have to bail out these banks and countries, and we – the taxpayers – have to pay for it and the countries around the world have to suffer such austerity measures as a result and those at the top, running the planet, just laugh their heads off! And those who have money can just buy up all the properties and land at a much reduced price (at auctions, etc. or get remortgages), then rent them out to people who can' t afford to buy a house, flat or apartment because they are not being paid enough or have lost their jobs or are claiming Housing Benefits. And then when the prices of these properties and land go up again, they can buy more or sell them off at a huge profit. It is nice for some but what about the rest of us?

Why don't the assholes at the top just press the button and blow the planet up and then we will soon find out the truth about God and the afterlife and then they can have the planet all to themselves, as they live in their self-sustaining underground cities and bunkers –and their chosen minions can lick their asses and they can all have so much fun together? Better this to happen than to have the possible future that they are planning right now for us. No, they LIKE and want us to suffer, be in pain, have little or no money and only they have all the money and power. They want us to be kept in the dark about who we really are and where we came from and they want us to get the education THEY dictate – can't have people thinking for themselves and coming up with newer ways to help people and improve things on this planet, oh no. And the experts know it all anyway. Yes keep the masses, the riff-raff and common people down and invent new and more ways to get them even more down and keep them there. Then THEY are happy and smiling. This IS their motivation and their purpose in life and has been for a long time. Ignore the hype and propaganda and false impressions that the media portrays about them and how this planet really is: this is all rubbish and this planet and society is going down fast.

And just recently, in November 2014, the G20 met in Australia and what do you know: they have agreed to put 2 trillion into the world economy to jumpstart it. That's nice of them. And who is going to pay for this money and from whom will they borrow it from or how will they raise this money? I wonder who will pay it back, huh? Look in that lovely mirror again: you and I will pay it back in some form or another. I promise you that! This is more world debt on top of the already growing total world debt, with many countries still paying back their old and current debts and loans to the IMF. According to Bloomberg.com, total world debt has now exceeded 100 trillion, up 40% prior to the Recession. What a nice mess they have put us all in?

It is the same in the United States of America (the USA, its real, good and honest people I mean [not those *really* running the Government and in government and those high up in the higher echelons right now] which used to stand for '**FREEDOM!**' Where has that ideal and message gone? Now the US invades and pretty much does whatever it wants (what the Powers-That-Be want, not what the real, genuine, ordinary US people really want; but then the US people are duped all the time by the Propaganda and Black PR in the Media and by the leaders and the Government). And, dare I say, is it not time now for the American people to wake up to what THEY are allowing their own country and Government to do around the World and to take responsibility for what they have been doing for more than 50 years? It is the same in most Governments around the world: we, the people, do not fully know what they have been doing and planning anymore; and most of these Mother F*****s are actually criminals (legal criminals I call them - because they have laws and rules to protect themselves, right?), guilty of high treason and treason against their own country, people and in particular: MANKIND!!! They probably all know each other very well and meet up at some very nice exclusive locations and have private (by invitation only) parties (orgies, drug-parties, sex with young boys and girls, prostitutes and a whole load of other sordid stuff I am sure, while their girlfriends, wives and children are at home, oblivious.) These are the low-life types of people who are running our Governments and the same for the 'ELITE' Powers-That-Be: The Lords of Death, Destruction and Evil: who think they are the chosen God-Like or 'Illuminati' owners and rulers (they are not people, but Slime, sub-humans) who run and control Earth, and WE are all *their* slaves. If you ever met these people you would probably feel very sick. And how they sleep at night, I do not know?

And I am not saying that all politicians are bad or scum: some (a few) people in our Governments are good and want to do good and they have (or had) all these great and good ideals, principles and ideas.

But when they get voted in, they get sucked into the system and become puppets, afraid to lose their jobs and pensions (or whatever the case may be) and have to toe-the-line of the party they are in or they get sacked or destroyed by the media or jailed on some trumped-up charge. Bear with me on this but these Powers-That-Be and their Minions will stop at nothing to get what they want: they actually started, financed and armed both sides of World War I & II and many other wars. Iraq was all just about oil and gas. Other surrounding countries around Iraq are the same. They get the CIA or Secret Ops or some other covert group in to start a war to get what they want (or to get someone in power who will do what they want) and it is so strange that the leaders and rulers in that country oblige them (they get looked after OR are threatened OR they are forced to resign OR are killed and then replaced with someone who will do what THEY say) and allow them to use and control the media. *They* destroy or kill (make it look like an accident or a suicide) all who get in their way or they destroy their reputations.

[Can I just interject here and say something more about Governments. There are probably really three Governments of any country (at least those of developed ones): One is the one we (wrongly) elected into power, the one they want us to see and think 'Oh, these boys are doing so much good for us and they are working oh so hard to help us and our country: NOT!; Two, is the inner-circle Government governing itself, wherein it is secretly running its own hidden agendas and advancing its own interests (doing illegal deals, or giving their family [nepotism] and friends contracts, etc. or doing deals and other dirty work for large commissions and backhanders and all the other self-interest covert rubbish they get up to) and also those of the elite businessmen/ Companies/Multi-Nationals, etc., in that country and its Royal Family (if it has one) and the Super-Rich or Super Powerful Families that Governments collude with -- we *only* know about their policies and agendas when they are found out; someone gets caught or it is leaked out or discovered somehow. Third, is the secret and very, very, VERY exclusive elitist supremist club: The Government's Government. Those handful of super-rich (they are richer than all of the top 100 Richest People in the World put together!!!) and super powerful families, who Govern pretty much all or most of the other governments and countries extant on planet Earth today. Now you can believe and think what you want about all of this – however; what I and others (in various books and Wikileaks, etc., open your eyes will you) have been saying for some time now is actually TRUE and you can and should check it out for yourself. Discover what is true for yourself and do not be a slave to only what 'others' purport or say is true.]

Some leaders/rulers are good (a small few today) too but they have to pay the price for getting to the top – and are usually financed by the Lords of planet Earth. And they are at risk if they do not do what the people at the top want or if they are a threat to the New World Order, they are taken out. Simple as that. Martin Luther King, Gandhi and President Kennedy paid the price. As did many others you would not even think about. Most just do their dirty work (they do some minor good activities but just to appease the masses and show them that they care a little bit about them and this will hopefully get them voted back in again) and then they retire or do not get elected back in again: funny how we never here of any poor EX-Presidents, Prime Ministers, Rulers or Leaders after they are out of office!!!??? No, they are looked after, including their henchmen, minions and ministers (commissions, backhanders: god - if we only knew what monies were in all those Swiss Bank accounts and off-shore accounts and where they all came from? WOW!!!! Maybe someday we will? Well only we can cause this to happen as with other topics and changes that I mention in this book). Clinton, Tony Blair, Bush, Nixon? And how many good people and leaders have been assassinated for speaking out against them, speaking the truth and for going up against them? Are you afraid? Well I am not and neither should you be or anyone else. They are human (or alien or part-alien – or whatever pieces of scum they are) like us and therefore they can be killed and better still, they can be tried and slung in jail for their crimes against humanity. More on this later…

Why can't we see the financial books of our own Governments? Why do they not tell us what they are REALLY up to and what their actual plans are? Not the rubbish they give us (most of what you hear in the media is lies, have-truths or altered truths, but mainly lies and false data and information to just control how you think, make you act or think how THEY want you to or just to make you feel crap, et al). What secrets

93

do they have which are above Top Secret and will never be revealed? If they were, they know they would all be jailed or even killed and the Governments toppled. What secrets do our wonderful Royal Families around Europe and the rest of the world have, because they are well in with the Powers-That-Be and probably are their puppets by now. The only reason Julian Assange of WikiLeaks is still alive today, is because he has enough on them to put them away; or they do not want to take the risk of having what he has on them revealed to the rest of the World; but they still try (as they have done with many other people) to get him in jail on trumped-up charges. And this shows us that they have most of the top judges and Senior legal people in their pockets too. Also, I am fairly certain Wikileaks is funded and protected by the good guys (thank god!) and maybe some secret, behind-the-scenes people, who are probably old now and regret what they have done in their lives or they just know what is going on and are not happy about it and just want to do their bit to help mankind. Whatever the case may be it is very admirable and laudable and for this, I thank you Julian Assange and all those who help, support and submit true factual articles and data to WikiLeaks and other websites and groups! But is no-one else going to help Mankind? Why is it always left to a handful of people or even worse - why do we wait until a huge disaster happens for people to act? It's too late then! Surely it is better to prevent a disaster or war from happening in the first place?

And so, where are all the other rich and powerful rulers, leaders and businessmen of the world? Are they working with the Powers-That-Be or are they afraid of them or are they just looking after Number One and their OWN interests and to hell with everyone else, including this lovely planet we live on? What men will do for money, wealth, fame, success and power is beyond belief and yet they (most of them) just believe in one life: when your body is dead that is the end of you. I can tell you that this is not true. Whether you believe it or not, it IS true that you go on living!!!

According to Wikipedia, the approximate population of planet Earth in 1350, was 300 million. Now it is almost 7 billion. Can anyone account for this growth and if we are all Spiritual Beings entering bodies at birth (and departing them at body-death), then where are all these billions of Beings or Souls coming from? If God is making them then fine – but if not? With this one fact in mind, one has to surmise and consider that the number of people dying every year is far below those being born, and supposedly these Beings are all going to Heaven, Hell or Purgatory or just back down to Earth again or whatever happens to Spiritual Beings when their bodies die (I personally strongly believe in reincarnation, of which there is much evidence: young children being born who can speak different languages, play piano, etc. and some even know who their brothers, sisters, sons/daughters/ mother/ father are and where they live, and the experts checked these out and found them to be correct!!!! Lots of other religions and people strongly believe in reincarnation too); this does make one think and question what is actually going on this planet and in this sector of the Universe? And this is not attacking religious beliefs; God; Allah; Buddha; Mohammed or anyone or anything else. There should always be freedom of speech and freedom of religious or non-religious belief – always; as long as those beliefs are good and actually do benefit and help people (not tricking, deceiving and conning them!) It does not mean that what someone believes to be true IS actually true – but one cannot force people to believe something they do not want to; it doesn't work ever, even if you beat them up or burn them at the stake: which the Catholic church did quite a lot (strange too that the Catholic Church has plenty of forbidden books, which the normal public are not allowed to read: why is that I wonder? It has plenty of land and wealth too.) But, do not forget that the Bible and all those other great books, were written thousands of years ago, when Mankind and his technologies were very young and primitive. And as indicated and hinted at in 'Rule by Secrecy' by Jim Marrs, those great religious people and leaders (including the true and real Mystics, Magicians and Philosophers of ages old) did either not tell us everything (kept the real secrets to themselves concerning who and what Mankind was and were he actually came from and how he evolved; and they only indoctrinated the chosen few so they could keep the knowledge and power for themselves and put and keep Mankind in *their* control, power and enslavement and in a state of ignorance) or they themselves did not know all the answers: one of the other? Witness the recently discovered Dead Sea Scrolls and in particular, the Sumerian (roughly where present day Iraq is today) Tablets and all those other ancient texts, papers and books: Thoth's Book of the Dead; Emerald Tablets,

Roger Bacon's books – check these out to find out more. Getting back to my point: Why can we not see the books of the banks that we the taxpayers had to bail out? Oil and gas prices keep going up and up, yet more and more oil and gas is being found all the time. And most of what we pay on fuel is tax to the Governments and they say they can't do anything about it and neither can OPEC: the major oil producing countries. What a load of baloney! They can't do anything about it or they do not want to do anything about it? You decide.

How did Greece and Italy (and many other countries in Europe and around the World) get into such huge debt? How do we know it is true? They were not involved in any recent wars? Where has all the money gone and what was it spent on? The UK has about 5 Trillion in national debt and the US about 17 trillion: what was the money spent on? Surely rich countries should not have any debt at all? Why are they all being forced to borrow from the IMF, the World Bank or the now new European Central Bank? (All owned and funded by the Powers-That-Be, the so-called Lords of Death and Destruction. Did you know that?)

The Bank of England and the Federal Reserve Bank are all owned by them too but they keep changing how they run each one and how they are involved: but regardless of how it may seem to us and how they portray it in the media: they own and run them (and make money from the Treasury and inter-bank lending, etc. – they are geniuses at finance but also at deception and subterfuge!!!!) and pretty much have most of the total wealth on the entire planet! Wow, now that is saying something or what?

Remember before, at the start of this book. I told you to look and see what is going on around you and that you may experience some stuff while reading this book? Well keep going and keep reading – do not stop. (Note: If one can look and see, then one can CONFRONT (face) one's own existence and the state of Mankind AND the Lords of Death and Destruction: and no-one else is going to do this and sort these problems out except US!!!!! The rest don't even care or are in no physical and/or mental state to be of any help anyway, and others are just so happy being HUMAN and being BODIES that they are not aware in the slightest that they are Spiritual Beings and that they CAN be Spiritually Free and

Exterior from their bodies and have the problems of their Unconscious Minds resolved all in ONE lifetime: We can all know the TRUTH AND be SPIRITUALLY FREE without having to wait until our bodies die!!!

How many millions of people in the last 100 years, have died, been raped, murdered, blown up, maimed, drugged, tortured and suffered in all these wars and World Wars? They were ALL caused and funded by the Lords of Death and destruction!!!!!!!!!!!! I kid you not. I know that this sounds insane and supremely evil, despicable and beyond words and comprehension – and it is – but that still does not mean it is not true and that what has happened is still continuing to happen - a complete violation of the highest and most basic tenets, rights and moral and ethical beliefs of Mankind: I print for you here (from the Universal Declaration of Human Rights as agreed my most countries in the World and it is pretty much intended and understood to be Worldwide Law and most, if not all, have actually been made into laws and legally binding in most countries around the world!) the:

The Human Rights of Mankind

Article 1.

All human beings are born free and equal in dignity and rights. They are endowed with reason and conscience and should act towards one another in a spirit of brotherhood.

Article 2.

Everyone is entitled to all the rights and freedoms set forth in this Declaration, without distinction of any kind, such as race, colour, sex, language, religion, political or other opinion, national or social origin, property, birth or other status. Furthermore, no distinction shall be made on the basis of the political, jurisdictional or international status of the country or territory to which a person belongs, whether it be independent, trust, non-self-governing or under any other limitation of sovereignty.

Article 3.

Everyone has the right to life, liberty and security of person.

Article 4.

No one shall be held in slavery or servitude; slavery and the slave trade shall be prohibited in all their forms.

Article 5.

No one shall be subjected to torture or to cruel, inhuman or degrading treatment or punishment.

Article 6.

Everyone has the right to recognition everywhere as a person before the law.

Article 7.

All are equal before the law and are entitled without any discrimination to equal protection of the law. All are entitled to equal protection against any discrimination in violation of this Declaration and against any incitement to such discrimination.

Article 8.

Everyone has the right to an effective remedy by the competent national tribunals for acts violating the fundamental rights granted him by the constitution or by law.

Article 9.

No one shall be subjected to arbitrary arrest, detention or exile.

Article 10.

Everyone is entitled in full equality to a fair and public hearing by an independent and impartial tribunal, in the determination of his rights and obligations and of any criminal charge against him.

Article 11.

(1) Everyone charged with a penal offence has the right to be

presumed innocent until proved guilty according to law in a public trial at which he has had all the guarantees necessary for his defence.

(2) No one shall be held guilty of any penal offence on account of any act or omission which did not constitute a penal offence, under national or international law, at the time when it was committed. Nor shall a heavier penalty be imposed than the one that was applicable at the time the penal offence was committed.

Article 12.

No one shall be subjected to arbitrary interference with his privacy, family, home or correspondence, nor to attacks upon his honour and reputation. Everyone has the right to the protection of the law against such interference or attacks.

Article 13.

(1) Everyone has the right to freedom of movement and residence within the borders of each state.

(2) Everyone has the right to leave any country, including his own, and to return to his country.

Article 14.

(1) Everyone has the right to seek and to enjoy in other countries asylum from persecution.

(2) This right may not be invoked in the case of prosecutions genuinely arising from non-political crimes or from acts contrary to the purposes and principles of the United Nations.

Article 15.

(1) Everyone has the right to a nationality.

(2) No one shall be arbitrarily deprived of his nationality nor denied the right to change his nationality.

Article 16.

(1) Men and women of full age, without any limitation due to race, nationality or religion, have the right to marry and to found a family. They are entitled to equal rights as to marriage, during marriage and at its dissolution.

(2) Marriage shall be entered into only with the free and full consent of the intending spouses.

(3) The family is the natural and fundamental group unit of society and is entitled to protection by society and the State.

Article 17.

(1) Everyone has the right to own property alone as well as in association with others.

(2) No one shall be arbitrarily deprived of his property.

Article 18.

Everyone has the right to freedom of thought, conscience and religion; this right includes freedom to change his religion or belief, and freedom, either alone or in community with others and in public or private, to manifest his religion or belief in teaching, practice, worship and observance.

Article 19.

Everyone has the right to freedom of opinion and expression; this right includes freedom to hold opinions without interference and to seek, receive and impart information and ideas through any media and regardless of frontiers.

Article 20.

(1) Everyone has the right to freedom of peaceful assembly and association.

(2) No one may be compelled to belong to an association.

Article 21.

(1) Everyone has the right to take part in the government of his country, directly or through freely chosen representatives.

(2) Everyone has the right of equal access to public service in his country.

(3) The will of the people shall be the basis of the authority of government; this will shall be expressed in periodic and genuine elections which shall be by universal and equal suffrage and shall be held by secret vote or by equivalent free voting procedures.

Article 22.

Everyone, as a member of society, has the right to social security and is entitled to realization, through national effort and international co-operation and in accordance with the organization and resources of each State, of the economic, social and cultural rights indispensable for his dignity and the free development of his personality.

Article 23.

(1) Everyone has the right to work, to free choice of employment, to just and favourable conditions of work and to protection against unemployment.

(2) Everyone, without any discrimination, has the right to equal pay for equal work.

(3) Everyone who works has the right to just and favourable remuneration ensuring for himself and his family an existence worthy of human dignity, and supplemented, if necessary, by other means of social protection.

(4) Everyone has the right to form and to join trade unions for the protection of his interests.

Article 24.

Everyone has the right to rest and leisure, including reasonable limitation of working hours and periodic holidays with pay.

Article 25.

(1) Everyone has the right to a standard of living adequate for the health and well-being of himself and of his family, including food, clothing, housing and medical care and necessary social services, and the right to security in the event of unemployment, sickness, disability, widowhood, old age or other lack of livelihood in circumstances beyond his control.

(2) Motherhood and childhood are entitled to special care and assistance. All children, whether born in or out of wedlock, shall enjoy the same social protection.

Article 26.

(1) Everyone has the right to education. Education shall be free, at least in the elementary and fundamental stages. Elementary education shall be compulsory. Technical and professional education shall be made generally available and higher education shall be equally accessible to all on the basis of merit.

(2) Education shall be directed to the full development of the human personality and to the strengthening of respect for human rights and fundamental freedoms. It shall promote understanding, tolerance and friendship among all nations, racial or religious groups, and shall further the activities of the United Nations for the maintenance of peace.

(3) Parents have a prior right to choose the kind of education that shall be given to their children.

Article 27.

(1) Everyone has the right freely to participate in the cultural life of the community, to enjoy the arts and to share in scientific

advancement and its benefits.

(2) Everyone has the right to the protection of the moral and material interests resulting from any scientific, literary or artistic production of which he is the author.

Article 28.

Everyone is entitled to a social and international order in which the rights and freedoms set forth in this Declaration can be fully realized.

Article 29.

(1) Everyone has duties to the community in which alone the free and full development of his personality is possible.

(2) In the exercise of his rights and freedoms, everyone shall be subject only to such limitations as are determined by law solely for the purpose of securing due recognition and respect for the rights and freedoms of others and of meeting the just requirements of morality, public order and the general welfare in a democratic society.

(3) These rights and freedoms may in no case be exercised contrary to the purposes and principles of the United Nations.

Article 30.

Nothing in this Declaration may be interpreted as implying for any State, group or person any right to engage in any activity or to perform any act aimed at the destruction of any of the rights and freedoms set forth herein.

These ARE our rights and if they are being violated (and many are being violated every day all over the world - fact! But strange how many countries, governments and other worldwide organizations completely ignore this, like the USA and the UK and others and the rest of the world sits back and does nothing as they know who is really giving the orders to these countries – more on this later?) then do contact your Embassy, any relevant government/legal department, Amnesty International, the European Court of Human Rights, the Citizen's Commission of Human Rights (they all have websites and are worldwide) or some other such independent organizations. Or contact someone by e-mail, Facebook, Skype, Twitter, letter, fax, text message, etc. - anything but get your case heard and something done about it and make it known internationally too, if you can; but do something about it and do not give up – ever!

You will also probably have special rights and laws that apply to one's own country or state only and one should check and find out what they are?

But we also now have criminals using Human Rights to protect themselves. Well, I am sorry but they lost their rights when they became criminal. And how many other laws and rules are there to protect the criminals, not us, but to protect them. Oh, the poor criminals. I feel so sorry for them.

Many of the Leaders/Rulers/Presidents/Prime Ministers (they know who they are and what crimes they have committed, and they have to live with them every day for the rest of their lives and beyond!) of many countries around the world are actually and factually guilty of violating these human rights; the constitutional rights of their own country and are guilty of treason and high treason; especially the Lords of Death and Destruction!!!!! They should be brought to justice or at the very least be made to reform and cease their evil ways and wrongdoings or be justly and fairly tried and jailed and prevented from further interfering in Mankind's affairs.

THE EEC & THE USA

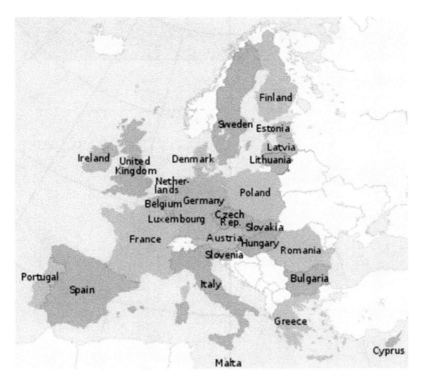

htt/commons.wikimedia.org/wiki/File:Member_States_of_the_European_Union_%28polar_stereographic_projection%29_EN.svg

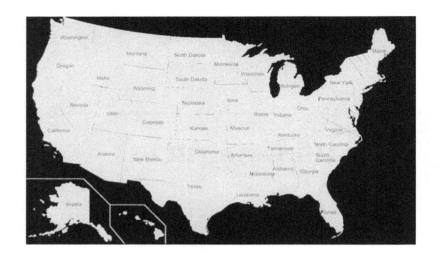

https://commons.wikimedia.org/wiki/File:Map_of_USA_States_with_names_white.sv

EEC POLITICAL STRUCTURE   USA POLITICAL STRUCTURE

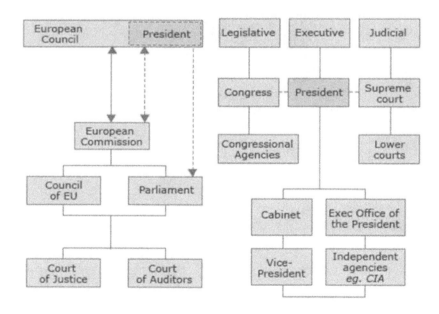

SHORT HISTORY OF THE EEC:

The original purpose of the EEC was to help rebuild Europe after

World War II, improve trade and to make sure a world war did not happen again.

The founding fathers of this new Europe were (according to the EEC & Brussels itself): Joseph Bech, Paul- Henri Spaak, Winston Churchill, Walter Hallstein, Robert Shuman, Sicco Mansholt, Johan Willem Beyen, Konrad Adenauer, Alterio Spinelli, Acide de Gasperi and Jean Monnet. I have not fully checked out all these people but I am sure they had some dealings with or connections with those who rule and run Earth today and most of the above gentlemen were advocating far more than just free trade; but a 'union' of states or a Superstate like in the USA. Which can then be merged with the USA, Canada and the other G8 or G 20 countries, other regions and continents. And then, we can – if evil people and beings prevail – kiss our asses, minds, spirits and souls goodbye!

As the Powers-That-Be's plan to take over Earth and Mankind using Hitler (who they created {mentally}, financed and shaped into the monster he became) had failed, they then resorted to the underhanded, behind-closed doors and legal and paperwork method and enlisted or forced or paid to-work-for-them those politicians who would do their bidding. This is NOT a conspiracy theory, which many scoff and laugh at and ignore. Well, they are actually laughing at themselves as all that I have said and will say in this book has either already happened, is happening or will happen very soon. Not theory but actual fact. Check it out for yourself and decide? I also invite you to think for yourself about the state you yourself are in, that of one's family, one's business or job; one's country and the entire planet as a whole?

Then later, the EEC become 'Free trade amongst member nations' and they now want to and are creating a giant Superstate, are destroying our cultures –slowly but surely - and changing us into how 'THEY' want us to be: their slaves. THEY are telling US and our wonderful Governments how to run our OWN countries???!!! They also want to expand the EEC and make it the rest of the World: Complete Domination, with us at the bottom, some in the middle and a very small few at the top. But they do it all under the false 'guise' that they are helping us: so kind of them! You have all heard of George Orwell's 'Animal Farm' and his prophetic '1984' (I am certain he knew or found out by some means what was really happening and is still happening on Earth today and who was doing it. He wanted to help us and to get us to take action. His books are not just fiction! They were and still are based on fact!) And see the Matrix and other books and films. Well, I do not jest: our possible future, and those of our children could be a version of this, if we do nothing about what 'THEY' have planned for us and what they are actually RIGHT NOW doing behind closed doors. Some may laugh or scoff at this or it is beyond their comprehension, imagination or understanding; some do not care at all and others just look the other way and/or look after Number One (sadly all too common in this, the modern society we live in today). And some want to do something about their lives, their countries and the destiny and future of Mankind and planet Earth. They are afraid, confused on how to act or just do not know what to do about it all or who to blame or even attack. Well, to be honest, we have every type of Human being (stupid, intelligent, genius, artist, killer and murders, et al), culture, knowledge (whether right or wrong), religion, cult, science, philosophy and everything else, all mixed up and co-existing together on this unique blue planet we live on. And with this in mind it is a real wonder, with all of this Global Concoction going on, on a daily basis, how Mankind has even got this far? It is the miracle of miracles when you also add in all the savage, terrible, violent and insane HISTORY man has experienced and yet still he survives and endures. But just. WOW, is that not amazing!

[Note: I must add in here again that not all men, women, teenagers, children are bad or evil. In times of stress or life-threatening dangers, anyone can be temporarily criminal, dangerous or do bad to protect themselves or their family; and alcohol and drugs do not help either. But this is different. What I am saying is that most of Mankind – the MAJORITY – thank god! - are good because if this were not the fact, then Man would have destroyed himself years ago and the evil people (small MINORITY) would have taken over and completely dominated us all by now. And what I am predicting as to potentially what our future could be, would have manifested itself by now. Luckily, we still have a chance (VERY slim) to act and create a future for mankind which is free from the influences of evil men and beings, and which is good, more equal and fair – but ONLY if we act now and act in the right, proper, sane and logical manner! One cannot just go and kill the entire staff of your Government or blow them up and then have it replaced by an even worse Government, Dictator or Despot, which/who then kill/s and tortures anyone who threatens or goes against him and no-one has any freedom, rights and everything in the economy and country is controlled by them or him and his minions. How would that work and how would that be better than the current corrupt Government you have in your country? I just give this as an example of how not to act. I cover this later in another chapter in more detail.]

But getting back to the EEC, we do not need Brussels to tell each country in Europe what to do and how to run their own countries and how to run their own finances and economies. Free trade yes, but how has free trade been turned into telling us how our lives and countries should be? Why should we allow OUR wonderful governments to give **our** rights and the sovereignty of our hard-won and fought-for countries (which WE have developed and our ancestors have paid for, died for and advanced over the centuries) to a bunch of dickheads in Brussels, who honestly do not give a shit about what WE want but ONLY what they want and the appeasement of the dark Powers-That-Be!!!

The International Institute for Labour Studies says:

"On average, more than **40 %** of jobseekers in advanced economies have been without work for more than a year."

At 19.8 % of GDP in 2010, global investment remains 3.1 percentage points lower than the historical average, with a more pronounced downward trend in advanced economies." Employment rates have increased in only 6 of 36 advanced economies (Austria, Germany, Israel, Luxembourg, Malta and Poland) since 2007."

Youth unemployment rates have increased in about 80 % of advanced countries and in 66 % of developing countries." Poverty rates have increased in half of developed economies and in one third of developing economies." Involuntary part-time employment has increased in two-thirds of advanced economies." The share of informal employment stands at more than 40 % in two-thirds of emerging and developing countries."

…and raising the risk of poverty and social unrest.

In 2010 16.4 percent of the population in the EU had been at risk of poverty. The figure is even higher for young people aged 18-24 at 21.2 per cent. These trends are on the rise…
Austerity measures have had a negative impact on labour markets and business investment

…This has led a number of EU member states to introduce lower employment protection regulations and decentralized collective bargaining, among them Estonia, France, Greece, Hungary, Italy, Latvia, Lithuania, Romania, Slovakia, and Spain.

Investment activity in the European Union is still weak with an investment/GDP ratio about 16 per cent below its historical average and only slightly above its all-time low…

Large businesses have built-up unprecedented large cash stocks since 2008. Between 2007 and 2011, the 50 European companies on the benchmark Euro Stoxx 50 Index **increased their cash holdings by 77 per cent and the increase was 32 per cent between 2010 and 2011.**

World of Work 2012: Better jobs for a better economy is available at (www.ilo.org/INST). For further comment, journalists are invited to contact Daniel Samaan (tel: +41 22 799 7539, email: samaan@ilo.org); or Raymond Torres (tel: +41 22 799 7908, email: torresr@ilo.org), Director of the ILO's International Institute for Labour Studies.

Here are some examples of the rubbish coming from Brussels:

Financial transactions tax in Europe given go-ahead

SOURCE: BBC NEWS BUSINESS: http://www.bbc.co.uk/news/business-21138494
Another Wikipedia link on this: http://en.wikipedia.org/wiki/European
Union financial transaction tax
This tax is expected to be charged at a rate of one euro for every 1,000 euros

of shares traded. It is intended to stop speculative trading. The UK and 15 other EU nations will not introduce the tax The tax - also known as a Tobin tax - is expected to be charged at a rate of 0.1% of the value of any trade in shares or bonds, and 0.01% of any financial derivative contract.

The other nine going ahead with the tax are Spain, Portugal, Italy, Belgium, Austria, Slovakia, Slovenia, Greece and Estonia.

>It is not yet clear how the proceeds of the tax will be used, but one possibility is that they will be collected by the European Commission to finance a bailout fund for eurozone banks. Then we have the IMF telling other countries what to do. For example: Ukraine was told to raise household gas and heating prices if it wanted to gain access to 15.6 billion bailout loan. Now look at what has happened in Ukraine recently in March 2014. This is current and a prime example of what the Powers-That-Be can do and illustrates how they operate. The Prime Minister, government and people of Ukraine were heading towards greater unity with Russia and better trade and relations instead of greater unity with the EEC. So what did the Powers-That-Be do? They got their minions and their Global Security Fund to work by getting rid of the Prime Minister, changing Ukrainian opinion and getting them back to increasing relations with the EEC again and to eventually joining it. And, of course, they also dangle the carrot by offering billions in loans from the wonderful IMF and then they own the country, as they have done with the rest of the EEC countries. Nice that. They are so helpful those people at the IMF and other such finance organizations. Anyway, they changed the entire country around from heading in Russia's direction to now being a nearly full member of the wonderful EEC. What's wonderful about being in the EEC, I really do not know? Russia, which must have got pissed of being told what to do by Europe and the USA (what the USA has got to do with Europe I do not know and it has nothing to do with Ukraine at all, has it? Oh, but the governments and those at the top of the UK, the rest of the EEC and the USA are all working with or pretty much owned by the Powers-That-Be. And I thought they served us, their people. Anyway, Putin or Russia got pissed off and basically took Crimea. So this is a very good example of how they work and what they can do and there are no limits to how far they are willing to go to attain their nefarious goals and further enslave mankind.

And recently, we have had Cameron saying that the UK should stay in the EEC and Obama agrees. What has Obama and the USA got to do with the UK or the EEC? Now David Cameron is saying there should be free trade between the US and the EEC. They just want to expand the countries they run and control and get them all joined together into one big happy family, create a giant World Superstate, which will allow (by dangling carrots or financial or other rewards/ commissions and other lucrative deals to the elite and those who do their bidding; and thus expand this Superstate into a giant World state, with one World Government, a new World Order (with no votes or referendums on anything [or if they are allowed, they will be fixed]), and then, my friends, you can kiss your ass goodbye and any good future and freedom that Mankind may be able to have – as it will be too late then. This is all happening, right now - TODAY! Look at the news and the newspapers. Nearly every country in the world now owes huge sums of money (for what I don't know and how these countries ended up borrowing so much money, when at least 50% of them are supposed to be rich, I cannot understand this – can you?) to the IMF, World Bank or some other bank, financial body or Central Bank. Only countries like China, Brazil and India are holding their own – but I am fairly certain that they have some kind of deals in place with the Powers-That-Are on Planet Earth today or are working with them behind the scenes. And look at the financial and pay inequalities that is going in in China, India and Brazil: the gap between the Super-rich, the rich and the working class and poor is huge and growing. All the wealth in these countries (and around the world for that matter) is all being hoarded by the few and not being shared out China and around the world. They are not paying us here in the UK, the EEC and around the world, good wages – just enough to survive, eat and rent a property – not enough to buy a property. Only the mangers, the skilled and highly skilled; those successful artists and the successful business owners and those with money, are earning a good wage and making more and more money. Who is benefiting and gaining from these so-called huge Sovereign Wealth Funds? It is not the working class and the poor, is it? Who owns these Sovereign Wealth Funds? Surely it is the peoples of the countries it is in? No? Or is it only those at the top, who are the rich millionaires and billionaires who benefit from them and that countries leaders and its top businesses. Funny, I thought the people owned everything in a communist country and it was all shared out equally?<

I thought I would now just briefly mention Sovereign Funds below (and I wonder how many other secret and hidden funds and accounts our governments have and this money is meant to be ours?):

FROM: Global Finance:-

http://www.gfmag.com/global-data/economic-data/largest-sovereign-wealth-funds

Largest Sovereign Funds (SWFs) – 2012 Ranking
November 19, 2012
Author: Tina Aridas, Valentina Pasquali
Writer: This article explains that: A Sovereign Wealth Fund is a state-owned investment fund made up of financial assets such as stocks, bonds, real estate or other instruments and funded by foreign exchange assets. In 2012, the Abu Dhabi Investment Authority tops the list at US$627 billion, with Norway's Government Pension Fund–Global (US$611 billion) second and China's SAFE Investment Company (US$568 billion) third. Most are financed from oil revenue, such as in the case of the Abu Dhabi and Norway.
Data is from the Sovereign Wealth Fund Institute, 2012 Sovereign Wealth Fund Allocation Report.

Ten Largest SWFs in 2012 (in US$ Millions)

The world's top 36 SWFs, in 2012 totalled nearly $5 trillion. Oil and gas-related SWFs totalled 57.3%; with Asia having 40.5%, followed by the Middle East with 35.6%.

Largest SFWs – 2012
Data is from the Sovereign Wealth Fund Institute, 2012 Sovereign Wealth Fund Allocation Report.

Country	Sovereign Fund Name	Assets $ Billion	Inception	Origin

UAE - Abu Dhabi	Abu Dhabi Investment Authority	$627.00	1976	Oil
Norway	Government Pension Fund - Global	$611.00	1990	Oil
China	SAFE Investment Company	$567.90	1997	Non-commodity
Saudi Arabia	SAMA Foreign Holdings	$532.80		Oil
China	China Investment Corporation	$439.60	2007	Non-commodity
Kuwait	Kuwait Investment Authority	$296.00	1953	Oil
China - Hong Kong	Hong Kong Monetary Authority Investment Portfolio	$293.30	1993	Non-commodity
Singapore	Government of Singapore Investment Corporation	$247.50	1981	Non-commodity
Singapore	Temasek Holdings	$157.20	1974	Non-commodity
Russia	National Wealth Fund*	$149.70	2008	Oil
China	National Social Security Fund	$134.50	2000	Non-commodity
Qatar	Qatar Investment Authority	$100.00	2005	Oil
Australia	Australian Future Fund	$80.00	2006	Non-commodity
UAE - Dubai	Investment Corporation of Dubai	$70.00	2006	Oil
Libya	Libyan Investment Authority	$65.00	2006	Oil
Kazakhstan	Kazakhstan National Fund	$58.20	2000	Oil
UAE - Abu Dhabi	International Petroleum Investment Company	$58.00	1984	Oil
Algeria	Revenue Regulation Fund	$56.70	2000	Oil
UAE - Abu Dhabi	Mubadala Development Company	$48.20	2002	Oil
South Korea	Korea Investment Corporation	$43.00	2005	Non-commodity
US - Alaska	Alaska Permanent Fund	$40.30	1976	Oil
Malaysia	Khazanah Nasional	$36.80	1993	Non-commodity
Azerbaijan	State Oil Fund	$30.20	1999	Oil
Ireland	National Pensions Reserve Fund	$30.00	2001	Non-commodity
Brunei	Brunei Investment Agency	$30.00	1983	Oil
France	Strategic Investment Fund	$28.00	2008	Non-commodity
US - Texas	Texas Permanent School Fund	$24.40	1854	Oil & Other
Iran	Oil Stabilisation Fund	$23.00	1999	Oil
New Zealand	New Zealand Superannuation Fund	$15.90	2003	Non-commodity
Canada	Alberta's Heritage Fund	$15.10	1976	Oil
Chile	Social & Economic Stablization Fund	$15.00	2007	Copper
US - New Mexico	New Mexico State Investment Council	$14.30	1958	Non-commodity
Brazil	Sovereign Fund of Brazil	$11.30	2008	Non-commodity
East Timor	Timor-Leste Petroleum Fund	$9.90	2005	Oil & Gas
Bahrain	Mumtalakat Holdings	$9.10	2006	Non-commodity

Oman	State General Reserve Fund	$8.20	1980	Oil & Gas

WRITER: The UK, Ireland and many other European countries (Ireland was booming before it joined the Euro - the Celtic Tiger. The UK [probably breaking apart as Scotland may probably leave and maybe Wales will follow to as, let's be honest here, they were only beaten into being a UK, not by their own choice] or England has been doing very well since its British Empire and Colonial times and the Industrial Revolution (but inflation and taxes in the UK have been going up almost continuously since these times.) So were many other European countries doing well before they joined the EEC and the wonderful Euro came along. But the leaders of our Governments (all bribed or given deep sleep therapy, brainwashing or some such action – or they just want to advance their own bank accounts, power, status and interests – or they just don't give a shit – whatever the case may be) tell us it is so vital and important and beneficial to stay in the EEC, and that our businesses and banks need the Euro and we must all join together and integrate all the European nations EVEN MORE and blah, blah, blah and more blah!

Why did the people of Ireland say yes to the Lisbon Treaty? Or did they? Maybe the results were tampered with and they were definitely all hoodwinked by the media and the oh-so-honest Irish Government. Why was the Maastricht Treaty (signed by our wonderful political leaders in 1992 without a referendum? Are referendums banned now or what?) ratified and more of the powers and control of our countries given to Brussels? Funny, it was written in such a manner that no-one could quite understand it and it was so huge in page numbers, that no-one would want to read it. Thus they can do whatever they want: which is what they pretty much do right now. Why does the UK and other European countries allow so many foreign people and Eastern Europeans (I have nothing against foreign people just that there are too many coming in to Europe and taking any jobs they can get, and of course business benefits by getting cheap labour.) And why do we not have a European Vote or Referendum on which countries are allowed to join the EEC? Some countries that have been allowed to join the EEC should NOT have been allowed to become members and that is a fact! It's sad, but now most of the countries in Europe just do what

Brussels tells them to? Witness all the events and changes that have taken place in Europe in just the last 10 years, to say nothing of the previous twenty years of its history?

And what do WE - the peoples of Europe - do about it?

NOTHING!!!!!

Nice fact to know that. If people do not do something about their own countries problems; then those at the top will be doing something to them to make matters worse - rest assured.

And all those countries who have recently joined the EEC – the Eastern Bloc countries (Poland, Hungary, Slovakia, Slovenia, and all the rest) are Oh so happy because they can legally and illegally come to the richer countries in Europe and take as many jobs/money as they can; and - get this - this was all planned. Yes, pre-planned years ago. Poor/underdeveloped countries should really not be allowed to join the EEC. And the rich EEC countries should not have to support the poorer European countries or other countries for that matter. And those countries in the EEC should operate an entry policy like they have in Australia and the same for those countries who want to join the EEC. Racism is not giving someone a job because they are black, white, Jewish, Irish, Polish, etc. or it is beating someone up because of their colour, religion or nationality – now that IS racism and I am not talking about that. I am talking about the fact that a country should look after its OWN first and I am talking about financial success, economics and rights/fairness. I do not know what our children and graduates are going to do for good-paid work in the future? O yes, if Mammy and Daddy have money or have a wealthy successful business, then they can work with them and have everything paid for: but what about the rest of us, what do we do?

The other factor is this: mix up all the races and cultures of Europe (and the world for that matter) and then you have none, none that is good anyway; just a culture of jeans, t-shirts, i-phones, laptops, slavery, taxes, bills and more suppressive laws and 'do-not-think-for-yourself' or question anything because: THEY know it all and they are your leaders and they have degrees in Politics, Economics or Political science (a science, huh?) and just enjoy what they give us and be so happy. Thank you so much – our wonderful Government Leaders for being so kind and thoughtful of us! We thank you SO much - NOT. This has and is happening as a pattern all over the world right now and it was all masterminded many years ago, even before the USA was founded and probably even before the time of Egyptian Pharaohs (yes, I know it is hard to believe this but there is evidence that this is the case. Do you think we are the only Life forms in existence in the entire Universe? I find that very hard to believe. But you are entitled to think what you want on this as it does not change the current condition Mankind is in today but it is food for thought.)

Strange how Germany, after the Berlin wall come down, became such a staunch supporter, financier and everything else of the EEC and the Euro (which nearly bankrupt their country to bring it in)? Is this World War III but being done on paper and behind closed doors, instead of all-out violent warfare? I think YES but check out the facts for yourself.

Not one country that I Know off has done better economically and financially by accepting (forced on us but still WE accept it – why?) and bringing in the Euro. Maybe Germany but they were the ones who introduced it (nearly bankrupting themselves I may add) on their own terms and now Germany (and I have nothing against the German people, just their government and a handful of certain people behind the scenes and at the top levels who are pulling al the strings) wants to force ITS terms, conditions and contracts on the rest of those poorer and richer European countries (who were meant to have been helped so much by the Euro?) if they want to borrow money because they are in so much debt.

You cannot have one same-currency-valued-Euro for all European countries. Why? Because not every country is the same: different industries, finances, exports/imports and all the rest, and some are rich, poor or in-between. That is why the Euro will NEVER work, has not worked and why it does not now work. The Euro actually has no real intrinsic value and is backed by nothing except Germany, France (strange how France is always close behind Germany on almost everything they do – why is that?) and the great Brussels. All bow down to Brussels and kiss their asses, because they do so much good for us and only have our best interests at heart. O thank you Brussels, the IMF, World Bank, European Central Bank, OPEC, Bank of England, Federal Reserve Bank, the US Government, all those wonderful Royal/Ruling Families, and all the rest, including the Globalist/Elitist/ Supremist Leaders, Capitalists, Communists and THEIR Powers-That-Be. You are so kind for allowing us to live and to be your loyal subjects and slaves and for allowing us to work so hard to pay taxes to them.

And another point to make about this Recession and Global situation, which our great political and economic 'experts' are trying so hard to handle, is this: if people are being taxed to the hilt, with their wages going down or staying the same, then if they have less money in their pockets or no free money because it is all being spent on bills, taxes, new taxes, increased taxes, increased fuel and energy bills, VAT (Value Added Tax: what value?), increased VAT, rates, increased car insurance, council tax, corporate tax, debts, rent, mortgage, food and other living expenses, then how in the hell are businesses going to make any money (except from those who have money)and therefore be able to pay their expenses and survive? Now that is why quite a few have closed down or gone bankrupt. The only businesses that are surviving are those that are selling products/services that people vitally need and the rest just target the rich and those with some spare extra money or savings put away: who are not much affected by this recession anyway. And the rest of us?

And very recently, on the 21.1.2015, that wonderful European Central Bank, has announced it is going to start in March it's Quantitative Easing (QE) – which means buying, in cash, public and private/corporate sector bonds and securities, including government/sovereign bonds - at a rate of about 50-60 billion Euros a month, continued until 2016; which in total will amount to 1 trillion Euros being injected in to the European Countries, Business and Economy. That's all good and well, but it is a little bit too late, as this should have been done 4 years ago? And who is going to get all of this money? Who is going to benefit? Will it benefit you and I? Will we get pay rises and cheaper mortgages and housing? As usual, those at or near the top will get or benefit from this 1 trillion – not us at or near the bottom. But hey, maybe a few crumbs will trickle down to us somehow after those at the top have made a killing and made some profit?

It would far better to share out equally 50% of that 1 trillion (or all of it) amongst those who earn less than 30,000 Euros a year. Then this would help kickstart the European economy, with those people then having more money to spend on and put in to business. If you do it the other way around, it usually does not come down to those at or near the bottom; or not much of it does anyway. But hey – this is how these people at the top want it. And they don't consult with us because they know it all or *think* they do. Which is one reason why the world and Mankind are in the state they are today. They, and they know who they are, serve themselves and others – but not US. I strongly hope you get that please; for all our sakes!

I must now talk about the USA, because I really like these people a lot and I have met some and they are SO nice and they CAN communicate and say what they want; and they are so larger than life – which I like. Big Spiritual and Capable Beings – but they are also, sadly so gullible and easily tricked and beguiled by the media and their own leaders.

Below is a picture I found of a timeline of the wars that the USA has been involved in. And all of these have been financed by the American people and paid back by them in inflation and taxes. Nice. Huh? Maybe this is why national debt is about 17 trillion, and this debt is for the richest country in the world, with the richest individuals residing there. How can a rich country have so much debt and debt for what and to who?

THE USA BOMBING LIST SINCE WW2

Korea and China 1950-1953 (Korean War)
Guatemala 1954
Indonesia 1958
Cuba 1959-1961
Guatemala 1960
Congo 1964
Laos 1964-1973
Vietnam 1961-1973

Cambodia 1969-1970
Guatemala 1967-1969
Grenada 1983
Lebanon 1983, 1984
Libya 1986
El Salvador 1980s
Nicaragua 1980s
Iran 1987
Panama 1989
Iraq 1991 (Persian Gulf War)
Kuwait 1991
Somalia 1993
Bosnia 1994, 1995
Sudan 1998
Afghanistan 1998
Yugoslavia 1999
Yemen 2002
Iraq 1991-2002 (USA/UK on regular basis)
Iraq 2003 – present
Afghanistan 2001 – present
Pakistan 2007 – present
Somalia 2007/8, 2011
Yemen 2009, 2011
Libya 2011

The American people have been tricked, conned, cheated, misinformed and abused for a long time now, and they have themselves to blame for this, for not knowing who was doing it to them or for not finding out earlier. I wish the American people would wake up as to what is going in their own country and around the world, and it, being a world leader and Superpower, should oust those out of power at the top and handle the '*real*' Powers-That- be in their own country and on this planet and stop them no matter what it takes; and take and get back the power to the good peoples of planet Earth. Now that would be something if they just had the guts to do it and not be so worried about just their own lives, money, car, house, mortgage (and this applies to everyone on planet Earth today, not just Americans! It applies to YOU, the person reading this book. Yes YOU!!!!) and decide to change the Governmental' systems and other systems in existence today, so we can ALL win and begin to have a happy or happier life again. Not a miserable one or one badly controlled by others. Nothing wrong with being controlled just as long as it is good control. Nothing wrong with having leaders or rich people running the country, the businesses, the planet, just so long as they are good and that measures, laws and systems are in place to get rid of them should they decide to be bad and do bad to us. You cannot give all power and trust and control to a handful of individuals and let them do what they want and have no way to controlling them or taking the power back and giving it to those who are good and who deserve and who WILL serve US, the peoples of Earth. There must be some way of also monitoring what Governments and World Leaders actually do. And this applies to businesses too. And we, the peoples of Earth, must be more involved in this and in economics, finances, laws and politics and not let it all be run on automatic or left to a 'few' who are a rotten as hell and legal criminals (they have the law on their sides), and who just lie, cheat, kill, maim, ruin, harm, swindle and destroy us all and our countries and our lovely planet. And WE ARE the ones letting them do it – yes or no – well?????

I should not really say this but I will (I did tell you at the start of my little book here that I would hold nothing back, remember?) – I think that probably (and that means I am not 100% certain and I do not have all the facts, data and the truth – just like it was with the assassination of President Abraham Lincoln, President Kennedy, Martin Luther King and MANY others [which I am sure we do not even know about because these assholes, who are running planet Earth do not normally do their evil deeds in public; but mainly in covert/ secretive operations and actions, and sometimes in overt/public ways but very rarely unless they themselves or their minions go insane or nuts; they get found out or something like this] the 9/11 disaster was most probably caused by THEM (you know the ones I am talking about but I have no proof and their probably never will be any because they and their minions have made it so). But even if it wasn't set up by them (the 9/11 disaster)) they still jumped on it and made it a VERY big excuse to then do pretty much whatever they want (pass this and that law; raise and borrow money [which we have to pay back –how kind of them?] to detect and prevent these so-called terrorists, which they probably covertly fund; and these terrorists are apparently everywhere: one could be hiding in your office somewhere or in your back garden. They do all this to scare everyone and to justify all their evil and unjust {if you think they give a damn about me or you or anyone, then let me put you straight: they DON'T! They only care about themselves and their own evil purposes and on making sure we suffer more and more} global activities and wars which, once again – get this – **WE** have to pay for and which is why the USA, the UK and other countries are billions and trillions of pounds in depth – which was borrowed from the Lords of Evil.

Is this not insane or what?

THEY cause the wars and terrorism: lend money to pay for the wars, lend money to rebuild the countries that are destroyed in the wars caused by them and then WE (the stupid slave workers and taxpayers) have to pay it all back in taxes and inflation! They also lend to countries and if they do not pay it back and keep to their terms and conditions, like the current IMF does (they either get rid of that President or Prime Minister or all top-level government heads; destroy them and their reputations using Black Propaganda, PR and the media; or they just send in the troops with some concocted excuse for a war or they send in Cover Ops to start a war, etc., etc. I do not lie about this!) Look at the USA national debt as a classic example: nearly 18 trillion and rising. And that my friends is how they work and which is why there has been inflation after every major war on the planet and globally inflation has been going up for years regardless of wars. They pretty much do whatever they want around the planet in the name of CAPITALISM, HUMANITY, COMMUNISM & TERRORISM but they say they are helping and protecting us – why they are so kind. Let's all thank them so much and be nice little slaves to them and the economic, banking and other wonderful systems and politics they have set up around the globe (which we, innocently and naively allowed them to do because they duped us.) And the USA people and the rest of populaces around the world lap it all up and believe it to be mostly true because the leaders say blah, blah, blah and the media says and shows blah, blah, blah and (sorry to say this but I am actually trying to help you here - believe me!) most of peoples of Earth agree with their governments policies and lies (and even if we don't agree with them; they force it through anyway because they have the Governments, Senate, Congress, House of Lords and all the rest in the grip of their very dirty hands; and they have people/ experts who influence and guide the Senate and Congress and some are paid-off and offered bribes, backhanders, commissions and all the political and big business bullshit that goes on. Come on. Be real. Do not be so naive: we know what some or a lot of our politicians are up to and this has been going on since even before the Roman, Greek and Egyptian times, o yes it has!). And what I am going to say to you now is very important, not just for the USA but also for the rest of the whole entire population of Mankind: we all have an unconscious mind and this can be affected and made to make us (without our knowing) behave and act in an unknowing, sometimes bad or illogical/insane way (we do not know why we reacted, did or said what we did. Hypnosis works on and uses this basis and fact too and so does deep sleep therapy, Psychiatry/Psychology, alcohol/drugs, brainwashing, and all this CIA/FBI and other torture/controlling and mind-programming bullshit they do – WHY – this is how they control people and one way of making us do what THEY want, not what we want! And they want us to be their slaves and do what they want and die or suffer how they want. I know on the surface, superficially, it doesn't appear that way – but I can tell you it *IS* the way I say it is. It is hard enough to lives one's life with an Unconscious Mind and not fully knowing what or who one is and what to believe in or not believe in anything: without having these additional evil anti-social deeds, acts and crimes making planet Earth even worse.

Please wake up America [and the rest of the world!] from the stupor **YOU** are all in and realize and become aware of who you really are and actually what you are capable off!!! I implore you because the USA alone (its good people I mean, not those in high up places who have evil vested interests and who serve the Powers-That-Be), with maybe the help of a few more good and powerful countries, could actually and truly be SO instrumental in sorting out the bad mother fuckers who are messing and fucking up planet Earth; and they could make this – OUR LOVELY BEAUTIFUL planet- a *free* planet: where Mankind can be free (whatever that means to you reading this book is fine - just so long as it is good!) in which people can flourish and prosper, be happy, successful, be able to have the faith or religion (or not) that they want and achieve their goals, purposes and dreams; young virgin girls can run free without the threat of being raped or killed; our babies/children/ teenagers can be free from the harmful influences of drugs and alcohol (and I am not saying ban them all, no!), the Psychiatrists and their illegal (should be) cure-all (not) drugs and brain operations and shock treatments, etc.; and where Mankind can be free to rise to heights he has only dreamed off in this entire existence thus far!!!

This is my request to the USA and to the rest of the World. This is my personal request to YOU reading my book?! And, on the EEC, I would be so happy if one self-determined and sane/ rational country/ member state of the EEC could/would decide to leave the EEC and its dreaded EURO and stick their fingers up at Brussels and tell them to go FUCK themselves!!! And maybe then the rest of the member countries/ nations of Europe will wake up, follow suit and tell Brussels and it's behind the scene rulers to FUCK OFF too!!!! J Then we might get some peace and quiet and be allowed to run our countries and live our lives as WE wish; not how THEY want us to: get it? (I do not apologize for my language, why should I: I am right and you and they know it, right?!)

>I must interject here a fact: not all beings or people on Earth are the same. Some are geniuses, very clever, good or great at art or music or sports, etc. Some can build things; others can write masterpieces or compose or play great music; some are great managers; some are talented as leaders (if they would only lead honestly, correctly and ethically), some can fix things or make machine parts; others can teach; others have limited intelligence and many others cannot study and learn things. Others are stupid. Others do not want to work and are allowed to get away with it (Welfare States). Others are criminal and fewer still are VERY, VERY evil. Others just can never make or get enough money and so many others are stuck in a rut, with a fixed income, fixed low wage/pay, with no way of ever getting out of the trap. Others inherit or are born into wealth and/or power. Others are the top people in their fields and they command huge salaries. What I am saying is that we are all different, with different circumstances and abilities, different families and different countries. But that does not mean that we cannot still get paid a good decent wage from the rich and wealthy business owners and businesses and the ordinary ones too. There **IS** plenty of money to go around and be shared around and there is enough land

and food on this planet so we can all have plenty. Not just the rich few and the landlords and farmers owning all the land and hoarding all the money. This condition is very wrong indeed. With power, knowledge and wealth; and all Leadership, their comes responsibility, not just for oneself but for others too and that includes planet Earth and all life on this planet. There are some who think they are above other humans and there are those who look down on other humans. Why I do not know. But they do. Well it is ok to be above other humans and some humans are indeed above other humans in terms of ability, wealth and riches. This is true. But that is still no excuse to look down on other humans and to mistreat other humans and to intentionally keep them down. We all want a piece of this big cake and we all want to be able to eat it and also have some dessert. And so those at or near the top need to change their way of operating and their point of view on these issues and start treating other humans lower than them in a better manner and also to start paying them better wages.

Then we can all have a good life, not just the few. Have I made my point clear enough on this?

OVERVIEW OF GLOBAL ECONOMY

Every country and person on this planet should be allowed to lead a good and happy life – if they want it. Yes, we have powerful and rich countries and multi-nationals. Yes we have powerful and wealthy individuals, whether they made their money or inherited it. And yes we have powerful and rich finance houses and banks. And we have stock exchanges; Oil and OPEC; Gold and Foreign Exchange markets and all the rest which makes up that wonderful word called: Capitalism. And we have people working all over the world, from the lowest to the highest echelons of life, either as self-employed or for other companies and all competing for jobs. And we have millions of companies competing with each other. And we have many countries competing with, attacking or helping each other. It is a fiercely competitive world we live in right now with fast transport and super-fast communications and most employers can pick and choose who they employ and give contracts to; and countries can pick and choose who they deal with. But the essence of being Human is being humane to others. And the main purpose of life and most people is not just to survive but to be happy, enjoy the life and SURVIVE WELL, not just eke out some low-life or miserable, depressing, sad existence. Why can't Mankind get into and stay in the festive mood of Christmas, which is: goodwill, merriment and cheer to all Mankind?! Now that is how this planet should be ALL the time. Presents, toys, food, drink and gadgets are OK for a while but nothing can replace real **love** - just for the sake of love - for one another and treating of each other with honesty, decency, fairness and respect. Now that is how Mankind should be and the business and workaday world. I'm not talking a false Utopia or one that cannot be attained. This is doable and can be attained quite easily if everyone tried to their best in this every day instead of just thinking of themselves and looking out for number one and/or their friends and family.

When all is said and done, it is these unmaterialistic virtues which make life worthwhile and make man NOT an animal (even though I wonder about some people I have met or seen so far on this planet?). And furthermore: you come in to this world with just oneself (as a spirit in whatever state one is in) and one leaves the same way; taking not one dollar with you, except one's memories: whether they be good or bad. So why not make the most of one's life while one is on Earth with a body and make the most of one's life to help others also have a nice, happy life? If we ALL help each other for real, instead of all this: grab and get as much money as we can and fuck everyone else, then Mankind, this planet and all life on it, has a chance. If not, well? Most of the major religious books of the world were all pushing this message: love and help one another; be good; work hard; do one's best to achieve one's goals and purposes; be honest, faithful, loyal, trustworthy as best one can and try not to sin. All those great books, God (in all his different forms and names) and all those great enlightened ones could all not have been wrong. Well – could they?

I think not!!!!!

Yes we need money, economics, possessions and all the rest – but they are not paramount in the broader picture of life. It seems that way; but they are not as important than what I mentioned above. We only get obsessed with them because we are being forced too because of how those at the top and those who run this planet are shaping this planet. They are causing it to be the way it is. And those vested interests and those who want it all for themselves. And **WE** are letting them do it and get away with it!!!!???

Read on for some more economic insanity:

Economic inequality

See also: WEALTH INEQUALITY IN THE UNITED STATES: http://en.wikipedia.org/wiki/Wealth_inequality_in_the_United_States
From Wikipedia, the free encyclopaedia

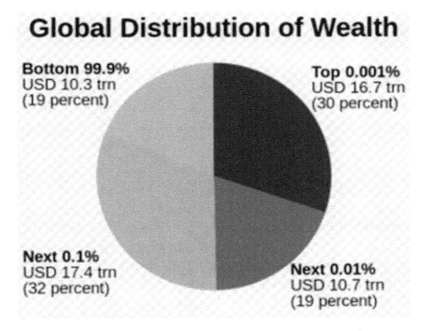

http://commons.wikimedia.org/wiki/File:U.S._Distribution_of_Wealth,_2007.jpg Edward N. Wolff

Brazil is South America's most influential country, an economic giant and one of the world's biggest democracies.

It is one of the rising economic powers - otherwise known as BRIC nations - together with Russia, India, China and South Africa. Over the past few years it has made major strides in its efforts to raise millions out of poverty. The discovery of major offshore oil reserves could propel the country into the top league of oil-exporting nations.

OVERVIEW

The exploitation of the Amazon rainforest, much of which is in Brazil, has been a major international worry, since the wilderness is a vital regulator of the climate. It is also an important reservoir of plant and animal life....

In 2005 the government reported that one fifth of the Amazon forests had been cleared by deforestation.

AT-A-GLANCE

Economy: Brazil has Latin America's largest economy; there has been steady growth
International: Brazil wants a permanent seat at the UN Security Council; relations with Bolivia suffered in 2006 over access to Bolivian gas

Brazil's natural resources, particularly iron ore, are highly prized by major manufacturing nations, including China. Thanks to the development of offshore fields, the nation has become self-sufficient in oil, ending decades of dependence on foreign producers. **There is a wide gap between rich and poor,** but the World Bank has praised the country for progress in reducing social and economic inequality... Social conditions can be harsh in the big cities of Rio de Janeiro and Sao Paulo, where a third of the population lives in favelas, or slums.

FACTS

Full name: **Federative Republic of Brazil.**

Population: 196.6 million (UN, 2011)
Capital: Brasilia

Largest city: Sao Paulo
Area: 8.55 million sq km (3.3 million sq miles)
Major language: Portuguese
Major religion: Christianity
Life expectancy: 71 years (men), 77 years (women) (UN)
Monetary unit: 1 real = 100 centavos
Main exports: Manufactured goods, iron ore, coffee, oranges, other agricultural produce
GNI per capita: US $9,390 (World Bank, 2010)
Internet domain: br
International dialling code: +55

LEADERS

President: Dilma Rousseff
A study by the World Institute for Development Economics Research at United Nations University reports that the **richest 1% of adults alone owned 40% of global assets in the year 2000. The** *three* **richest people possess more financial assets than the lowest 48 nations combined.**[12] **The combined wealth of the "10 million dollar millionaires" grew to nearly $41 trillion in 2008.**[13] In 2001, 46.4% of people in sub-Saharan Africa were living in extreme poverty.[14] Nearly half of all Indian children are undernourished, however, even among the wealthiest fifth one third of children are malnourished.

BRAZIL:
(from Wikipedia)
Brazil country profile

http://commons.wikimedia.org/wiki/File:Montagem_RJ.jpg Chronus

| FROM: | World Bank: Development Indicators 2000. |

Writer: It specifies there that in Brazil, despite a government program against illiteracy developed in 1971, 15 percent of the population aged 15 and higher were illiterate in 1999. Among the upper-middle class this was 10 percent. Education is free at the school and university levels. Secondary school is the responsibility of the municipalities, and universities are the responsibility of the federal and state governments. **The biggest social challenge facing the Brazilian government and society is the lack of education, housing, health care, and nutrition for the homeless children of Brazil. Thousands of children live in the streets, abandoned by their parents who cannot afford to raise them. Confronting starvation and living in deplorable conditions, these children abuse drugs, commit crimes, and resort to prostitution in order to survive.** The government has developed programs through the Ministry of Social Assistance to combat the poverty and starvation of homeless children.

Read more: http://www.nationsencyclopedia.com/economies/Americas/Brazil-POVERTY-AND-WEALTH.html

INDIA:

Poverty in India is widespread, with the nation estimated to have a third of the world's poor. In 2010, the World Bank reported that 32.7% of the total Indian people fall below the international poverty line of US$1.25 per day (PPP) while 68.7% live on less than US$ 2 per day.[1]

According to 2010 data from the United Nations Development Programme, an estimated 29.8% of Indians live below the country's national poverty line.[2] A 2010 report by the Oxford Poverty and Human Development Initiative (OPHI) states that 8 Indian states have more poor people than 26 poorest African nations combined which totals to more than 410 million poor in the poorest African countries.[3][4]

A study by the Oxford Poverty and Human Development Initiative using a Multi-dimensional Poverty Index (MPI) found that there were **650 million people (53.7% of population) living in poverty in India**, of which **340 million people (28.6% of the population) were living in severe poverty**, and that a further 198 million people (16.4% of the population) were vulnerable to poverty. This number is higher than the 410 million poor living in the 26 poorest African nations.[14]

In 1947, the average annual income in India was US$619, compared with US$439 for China, US$770 for South Korea, and US$936 for Taiwan.

Persistence of malnutrition among children[edit]

According to the *New York Times*, it is estimated that about 55% of the children in India suffer from malnutrition.[52] The World Bank, citing estimates made by the World Health Organisation, states that "About 49 percent of the world's underweight children, 34 percent of the world's stunted children and 46 percent of the world's wasted children, live in India." ...

The United Nations had estimated that "**2.1 million Indian children die before reaching the age of 5 every year – four every minute.**"[56]

India

SOURCE: G L O B A L   E D I T I O N

October 30, 2012, 1:31 am

Is India's Rising Billionaire Wealth Bad for the Country?
By VIVEK DEHEJIA
WRITER: ACCORDING TO THIS ARTICLE, Mukesh Ambani, chairman of Reliance Industries, is the richest Indian according to the Forbes Billionaires list 2012.

48 of the 1,153 billionaires are from India!!!!!! Can you believe this and there is so much extreme poverty there. This is insane and must be changed. Just the same as the wealth distribution round the entire world must be changed so it is much fairer and everyone gets a little slice of the pie instead of some taking HUGE slices.

In 2012, billionaire's wealth accounted for about 10% of the national income of India.

India is now fairly equal with the United States and Mexico, where billionaires' wealth in both of these countries account for about 10 percent of national income. India is even above Brazil regarding disparities in wealth and income. Only Russia has a higher percentage of Billionaire oligarchs who have 20% of their nation's total income.

Can you believe this?

A lot of these big Indian companies get very generous privileges; and I am sure those in Government get their backhanders and perks for 'helping' these Billionaires!

It's a nice planet we live, huh?

How the hell can there be so many billionaires in India, Russia, Brazil and China and yet so many hungry, starving and low to very low paid people. This does NOT make sense? Does it make sense to you? Something has to be done about this, and fast! And it is not much different in most of the countries on this planet. I have nothing against the rich and super rich; but there is a point where one has to draw the line and where one has to consider why these people want so much money, money they will never spend, and why the working classes and those in poverty have to suffer and why they are intentionally kept down?

RUSSIA

(**Writer:** Was Communist now trying to be Capitalist but still the wealth is not being shared around/out as it should be. And how democratic is it really? What happened to all that wealth, business, land, factories, etc. that Communist Russia had before it became Capitalist? Strange how there are so many Billionaires and Oligarchs who own and control all the oil, gas, wealth, etc. and the rest of the people are on low wages. Surely the peoples of Russia should have gotten a share of the profits from these, as apparently they 'owned' them under Communism?)

The **economy of Russia** is the Eighth largest economy in the world by nominal value and the sixth largest by purchasing power parity (PPP). [18] Russian economy is today considered by IMF and World Bank a developing one. Russia has an abundance of Fossil Fuels (Oil, Natural gas and coal) and precious metals. Russia has undergone significant changes since the collapse of the Soviet Union, moving from a centrally planned economy to a more market-based and globally integrated economy. Economic reforms in the 1990s privatized many sectors of the industry and agriculture, with notable exceptions in the energy and defense-related sectors. Nonetheless, the rapid privatization process, including a much criticized "loans-for-shares" scheme that turned over major state-owned firms to politically connected "oligarchs", has left equity ownership highly concentrated. As of 2011, Russia's capital, Moscow, now has the highest billionaire population of any city in the world.[19][20]

In late 2008 and early 2009, Russia experienced the first recession after 10 years of experiencing a rising economy, until the stable growth resumed in late 2009 and 2010. Despite the deep but brief recession, the economy has not been as seriously affected by the global financial crisis, largely because of the integration of short-term macroeconomic policies that helped the economy survive, as well as low sovereign debt levels which made austerity unnecessary. The Russian Government predicts stable growth rates for future years of around 3.4% of GDP.[21]

Economy of Russia
From Wikipedia, the free encyclopedia

Economy of Russia

http://en.wikipedia.org/wiki/Economy_of_Russia Kirill Vinokurov
Moscow International Business Center

Rank	8th (nominal) / 6th (PPP)
Currency	Russian Ruble (RUB)
Fiscal year	calendar year
Trade organizations	WTO, CIS, APEC, EURASEC, G-20, G8 and others
Statistics	
GDP	$ 2.022 Trillion (2012, IMF) (nominal;8th) [1] $ 2.053 Trillion (2013 CIA[2] and RIA[3]) (nominal; 8th) $2,513,299 Trillion (2012, IMF) (PPP;6th) [4]
GDP growth	3.4% (2012) [5] (1.8% Jan-Apr. 2013)[6]
GDP per capita	$14,247 2012 (nominal; 47th) $17,709 (2012 IMF) PPP 55th [7]
GDP by sector	agriculture: 4.4% industry: 37.6% services: 58% (2012 est.) [8]
Population below poverty line	12.5% with income below $217.8 /month (November 2012) [9]
Labour force	75.24 million (2012 est.)

Labour force by occupation	Agriculture: 4.4% Industry: 37.6% Services: 58% (2012 est.)
Unemployment	5.3% (January 2013) [10]
Average gross salary	26,690 Rubles - Average net income 22861 rubles (Rosstat January 2013 on 2012)
Main industries	complete range of mining and extractive industries producing coal, oil, gas, chemicals, and metals; all forms of machine building from rolling mills to high-performance aircraft and space vehicles; defense industries including radar, missile production, and advanced electronic components, shipbuilding; road and rail transportation equipment; communications equipment; agricultural machinery, tractors, and construction equipment; electric power generating and transmitting equipment; medical and scientific instruments; consumer durables, textiles, foodstuffs, handicrafts
Ease of Doing Business Rank	112th (2013) [11]
External	
Exports	$542.5 billion (2012 est.) [12]
Export goods	petroleum and petroleum products, natural gas, metals, wood and wood products, chemicals, and a wide variety of civilian and military manufactures
Main export partners	Netherlands 12.3%, China 6.5%, Italy5.6%, Germany 4.6%, Poland 4.3% (2011)
Imports	$358.1 billion (2012 est.) [13]
Import goods	machinery, vehicles, pharmaceutical products, plastic, semi-finished metal products, meat, fruits and nuts, optical and medical instruments, iron, steel
Main import partners	China 15.6%, Germany 10%, Ukraine6.6%, Italy 4.3% (2011)
Gross external debt	$455.2 billion (31 December 2012 est.)
Public finances	

Public debt	11% of GDP (2012 est.)[14]
Revenues	$469 billion (2012 est.)
Expenses	$414 billion (2012 est.)
Credit rating	Standard & Poor's:[15] BBB+ (Domestic) BBB (Foreign) BBB (T&C Assessment) Outlook: Stable[16] Moody's:[16] Baa1 Outlook: Stable Fitch:[16] BBB Outlook: Positive
Foreign reserves	$561.1 billion (December 2012)[17]

Main data source: CIA World Fact Book
All values, unless otherwise stated, are in US dollars

UK (in the EEC):

The **economy of the United Kingdom** is the sixth-largest national economy in the world measured by nominal GDP and eighth-largest measured by purchasing power parity (PPP), and the third-largest in Europe measured by nominal GDP and the second-largest in Europe measured by PPP. The UK's GDP per capita is the 22nd highest in the world in nominal terms and the22nd highest measured by PPP. The British economy encompasses (in descending order of size) the economies of England, Scotland, Wales and Northern Ireland. The UK has one of the world's most globalised economies.[15] London is the world's largest financial centre alongside New York[16][17][18] and has the largest city GDP in Europe.[19] As of December 2010 the UK had the third-largest stock of both inward and outward foreign.[20][21] The aerospace industry of the UK is the second- or third-largest national aerospace industry, depending upon the method of measurement.[22][23] The pharmaceutical industry plays an important role in the UK economy and the country has the third-highest share of global pharmaceutical R&D expenditures (after the United States and Japan).[24]

[25] The British economy is boosted by North Sea oil and gas reserves, valued at an estimated £250 billion in 2007.[26] The UK is currently ranked seventh in the world in the World Bank's Ease of Doing Business Index.[8]

http://en.wikipedia.org/wiki/File:Canary_Wharf_at_night,_from_Shadwell_cropped.jpg Pointillist
Canary Wharf business district in London

Rank	6th (nominal) / 8th (PPP) (2nd in Europe)
Currency	Pound sterling (GBP)
Fiscal year	6 April – 5 April
Trade organisations	EU, BCN, OECD and WTO
Statistics	
GDP	$2.433 trillion (2012)[1](nominal; 6th) $2.316 trillion (2012)[2] (PPP; 8th)
GDP growth	0.3% Q1 2013 (0.6% y/y) (ONS)[3]
GDP per capita	$38,591 (2012)[2] (nom; 20th) $36,728 (2012)[2] (PPP; 17th)
GDP by sector	agriculture: 0.7%, industry: 21.5%, services: 77.8% (2011 est.)
Inflation (CPI)	CPI:2.4%, RPI 2.9% (April 2013)
Population below poverty line	16.1% with household income below 60% of UK median income (2010-11 est.)[4]

139

Gini coefficient	0.34 (2010-11)[5]
Labour force	29.71 million (May 2013)[6]
Labour force by occupation	agriculture: 1.4%, industry: 18.2%, services: 80.4% (2006 est.)
Unemployment	7.8% (2.52 million)
Average gross salary	€4,108 / $5,546, monthly (2006)[7]
Average net salary	€2,749 / $3,712, monthly (2006)[7]
Main industries	List[show]
Ease of Doing Business Rank	6th[8]
External	
Exports	$479.2 billion (2011 est.)[9]
Export goods	Manufactured goods, sup, chemicals, food, beverages, tobacco, automotive vehicles and components, computer programming, finance, entertainment, clothes, fuel oil and petroleum products, industrial supplies and materials, military arms and equipment, pharmaceuticals, other.
Main export partners	Germany 11.6%, US 10.6%, Netherlands 8.4%, France 7.8%, Republic of Ireland 6.4%, Belgium5.7% (2011)[9]
Imports	$639 billion (2011 est.)[9]
Import goods	Manufactured goods, machinery, fuels; foodstuffs
Main import partners	Germany 13.2%, China 8.7%, Netherlands 7.5%, US 6.1%, France6%, Norway 5%, Belgium 5% (2011)[9]
FDI stock	$1.169 trillion (31 December 2010 est.)
Gross external debt	$9.836 trillion (30 June 2011) (2nd)
Public finances	
Public debt	£977 trillion 88.7% of GDP (2012 est.)[10]
Budget deficit	£155 billion[10] (2009–10 FY) £120 billion (2011-12 FY). Budget deficit proposed for 2012-2013 is £90 billion (6% of GDP)
Revenues	£592 billion (2012-2013 FY)
Expenses	£682 billion (2012-2013 FY)
Economic aid	$10 billion (2012) (donor)

Credit rating	Standard & Poor's:[11] AA1 (Domestic) AA1 (Foreign) AA1 (T& C Assessment) Outlook: Negative[12] Moody's:[13] Aa1 Outlook: Negative Watch Fitch: AAA[14] Outlook: NEGATIVE
Foreign reserves	$127.8 billion (Aug 2012)
Main data source: CIA World Fact Book **All values, unless otherwise stated, are in US dollars**	

The economy of the United Kingdom is the sixth-largest

Sectors[edit]
Taxation and borrowing[edit]
Main article: Taxation in the United Kingdom

http://commons.wikimedia.org/wiki/File:Government_Offices_Great_George_Street.jpg Carlos Delgado

The headquarters of HM Revenue & Customs in London
Taxation in the United Kingdom may involve payments to at least two different levels of government: local government and central government (HM Revenue & Customs). Local government is financed by grants from central government funds, business rates,

council tax and increasingly from fees and charges such as those from on-street parking. Central government revenues are mainly income tax, national insurance contributions, value added tax, corporation tax and fuel duty.

These data show the tax burden (personal and corporate) and national debt as a percentage of GDP. Samples are taken at 10 year intervals (snapshots, but the rolling averages are very close).

Year	Tax	Debt
1975/6	54%	43%
1985/6	44%	43%
1995/6	43%	38%
2005/6*	46%	40%
2009/10	57%	68%

(Source: HM Treasury Public Finances Databank)

(* — **Projected**)

WRITER: As I live in the UK, I wanted to add excerpts of an interesting article – WELL worth reading – from: **www.moneyweek.com (see below)**

The End of Britain (from **Moneyweek**)

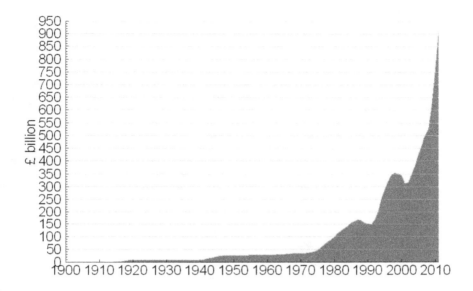

Source: ukpublicspending.co.uk

But for all that, our national debt is still growing at an incredible rate. Despite David Cameron's talk of "austerity", he's going to add an estimated £700 billion to the national debt in just five years. That's more than Tony Blair and Gordon Brown added to the national debt in eleven years. It's more than every British government of the past 100 years *put together.* The fact is, when you look at our finances as a whole, the Coalition *isn't cutting anything*. State spending is going up… our national debt is going up… and our interest payments are going up.

By the next general election in 2015, our national debt is estimated to stand at almost £1.4 trillion, as this chart shows:

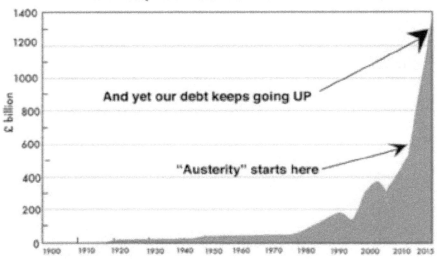

Source: ukpublicspending.co.uk

Compared to the size of our economy, Britain is now one of the most heavily indebted countries in the Western world. That's official. Our total debts stand at more than FIVE TIMES what our entire economy is worth. Proportionally, that's more debt than Italy... Portugal... Spain...and almost twice as much debt as Greece. Those are four countries already in the throes of financial crisis. We're the odd one out because we haven't collapsed – yet. But things can't stay that way for long. You see, the only countries that have more debt than us are Japan, where the economy has stagnated for 20 years and the stock market has crashed by 75%... and Ireland, where the housing market has crashed 50%, and the government has been forced to accept a bailout. In fact, our debts tower above almost every other nation's – here are the figures that prove it:

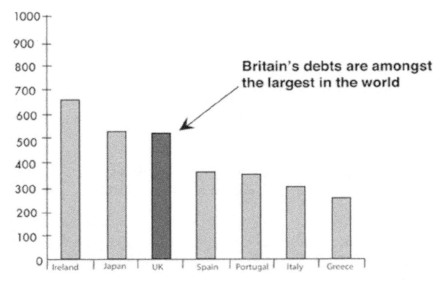

Source: Haver Analytics; Bank for International Settlements; national central banks; McKinsey Global Institute Because when you add in all of Britain's "unfunded obligations" – promises the Government has made on things like public sector pensions – our debts swell to 900% of our economy. That's right – when you add everything up, we owe TEN TIMES what our entire economy is worth. Our political leaders still like to see Britain as a world power. But let's not delude ourselves. It's clear to see: we're totally broke. It doesn't matter which set of figures you use, or which way you look at Britain's debts. We're merely talking about different shades of disaster here. A country can either pay back its debts or it can't. And it is very clear to us that Britain can't. But how did we get here? After all, **we were once the richest and most powerful nation on earth. What happened to all of our money?**

A dangerous experiment gone wrong

On the 1st of January, 1909, something happened for the first time in British history.

The government agreed to redistribute taxes to support people in their old age. On that day, more than any other, the modern welfare state began in earnest…

Lloyd George initiated a social experiment that would soon spiral out of control.

It wasn't until the Second World War was finally over that the welfare state really began to grow... Welfare was seen as a major part of "Winning the Peace"; keeping the forces of Socialism and Fascism at bay. Of course, politicians soon realised welfare wasn't just a tool to win the peace. It was also incredibly effective at winning votes too.

This same scenario came to be repeated across the world – in the USA, Japan and across Europe. Seemingly limitless economic growth and prosperity allowed politicians to make an essentially unlimited promise:

The government promised to look after you "from Cradle to Grave". This single, powerful idea gave government the licence to swell to a size unimaginable just half a century earlier.

The promises got bigger, and so did the cost.

In just a few short years, the size of the welfare state grew, almost uncontrollably, in a flurry of new laws. There was *The Butler Act*, which reformed schooling. *The Family Allowance Act. The National Insurance Act. The National Health Act.* The list went on. The problem was, this all came with a nasty side effect. It was immensely expensive. Everyone assumed we'd be able to pay for it forever.

But they were wrong.

Politicians found themselves totally and utterly caught in this trap. Any attempt to reduce the size of the welfare state was met with often violent resistance in the form of strikes and protests...

Since public pensions were first introduced, average life expectancy has grown from 48 to 80 – a 67% increase. But the age at which we retire has remained essentially the same. This has resulted in an estimated £5 trillion worth of pension promises the state has made to its citizens – roughly five times what our entire economy is worth. No one has any idea how we'll pay these. The recent attempts by the government to change the retirement age don't go anywhere near solving the problem.

As people have lived longer, the strain on the NHS – the demand for medication, more doctors, nurses and other staff, as well as a skyrocketing cost of caring for the elderly – has pushed our finances to breaking point.

In fact, as state spending has grown, so has the cost of running the welfare system itself. For instance, the state employs half a million civil servants. To put that into perspective, during the height of the British Empire, when Britain ran a quarter of the planet, the state employed just 4,000 civil servants.

If you're in any doubt just how out of control state spending has become, simply take a look at this:

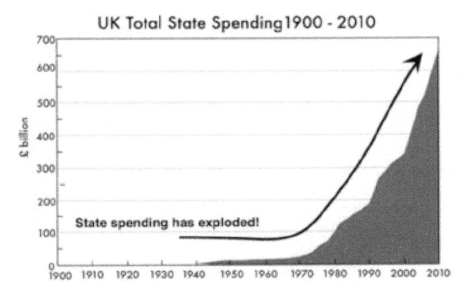

Source: ukpublicspending.co.uk

In 2012, for example, the government will spend roughly £120 billion more than it collects in taxes.

Government over-spending = BORROWING

If the UK had been a business or an individual, we'd have been declared bankrupt by now...

The explosion of government spending and government debt has mostly come in the past 30 years. And during that time, it's been easy and cheap for the government to borrow money. You see, interest rates on the government's debt have been steadily falling for thirty years. Here, let us show you...

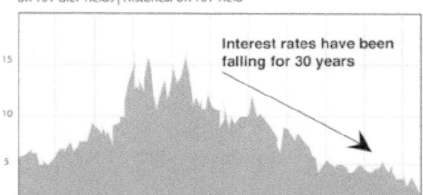

Source: Gecodia.com

It's simple maths. If interest rates moved back towards the normal 5% level, our cost of borrowing would triple. Just to put that into context, if our current debt repayments tripled, the government would have to take drastic action – like abolishing the state pension. Or privatising the NHS. Or pushing tax rates back up to 90%, as they were in the 1960s.In short, Britain would change radically.

And that's just if interest rates move back to "normal" levels.

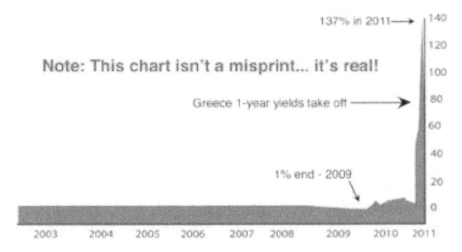

Source: Bloomberg

This is an extreme example of what happens when interest rates take off. As you can see, in 2009, the Greek government could borrow money at just 1%. Then in the wake of the financial crisis, the Greek economy hit the rocks, fell into recession and the markets realised what a complete mess the country was in. Interest rates shot up vertically. And Greece imploded. Not just financially, but socially and politically too…

In Britain, interest rates on government borrowing now stand at record lows. If we're not at rock bottom, then we're incredibly close.

That means the most important trend of the next twenty years is almost certainly rising interest rates.

Debt has been getting cheaper for thirty years. Now it's about to start getting much more expensive.

We're now facing an unprecedented crisis. As interest rates rise, our record debts will become impossible to bear.

The important thing to realise is that Britain is going to change – very significantly. Things might never be the same again.

A warning from history

…Most people think Britain's debt collapse can't happen. Of course, it's hard to picture. Banks look safe until they announce they're broke. Governments say everything's under control, until they beg for bailouts… The Victorians thought the British Empire would last forever. Americans in the 20s thought the stock market boom would never end. And here in the UK, during the 90s and early 2000s, we thought we could keep borrowing and spending forever.

…In the early 20th century Argentina was one of the world's largest economies. Rich in natural resources, a massive industrial sector, so cultured they called Buenos Aires the Paris of South America. In fact, a popular saying 100 years ago was as 'rich as an Argentine.'

But fast forward to the end of the 20th century, and things looked very different. Argentina's borrowing spiralled out of control…

As Argentina's debt accumulated in the late 90s, its financial system buckled. Austerity measures were put in place (sound familiar?), businesses closed, trade fell off a cliff and investment fled the country by the billion…

… you need to listen to our man in Argentina, Federico Tessore. Federico is one of our private network of analysts. He worked as a Financial Advisor for Citibank in Buenos Aries at the time, experiencing the chaos first hand.

He's got quite a story to tell…

"It was 2001… the US had just suffered the 9/11 attacks, many Argentines were frightened about what could happen in America. It was chaos. So they decided to bring back their money to Argentina…

But that was a terrible mistake, because in December of 2001 the Argentinian government created the "corralito". In English you would say "playpen", I think… we called it a "money prison".

This meant that you could only get out 500 US dollars per week in cash from your bank account. It didn't matter if you had $1 million in the bank, in *cash... you could only get $500 per week.*

For two months this madness continued, until the government decided to convert the US dollar deposits into Argentinian pesos...

The official exchange rate was 1.4 to 1, but the illegal market exchange rate was 3 to 1. Even worse, this conversion was not in cash. The government created a 10-year bond for the depositors.

So, people that had a $100,000 deposit in the bank were given an Argentina pesos 140,000 10-year bond...

This of course enraged people, who stormed into the banks very angry. I was working at the Citibank bank at the time. I saw what was happening from the inside. More than once my life was threatened by desperate customers who just wanted to get their money back. I had to talk with thousands of people per day, many old people, and try to explain what was happening... it was almost impossible.

One of the hardest parts, was to explain why the international banks like Citibank, decided not to recognize the dollar deposits to their customers. They had the money abroad to do that. But they didn't do it. They basically defrauded their own customers...

The depositors attacked the banks, rioting outside, smashing the windows... all the walls where painted with insults and complaints. We had to enter the bank escorted by the police... it was like living in hell."...

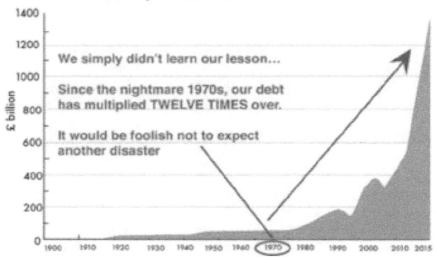

Source: ukpublicspending.co.uk

Escape is impossible

If you take one thing away from this presentation, it should be this:

In recorded economic history, every single country with debts as big as ours – *every single one* – has suffered a devastating economic collapse. There are NO exceptions.

For example…

During the Great Depression – when thousands of ordinary people lost everything – America's total debt hit 252% of GDP. In any circumstances, that's bad.

But things can get worse. During the Japanese economic collapse – which triggered more than two decades of deflation and a 75% drop in the stock market – Japanese total debt hit 498% of GDP. That's twice as bad as the level of debt seen in America during the Great Depression.

If Britain's current debts were at those kinds of levels, it would be worrying. But in truth, our debts are now much worse than either of those two examples.

Shockingly, our debt load is now on a scale comparable with one of the most frightening economic disasters of the 20th century...

We're talking about the Weimar Republic.

Back then, suffering under the weight of brutal war reparations, civil unrest and shattered public finances, the Weimar Republic's total debt equalled 913% of its economy.

I'm sure you know what happened next: the government printed money and hyperinflation took off. In the end, it was cheaper to decorate your home with bank notes than wallpaper. Ultimately, the country descended into a period of economic and social crisis... a catastrophe that ended with the rise of the Nazi party. And that was with debts worth 913% of the economy. Today, Britain's total debt equals 900% of the economy.

When interest rates rise – and they WILL rise – Britain will face the greatest crisis in generations.

And there's one more thing you need to consider.

The first danger you face won't be the falling price of your shares... nor will it be the insolvency of the banks. Those things, we believe, will happen. But first, you face an even more immediate threat:

The desperate actions of our own government.

How the government could seize your wealth

...In a desperate attempt to pay off the debts and try to regain control, politicians will cast around for any sources of money available, and use almost any means to seize it.

Invariably, that means they'll turn to their primary source of income: you.

It goes as far back as Ancient Rome. As the Empire crumbled and inflation raged, the Emperors raised taxes over and over, squeezing as much coin as they could from their subjects.

"A nation trying to tax itself into prosperity is like a man standing in a bucket and trying to lift himself up by the handle". Winston Churchill

Remember how Britain got into this dangerous situation in the first place:

The enormous cost of welfare started spiralling. We had to borrow hundreds of billions to service it. We had to pay interest on that borrowing. The debt has grown and grown. Soon the rates of interest could rocket. At that point the government cannot function. And very soon we believe they will target **YOU** and your wealth to pay for everything!!!

FROM: WIKIPEDIA https://en.wikipedia.org/wiki/Economy_of_Germany

GERMANY (in the EEC):

Germany is the largest national economy in Europe, the fourth-largest by nominal GDP in the world, and fifth by GDP (PPP) in 2008.[14] Since the age of industrialisation and beyond, the industrial capitalism,[15][16] the country has been a driver, innovator, and beneficiary of an ever more globalised economy. Germany is the world's second largest exporter with $1.408 trillion exported in 2011 (Eurozone countries are included).[17][*dated info*] Exports account for more than one-third of national output.[18][*dated info*]

Germany is relatively poor in raw materials. Only lignite and potash salt are available in economically significant quantities. Power plants burning lignite are one of the main sources of electricity in Germany. Oil, natural gas and other resources are, for the most part, imported from other countries. Germany imports about two thirds of its energy. **The service sector contributes around 70% of the total GDP, industry 29.1%, and agriculture 0.9%. Most of the country's products are in engineering, especially in automobiles, machinery, metals, and chemical goods.[19] Germany is the leading producer of wind turbines and solar power technology in the world. The largest annual international trade fairs and congresses are held in several German cities such as Hanover, Frankfurt, and Berlin.[20] Combination of service-oriented manufacturing,[21] R&D spending,**

links between industry and academia, international cooperation and SME contribute to the overall competitiveness of the economy of Germany.[22][23]

Of the world's 500 largest stock market listed companies measured by revenue, the Fortune Global 500, 37 are headquartered in Germany. In 2010 the ten largest were Volkswagen, Allianz, E.ON, Daimler, Siemens, Metro, Deutsche Telekom, Munich Re, BASF, and BMW.[24] Other large German companies include: Robert Bosch, ThyssenKrupp, and MAN(diversified industrials); Bayer and Merck (pharmaceuticals);Adidas and Puma (clothing and footwear); Commerzbank and Deutsche Bank (banking and finance); Aldi, Lidl and Edeka (retail); SAP (computer software); Infineon (semiconductors);Henkel (household and personal consumer products); Deutsche Post (logistics); and Hugo Boss (luxury goods). Well-known global brands are Mercedes Benz, BMW, Adidas, Audi, Porsche, Volkswagen, Bayer, BASF, Bosch, Siemens, Lufthansa, SAP andNivea.[25]

Between 1991 and 2010, 40,301 mergers and acquisitions with an involvement of German firms with a total known value of 2,422 bil EUR have been announced.[26] The largest transactions[27] since 1991 are: the acquisition of Mannesmannby Vodafone for 204.8 bil. EUR in 1999, the merger of Daimler-Benz with Chrysler to form DaimlerChrysler in 1998 valued at 36.3 bil. EUR.

http://commons.wikimedia.org/wiki/File:FrankfurtSkyline2014.jpg Stefan Zinsmeister

Frankfurt, financial capital of Germany.

Rank	4th (nominal) / 5th (PPP)
Currency	Euro (EUR)[1]
Fiscal year	calendar year
Trade organisations	EU, WTO (via EU membership) and OECD
Statistics	
GDP	$3.577 trillion, €2.570 trillion (2011)[2]
GDP growth	0.9% (2012 est.)[3]
GDP per capita	Nominal: $43,741, €31,437 (2011)[2]
GDP by sector	agriculture: 0.8%, industry: 28.6%, services: 70.6% (2011 est.)
Inflation (CPI)	1.3% (October 2010)[4]
Gini coefficient	.27 (2006)

Labour force	44.01 million (2012 est.)
Labour force by occupation	agriculture (2,4%), industry (29,7%), services (67,8%) (2005)
Unemployment	5.3% (January 2013)[5]
Average gross salary	4,217 € / 5,692 $, monthly (2006)[6]
Average net salary	2,040 € / 2,754 $, monthly (2006)[6]
Main industries	automobiles, iron, steel, coal, cement, chemicals, machinery, vehicles, machine tools, electronics, food and beverages, shipbuilding, textiles,
Ease of Doing Business Rank	20th[7]
External	
Exports	$1.492 trillion (2012 est.)[8]
Export goods	motor vehicles, machinery, chemicals, computer and electronic products, electrical equipment, pharmaceuticals, metals, transport equipment, foodstuffs, textiles, rubber and plastic products
	France 9.4%, United States 6.8%, Netherlands 6.6%, United Kingdom 6.2%,
Main export partners	Italy 6.2%, China 5.7%, Austria 5.5%, Japan 4.8%, Belgium 4.7%, Switzerland 4.4%, Turkey 4.1%, Brazil 3.3% (2012 est.)
Imports	$1.276 trillion (2012 est.)[8]
Import goods	machinery, data processing equipment, vehicles, chemicals, oil and gas, metals, electric equipment, pharmaceuticals, foodstuffs, agricultural products

Main import partners	China 9.7%, Netherlands 8.4%, France 7.6%, United States 6.2%, Japan 5.4%, Italy 5.2%, United Kingdom 4.7%, Belgium 4.2%, Austria 4.1%, Switzerland 4.1%, Brazil 2.9%, Turkey 1.7% (2012 est.)
FDI stock	$1.057 trillion (31 December 2010 est.)
Gross external debt	$5.624 trillion (30 June 2011)
Public finances	
Public debt	83% of GDP (2012 est.)[9]
Revenues	$1.511 trillion (2012 est.)
Expenses	$1.507 trillion (2012 est.)
Economic aid	donor: $7.5 billion (€5 billion), 0.28% of GDP GDP Germany is ranked on the CPI [2] 2009 as 14th for the perceived level of public sector corruption, with a confidence range between 7.7-8.3. (2004)[10]
Credit rating	Standard & Poor's:[11] AAA (Domestic) AAA (Foreign) AAA (T & C Assessment) Outlook: Stable[12] Moody's:[12] Aaa Outlook: Stable Fitch:[12] AAA Outlook: Stable
Foreign reserves	$233.813 billion, €200 billion (April 2011)[13]

> Main data source: CIA World Fact Book
> All values, unless otherwise stated, are in US dollars

FROM: WIKIPEDA https://en.wikipedia.org/wiki/Economy_of_Norway

NORWAY

(Not in the EEC yet it is a rich country; seems to be doing fine without being in the EEC?):

The **economy of Norway** is a developed mixed economy with heavy state-ownership in strategic areas of the economy. Although sensitive to global business cycles, the economy of Norway has shown robust growth since the start of the industrial era. Shipping has long been a support of Norway's export sector, but much of Norway's economic growth has been fuelled by an abundance of natural resources, including petroleum exploration and production, hydroelectric power, and fisheries. Agriculture and traditional heavy manufacturing have suffered relative decline compared to services and oil-related industries, and the public sector is among the largest in the world as a percentage of the overall gross domestic product. The country has a very high standard of living compared with other European countries, and a strongly integrated welfare system. Norway's modern manufacturing and welfare system rely on a financial reserve produced by exploitation of natural resources, particularly North Sea oil. [7][8][9][10][11]

Economy of Norway

http://en.wikipedia.org/wiki/File:Norwegianeconomy.png Oro2

Currency	1 Norwegian krone (NOK) = 100 øre
Fiscal year	Calendar year
Trade organisations	OECD, WTO, European Economic Area and others
Statistics	
GDP	$499.8 billion (2012 est.)
GDP growth	3.1% (2012 est.)
GDP per capita	$53,269 (2009 est.) (PPP) (3rd)
GDP by sector	agriculture: 2.2%; industry: 45.1%; services: 52.7% (2009 est.)
Inflation (CPI)	2.7% (2011 est.)
Gini coefficient	25 (2008)
Labour force	2.645 million (2012 est.)
Labour force by occupation	agriculture: 2.9%; industry: 21.1%; services: 76% (2008)

Unemployment	3.0% (September 2012)[1]
Average gross salary	38,100 NOK / $6909, monthly (May 2011)[2]
Main industries	petroleum and natural gas, food processing, shipbuilding, wood pulp and paper products, metals, chemicals, timber, mining, textiles, fishing
Ease of Doing Business Rank	6th[3]
External	
Exports	$162.7 billion (2012 est.)
Export goods	petroleum and petroleum products, machinery and equipment, metals, chemicals, ships, fish
Main export partners	United Kingdom 27%, Germany12.8%, Netherlands 10.4%, France9.4%, Sweden 6.5%, United States4.5% (2008)
Imports	$86.78 billion (2012 est.)
Import goods	machinery and equipment, chemicals, metals, foodstuffs
Main import partners	Sweden 14.3%, Germany 13.4%, Denmark 6.8%, China 6.4%, United Kingdom 5.9%, United States 5.4%, Netherlands 4.1% (2008)
FDI stock	$93.88 billion (31 December 2009 est.)
Gross external debt	$548.1 billion (30 June 2009)
Public finances	
Public debt	30.3% of GDP (2012 est.)
Revenues	$282.9 billion (2012 est.)
Expenses	$206.7 billion (2012 est.)
Economic aid	$2.20 billion (donor), 0.87% of GDP (2004) [1]

Credit rating	Standard & Poor's:[4]
	AAA (Domestic)
	AAA (Foreign)
	AAA (T & Assessment)
	Outlook: Stable[5]
	Moody's:[5]
	Aaa
	Outlook: Stable
	Fitch:[5]
	AAA
	Outlook: Stable
Foreign reserves	US$54.504 billion (March 2011)[6]

Main data source: CIA World Fact Book
All values, unless otherwise stated, are in US dollars

FROM: WIKIPEDIA https://en.wikipedia.org/wiki/Economy_of_Japan

Japan:

(**WRITER:** We could all learn a lot from Japan, at least on how it runs its economy and they only import what they need. All the smaller companies support the bigger companies and multi-nationals, so the wealth and jobs, etc., are kept *IN* the country. Why the rest of the world does not do this instead of getting their products made in China, India, Brazil or some other place, I do not know? But then the businesses and capitalists have to make their profits at the expense of everyone else, right? I should also add that workers apparently in Japan work very long hours. Sometimes 7 days a week, with little or no holidays. I cannot support this. And some do not have children because they want to save money. I cannot see how one can enjoy life if one is working all the time, regardless of how much money one has in the bank? Sounds like a trap to me and how many of us on this planet are trapped in a myriad of ways, not just financially? Japan also has a very high suicide rate!)

The **economy of Japan** is the third largest in the world by nominal GDP and fourth largest by Purchasing power parity [8]and is the world's second largest developed economy.[9] According to the International Monetary Fund, the country's per capita GDP (PPP) was at $34,739 or the 25th highest in 2011. Japan is a member of Group of Eight. Japanese economy can be forecasted by Quarterly Tankan survey of business sentiment by the Bank of Japan.[10] See also Economic relations of Japan.

Japan is the world's 3rd largest automobile manufacturing country, has the largest electronics goods industry, and is often ranked among the world's most innovative countries leading several measures of global patent filings.[11] Facing increasing competition from China and South Korea, manufacturing in Japan today now focuses primarily on high-tech and precision goods, such as optical equipment, hybrid cars, and robotics.

Japan is the world's largest creditor nation,[12] generally running an annual trade surplus and having a considerable net international investment surplus. As of 2010, Japan possesses 13.7% of the world's private financial assets (the 2nd largest in the world) at an estimated $14.6 trillion.[13] As of 2011, 68 of the Fortune 500 companies are based in Japan.

In the three decades following 1960, Japan ignored defense spending in favour of economic growth,[14] thus allowing for a rapid economic growth referred to as the Japanese post-war economic miracle. By the guidance of Ministry of Economy, Trade and Industry,[15] with average growth rates of 10% in the 1960s, 5% in the 1970s, and 4% in the 1980s, Japan was able to establish and maintain itself as the world's second largest economy from 1978 until 2010, when it was supplanted by the People's Republic of China. By 1990, income per capita in Japan equalled or surpassed that in most countries in the West.[16]

However, in the second half of the 1980s, rising stock and real estate prices caused the Japanese economy to overheat in what was later to be known as the Japanese asset price bubble caused by the policy of low interest rate by Bank of Japan. The economic bubble came to an abrupt end as the Tokyo Stock Exchange crashed in 1990–92 and real estate prices peaked in 1991. Growth in Japan throughout the 1990s at 1.5% was slower than growth in other major developed economies, giving rise to the term Lost Decade. Nonetheless, GDP per capita growth from 2001-2010 has still managed to outpace Europe and the United States.[17] Japan had recently embraced the new strategy of economic growth with such goals to be achieved in 2020 as expected.[18]

The modern ICT industry has generated one of the major outputs to the Japanese economy.[19][20][21][22][23][24][25][26][27] Japan is the second largest music market in the world.[28]

A mountainous, volcanic island country, Japan has inadequate natural resources to support its growing economy and large population, and therefore exports goods in which it has a comparative advantage such as engineering-oriented, Research and Development-led industrial products in exchange for the import of raw materials and petroleum. Japan is among the top-three importers for agricultural products in the world next to the European Union and United States in total volume for covering of its own domestic agricultural consumption.[29] Japan is the world's largest single national importer of fish and fishery products.[30][31][32][33][34] Tokyo Metropolitan Central Wholesale Market [35][36] is the largest wholesale market for primary products in Japan, including the renowned Tsukiji fish market.[37][38] Japanese whaling, ostensibly for research purposes, has been challenged as illegal under international law.

Although many kinds of minerals were extracted throughout the country, most mineral resources had to be imported in the postwar era. Local deposits of metal-bearing ores were difficult to process because they were low grade. The nation's large and varied forest resources, which covered 70 percent of the country in the late 1980s, were not utilized extensively. Because of political decisions on local, prefectural, and national levels, Japan decided not to exploit its forest resources for economic gain. Domestic sources only supplied between 25 and 30 percent of the nation's timber needs. Agriculture and fishing were the best developed resources, but only through years of painstaking investment and toil. The nation therefore built up the manufacturing and processing industries to convert raw materials imported from abroad. This strategy of economic development necessitated the establishment of a strong economic infrastructure to provide the needed energy, transportation, communications, and technological know-how.

Deposits of gold, magnesium, and silver meet current industrial demands, but Japan is dependent on foreign sources for many of the minerals essential to modern industry. Iron ore, copper, bauxite, and alumina must be imported, as well as many forest products.

Economy of Japan

http://commons.wikimedia.org/wiki/File:Skyscrapers_of_Shinjuku_2009_January.jpg Morio
Financial centre in Tokyo

Rank	3rd in GDP(nominal) and 4th in GDP(PPP), 25th in GDP per capita (PPP)
Currency	Japanese Yen (JPY)
Fiscal year	1 April – 31 March
Trade organisations	APEC, WTO, OECD, G-20, G8 and others
Statistics	
GDP	$5.964 trillion (2012 est.) (nominal;3rd) $4.628 trillion (2012 est.) (PPP; 4th)
GDP growth	0.9% (Q1 2013)
GDP per capita	$46,736 (2012 est.) (nominal; 14th) $36,266 (2012 est.) (PPP; 23rd)
GDP by sector	agriculture: 1.2%, industry: 27.5%, services: 71.4% (2012 est.)
Inflation (CPI)	0.3% (April 2011)[1]
Population below poverty line	15.7%[2]
Gini coefficient	38.1 (2002)
Labour force	65.93 million (2011 est.)
Labour force by occupation	agriculture: 3.9%, industry: 26.2%, services: 69.8% (2010 est.)
Unemployment	4.6% (2011 est.)[1]

Main industries	among world's largest and technologically advanced producers of motor vehicles, electronic equipment, machine tools, steel and nonferrous metals, ships, chemicals, textiles, processed foods
Ease of Doing Business Rank	24th[3]
External	
Exports	$788 billion (2011 est.)
Export goods	motor vehicles 13.6%; semiconductors 6.2%; iron and steel products 5.5%; auto parts 4.6%; plastic materials 3.5%; power generating machinery 3.5%
Main export partners	China 19.7%, United States 15.5%, Russia 11.3%, South Korea 8%, Germany 7.9%, Hong Kong 5.2%, Singapore 4.7%, Thailand 4.6% (2011), France 2.1 %, United Kingdom 0.3% (2012 est.)
Imports	$808.4 billion (2011 est.)
Import goods	petroleum 15.5%; liquid natural gas 5.7%; clothing 3.9%; semiconductors 3.5%; coal 3.5%; audio and visual apparatus 2.7%
Main import partners	China 21.5%, Russia 16.1% United States 8.9%, Australia 6.6%, Saudi Arabia 5.9%, United Arab Emirates 5%, South Korea 4.7% (2012 est.)
FDI stock	$161.4 billion (31 December 2010 est.)
Gross external debt	$2.719 trillion (30 June 2011)

Public finances	
Public debt	$13.64 trillion / 229.77% of GDP (2011 est.)[4]
Revenues	$1.1trillion (2011 est.)
Expenses	$1.157trillion (2011 est.)
Economic aid	$9.7 billion ODA (February 2007)
Credit rating	Standard & Poor's:[5] AA- (Domestic) AA- (Foreign) AAA (T & C Assessment) Outlook: Stable[6] Moody's:[6] Aa2 Outlook: Negative Fitch:[6] A- Outlook: Negative
Foreign reserves	US$1.154 trillion (April 2011)[7]

Main data source: CIA World Fact Book
All values, unless otherwise stated, are in US dollars

The **economy of Japan** is the third largest in the world

The government's liabilities include the second largest public debt of any nation. Former Prime Minister Naoto Kan has called the situation 'urgent'.[66]

Japan's central bank has the second largest foreign-exchange reserves after People's Republic of China.

FROM: WIKIPEDIA https://en.wikipedia.org/wiki/Economy_of_Switzerland

SWITZERLAND

(**N**ot in EEC and where most of the money, Diamonds and Gold of the world resides. It seems, for some reason, to be a charmed and protected country. Why?):

The **economy of Switzerland** is one of the world's most stable economies. Its policy of long-term monetary security and political stability has made Switzerland a safe haven for investors, creating an economy that is increasingly dependent on a steady tide of foreign investment.

Because of the country's small size and high labor specialization, industry and trade are the keys to Switzerland's economic livelihood. Switzerland has achieved one of the highest per capita incomes in the world with low unemployment rates and a balanced budget. The service sector has also come to play a significant economic role.

History [edit]

19ᵗʰ century [edit]

Switzerland as a federal state was established in 1848. Before that time, the city-cantons of Zurich and Basel in particular began to develop economically based on industry and trade, while the rural regions of Switzerland remained poor and under-developed. While a workshop system had been in existence throughout the early modern period, the production of machines began in 1801 in St. Gallen, with the third generation of machines imported from Great Britain. But in Switzerland, hydraulic power was often used instead of steam-engines because of the country's topography while there are no significant deposits of coal. By 1814, hand weaving had been mostly replaced by the power loom. Both tourism and banking began to develop as an economic factor from about the same time.

Its industrial sector began to grow in the mid-19ᵗʰ century, but Switzerland's emergence as one of the most prosperous nations in Europe, sometimes termed the "Swiss miracle" was a development of the short 20ᵗʰ century, among other things tied to the role of Switzerland during the World Wars.[7]

20ᵗʰ century [edit]

During World War I, Switzerland suffered an economic crisis. It was marked by a decrease in energy consumption, energy being mostly produced by coal in the 1910s, 1920s, 1930s and 1940s. The war tax-[specify] was introduced. As imports were difficult, attempts were made to strengthen the Swiss economy. The cultivation of grain was promoted, and the Swiss railway became the first to use electric instead of coal-burning, steam-driven engines[citation needed].

In the 1920s Switzerland's energy consumption increased[citation needed].

Throughout the 1930s Switzerland's energy consumption stagnated[citation needed].

In the 1940s, particularly during World War II the economy profited from the increased export and delivery of weapons to the German Reich, France, Great Britain, and other neighbouring and close countries. However, Switzerland's energy consumption decreased rapidly. The conduct of the banks cooperating with the Nazis, but not exclusively, they also cooperated extensively with the British and French. [citation needed] and the commercial relations with the axis powers during the war became the subject of sharp criticism, resulting in a short period of international isolation of Switzerland from the world. After World War II, Switzerland's production facilities remained to a great extent undamaged which facilitated the country's swift economic resurgence[citation needed].

Year	Gross Domestic Product	US Dollar Exchange
1980	184,080	1.67 Francs
1985	244,421	2.43 Francs
1990	330,925	1.38 Francs
1995	373,599	1.18 Francs
2000	422,063	1.68 Francs
2005	463,799	1.24 Francs
2006	490,545	1.25 Francs
2007	521,068	1.20 Francs
2008	547,196	1.08 Francs
2009	535,282	1.09 Francs
2010	546,245	1.04 Francs
2011	in progress	0.75 Francs

The CIA World Factbook estimates Switzerland's 2011 exports at $308.3 billion and the 2010 exports at $258.5 billion. Imports are estimated to be $299.6 billion in 2011 and $246.2 billion in 2010. According to the World Factbook numbers, Switzerland is the 20th largest exporter and the 18th largest importer.[12]

The United Nations Commodity Trade Statistics Database has lower numbers for Switzerland's exports and imports. The UN calculates exports at $223.5 billion in 2011 and $185.8 billion in 2010. The value of all imports in 2011 was $197.0 billion and in 2010 it was $166.9 billion.[18]

Switzerland's largest trading partner is Germany. In 2009, 21% of Switzerland's exports and 29% of its imports came from Germany. The

United States was the second largest destination of exports (9.1% of total exports) and the fourth largest source of imports (6.7%).[19]

Switzerland's neighbors made up next largest group; Italy was third for exports (8.6%) and second for imports (10%), France was fourth for exports (8%) and third for imports (8.1%) and Austria was fifth for exports (4.6%) and sixth for imports (3.7%). Major non-European trading partners included; Japan (seventh for exports with 3.6% and twelfth for imports with 2%), China (eighth for exports and imports with 3.1% and 2.5% respectively) and Turkey (sixteenth for exports with 1.2% and ninth for imports with 2.3%).[19]

As a first world country with a skilled labor force, the majority of Swiss exports are precision or 'high tech' finished products.

Banking [edit]

http://commons.wikimedia.org/wiki/File:BIZ_Basel.jpg Wladyslaw Sojka

The Bank of International Settlements in Basel.
Main article: Banking in Switzerland

In 2003, the financial sector comprised an estimated 11.6% of Switzerland's GDP and employed approximately 196,000 people (136,000 of whom work in the banking sector); this represents about 5.6% of the total Swiss workforce.[24]

Swiss neutrality and national sovereignty, long recognized by foreign nations, have fostered a stable environment in which the banking sector was able to develop and thrive. Switzerland has maintained neutrality through both World Wars, is not a member of the European Union, and was not even a member of the United Nations until 2002. [25][26]

Currently an estimated 28 percent of all funds held outside the country of origin (sometimes called "offshore" funds) are kept in Switzerland.[27] In 2009 Swiss banks managed 5.4 trillion Swiss Francs.[28]

The Bank of International Settlements, an organization that facilitates cooperation among the world's central banks, is headquartered in the city of Basel. Founded in 1930, the BIS chose to locate in Switzerland because of the country's neutrality, which was important to an organization founded by countries that had been on both sides of World War I.[29]

Foreign banks operating in Switzerland manage 870 billion Swiss francs worth of assets (as of May 2006).[30]

Switzerland is among the world's most prosperous countries in terms of private income. In 2007 the gross median household income in Switzerland was an estimated 107,748 CHF, or USD 137,094 at purchasing power parity(PPP).[citation needed] The median income after social security, taxes and mandatory health insurance was 75,312 CHF, or USD 95,824 at PPP.[citation needed][dubious - discuss]

In October 2011, Switzerland had the highest average wealth per adult, at USD 540,000 (c. 325,000 at PPP)[31] This development was tied to the exchange rate between the US Dollar and the Swiss franc, which caused capital in Swiss francs to more than double its value in dollar terms during the 2000s and especially in the wake of the financial crisis of 2007–2008, without any direct increase in value in terms of domestic purchasing power.[32]

At the same time, wealth distribution of Switzerland has the high Gini coefficient of 0.8, indicating unequal distribution, see list of countries by distribution of wealth.[33] The high average wealth is explained by a comparatively high number of individuals who are extremely wealthy and says nothing about a typical Swiss citizen. The median wealth of a Swiss adult (50th percentile) is five times lower than the average, at USD 100,900 (c. USD 61,000 at PPP).[34]

Swiss and EU finance ministers agreed in June 2003 that Swiss banks would levy a withholding tax on EU citizens' savings income. The tax would increase gradually to 35% by 2011, with 75% of the funds being transferred to the EU. Recent estimates value EU capital inflows to Switzerland to $8.3 billion.

International comparison [edit]

Countries	Agricultural sector %	Manufacturing sector %	Services sector %	Unemployment rate %	Unemployment rate (females) %	Unemployment rate (males) %	Average hours worked per week
Switzerland (2006) [11]	3.8	23	73.2	4.0	4.7	3.4	41.6
European Union-25 countries (2006)[35]	4.7	27.4	67.9	8.2	9	7.6	40.5
Germany (2006)[36]	2.2	29.8	68	10.3	10.1	10.4	40.3
France (2006)[37]	3.9	24.3	71.8	8.8	9.5	8.1	39.1
Italy (2006) [38]	4.2	29.8	66	6.6	8.5	5.2	39.3
United Kingdom (2006)[39]	1.3	22	76.7	5.3	4.8	5.7	42.4
United States (2005) [40]	1.6	20.6	77.8	5.1[41]	5.6 [42]	5.9 [42]	41[43]

FROM: WIKIPEDIA https://en.wikipedia.org/wiki/Economy_of_the_United_States

And last but not least: the USA - the land of freedom (for the few) and economic slavery for the rest?

Throughout this article, the unqualified term "dollar" and the $ symbol refer to the US dollar.

The **economy of the United States** is the world›s largest national economy and the world›s second largest overall economy, the GDP of the European Union being approximately $2 trillion larger. The United States› nominal GDP was estimated to be $15.7 trillion in 2012,[1] approximately a quarter of nominal global GDP.[2] Its GDP at purchasing power parity is also the largest in the world, approximately a fifth of global GDP at purchasing power parity.[2] The United States has a mixed economy[20][21] and has maintained a stable overall GDP growth rate, a moderate unemployment rate, and high levels of research and capital investment. Its five largest trading partners are the European Union, Canada, China, Mexico and Japan.

The US is one of the world's wealthiest nations, with abundant natural resources, a well-developed infrastructure, and high productivity.[22] It has the world's sixth-highest per capita GDP (PPP).[2] The U.S. is the world's third-largest producer of oil and second-largest producer of natural gas. It is the second-largest trading nation in the world behind China.[23] It has been the world's largest national economy (not including colonial empires) since at least the 1890s.[24] As of 2010, the country remains the world's largest manufacturer, representing a fifth of the global manufacturing output.[25] Of the world's 500 largest companies, 132 are headquartered in the US, twice that of any other country.[26] The country is one of the world's largest and most influential financial markets. About 60% of the global currency reserves have been invested in the US dollar, while 24% have been invested in the euro. The New York Stock Exchange is the world's largest stock exchange by market capitalization.[27]Foreign investments made in the US total almost $2.4 trillion, which is more than twice that of any other country.[28] American investments in foreign countries total over $3.3 trillion, which is almost twice that of any other country.[29] Consumer spending comprises 71% of the US economy in 2013.[30] The labor market has attracted immigrants from all over the world and its net migration rate is among the highest in the world. The U.S. is one of the top-performing economies in studies such as the Ease of Doing Business Index, the Global Competitiveness Report,[31]and others. The US is ranked first globally in the IT industry competitiveness index.[32] The US economy is currently embroiled in the economic downturn which followed the Financial crisis of 2007–2008, with output still below potential according to the CBO[33] and unemployment still above historic trends.[34] As of March 2013, the unemployment rate was 7.6% or 11.7 million people,[35] while the government's broader U-6 unemployment rate, which includes the part-time underemployed, was 13.9%.[36] With a record proportion of long term unemployed, continued decreasing household income, and new federal budget cuts, the US economy remained in a jobless recovery.[37] At 11.3%, the U.S. has one of the lowest labor union participation rates in the OECD world.[38] Extreme poverty, meaning households living on less than $2 per day before government benefits, doubled from 1996 levels to 1.5 million households in 2011, including 2.8 million children.[39] In 2013, child poverty reached record high levels, with 16.7 million children living in food insecure households, about 35% more than 2007 levels. [40] There were about 643,000 homeless people in the US in January 2009, about two thirds of whom stayed in an emergency shelter or transitional housing program and the other third were living on the street, in an abandoned building, or another place not meant for human habitation.[41] In 2008, the US spent more on health care per capita ($7,146), and as percentage of GDP (15.2%), than any other nation. But in 2013, life expectancy was less than 17 other high-income countries.[42] In 2010, 49.9 million residents or 16.3% of the population did not carry health insurance, the lack of which causes roughly 48,000 unnecessary deaths per year.[43] In 2007, 62.1% of filers for bankruptcy blamed medical expenses. About 25% of all senior citizens declare bankruptcy due to medical expenses, and 43% are forced to mortgage or sell their primary residence.[44]

Total public and private debt was $50.2 trillion at the end of the first quarter of 2010, or 3.5 times GDP.[45] In October 2012, the proportion of public debt was about 1.0043 times the GDP.[46]Domestic financial assets totalled $131 trillion and domestic financial liabilities totalled $106 trillion.[47] The US economy is regularly reviewed with comprehensive economic data analysis in the Beige Book[48] of the Federal Reserve System,[49] the Bureau of Economic Analysis of the Department of Commerce,[50][51] the Bureau of Labor Statistics[52] of the Labor Department and economic indicators[53] of the US Census.

Economy of the United States of America

http://commons.wikimedia.org/wiki/File:Above_Gotham.jpg Anthony Quintano
New York City, financial center of the United States

Rank	1st (nominal) / 1st (PPP)
Currency	US$ (USD)
Fiscal year	October 1 – September 30
Statistics	
GDP	$15.685 trillion (2012) [1][2]
GDP growth	2.2% (2012) [1]
GDP per capita	$49,601 (2012)[2] (12th, nominal; 6th, PPP)
GDP by sector	agriculture: 1.2%, industry: 19.2%, services: 79.6% (2011 est.)
Inflation (CPI)	1.6% (January 2012 – January 2013)[3]
Population below poverty line	15.0% (2011)[4]
Gini coefficient	0.477 (2011) (List of countries)[5]
Labor force	155.028 million (includes 11.742 mil. unemployed, March 2013)[6]

Labor force by occupation	farming, forestry, and fishing: 0.7% manufacturing, extraction, transportation, and crafts: 20.3% managerial, professional, and technical: 37.3% sales and office: 24.2% other services: 17.6% (2009) [note: figures exclude the unemployed]
Unemployment	7.5% (April 2013)[6] ▼(−0.1%)
Average gross salary	$45,230 (May 2011)[7]
Main industries	Highly diversified, world-leading, high-technology innovator, second-largest industrial output in world; petroleum, steel, motor vehicles, aerospace, telecommunications, chemicals, electronics, food processing, consumer goods, lumber, mining
Ease of Doing Business Rank	4th [8]
External	
Exports	$1.564 trillion (2012)[9]
Export goods	Capital goods, 27.9%; industrial supplies and materials (except oil fuels), 24.8%; consumer goods (except automotive), 11.8%; automotive vehicles and components, 9.4%; food, feed, and beverages, 8.6%; fuel oil and petroleum products, 7.6%; aircraft and components, 6.1%; other, 3.8%.
Main export partners	Canada 18.9%; Mexico 14.0%; China, 7.1%; Japan, 4.5%; United Kingdom, 3.5% (2012)
Imports	$2.299 trillion (2012)[9]
Import goods	Consumer goods (except automotive), 22.7%; capital goods (except computing), 18.7%; industrial supplies (except crude oil), 18.4%; crude oil, 13.7%; automotive vehicles and components, 13.1%; computers and accessories, 5.4%; food, feed, and beverages, 4.8%; other, 3.1%.
Main import partners	China, 18.7%; Canada, 14.2%; Mexico, 12.2%; Japan, 6.4%; Germany, 4.8% (2012)
FDI stock	$2.824 trillion (2012)[10]
Gross external debt	$14.71 trillion / 98% of GDP (June 2011)[11]
Public finances	

Public debt	$16.687 trillion[12] / 105% of GDP[13]
Budget deficit	$1.09 trillion (2012)[14]
Revenues	$2.45 trillion (individual income tax, 46.1%; social insurance, 34.7%; corporate taxes, 9.9%; other, 9.3% – 2012)[14]
Expenses	$3.54 trillion (Social Security, 21.5%; defense, 18.4%; Medicare, 13.2%; interest, 7.3%; Medicaid, 7.1%; other, 32.4% – 2012)[14]
Economic aid	ODA $19 billion, 0.2% of GDP (2004)[15]
Credit rating	Standard & Poor's:[16] AA+ (Domestic) AA+ (Foreign) AAA (T & C Assessment) Outlook: Negative[17] Moody's:[17] AAA Outlook: Negative[18] Fitch:[17] AAA Outlook: Negative
Foreign reserves	$151.866 billion (Dec. 2012) [19]
Main data source: CIA World Fact Book All values, unless otherwise stated, are in US dollars	

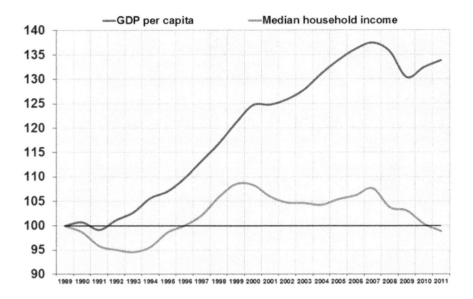

http://en.wikipedia.org/wiki/File:Gdp_versus_household_income.png Frichmon

The growth in total US GDP vs median US household income, 1989–2011

WRITER: According to Credit Suisse, in 2013, the USA had 42% of the world's total number of millionaires – wow!

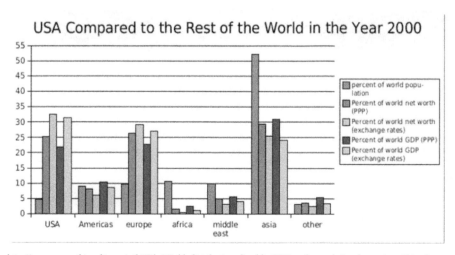

http://commons.wikimedia.org/wiki/File:World_distributionofwealth_GDP_and_population_by_region.gif Analoguni

United States wealth compared to the rest of the world in the year

2000.

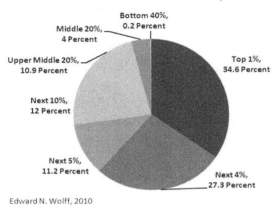

Edward N. Wolff, 2010

http://commons.wikimedia.org/wiki/File:U.S._Distribution_of_Wealth,_2007.jpg Edward N. Wolff

The distribution of net wealth in the United States, 2007. The chart is divided into the top 20% (blue), upper middle 20% (orange), middle 20% (red), and bottom 40% (green). (The net wealth of many people in the lowest 20% is negative because of debt.)

Notable companies and markets [edit]
In 2011, the 20 largest U.S.-based companies by Revenue were Walmart, ExxonMobil, Chevron, ConocoPhillips, Fannie Mae, General Electric, Berkshire Hathaway, General Motors, Ford Motor Company, Hewlett-Packard, AT&T, Cargill, McKesson Corporation, Bank of America, Federal Home Loan Mortgage Corporation, Apple Inc., Verizon, JPMorgan Chase, and Cardinal Health.
In 2011, four of the world's ten largest companies by market capitalization were American: Exxon Mobil, Apple Inc., Chevron Corporation, and Microsoft.
According to Fortune Global 500 2011, the ten largest U.S. employers were Walmart, U.S. Postal Service, IBM, UPS, McDonald's, Target Corporation, Kroger, The Home Depot, General Electric, and Sears Holdings.
Apple, Google, IBM, McDonald's, and Microsoft are the world›s five most valuable brands in an index published by Millward Brown.[168]
A 2012 Deloitte report published in *STORES* magazine indicated that

of the world›s top 250 largest retailers by retail sales revenue in fiscal year 2010, 32% of those retailers were based in the United States, and those 32% accounted for 41% of the total retail sales revenue of the top 250.[169] Amazon.com is the world›s largest online retailer.

Half of the world's 20 largest semiconductor manufacturers by sales were American-origin in 2011.[170]

Most of the world's largest charitable foundations were founded by Americans.

American producers create nearly all of the world's highest-grossing films. Many of the world's best-selling music artists are based in the United States. U.S. tourism sector welcomes approximately 60 million international visitors every year.

Forbes top 10 U.S. corporations by revenue [edit]

Top 10 U.S. corporations by revenue in 2012[171]

Rank	Corporation	Revenue $ millions 2012[172]	Profit $ millions 2012[173]	Assets 12/31/12[174]	Debt Ratio 12/31/12[175]	Headquarters	Employees 2012	Market cap 4/1/13 $ billions[176]	Industry
1	Exxon Mobil	454,926	41,060	334	50%	Irving, TX	99,100	403	Energy
2	Wal-Mart Stores	446,950	15,699	203	62%	Bentonville, AK	2,200,000	246	Retail
3	Chevron	245,621	26,895	233	41%	San Ramon, CA	61,189	230	Energy
4	ConocoPhillips	245,621	12,436	117	59%	Houston, TX	29,800	73	Energy
5	General Motors	150,476	9,190	149	76%	Detroit, MI	202,000	38	Auto
6	General Electric	147,616	14,151	685	82%	Fairfield, Connecticut	301,000	240	Diversified
7	Berkshire Hathaway	143,688	10,254	427	56%	Omaha, NE	288,500	259	Diversified
8	Fannie Mae	137,451	-16,855	3,221	99%	Washington D.C.	7,300	1	Finance
9	Ford Motor	136,264	20,213	190	91%	Dearborn, MI	164,000	50	Auto
10	Hewlett-Packard	127,245	7,074	108	80%	Palo Alto, CA	350,610	43	Computers

http://commons.wikimedia.org/wiki/File:Houston_Ship_Channel_Barbours_Cut.jpg U.S. Army Corps of Engineers Digital Visual Library

Internet was developed in the U.S. and the country hosts many of the world's largest hubs.

Finance [edit]

http://commons.wikimedia.org/wiki/File:NYC_NYSE.jpg Arnoldius

The New York Stock Exchange is the largest stock exchange in the world.

Main articles: Banking in the United States and Insurance in the United States

Top ten U.S. banks by assets

Rank	Bank	Assets $ millions 12/31/12	Profit $ millions 2012	Headquarters	Employees
1	JP Morgan Chase[191]	2,359,000	21,280	New York, NY	258,965
2	Bank of America[192]	2,209,000	4,188	Charlotte, NC	276,600
3	Citigroup [193]	1,865,000	7,415	New York, NY	259,000
4	Wells Fargo[194]	1,422,000	18,890	San Francisco, CA	265,000
5	Goldman Sachs[195]	923,220	7,475	New York, NY	57,726
6	Morgan Stanley [196]	749,890	–19,000	New York, NY	57,726
7	U.S. Bancorp[197]	353,000	5,600	Minneapolis, MN	62,529
8	Bank of NY Mellon[198]	359,301	2,569	New York, NY	48,700
9	HSBC North American Holdings[199]	318,801	N/A	New York, NY	43,000
10	Capital One Financial[200]	286,602	3,517	Tysons Corner, VA	35,593

THE RICH, THE WORKING CLASS & THE POOR

I have nothing against prosperous, rich, successful and wealthy people! They make the world go around and keep world economies going and provide us with jobs, etc. One will always have a certain percentage of the worlds' population who will make it close to, midway to or to the top. This is a fact! This is called competition and that we all have certain abilities and knowledge, talents, IQs, etc. But what I do not like is too many of these people are greedy and just want more and more. Once they have enough – I think about a 50 or 100 million is more than enough for any one person to have - they should then pay any workers they employ better wages, so they too can have a nice life and a good standard of living? This applies to big multi-million and multi-billion companies too. How some of these people and companies can live with themselves, and make so much money at the expense of others (look at the poverty, inhumanity and how some of the poor and working class live?) I really do not understand this? Yes they inherit the world and most of the wealth: but the rest of us would like our fair portion too? If I am wrong on this, then fine. You let me know. But I do not think I am. You decide. But something has to be done about the wages, living conditions and wealth distribution on this planet; as it is totally not fair. I've seen humans treat their pets better than they treat their servants and even, dare I say, their own wives, sons and daughters – and that is saying a lot!

SLUMS WORLDWIDE: (source: Wikipedia)

Slums are on the increase. In 2008, it was calculated that, for the first time in history, more people are living in urban environments than in rural areas. And one in three city dwellers lives in a slum. That represents a total of one billion slum dwellers worldwide, and this number is growing rapidly.

http://commons.wikimedia.org/wiki/File:Shanty_housing_in_Hong_Kong.jpeg Stephen Codrington

http://commons.wikimedia.org/wiki/File:A_young_boy_sits_over_an_open_sewer_in_the_Kibera_slum,_Nairobi.jpg Trocaire

Welcome, to Global Poverty Crisis.

What could be causing such financial struggle in Mumbai, sharing the same space as such financial success?

Corruption? Disordered politics? Temporary transition? Vast gaps in financial intelligence? Complex global finance? Inevitable effects? The GFC?

Consider these words and figures on worldwide financial famine:

- Over 25% of the planet is living in absolute poverty crisis – lacking basic needs for survival.
- Over 35% of the countries on planet Earth would qualify for assistance from the IMF Poverty Reduction and Growth Facility or PRGF (now known as the Extended Credit Facility).
- The number of people at risk of falling into poverty crisis has risen by over 15% in the past three decades.
- **Nearly half of the planet is living on less than \$2.50 per day**.
- Nearly a billion people entered the 21st century unable to read a book or sign their names.

A USD would purchase much less in the United States than a USD in India. PPP would value a \$1.25 in India as the equivalent of \$6.25 in the United States.

A large percentage of the world is living on less than \$1.25 per day in purchasing power parity.

(Source: Tony 0106) – Percentage of World Living on < \$1.25/day (PPP) – 2009 –

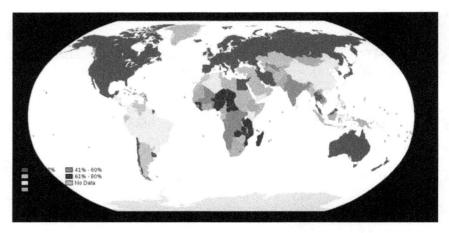

http://commons.wikimedia.org/wiki/File:Percentage_population_living_on_less_than_$1.25_per_day_2009.svg BokicaK

Global Income Inequality – Global Gini Coefficient – 2009 –

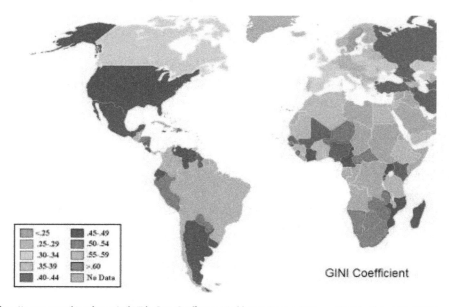

http://commons.wikimedia.org/wiki/File:Gini_Coefficient_World_CIA_Report_2009.png Gini Coefficient World CIA Report 2009

URBAN POPULATION LIVING IN SLUMS (below)

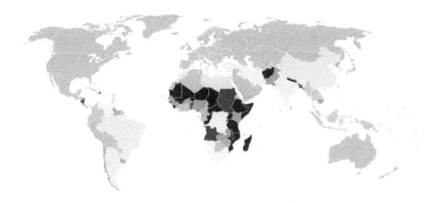

http://commons.wikimedia.org/wiki/File:Urban_population_living_in_slums.png • Map background from Image:BlankMap-World-v5.png. Data from UN-HABITAT, Global Urban Observatory, 2001 estimates

Urban population living in slums, as of 2001. 0-10% 10-20% 20-30% 30-40% 40-50% 50-60% 60-70% 70-80% 80-90% 90-100% No data

http://commons.wikimedia.org/wiki/File:Child_in_slum_in_Kampala_%28Uganda%29_next_to_open_sewage_%283110617133%29.jpg https://www.flickr.com/photos/gtzecosan/3110617133 SOURCE: SuSanA Secretariat
PHOTO BY: I. Jurga

Child in slum in Kampala (Uganda) next to open sewage

Gap between rich and poorest widest since the nineties

(from: Save the Children http://www.savethechildren.org.uk/news-and-comment/news/2012-10/gap-between-rich-and-poorest-widest-nineties)

The gap between rich and poor is at its highest since the 1990s and is growing – with children hit hardest, according to our new report, Born Equal, published today.

Thursday 1 November 2012

In some countries, the gulf between the richest and poorest families has increased by up to 179% over the past two decades according to the findings of Born Equal.

What's more, the gap between rich and poor children has grown by 35% and in some countries more than twice the numbers of poor children die before the age of five than rich children.

Our report, which comes as David Cameron prepares to co-chair a high level UN panel on global poverty today, highlights that children are hit twice as hard by inequality, despite its causes not being of their making.

Poorest of the poor excluded

The report argues that against a backdrop of overwhelming progress (extreme income poverty has dropped from 2 billion in 1990 to less than 1.3 billion today and child mortality has almost halved) the poorest of the poor have too often been excluded.

This means that children living in the same country may have vastly different chances of surviving to the age of five, getting a good education and eating a nutritious diet.

According to the report, now that 70% of the world's poorest people live in middle income countries, tackling inequality is one of the most effective ways to accelerate progress towards eradicating global poverty.

Inequality must be addressed

Save the Children's Chief Executive, Justin Forsyth, said: "In recent decades the world has made dramatic progress in cutting child deaths and improving opportunities for children; we are now reaching a tipping point where preventable child deaths could be eradicated in our lifetime.

"But this will only happen if we redouble our efforts and tackle inequality. Unless inequality is addressed, the MDGs and any future development framework will simply not succeed in maintaining or accelerating progress.

"What's more, it will hold individual countries – and the world – back from experiencing real growth and prosperity," he added.

Born Equal also highlights:

That in most of the 32 developing countries looked at the rich increased their share of national income since the 1990s.:

In almost a fifth of the countries (Bolivia, Peru, Zambia, Côte d'Ivoire, Ghana and Cameroon) the incomes of the poorest had fallen.

In Nigeria the poorest children are more than twice as likely to die before their fifth birthday than the richest children.:

In Tanzania child mortality in the richest quintile fell from 135 to 90 per 1,000 births over the research period while the poorest quintile hardly saw any progress with a modest fall of 140 to 137 per 1,000 births.

Disparities also affect rich countries such as Canada where low-income children are 2.5 times more likely to have problems with vision, hearing, speech or mobility.

In Brazil – one of eight countries researchers focused on in-depth – rapid economic growth has been accompanied by a decline in the country's income inequality alongside dramatic poverty reduction and improvements for child well-being.

Inequalities in gender, race and geographic location also affect children's opportunities to thrive.

See more at: http://www.savethechildren.org.uk/news-and-comment/news/2012-10/gap-between-rich-and-poorest-widest-nineties#sthash.ALQeVNbW.dpuf

SOURCE: The Independent, Tuesday 17 July 2007

http://www.independent.co.uk/news/uk/this-britain/gap-between-rich-and-poor-widest-in-40-years-457609.html

Writer: This article informs us not surprisingly that the **Gap between rich and poor 'widest in 40 years' in the UK!** You can read this at the above link

Nice!

Most of the richest people on the planet have seen their fortunes

soar in the past few years! Is this why they do not pay (the rich and super rich and the top 500 hundred companies on the planet) their workers a good decent wage, so they can have a nice standard of living too? We must all suffer because the rich and those in power just want more and more wealth, more and more personal and national debt for us and our countries and more and more power for them. Please go to the Forbes website and check out the stats on the number of millionaires and billionaires on the planet and their increase in wealth every year? This makes me sick. I am not against someone or a company making some money – but not at the expense of everyone else and the planet? I don't think this is right or fair!?

SOURCE: https://www.statista.com/statistics/272047/top-25-global-billionaires/:
The world's top 25 billionaires in 2017 based on assets (in billion U.S. dollars)

Bill Gates (United States) 86 Warren Buffet (United States) 75.6 Jeff Bezos (United States) 72.8 Armancio Ortega (Spain) 71.3 Mark Zuckerberg (United States) 56 Carlos Slim Helú (Mexico) 54.2 Larry Ellison (United States) 52.2 Charles Koch (United States) 48.3 David Koch (United States) 48.3 Michael Bloomberg (United States) 47.5 Bernard Arnault (France) 41.5 Larry Page (United States) 40.7 Sergey Brin (United States) 39.8 Liliane Bettencourt (France) 39.5 S. Robson Walton (United States) 34.1 Jim Walton (United States) 34 Alice Walton (United States)33.8 Wang Jianlin (China) 31.3 Li Ka-shing (China) 31.2 Sheldon Adelson (United States) 30.4 Steve Ballmer (United States) 30 Jorge Paulo Lemann (Brazil) 29.2 Beate Heister & Karl Albrecht Jr. (Germany) 27.2 David Thomson (Canada) 27.2 Jacqueline Mars (United States) 27

SOURCE: https://www.statista.com/statistics/299513/billionaires-top-countries/

The 20 countries with the most billionaires in 2017

China (knocking the USA off the top spot!) – 609
USA – 552
GERMANY – 109
India – 100
UK – 89

Swizerland – 77
Russia – 68
France – 50
Brazil – 43
Japan – 42
Italy – 41
Canada – 35
South Korea – 34
Turkey – 29
Singapore – 28
Australia – 27
Thailand – 26
Spain – 23
UAE – 21
Indonesia – 17
Sweden – 17

The USA, is still, overall, the richest country in the world in terms of total number of millionaires and billionaires.

The richest 3% of the world's population own 50% of the world's total wealth!!!!!!

Something is grossly wrong with these stats. These people are rich at the expense of everyone else! And overall, the worldwide minimum and average wage must be too low if these people and companies are making so much money and profit???? Where is all going to end? Something effective yet fair must be done about this!?

THE WEALTH REPORT

Robert Frank looks at the culture and economy of the wealthy.
October 19, 2011, 12:46 PM

Millionaires Control 39% of Global Wealth

Writer: In this report, millionaires and billionaires now control 38.5% of the world's wealth!

Less than 1% of the world's population controls about $89 trillion.

This is up on 2010 and their wealth increased by $20 trillion. Total world wealth, in 2011, was £231 trillion.

Something is drastically wrong here my readers.

Of course the U.S. is still the overall wealthiest country.

The fastest growth will be in China, India and Brazil. Russia, who knows what will happen there?

WRITER: I have nothing against people making and having money; being successful; and making a profit. And many have really worked hard for their money. This is true. And this does not include the wealth which companies own. However, we **ALL** need money and not just the minimum wage salary. There is enough money on this planet for everyone to have a good, decent life! Companies and rich individuals/families could pay the lower and working class peoples better wages and they would still have lots of money in the bank and make a profit for the shareholders. If people have more money then they buy and spend more, then businesses make more in sales and governments make more in taxes and so everyone wins. Does that not sound good? It does to me. But no, some people do not want this scenario of sharing the money around and paying good wages so EVERYONE can have a good life and standard of living. No, they are just greedy and most just think about themselves and to hell with everyone else.

There is no need for about 30 million people (this is 0.43% of total world population) to control nearly 40% of the world's wealth, while the rest of us are barely surviving or do not know where our next meal will come from. What the fuck is going on here? This is NOT right, is not fair and is insane! The minimum wage needs to be hugely raised around the whole planet, so we can **ALL** have and lead a good life and be able to buy a fairly decent car and house and have some nice luxuries in life. I would like to see any politician or wealthy individual live on 7 dollars or 7 pounds an hour? This has to be sorted out and the line has to be drawn somewhere. And you know what is even funnier: no-one takes one cent of money or possession with them when their body dies. Death of one's body IS a certainty in this life but how many people ignore, hide from or do not confront this fact?

How many wrongly believe that when their body dies that this is the end of them. Ha, little do they know! So why all this injustice and unfairness between the Rich, the Working Class and the Poor. The Middle Income earners are also being hit harder and harder in these times but they tend to care little about the Working Class and the Poor (OK they and the Rich do contribute to charities [of which there are thousands and thousands of but yet still the problems of the poor continue?] but as long as they have/own a house and a car or two and get to go on holidays and their children go to University, they usually and mostly do not give a damn about anyone else. And VERY sadly this tends to be the general attitude and opinion of most of the peoples and races of Earth: this HAS to change for the good of us all!!!

I can only conclude that there are some people on this planet who do not give a fuck about the Working Class and the Poor (or anyone else for that matter, and in fact, want to keep them down and have all the money for themselves. As just like in Victorian times, when some people saw the injustices and read about them in Charles Dickens' novels, they made good (but basic) changes for the working class and the poor. Well, it is well overdue for this to happen again but on a very large planetary scale so the gap between the rich/upper/middle income earners (in particular the rich and supper rich) and the working classes and poor are far more reduced. Otherwise, some people might get really pissed off and there could be a Class World War and I do not know if that would end well for anyone since the largest Class on this planet is the Working Class and the Poor. Fact. But, change IS needed on this fiery subject and that is a fact and if a Class War or a World War for equality and good change for all is needed, then so be it, regardless of the consequences.

SLAVERY

https://pixabay.com/en/handcuffs-punishment-crime-law-2185221/

This is a subject that really pisses me off. Why? Because there is no need for it. But also, to some extent (to varying degrees), we are slaves to the current economic, financial, governmental and work-a-day-world systems we have in operation today. You don't eat, your body dies. You have no money, you die - unless you are totally self-sufficient and live off the land or in the jungle somewhere (and this is being stopped too because '*they*' cannot control you then, can they?) It may also be said, to some extent we are all slaves to or on this planet or even dare I say prisoners, as I do not think anyone is going anywhere when their body dies: not that I know off. I know of no-one who has departed this life, gone somewhere else off of Earth and then come back again to tell us all about where they were and what happened to them when their body died? If you know of someone then do let me know. Maybe a few unique individuals could leave their bodies while still alive and go sit on the Moon or in the Sun (and I don't mean astral bodies or astral projection and stuff like this) or go to another part of this Universe, but that would be very small percentage and they would not reveal themselves as being able to do this anyway. And, obviously such individuals could go to any part of Earth too and with full perception and consciousness. But most do not even know who they are and what a Spirit Being is and what it can do? Most are unconscious as Spirits or Souls and so must have a body to perceive at all. Plus, the population of this planet is increasing, not decreasing. And this has nothing to do with God or any Supreme Being and I am not saying anything here to question your faith in God and I am not saying that there is no God, there is. I am just talking here about the state of man and how things are on this planet right now. Having a good religious faith and religion and a belief in God is definitely a very good and healthy thing to have. Better to have faith in something and something to look forward to, than to belief in nothing and have nothing or no future goals to work toward or to look forward to. A fair amount of people today (and the number is growing because of various factors occurring on this planet today: Psychiatry; Psychology; Scientists; Physicists; the Media and general education basically saying we are all bodies and animals and everything is decided by and controlled by our brains, DNA and our genes) believe in nothing and when our body dies that is the end of them. Well, I can tell you, that this is not true. Charles Darwin had a big problem with his discoveries about evolution and its conflict with the church, the soul and God. Well he needn't have had this because he was only right about and talking about the evolution of human bodies (the human body would be just an animal if there was no Spiritual Being inhabiting and controlling it. And a body and all animals and plants too, all have life and life force energy in them; otherwise they could not do what they do. A body is alive. So is a plant. All those cells talk to one another and communicate. And they think. Bodies, with or without a Soul in them, do have an Unconscious Mind and they also must have a small thinking Conscious Mind, otherwise they would not be able to recognize and perceive anything. The same for plants but on a lesser scale. A cell knows what it is doing, where it is and what is going within itself and outside of itself. A cell is like a factory powerhouse. And there is no way that a human or animal female cell and a male cell can conceive and be joined together to form a Zygote and then embryo and grow on to form a full-sized body or animal, if it did not know what it was doing and what do with all the food, water and milk it gets. And a single celled organism just divides itself into another complete and exact copy of itself and grows to a complete organism that way. But still each cell or stem cell [basic cell that has not been assigned a function yet] is aware of itself and other cells and chemicals; and these cells are able to unite together to grow into bodies, animals and plants. And they can even heal and repair themselves. This is all quite amazing I think!) This evolution of animals has nothing to do with us as Spirits or Souls and does not infringe into the realm of God. But this is where this idea of us being just animals and bodies came from and it was supported and developed by others to control, falsely educate Man with lies, and to pull him down and make him as their slaves: which is very much in vogue and happening on a worldwide scale as I write this book. I just wanted to make sure you understand these important facts. They are important. Why? Because they are about YOU, ME and EVERYONE on this planet.

There are far more facts and truths I could give you in this book but, to be honest, you would not believe them and most probably could not handle or understand them. So there is no point in mentioning them.

But I just wanted you to know that there is more to this planet and this sector of this Universe, more to you as a Spiritual Being and more this Universe than you think. I suppose one day soon, Mankind will get the chance to have these facts and truths revealed to him and be able to experience them for real himself and not just read about them or listen to someone else discuss them. But that will only happen if Mankind remains free to attain and reach these facts and truths and does not end up in utter, complete slavery and totally forgets himself and who and what he is. For, if that happens, he may be lost forever, unless by a slim chance, some wise, savant and genius savior happens to appear or rise above it all and once again bring Mankind back into the light. But why let that happen, when we have the chance of attaining the fullest and highest states of Spiritual existence Man has ever known or dreamed of. This is what I am communicating to you now in my book and what I would like to ponder and understand that what I am saying to you now is the truth. And if, you can look deep inside oneself, you may see that what I say is TRUTH. And the ultimate truth is: we are all Spiritual Beings and there is nothing we cannot do, cause or create. Let's continue on with my book....

Slavery has existed since the very earliest times of Man – but really there is no need for it any more, is there? Indeed Man may well be a slave himself but we are not going there. Slavery comes in many forms. How another man or fellow human being, can make another man, woman or child a slave is beyond my comprehension and is indicative of how insane Mankind can really be. And the other mentally and spiritually sick people are the rapists, the paedophiles, the murderers and those who eat people. And one also has those evil, one-minded and sadistic assholes who keep Mankind down intentionally (and in particular keep the working classes down and the poor poor, intentionally I may add!) by passing stupid laws, raising and forever raising and creating more and more taxes; and making sure that THEY get most of the money and they keep most of the money all for their love, wonderful selves – with little left for anyone else. This creates slavery too – economic and financial slavery. Heard the sheep up, give them enough just food and money to just survive and keep them stupid and as robots (like in Animal Farm). Well, I have to say that this IS all going to change in the next few years. Believe it will, if I have anything to do with it. And if it doesn't, well we can all just kiss our asses goodbye and enjoy complete and total slavery, domination and even oblivion – like it would have been if Hitler had of won! I am not kidding you in this my friend and if you are my enemy, I am definitely not kidding that some payback is coming, some much deserved justice and some punishment and some BIG changes to these enemies of planet Earth and Mankind and how they are free to operate and almost do whatever they want. The times, they are definitely a changing. We are either going to win (us, the good guys) and they (the bad guys) will lose; or we will lose and that is pretty much the end of Mankind as you currently know it.

I have included what others have said about this below and given you some stats. This makes me sick, so I do not want to talk any more about this.

This article gives a good history of Slavery:
http://en.wikipedia.org/wiki/Slavery
I've just shown some pictures but you can read the full article online if you want. Pictures usually speak louder than words:

Slavery

From Wikipedia, the free encyclopedia

http://commons.wikimedia.org/wiki/File:Slavezanzibar2.JPG http://www.untoldlondon.org.uk/news/ART38118.html
unknown photographer
Photograph of a slave boy in Zanzibar. 'An Arab master's punishment for a slight offence. 'c. 1890.

David P. Forsythe wrote: "In 1649 up to three-quarters of Muscovy's peasants, or 13 to 14 million people, were serfs whose material lives were barely distinguishable from slaves. Perhaps another 1.5 million were formally enslaved, with Russian slaves serving Russian masters."[62] Slavery remained a major institution in Russia until 1723, when Peter the Great converted the household slaves into house serfs. Russian agricultural slaves were formally converted into serfs earlier in 1679.[63] Russia's more than 23 million privately held serfs were freed from their lords by an edict of Alexander II in 1861.[64] State-owned serfs were emancipated in 1866.[65]

During the Second World War (1939–1945) Nazi Germany effectively enslaved about 12 million people, both those considered undesirable and citizens of countries they conquered.[66]

The Arab enslavement of the Dinka people.

Joseph Jenkins Roberts, born in Virginia, was the first president of Liberia, which was founded in 1822 for freed American slaves.

http://www.wikipedia.or.ke/index.php/File;Lehnert_et_Landrock_-_Bound_Slave,_Tunisia_c.1900.jpg Delcampe, Verdeau, Liveauctioneers, eBay

"Bound slave". Orientalist nude photograph by Lehnert & Landrock, Tunisia circa 1900.
(Source: from 'Abolition Media')

Modern Slavery Statistics

Writer: The mixed statistics from this article say:

> 27 million – Number of people in modern-day slavery across the world.

> 1 million – Number of children exploited by the global commercial sex trade, every year. In 2003- 2004. 80% – Percent of transnational victims who were women and girls.

> The UN Office on Drugs and Crime, says in April 2006, 32 billion – Total yearly profits generated by the human trafficking industry. $15.5 billion was made in industrialized countries. $9.7 billion in Asia $13,000 per year generated on average by each "forced laborer." This number can be as high as $67,200 per victim per year.

And other sources say:

161 Countries identified as affected by human trafficking:

127 countries of origin; 98 transit countries; 137 destination countries.

Prosecutions:
In 2006 there were only 5,808 prosecutions and 3,160 convictions throughout the world
This means that for every 800 people trafficked, only one person was convicted in 2006

According to **The New York Times**, in an article by *QUENTIN HARDY TITLED:* GLOBAL SLAVERY, BY THE NUMBERS
It says:
The lifetime profit of a brickmaking slave in Brazil is $8,700, and $2,000 in India. Sexual slavery brings the slave's owner $18,000 over the slave's working life in Thailand, and $49,000 in Los Angeles There are 27 million slaves worldwide, more than in 1860, when there were 25 million. Most are held in bonded servitude, particularly after taking loans they could not repay. Slaves cost slightly more now, with a median price of $140, compared with $134 per human then. Debt slaves cost on average $60; trafficked sex slaves cost $1,910.
"Life is cheaper than some bottles of wine!!!"

On average today, a person is a slave for six years, after which the person usually escapes, repays the debts holding them, or dies. Most of the world's slaves are in South Asia.

I do not think anything else needs to be said by me or anyone else on Slavery except that it **IS** sick and it should not exist on any part of this planet; there is enough food, land and wealth for everyone, so there is no need for slavery at all! Let's leave it at that. However, I must make this important point: as technology, drugs and methods to control Man develop and become more advanced; then the Powers-That-Be will be far more easily able to enslave us all; both mentally and spiritually. This is when we have a Super Technocratic Superstate. That's if we don't blow our-selves up before then or destroy ourselves and this lovely planet with pollution or some super virus or disease. Man does not really know how precarious his existence is on this little planet. One large meteor could wipe us all out just like that! Let's move on.

PSYCHIATRY/PSYCHOLOGY VS RELIGIOUS/SPIRITUAL/MENTAL FREEDOM

(This war *IS* happening as we speak – honest!!!)

I told you before that Man IS a *Spiritual Being*: **NOT** a body, a brain, piece of clay, dust, DNA, Genes, an animal, a non-thinking robot or whatever else he has been incorrectly told by 'the *experts*' he is – *they* (Psychiatry/Psychology/The Powers that are) tell us what we are. Ha! That's so nice of them to tell us lies. Well, it is only like this because Man gets born in a usually unknowing state. He is confused and spends the rest of his living life trying to find the answers before his body dies again. Thus he has to search around and discover < if he wants to know the facts and truth as some people do not want to know too much and avoid certain topics and some also intentionally avoid knowing the truth (it's too painful or confusing) > usually from his parents, education, growing up (life experiences: good and bad), TV, Radio, newspapers, magazines, books, internet, friends, family and all other sources of knowledge (whether true or not) and anything he may already know which could be called intuition or natural knowingness (not learned). If we, each and every one us on Earth, knew the ultimate truth about who/what we **REALLY** are and what we are capable off, then we probably would not be here at all. Or we could spiritually be somewhere else on this planet while our body is in another location; or we could be spiritually (not astral projection or Mind's Eye and all that) on another planet like Mars or Venus while our bodies sleep; or we could just have no body at all (all those Norse, Greek, Roman, Indian, Arabian, American Indian and other gods were real!!! Most myths and legends have some truth in them if you trace them back; but they usually get altered over time. Some of these gods were Ghosts and some Ghosts become gods when their bodies died; some gods were evil, some were god, some were nuts just as it is the same for modern-day Ghosts, just the same as it is for us Human Beings). But unless you could communicate with other Spiritual Beings or gods or ghosts (and that implies that there would have to be some Spiritual Beings, gods or ghosts around for this to happen), then you would be alone and have no-one talk too and know-one to play games with and have fun. So, it may be better to have a body and ALSO be able to go in and out of one at will; but be able to go as a fully aware, knowledgeable and capable Spiritual Being too. Then that would be fun and a lot of happiness could be had and a lot of amazing stuff could be done.

However; I know right now that some people will be reading these words and scoffing, laughing in disbelief and thinking 'What does he know?' Others will be scared or afraid. Others may ask 'Sounds good, but how do I get into that state?' And others more will just be quite happy to not know more than what they currently know and are quite content with their own state/condition/fate or destiny (some people say fate or destiny cannot be changed. I say rubbish. No-one else is going to do it but oneself) and are very happy with what they believe: religiously, spiritually or otherwise. More are also very happy that they are born, live and die as bodies or as spirits in bodies - over and over for thousands of years ever more until Earth dies or the Sun dies or life somehow is discontinued. And more still will just want to remain in a body or they believe they are no more than a body anyway and all they want is money, sex, a good job, a wife, girlfriend, a family, car, house and all this materialism. And more still are far lower than all the rest and do not even know they have a body or where they are as a human being> the totally lost and confused.

Well, I do not really care what you or people believe as long it is not bad or evil or harmful to yourself, others and the rest of mankind. You believe and think what you want. Whether it is true or not, it is what you believe and if you are happy with that, then I am fine with that too. No. Really, I am. What I am saying is this: No matter what you believe or what religion you have or don't have or whether you believe you are just a body or not, the main point I am making here is that we all living here together on planet Earth right now at this point in time, in the cosmic time of the broad Universe, and we - all of us together - compose the entire Human Race of living beings on Earth today. We are all that we know of that exists on this planet and in this sector of the Universe, at this time. There most certainly is life out there (this is my belief and others) but let us just deal in what we do 100% know. And so, for now, it is just us on this sea-blue planet; spinning through space and around the Sun and in danger of complete annihilation at any time or in very real and extreme danger of being in complete and total slavery to whoever is running this planet, be they human, alien, subhuman, slime, scum or whatever you want to call them or whatever they are. The fact is they exist and are very real and THEY ARE the ones making our lives and this planet the way they are. And to some extent we have been going along with all this for some time now and enjoying it because we have all this great new entertainment and technology and of course, there is fun and love to be had while on lives – but also pain and suffering and nowadays, there sadly seems to be more of the latter. And it DOES NOT HAVE TO BE LIKE THIS AT ALL!

Now, I would like to touch on two supposedly expert subjects which are so dear to my hear – NOT!!!!!!!!!

PSYCHIATRY and PSYCHOLOGY:- Some of the culprits in Psychiatric drug manufacturing are:

Johnson & Johnson; Roche; gsk GlaxoSmithKline; Novartis; Sanofe Aventis; AstraZeneca; ABBOT; MERK; BAYER, etc...

SOURCE: CCHR INTERNATIONAL

Psychiatrists/Physicians admit—Disorders are not a "Disease"

"There are no objective tests in psychiatry-no X-ray, laboratory, or exam finding that says definitively that someone does or does not have a mental disorder." "there is no definition of a mental disorder." "It's bull—. I mean, you just can't define it." — *Allen Frances, Psychiatrist and former DSM-IV Task Force Chairman*

"While DSM has been described as a 'Bible' for the field, it is, at best, a dictionary.... The weakness is its lack of validity. Unlike our definitions of ischemic heart disease, lymphoma, or AIDS, the DSM diagnoses are based on a consensus about clusters of clinical symptoms, not any objective laboratory measure. In the rest of medicine, this would be equivalent to creating diagnostic systems based on the nature of chest pain or the quality of fever." — *Thomas Insel, Director of the National Institute of Mental Health*

"Virtually anyone at any given time can meet the criteria for bipolar disorder or ADHD. Anyone. And the problem is everyone diagnosed with even one of these 'illnesses' triggers the pill dispenser." — *Dr. Stefan Kruszewski, Psychiatrist*

"Despite more than two hundred years of intensive research, no commonly diagnosed psychiatric disorders have proven to be either

genetic or biological in origin, including schizophrenia, major depression, manic-depressive disorder, the various anxiety disorders, and childhood disorders such as attention-deficit hyperactivity. At present there are no known biochemical imbalances in the brain of typical psychiatric patients—until they are given psychiatric drugs."
— *Peter Breggin, Psychiatrist*

While "there has been no shortage of alleged biochemical explanations for psychiatric conditions...not one has been proven. Quite the contrary. In every instance where such an imbalance was thought to have been found, it was later proven false." — *Dr. Joseph Glenmullen, Harvard Medical School psychiatrist*

"The theories are held on to not only because there is nothing else to take their place, but also because they are useful in promoting drug treatment." — *Dr. Elliott Valenstein Ph.D., author of Blaming the Brain*

"There is no blood or other biological test to ascertain the presence or absence of a mental illness, as there is for most bodily diseases. If such a test were developed ... then the condition would cease to be a mental illness and would be classified, instead, as a symptom of a bodily disease." — *Dr. Thomas Szasz, Professor Emeritus of Psychiatry, New York University Medical School, Syracuse*

"We do not have an independent, valid test for ADHD, and there are no data to indicate ADHD is due to a brain malfunction." — *Final statement of the panel from the National Institutes of Health Consensus Conference on ADHD*

"The way things get into the DSM is not based on blood test or brain scan or physical findings. It's based on descriptions of behavior. And that's what the whole psychiatry system is." — *Dr Colin Ross, Psychiatrist*

"Psychiatry has never been driven by science. They have no biological or genetic basis for these illnesses and the National Institutes of Mental Health are totally committed to the pharmacological line. ... There is a great deal of scientific evidence that stimulants cause brain damage with long-term use, yet there is no evidence that these mental illnesses, such as ADHD, exist." — *Peter Breggin, Psychiatrist*

"No claim for a gene for a psychiatric condition has stood the test of time, in spite of popular misinformation." — *Dr. Joseph Glenmullen, Harvard Medical School psychiatrist*

"In reality, psychiatric diagnosing is a kind of spiritual profiling that can destroy lives and frequently does." — *Peter Breggin, Psychiatrist*

"...modern psychiatry has yet to convincingly prove the genetic/biologic cause of any single mental illness...Patients [have] been diagnosed with 'chemical imbalances' despite the fact that no test exists to support such a claim, and...there is no real conception of what a correct chemical balance would look like." — *Dr. David Kaiser, Psychiatrist*

"There's no biological imbalance. When people come to me and they say, 'I have a biochemical imbalance,' I say, 'Show me your lab tests.' There are no lab tests. So what's the biochemical imbalance?" — *Dr. Ron Leifer, Psychiatrist*

"Virtually anyone at any given time can meet the criteria for bipolar disorder or ADHD. Anyone. And the problem is everyone diagnosed with even one of these 'illnesses' triggers the pill dispenser." — *Dr. Stefan Kruszewski, Psychiatrist*

"No behavior or misbehavior is a disease or can be a disease. That's not what diseases are. Diseases are malfunctions of the human body, of the heart, the liver, the kidney, the brain. Typhoid fever is a disease. Spring fever is not a disease; it is a figure of speech, a metaphoric disease. All mental diseases are metaphoric diseases, misrepresented as real diseases and mistaken for real diseases." — *Thomas Szasz, Professor of Psychiatry Emeritus*

"It has occurred to me with forcible irony that psychiatry has quite literally lost its mind, and along with it the minds of the patients they are presumably suppose to care for."— *David Kaiser, Psychiatrist*

"DSM-IV is the fabrication upon which psychiatry seeks acceptance by medicine in general. Insiders know it is more a political than scientific document... DSM-IV has become a bible and a money making bestseller—its major failings notwithstanding."— *Loren Mosher, M.D., Clinical Professor of Psychiatry*

"All psychiatrists have in common that when they are caught on camera or on microphone, they cower and admit that there are no such things as chemical imbalances/diseases, or examinations or tests for them. What they do in practice, lying in every instance, abrogating [revoking] the informed consent right of every patient and poisoning them in the name of 'treatment' is nothing short of criminal."— *Dr. Fred Baughman Jr., Pediatric Neurologist*

"Psychiatry makes unproven claims that depression, bipolar illness, anxiety, alcoholism and a host of other disorders are in fact primarily biologic and probably genetic in origin...This kind of faith in science and progress is staggering, not to mention naïve and perhaps delusional." — *Dr. David Kaiser, psychiatrist*

"In short, the whole business of creating psychiatric categories of 'disease,' formalizing them with consensus, and subsequently ascribing diagnostic codes to them, which in turn leads to their use for insurance billing, is nothing but an extended racket furnishing psychiatry a pseudo-scientific aura. The perpetrators are, of course, feeding at the public trough."— *Dr. Thomas Dorman, internist and member of the Royal College of Physicians of the UK*

"I believe, until the public and psychiatry itself see that DSM labels are not only useless as medical 'diagnoses' but also have the potential to do great harm—particularly when they are used as means to deny individual freedoms, or as weapons by psychiatrists acting as hired guns for the legal system." — *Dr. Sydney Walker III, psychiatrist*

"The way things get into the DSM is not based on blood test or brain scan or physical findings. It's based on descriptions of behavior. And that's what the whole psychiatry system is."— *Dr. Colin Ross, psychiatrist*

"No biochemical, neurological, or genetic markers have been found for Attention Deficit Disorder, Oppositional Defiant Disorder, Depression, Schizophrenia, anxiety, compulsive alcohol and drug abuse, overeating, gambling or any other so-called mental illness, disease, or disorder." — ***Bruce Levine, Ph.D., psychologist and author of Commonsense Rebellion***

"Unlike medical diagnoses that convey a probable cause, appropriate treatment and likely prognosis, the disorders listed in DSM-IV [and ICD-10] are terms arrived at through peer consensus." — ***Tana Dineen Ph.D., psychologist***

"It's not science. It's politics and economics. That's what psychiatry is: politics and economics. Behavior control, it is not science, it is not medicine." — ***Thomas Szasz, Professor of Psychiatry Emeritus***

Alternatives To Drugs

Why Safe, Effective Treatments to Mental Difficulties are Kept Buried

The larger problem is that the biological drug model (based on the bogus mental disorders are a disease marketing campaign) prevents governments from funding real medical solutions for people experiencing difficulty.

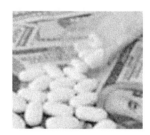

There is a great deal of evidence that medical conditions can manifest as psychiatric symptoms, and that there are non-harmful medical treatments that do not receive government funding because the psychiatric/pharmaceutical industry spends billions of dollars on advertising and lobbying efforts, including hundreds of their pharma funded "patient's rights" groups to counter any medical modality that does not support their biological drug model of mental disorders as a disease. This even includes people diagnoses psychotic or schizophrenic – and there have been workable, non-drug programs such as Soteria House which have not received the recognition they should have been afforded considering their success rate when compared to patients treated with drugs. Why? Billions of dollars in revenue for the psycho/pharma industry would have been lost. This is an industry that time and again, has been proven to put profit above patients lives.

SOURCE: CCHR INTERNATIONAL

PSYCHIATRY: HOOKING YOUR WORLD ON DRUGS

Introduction

What is one of the most destructive things in your world today?

If you answered drugs, then you share that view with the majority of people in your community. Illegal drugs, and their resultant violence and crime, are recognized as a major threat to children and society. However, very few people recognize that illegal drugs represent only part of the current drug problem. Today, we see a reliance on another type of drug, namely prescription psychiatric drugs.

Once reserved for the mentally disturbed, today it would be difficult to find someone—a family member, a friend or a neighbor—who hasn't taken some form of psychiatric drug. In fact, these have become such a part of life for many people that "life without drugs" is simply unimaginable.

Prescribed for everything from learning and behavioral problems, to bedwetting, aggression, juvenile delinquency, criminality, drug addiction and smoking, to handling the fears and problems of our elderly, from the cradle to the grave, we are bombarded with information pushing us towards this type of chemical "fix."

Little surprise then that worldwide statistics show that a rapidly increasing percentage of every age group, from children to the elderly, rely heavily and routinely on these drugs in their daily lives. Global sales of antidepressants, stimulants, antianxiety and antipsychotic drugs have reached more than $76 billion a year—more than double the annual US government budget spent on the war against drugs...

215

Understanding society's skyrocketing psychiatric drug usage is now even more critical than ever. Internationally, 54 million people are taking antidepressants known to cause addiction, violent and homicidal behavior.

How did millions become hooked on such destructive drugs? We need to look earlier than the drug.

Forcing widespread implementation of this diagnostic sham, **psychiatrists have ensured that more and more people with no serious mental problem, even no problem at all, are being deceived into thinking that the best answer to life's many routine difficulties and challenges lies with the "latest and greatest" psychiatric drug.**

Whether you are a legislator, a parent of school-aged children, a teacher, an employer or employee, a homeowner, or simply a community member, this report is vital reading.

Our failure in the war against drugs is due largely to our failure to put a stop to the most damaging of all drug pushers in society.

This is the psychiatrist at work today, busy deceiving us and hooking our world on drugs.

Sincerely,

Jan Eastgate
President Citizens Commission on Human Rights International
Source: http://healthworkscollective.com/rhona-finkel/43221/three-biggest-pharmaceutical-lawsuits-2012-psychiatric-drugs-focus-all-three

Three Biggest Pharmaceutical Lawsuits of 2012: Psychiatric Drugs Focus of All Three

Posted August 8, 2012 Posted by Rhona Finkel

Writer: This article details that landmark lawsuits against Johnson and Johnson resulted in them having to pay $1.1 billion in fines for improper marketing that violated various laws; Abbot Labs had to pay $1.5 billion for off-label promotion of Depakote to dementia patients in nursing homes and GlakoSmithKline had to pay $3 billion for its practices.

One has to ask ourselves why we allow these psychiatric drug companies to even be allowed to make and sell these drugs as they cure nothing and are the root cause of so much violence, killings and suicides! Why do the governments 1. Allow Psychiatry to even exist and 2. To be even able to use psychiatric drugs and other brutal so-called 'treatments' in their methods?

I think some people treat their pet animals better than they treat fellow human beings!

SOURCE: CCHR INTERNATIONAL

BEHIND TERRORISM: PSYCHIATRY MANIPULATING MINDS
Introduction

The terrorist attacks on the twin towers of New York's World Trade Center and the Pentagon in Washington, DC on September 11, 2001, will never be forgotten: the airplanes exploding into flames as they hit buildings; people leaping from the burning wreckage to certain death; firemen rushing into the crumbling towers only to become victims themselves; large swaths of lower Manhattan reduced to smoking rubble. A stunned world watched the news footage over and over, trying to come to grips with the criminal mind that could conceive of such a plan, much less execute it.

Unthinkably violent acts like this shock us all. What kind of person could be so cold-hearted and destructive—and be willing to give up his own life in the process? What kind of mindset methodically plans and executes mass murder—with utter disregard for humanity? Yet some "experts" claim that today's terror merchants are no more irrational than you or I—that we all have "demons" within.

Beware these experts, because their claims are blatant falsehoods.

Terrorism is created; it is not human nature. Suicide bombers are made, not born. Ultimately, terrorism is the result of madmen bent on destruction, and these madmen are often the result of psychiatric or psychological techniques aimed at mind and behavioral control. Suicide bombers are not rational—they are weak and pliant individuals psychologically indoctrinated to murder innocent people without compassion, with no concern for the value of their own lives. They are manufactured assassins.

Part of that process involves the use of mind-altering psychiatric drugs. Consider the roots of the word "assassin." In the year 1090, Hasan ibn al-Sabbah founded a terrorist group called the Ismaili Order in a mountain fortress south of the Caspian Sea. To train followers as killers, they were first drugged unconscious, then taken to a beautiful garden filled with luxuries and women. They were woken to enjoy the "delights" and then drugged again and returned to the "Grand Master" overseeing their training. He would assure them they had never left his side but had merely experienced a taste of the paradise that awaited them if they successfully carried out a killing assignment. Because of the heavy use of hashish to accomplish the intoxication, the killers became known as "Hashishiyn" (from Arabic, "user of hashish"), and later "Assassins."

The Japanese "kamikaze" pilots who launched suicide attacks against Allied shipping during World War II used amphetamines to override their natural impulse to survive. Amphetamine side effects include psychosis, euphoria and combativeness.

Beverly Eakman, author and educator says, "Unspeakable acts of terror, torture, and mass murder are not so much the results of individuals who have lost their minds as they are of individuals who have lost their conscience. The heinous suicide attacks on the World Trade Center and the Pentagon are traced to Osama bin Laden and…bin Laden's chief mentor is a former psychiatrist.…It would not be the first time psychiatrists had served as the manipulators behind charismatic, but essentially weak and flawed, human beings—systematically feeding their hatreds [and] stroking their egos—until eventually even the most barbaric act may appear plausible and rational in the name of some twisted cause."

From Hitler's "Final Solution" in Germany and the unthinkable "ethnic cleansing" and terrorist purges in Bosnia and Kosovo in the 1990s, to today's suicide bombers, the world has suffered greatly at the hands of *programmed* assassins and genocidal maniacs.

This report reveals hidden key players in the alarming and explosive upsurge in terrorism today—psychiatrists and psychologists. Publicly exposing this destructive source behind terrorism provides insight and solutions to an otherwise incomprehensible and devastating phenomenon.

Sincerely,

Jan Eastgate
President, Citizens Commission
on Human Rights International
Minding the Gap
Treatment and origins of schizophrenia and other mental illness
Charting ties between drug companies, psychiatrists, lawmakers
Posted on **December 19, 2012** by **Kristen French**
Writer: Summing up; this article is saying that antipsychotic drugs are being prescribed for illnesses which have not been approved by the FDA. Furthermore; many people are not told of their side-effects. Some Psychiatrists had failed to disclose millions of dollars they received from drug companies. What power do the drug companies have over Washington and its lawmakers?
These people should be all locked up for all the indirect harm they have and are doing! But no, they are sneaky and they have friends in high places: they look after their own, not us.
Source: http://www.offthegridnews.com/2012/08/14/psychiatric-drugs-and-mass-murder-exploring-the-connection/

Psychiatric Drugs And Mass Murder: Exploring The Connection

Aug 14th, 2012 | By Carmen | Category: Big Pharma and the FDA, Health, Top Headline | Print This Article

The writer of this article explains that before the 1980s the number of mass killings in America was averaging one or two per decade. Then after this period, the number of mass killings has just been going up and up with quite a few ghastly crimes being committed by people under the age of eighteen!!! These mass, senseless killings and murders have not just been increasing in America but around the world too and this includes terrorist related killings. This then makes people want to ban guns, as they are thought to be the cause or something.

The highest number of the most infamous mass atrocities were perpetrated by people who had been on powerful, mind-altering Psychiatric drugs weeks or months leading up to the killings. Most were on SSRIs (Selective-Serotonin Reuptake Inhibitors) and this includes the Columbine shooters, the Virginia Tech gunman who murdered thirty-two people in an on-campus rampage, a Louisville man who shot and killed nine people at the Standard Gravure Company, a sixteen-year-old Native-American boy who gunned down nine on the Red Lake Indian Reservation in Minnesota, etc.

I can only conclude that certain people want the US people to be defenceless and without guns; so they cannot defend themselves against the future enslavement and control plans they have in the pipeline.

Some bad reactions to: Prozac, Luvox, and Paxil and other similar drugs are:

- Manic reaction (kleptomania, pyromania, dipsomania, nymphomania)
- Hypomania (poor judgment, over spending, impulsivity, etc.)
- Abnormal thinking
- Hallucinations
- Personality disorder
- Amnesia
- Agitation
- Psychosis
- Abnormal dreams
- Alcohol abuse and/or craving
- Hostility
- Paranoid reactions
- Confusion
- Delusions
- Sleep disorders
- Akathisia (severe internal restlessness that can lead to suicide)
- Withdrawal syndrome

Impulsivity

Why and how these psychiatric drugs are still being allowed to be prescribed and used is beyond me?

You can read the full article at the link above.

PSYCHIATRY (FROM: CCHR)
REHAB FRAUD: PSYCHIATRY'S DRUG SCAM
Introduction

...Is all hope lost?

Before considering that question, it is very important to understand one thing about drug rehabilitation today. Our hope of a cure for drug addiction was not lost; it was buried by an avalanche of false information and false solutions.

First of all, consider psychiatrists' long-term propagation of dangerous drugs as "harmless":

- In the 1960s, psychiatrists made LSD not only acceptable, but an "adventure" to tens of thousands of college students, promoting the false concept of improving life through "recreational," mind-altering drugs.
- In 1967, US psychiatrists met to discuss the role of drugs in the year 2000. Influential New York psychiatrist Nathan Kline, who served on committees for the US National Institute of Mental Health and the World Health Organization stated, "In principle, I don't see that drugs are any more abnormal than reading, music, art, yoga, or twenty other things—if you take a broad point of view."
- In 1973, University of California psychiatrist, Louis J. West, wrote, "Indeed a debate may soon be raging among some clinical scientists on the question of whether clinging to the drug-free state of mind is not an antiquated position for anyone—physician or patient—to hold."
- In the 1980s, Californian psychiatric drug specialist, Ronald K. Siegel, made the outrageous assertion that being drugged is a basic human "need," a "fourth drive" of the same nature as sex, hunger and thirst.

- In 1980, a study in the *Comprehensive Textbook of Psychiatry* claimed that, "taken no more than two or three times per week, cocaine creates no serious problems."
- According to the head of the Drug Enforcement Administration's office in Connecticut, the false belief that cocaine was not addictive contributed to the dramatic rise in its use in the 1980s.
- In 2003, Charles Grob, director of child and adolescent psychiatry at the University of California Harbor Medical Center believed that Ecstasy (hallucinogenic street drug) was potentially "good medicine" for treating alcoholism and drug abuse.

Today, drug regulatory agencies all over the world approve clinical trials for the use of hallucinogenic drugs to handle anything from anxiety to alcoholism, despite the drugs being known to cause psychosis.

The failure of the war against drugs is largely due to the failure to stop one of the most dangerous drug pushers of all time: the psychiatrist. The sad irony is that he has also established himself in positions enabling him to control the drug rehab field, even though he can show no results for the billions awarded by governments and legislatures. Governments, groups, families, and individuals that continue to accept his false information and drug rehabilitation techniques, do so at their own peril. The odds overwhelmingly predict that they will fail in every respect.

Drug addiction is not a disease. Real solutions do exist.

Clearing away psychiatry's false information about drugs and addiction is not only a fundamental part of restoring hope, it is the first step towards achieving real drug rehabilitation.

Jan Eastgate
President
Citizens Commission
on Human Rights International

Another article you can read is:

http://www.naturalnews.com/031787_psychiatric_drugs_greed.html

(Source: CCHR: REPRINTED WITH PERMISSION)

Psychiatric drugs sales generate $80 billion dollars per year with Big Pharma spending $4.7 annually on TV and Print ads, and $1 billion a year on internet advertising.

As a result the number of people worldwide taking psychiatric drugs has skyrocketed to 100 million (20 million of them children) with documented side effects of worsening depression, mania, psychosis, violence, suicidal and homicidal ideation, birth defects, heart attack, stroke and sudden death to name but a few.

Ideation (idea generation), the process of creating new ideas.; **Suicidal**

Ideation - Wikipedia, the free encyclopedia

International drug regulatory warnings have increased by 400% in the last 10 years, yet the general public has nowhere to go to find this information online in an easy to search, concise format.

Until now.

CCHR International, the world's leading mental health watchdog, has created a free public search engine featuring:

* 160 psychiatric drug warnings from international drug regulatory agencies

* 151 drug studies from international medical journals

* 194,558 adverse reaction reports on psychiatric drugs filed with the FDA between 2004-2008 from doctors, pharmacists, other health care providers, consumers and lawyers.

People can search international drug regulatory warnings, or studies, or both. They can search by the brand name of a drug (such as Prozac, Zoloft, Ritalin) or by drug class (such as antipsychotic, stimulant, antidepressant, etc.) or by type of side effect or by country issuing the study/warning. All information is summarized and easy to read.

CCHR International has also decrypted the FDA's Adverse Drug Reaction reports which include psychiatric drug side effects reported to the FDAs Medwatch program. This lists who reported the side effect (Doctor, Pharmacist, etc.) the side effect of the drug and also the age range.

Any medical term that appears in the search results can be defined

simply by double clicking the word, and a small bubble will appear defining the word.

No other mental health watchdog or government agency is offering this service to the public. This is the world's only searchable online psychiatric drug database containing all international studies, warnings and adverse reaction reports on psychiatric drugs in existence.

You can try out the new Psychiatric Drug Search Engine here. Help get the word out. The information is free. CCHR Int Psychiatric Drug Database

Source: FightForKids.org

Facts and Statistics

This article states that **17 million children worldwide** have been prescribed psychiatric drugs. And these are so dangerous that regulatory agencies in Europe, Australia and the United States have issued warnings that these antidepressants can cause suicide and hostility in children and adolescents.

10 million of these are in the United States!

Even children as young as 5 years old and younger are being given these psych drugs, in particular Ritalin, which the U.S. Drug Enforcement Agency says is more potent than cocaine, has the same effects on the brain and has many harmful side-effects.

This is what the US Government and Psychiatry thinks of its children. And why do doctors prescribe them and why do parents give them to their children?

WRITER: Breaking news and this *IS* good: recently it has come to my attention that Psychiatry has admitted that even its own Mental Diagnosis Bible is wrong (witness below). Funny that, but I knew this all along and they and Psychology have previously even admitted that they do not know how the mind works. Strange but did you ever fix a car or something that you did not know how it worked? (sometimes you did just by sheer luck or accident or your strong will or intention – which can work too by the way – I have done it MANY times myself:

224

made things work by hitting, banging them (the Physical Universe loves force sometimes) or just by my decision and strong, VERY positive thought to fix something or to make it work or to heal myself and right there, we get into the realm of gods, God, Supreme Beings and the potential spiritual powers and abilities that Man <u>DOES</u> still possess but is not using them, for various reasons (I know this goes against the grain of Mankind's current and past thinking and it is sacrilege to say such things and that everything is caused by an Other, or Others or Destiny (whatever that is). If you brought your car in to a mechanic or your body to a doctor and they said: 'Well, we can try this and that or maybe this and see what happens; but to be honest we haven't got a clue...' You would not be going back to that mechanic or doctor anymore; same if it was a lawyer or engineer, scientist or physicist, politician or anyone else of that ilk, if they did not know their profession and relevant data and knowledge and could do what they claim: If it didn't work and they do not help you and do their jobs correctly, you would not pay them or you would never, ever go back to them again – would you? The same applies to Psychiatry and Psychology.

So this data about Psychiatry is as follows:

SOURCE: National Institute of Mental Health

Transforming Diagnosis

By Thomas Insel on April 29, 2013

In this article the Director Thomas R. Insel, of the National Institute of Mental Health (NIMH), publicly delivered a bombshell about the Diagnostic and Statistical Manual of Mental Disorders (DSM). He has left the psychiatric world in turmoil after saying of the DSM:

"The weakness is its lack of validity."

The DSM has been described as a "Bible" for the field, and is, at best, a dictionary, creating a set of labels and defining each.

WRITER: And these guys are meant to know all about the mind and be 'treating' and 'curing' so-called mental disorders? Are you joking! They just invent them so the drugs companies can have something to say what their drugs are for – but they are not what they say they are for and they cure nothing; based on the above data and other parts of my book, they actually cause crime, suicides, mass killings and insanity (or if a person is truly insane, they actually make them worse!). And this is ALL LEGAL and the FDA and Governments allow these to be prescribed and sold? This is like having a licence to kill people but they say they are helping and curing them.

Come on! Please wake up to the seriousness, the inhumanity; the barbarism Psychiatry and it's various so-called *cures* and *treatments* and drugs are doing to millions of people all over the world???!!!!!

To conclude this section, I want to bring to your attention some famous people who have died or committed suicide by taking street drugs and/or Psychiatric Drugs. This is only a very small percentage of a long list. It is not nice:

River Phoenix: The actor, 23, was set to perform with his friend, Flea, of the Red Hot Chili Peppers in 1993 at Hollywood's Viper Room nightclub when he snorted an overdose of cocaine and heroin in the bathroom. He collapsed on the sidewalk outside the club and after his brother Joaquin called 911 and sister Rain couldn't revive him, he died of drug-induced heart failure.

Marilyn Monroe: America's greatest screen sex symbol of all time was discovered dead in her Brentwood bedroom by her psychiatrist. The coroner determined Marilyn's death at 36 was the result of "acute barbiturate poisoning" and "probable suicide." But many fans have long questioned the strange circumstances of her death.

She was probably a 'Monarch' or pain-drug hypnosis slave to the Kennedys or someone else high up. She also probably knew too much, so it may not have been suicide but murder. Sad what happened to her; so beautiful and so young!

Heath Ledger: In 2008, Batman's Joker was found unconscious in bed by his housekeeper. Paramedics couldn't revive the star and Heath, 28, was later ruled to have died from "acute intoxication" from the combined effects of six different prescription drugs.

Whitney Houston: Last year, the world was shocked when the famed diva, 48, was found unconscious and submerged in the bathtub of her suite at the Beverly Hills Hotel, where she was getting ready for a pre-Grammy party. Attempts to revive her failed and although the coroner ruled the death accidental, cocaine and other drugs were found in Whitney's system.

Jim Morrison: The Doors' frontman died on July 3, 1971, at age 27. He was found in a Paris apartment bathtub. No autopsy was performed but it is believed Morrison was the victim of a heroin overdose.

Kurt Cobain: The Nirvana frontman was found in 1994 at his Lake Washington home by an electrician. Though he killed himself -- a suicide note was found -- a high concentration of heroin and traces of diazepam were also found in his body. He was 27; the same age as Jimi Hendrix when he died.

Michael Jackson, aged 50, died of a Demerol overdose, given to him by his doctor I may add (nice doctor). Neverland employees reported that Jackson was "taking ten-plus Xanax pills a night." When police raided Jackson's Neverland ranch in 2003 the drugs found there included bottles of Vicodin, Oxycontin, Versed, Promethazime, Xanax and Valium. He had been fighting addiction to psychedelic/psychiatric drugs for many years. Sadly the Superstar is not with us anymore.

And sadly, his daughter, Paris Jackson (only 15), is still in a Psychiatric Hospital 3 months after trying to commit suicide by slitting a wrist and taking a drug overdose.

Surely all of these people can be helped in other more saner, more humane and civil ways than this barbarism - ways that *DO* actually work and cure people?

I think some people treat their dogs and pets better than they treat their fellow human beings! And this is not a nice commentary on Man.

Elvis Presley: The King of rock and roll, 42, died on Aug. 16, 1977. After being found unresponsive on the bathroom floor at his Graceland home, Elvis was rushed to the hospital where he was pronounced dead. Although the coroner said the cause of death was cardiac arrhythmia, what had caused his heart to beat irregularly was an overdose of prescription drugs, including Codeine, Valium, Morphine, and Demerol.

The world has never mourned the loss of such a legend as he so much!

People forget that apart from the damaging mental/spiritual side-effects (highs and lows) of these psychiatric and street/prescription drugs; there are many, many harmful physical side-effects, and these build up and badly alter the body, mind and soul of the person taking them. And all of these side-effects are known by the Drug Manufacturing companies; the FDA, the doctors, the Governments and the Psychiatric Associations. Isn't it about time *WE* did something about it and them - well?

VIRUSES, CANCERS, FLUES AND DISEASES

http://commons.wikimedia.org/wiki/File:Rod_of_Asclepius2.svg SOURCE:**Ddcfnc** at the **English language Wikipedia**

We have or have had Swine Flue, Bird Flue, Mad Cow Disease, HIV/AIDS, so many different types of Cancer which seem to be growing in number – not decreasing I may add? And we also have: SARS (Severe Acute Respiratory Syndrome), Viral Hepatitis (A, B, C, E), Cholera, Meningitis, Smallpox, various Influenzas and Flue Viruses, Yellow Fever, various Plagues and more recently MERS (Middle East Respiratory Syndrome) and recently EBOLA.

Where are all they coming from and what will be coming next? The Human Extinction Syndrome that wipes out all mankind including those who create and release it unless they have a cure and/or hide in their underground bunkers and cities. I am not trying to scare everyone but just highlighting that there are too many viruses, flues and diseases that suddenly spring up from nowhere or some questionable source and no-one seems to know where they came from or how or what created them? I find this hard very to believe!

I am pretty certain that the Powers-That-Be are behind all or most of these viruses and cancers in one way or another. That's how evil, nefarious they are. The Spanish Flu, for example, in 1918 killed more than 22 million people worldwide. That's a lot of people and not even a war would kill that many people (except World War II, in which about 60 million people died). And that was just from one flu virus!

And now we have Ebola, which was actually first discovered in 1976. I have some data that can help you or anyone. For example: Milk Thistle will help anyone clean their Liver out and keep it healthy. Hydrangea will clean your Kidneys out. Green Tea, is quite amazing and does many good things for the body. It is a VERY strong anti-oxidant; it can help one lose weight and it is a very good detoxifier! It can keep one young looking too. It is also good for the immune system. High doses of Vitamin C are also good for the immune system. But there is one substance that will kill the Ebola (if it hasn't evolved or mutated into something else) or at least stop it from getting worse, and that is the seeds of the African Garcinia or 'bitter' Kola tree.

So some free advice for anyone out there: anyone can take Milk Thistle and Hydrangea every day and it will keep one healthy, as your Liver and Kidneys are always the ones that suffer from drugs and alcohol and just general living and they get in a worse state as one gets older. Vit C, in about 1,000 mg dose every day, will also keep one healthy (take much higher doses if one is sick). Green Tea is, I think, the BEST all-around elixur of life for humans. It does so many good things for the body! So all of the above be taken every day to keep one well and healthy and to also keep Ebola and other viruses/flues/cancers away.

But one can also eat or chew the Bitter Kola seeds or nuts (they contain a special Flavonoid) even if one does not have Ebola, as it will or should prevent one from getting it or it will kill it if one has it. I don't know how many seeds or nuts you need to eat or chew every day, but one can try it or check with someone who does know. Doctors know every little about the above, but you can check with them in case of any side effects or if you are taking medication, this applies to

230

the Green Tea, Milk Thistle, Hydrangea and Vitamin C too. But they are all natural, so they should only help one. I have e-mailed this to a friend in Africa and I am waiting for him to let me know the results as they have Ebola where he lives. The above is known data. It is not newly discovered. The native Americans have been taking Hydrangea for thousands of years. The Chinese have been drinking Green Tea for the same amount of time.

And then we have all the other Drug related deaths, Alcohol and Tobacco; Overweightness and Obesity, Suicides, chemical poisoning, Genetic related stuff and death-sources we don't even know about.

Can I also add that a lot of these cancers, viruses and many other ailments, illnesses and body problems Mankind has can, a lot of them, be alleviated or cured with the right amount and/or combination of natural herbs, minerals and vitamins. And a good diet, with some exercise. Doctors do a one day course on Vitamins as far as I know, so they would not know about and be able to help and advise on these. But other trained experts can, and there are many of these in China, Peru and other countries.

Does anyone know what the hell is going on? We are meant to be a superior race, with advanced or advancing technologies. And we now have so many radiations, Satellite, radio and TV signals, Microwave, Internet and Mobile Phone communication and electro-magnetic signals bouncing and going around our planet, atmosphere and ionosphere and into and through our bodies (and our heads!) and that affects all life on Earth, including our children, plants, water, air and animals. Plus all the other pollutants and chemicals mixed up in this Global Communications and Radiation System.

I don't think our bodies and life on Earth were made to endure this onslaught? What do you think? Unless our bodies evolve to adopt to this and into what, I do not know.

The following stats may be of interest:

SOURCE: **WORLD HEALTH ORGANIZATION**

The 10 leading causes of death in the world, 2000 and 2012

Ischaemic heart disease, stroke, lower respiratory infections and chronic obstructive lung disease have remained the top major killers during the past decade.

HIV deaths decreased slightly from 1.7 million deaths in 2000 to 1.5 million deaths in 2012. Diarrhoea is no longer among the 5 leading causes of death, but is still among the top 10, killing 1.5 million people in 2012.

Chronic diseases cause increasing numbers of deaths worldwide. Lung cancers (along with trachea and bronchus cancers) caused 1.6 million deaths in 2012, up from 1.2 million deaths in 2000. Similarly, diabetes caused 1.5 million deaths in 2012.

COPD = Chronic Obstructive Pulmonary Disease

SCIENCE/PHYSICS/MATHS/ EDUCATION/EXPERTS

Neither Maths, Physics, Science, Chemistry and most of the so-called 'experts' and 'savants' (except for a few, the good guys, have advanced and helped Mankind an awful lot, without them maybe not being fully aware of it) have been able to crack the code or find the ULTIMATE TRUTHS that mankind so craves, desires and deserves. No, they have not. Each has maybe solved a little piece of the big puzzle: but none have completely solved it. If you say 'yes they have' then please do let me know as thus far I have not found it or read about it?

I 1000% think and feel that the real answers we seek will only be found by all of these people, experts, professors, subjects, areas and fields joining together – including RELIGION - in solving the riddles and getting to the bottom of the truths we seek. I do not see it happening any other way. Each field says ours is the way but each are just composites and a little part of the VERY large puzzle: if they openly and freely – without prejudice, bigotism and vested interest; join together without thinking of money, patents, fame, power, glory and all the rest, then and ONLY then, will we: Mankind finally be able to get somewhere and be happy and free and able to get to the stars, achieve real and full Spiritual Freedom and beyond: or whatever we want actually (some Human Beings want to remain as Human Beings and do not want anything else. As long as they have their body, sex, food, house, car, mortgage, job, business, holidays, money and all they rest, they are happy. And this is fine – but get this – THIS is in extreme jeopardy too with the direction this planet is currently headed, believe and trust me on this!)

And can I just interject something on modern Physics and Science: nothing much has been developed (that we know of anyway; as we do not know what the USA Military and others may have developed?) since Classical Physics merged with Quantum Physics. Einstein's theories, most of them are actually incorrect or partly incorrect. Light is not a constant and not a constant speed and one CAN go faster than the speed of light. His Special Relativity Theory and $E = MC^2$ are incorrect (which is also why most people who read them, do not understand them.). And the reason he failed to find a true Unified Theory is because his previous theories and formulas were not entirely correct (some parts were) AND, this is more important, he never factored in the God, Soul/Spiritual Being and Life Energy factors. And in Bran Cox's 'Human Universe' he does not factor in these either. The Big Bang theory is also incorrect. And to get any Big Bang (maybe it explains the creation of Galaxies, of which this Universe is mainly composed off), there has to have been someone or something that created the something to be banged in the first go off, right? Matter may be being created like a very, VERY fast on/off switch: now it is there; now it is gone - but this is happening so fast that one never notices the gaps in its existence - rather like speeding up and slowing down a modern-day movie film real. If one could get a super, super, SUPER fast camera, that could minute shots of matter, one would probably find a shot of the matter or particles, then another shot would show nothing and then next shot would show some matter and on and on. My point is, that there has to be source or cause point or entity for this Universe and its component parts. It is not just creating itself; I can tell you that. I will publish another short paper I have written on this after this book is published, which should put more 'light' on all of this (do you get the joke?) And light itself is also a very big mystery, as no-one has a clue what it is really; they only know what it does and what can be done with it. If Mankind does get to exist until the end of this century and does get to be more free in the fields of Invention, Science and Physics, and the Arts - more so than what he currently is - then Man may find the answers he seeks and crack the riddles and codes and establish beyond any doubt, the true source of this Universe, and maybe any others that are out there. As who says this is the only Universe there is. There may well be many more out there, completely different or similar to this one. And getting to being able to travel up to the speed of light X 1,000 or 1,000,000 is the *only* way Man is ever going to be able to map and discover this Universe, like those warp drives in Star Trek and Star Wars. But this will only happen if Mankind is allowed to progress to and exist at higher levels than he presently is; which is another reason I wrote this book. This will all make sense at the end. Trust me.

But no, the Lords of Death and Destruction do not want us to think for ourselves and they have altered and messed with the educational systems we presently have for some time, especially since after World War II. Stupid and ignorant people can be easily controlled (and so can one-track minded people or those with blinkers on) and made easily into slaves and servants to them and their global systems: why, because if we were able to freely think and discover the truths ourselves (or at least freely think); AND find out about ***them*** (the Dark Ones) and who and what they really are and why they behave in this course of action they pursue; then we might actually destroy, kill or imprison them; and this drives them crazy! And what drives them even more crazy is that we might be happy and free beings! Why, because they are completely nuts and do not see what we see, think like we think, and act like we do because the rest of us do not speak and act like them: why because we are good and not extreme anti-socials like them. But get this: they think WE are evil despite the fact that 80% of us are doing good. But they do not see this. This is why they are nuts and insane. You judge a person or organization by their actions and deeds, not their words. Not if they shag well or smile at you and all the rest.

The 'experts' tell us this and that: well how do *we* know what they say is true? Were they there 2 thousand, 5 million or 5 billion years ago? NO. Or were they there at the start of existence (the Big bang theory) – I think not and no matter how much they test, analyze, do carbon dating and all the rest of this bullshit, they (the experts), without working together, will NEVER find all the answers. They have BIG blinkers on and only discover what they want and what they are aware of and can confront. Unconsciously or intentionally they avoid the rest – funny that! Oh, I could say that one day (a very small and insignificant being like I am: without wealth, power and riches [but I have my wisdom and FAR more superior: my knowledge; and I cannot tell you where I got it from but maybe I already knew it all (or most of it anyway), all along and I feel that is more closer to the truth) I was stumbling/ floundering/ playing around and in an emotional-all-seeing-all-knowing-moment of awareness and consciousnesses; I discovered the ULTIMATE TRUTHS and the ALLNESS-OF-ALL (like Buddha did under his tree but he did not discover the Global way or path for all to achieve Bodhi or the state of Self-Awareness or Self Consciousness and Awareness of All; but he was [as well as all the rest of the greats] **SO** influential in giving us another piece of the puzzle: but the Lords of Darkness, the assholes keep blocking/suppressing it in any way they can. Why? They do not want us to know who and what we are and what we are capable of as Humans but MORE importantly as Spiritual Beings!) Oh, you think I jest. Not in this, my friends! Or I could say that I have researched for hundreds or thousands of years and that I have now found ALL the answers and this COULD be true too. However, Mankind believes in facts and much more in and sadly, in PROOF: and I do have some personal proof of my knowledge and the data and facts in this book; but I do not have proof of everything. You will just have to trust me and what I say. But I have lived, studied and observed life and we all believe in bodies, men/woman and two-way sex, wealth, money, riches, power, fame, deception, treason, crime, fraud, drugs, our brains, genes/DNA, chemicals, wars, arms, nuclear power and weapons, pornography, exotic art, torture, racism, tit-for-tat, ignorance, rape, murder, dying, lying, being born or reborn; beating up or killing our enemies and foes – and all the other vices and 'accepted' modes of 'normal' thought and behaviour. Wow: what a planet we live on!! I say it again: WOW!!! I think if aliens do exist (and I personally know that they do! [Again, you do not need to know how I know some all of the data and info in this book – you would not believe me if I told you, so I won't – but I do know what I am talking about. Trust me on this please!] Plus, the chances of us being the only lifeform in this vast Universe is very slim. I am sure aliens have lived on this planet long before Man did), they would have it boldly marked on their star maps 'Stay Clear of Planet Earth! They are all nuts there!':)

But I have also seen lots of good deeds and selfless acts on this planet. And seen lots of funny things too and met lots of interesting people. I've led a very interesting life. I've had extreme highs and very low lows. So we have the good with the bad. But is there a need for the bad? And the evil? I say no! Maybe we have all grown used to it after seeing and experiencing it so much and for so long ourselves while growing up and living on Earth (and the history books and the films tell us this too) and if our parents do it or 'others' do it, then it must be OK, right? But that does not mean our lives, this planet and its peoples need to be the way they are, does it? It and we all need to change and that change can only be done by each individual and by co-ordinated groups.

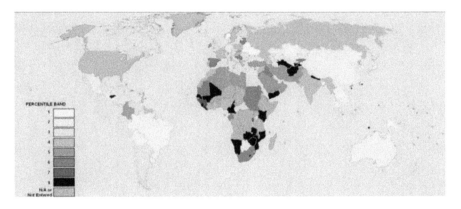

http://upload.wikimedia.org/wikipedia/commons/0/0b/Analfabetismo2013unesco.png UN Human Development Report 2011

DRUGS/ALCOHOL/CIGARETTES/SINS/ CRIMES/HAPPINESS

How freely available are drugs (both street and medical [that cure all of these wonderful diseases – not {some yes but mainly they just alleviate the symptoms. Why? Because they do not know the cause!) and alcohol in our society today. Drugs and alcohol slowly or quickly, depending on what the case may be, destroy your body and mind. They also - effect to a greater or lesser extent (as we are all different) - our perception and outlook on life; relationships, work, life in general; but they also affect our reaction time and literacy levels, reaction times and study speed. And many more side-effects can be added in here: it is a long list.

How many people of all ages smoke? Cigarettes contain lots of harmful chemicals (over 4,000 in the smoke [69 of which can cause cancer] and in 1994, the cigs in the USA, had 599 additives) including, of course, Nicotine. And its effects are cumulative on your lungs, blood vessels and heart.

How many people casually and ordinarily smoke joints of Cannabis, Weed and Marijuana, even in work or while driving? How many people take Cocaine and all the other deadly drugs? How many rich and famous people have died because of them? And how many crimes have been committed over them? I can say: it is a lot!!!!! And this does not include all those poor and working classes who die from drugs every year, including teenagers?

Then you have the wonderful prescription drugs which are so great, they can cure almost everything: sleeping tablets, Prozac and all the rest make the Drug Companies billions every year and trillions worldwide; and all supported and condoned by the medical professions (doctors and GPs) and our governments, and our wonderful Psychiatrists and Psychologists, I will cover these two later in more detail. OK some drugs do help patients with 'real' medical conditions but not to the extent that the Drug Companies claim, with most having so many more bad side-effects than benefits.

The thing about drugs, is they don't just have bad physical side-effects but mental and spiritual ones too. And all these drugs and alcohol are stored in the fatty tissues of the body; they do not disappear by themselves. And then, how much crime and sins are committed while under the influence or from the withdrawal or after-effects of these drugs (alcohol is a drug by the way)? How many people have died or are dying because of this? How many people are waiting for liver and kidney transplants, if they can get them in time?

Crime and suicide are up around the planet. Babies are being born addicts for god's sake!!! Children and woman are being raped while on them – whether they took the drugs themselves or whether they had their drinks spiked with Rohypnol? Street gangs murder and kill over them.

What I am saying is: IS ALL THIS REALLY NECESSARY? But it seems is that quite a few people on this planet, despite what they say, are clearly wanting to die and are heading in that direction whether intentionally or not.

I am not saying that one cannot have some alcohol or take some medical drug because it keeps you alive or something like this. This is OK and justified. Parties and having FUN are good. No, I am talking about the excessive and unnecessary use of drugs and smoking and drinking too much.

Sure they even give drug addicts Methadone (an addictive drug) to get them off the other drug they are addicted too, including alcohol. And they or the taxpayer pays for it! Now what does that tell you about our Governments? Then they become addicted to the Methadone. Now how does this cure and help them with their addictions? This is insane!

But back of all this, you will find the Lords of Darkness and their minions, including Psychologists and Psychiatrists and our wonderful Legal systems and Politicians: and of course, the big Drug Companies. Why, because they all make money out of it and they all get to see and watch people die every year around the world, in their millions. And crime rises and lives are destroyed. The bad and evil LOVE to cause these type of effects and they laugh and joke about it. We are low-life scum and sheep to them.

I do not jest in this my friends.

They are such nice and wonderful sub-people. They are **SUB-SCUM**!!!

But they tell us that 'We are *helping* you! And we are the experts,' and all this bullshit. Now these are the real enemies of mankind and who he should be fighting. Why do we fight ourselves, while the Powers-That-Be and their callous servants just sit there in their big guarded mansions, laughing their heads off or whatever it is that they do behind closed doors? And boy do they need a lot of armed guards. If someone could get to them, they would surely kill the mother-fuckers for what they have and are doing to Mankind.

It would be great if the mental, spiritual and physical side-effects of Drugs, Cigarettes and Alcohol were temporary or didn't even happen. This would be great. Drink as much as you want and wake up with no further liabilities or disadvantages and no hangovers. But sadly this is not the case. We all know this and so do the Lords of Darkness. They use our weaknesses; our unconscious minds; our state of unknowingness or not knowing the truth about ourselves and this planet and the media; our petty foibles and vices against us.

Is there a way out of all this mess? I would say YES! Firstly, YOU and WE can just decide to drink less and to smoke less, or even – dare I say it – quit! Now that would be something. And maybe your body might feel better; your mind and head would feel clearer; and YOU, as a Spiritual Being, would feel better too.

The second step we can all take, is to become more informed about all these drugs and what they are for, their actual *REAL* side-effects and what they actually do do (not what the FDA, Doctors and the Drugs' Companies tell us.) If in doubt; then DO NOT take them and seek independent advice! One can also contact a group like the Citizens Commission on Human Rights; Narconon or some other such free advisory or independent group.

People – and this should be thought to everyone in schools, colleges and Universities – should know all about vitamins, minerals and herbs; various food types: meats; vegetables; fruits and what they are for, when to take them and how much to take. Even GPs and Medical Doctors know very little about them (I mean vitamins, minerals and herbs and what they can cure, etc.) – why I do not know? You would be so surprised how much they can help and cure without taking any drugs. The food we eat today in this wonderful Capitalist world, which is all about making profit and cutting corners, is not as good as it once was, so taking balanced vitamins, minerals and herbs is a good idea. The Capitalists add water and other crap to meat and food just to increase the weight, so they get more money and profit. And they use lots of other tricks: growth hormones, genetics, drugs, chemicals and all the rest. Make a profit while we slowly kill them. That's their motto. And if you want the hopefully pure, organic food, vegetables and meat, you have to pay a fortune. Nice.

The Lords of Darkness are even trying to stop us from being able to take or buy Vitamins, Minerals and Herbs! This, through their paid lobbyists and minions, they are actually trying to make law. So that everyone will have to buy their Drugs and Cure-alls from the drug companies. Can you believe this?

Ignorance and stupidity are enemies of Man!

So it would be wise for Man to remedy this and get educated on the facts of his life, this planet; this Universe and who and what we are; where we can from; how we got here and more importantly how MANKIND CAN BE FREE AGAIN!!!! Yes, I say again (try getting your head around that one?)

And we have to handle ignorance and stupidity and the in-ability to learn which is more dominant than one may think: then everyone could be properly thought how to study and be able to learn anything!

If you do not know what a word or symbol means (or many words or symbols), and it doesn't matter how hard or simple it is or what subject or book it is; just get a simple but good dictionary, which YOU can understand, and BEFORE you progress any further in what you are learning – just look at, read and get defined the definitions or symbols in the dictionary. In this way YOU can learn ANYTHING. And it may take you some time to do this but eventually you will get faster and you WILL understand what you are learning or what you want to know about.

Thirdly, get some exercise. So many people and children today just sit around everywhere and do not get *enough* exercise to get their circulation going and get the blood and Oxygen around the body. So many things up with our bodies, even our minds and us as Spiritual Beings (they are all linked and can affect each other - one or all of them), could be helped just by doing this simple activity every week; every few days or every day (start off slow and nice and easy and just increase it – you will be amazed at the results!)

Also, just to show how far these Powers-That-Be can, have and WILL go: check out their covert proposals and plans for food and in particular vitamins, minerals and herbs. They have formed a new organization called: Codex Alimentarius, which is made of the World Health Organization and the FAO (Farming and Agriculture Association), which, strangely enough, they run too, and all the other organizations that are linked with this Codex. You can check this out and all that I have mentioned on this, on the internet and in other books. It is all there, if one would just look and find it.

Another point to mention on these Lords of Darkness assholes, is that they portray all their hundreds and hundreds of worldwide organizations, funds, banks, IMF. World Bank, educational grant/ charity organizations, et al, as all being so good and doing their utmost to HELP mankind (what a fucking joke!), and they say this on the websites for all these covert operational organizations and it is in their blurb and media relations to the rest of world. But this is ALL a cover-up for their *real* intentions, goals and purposes. They, as I said, are not stupid dickheads but intelligent ones and they know 1000% what they are doing and what is happening on this planet (the bad, evil stuff),

243

because **THEY** are the ones causing and doing it. I know the current social façade and superficial appearances seem to make it all look fine and that there is not much bad going on this planet; but this is all part of their plan: to dupe everyone into thinking everything is fine and it also (and they are VERY good at this) diverts attention away from them. They know full well that if WE: the peoples of planet Earth fully and truly knew what they were doing to us and our planet; we would either kill them or put them in jail and their entire families, cohorts and minions for the treason and high treason; for the thousands of evil crimes they are and have committed; the millions and millions of innocent people they have killed by their decisions and by the actions they have taken via their many companies and organizations; and via the numerous products they have and are selling (drugs, oil. etc.) and all their financial, banking and political crimes against humanity. And the list goes on and on, far too much to mention here. They know full well, that we would tear them apart and enjoy it. Just the same as how they feel about us right now! Fair is fair, right?

I even think these BIG Anti-social fuckheads may even be alien in origin (you may laugh at this but there is so much evidence which has come to light about Aliens being and having been on this planet before – that it is very hard to deny it); but I have no proof of this and this is not really that important unless (and please bear with me on this: you do not have to believe in aliens or that Science Fiction is part-factual or real (which makes Star Wars, Star Trek, The Matrix and all the rest not fiction but fact as regards our past and/present/ future) they are alien beings inhabiting human bodies (or have taken them over) and they send a message to their homeworld that they have lost control of Earth and to send the heavies down. Apart from this, you are fully capable of seeing that what has been happening on this planet for the last hundreds and few thousands of years, **has** to have been caused by someone or someones. It has not been chance, I can assure you of that! And it has nothing to do with God or the Devil – but if you think otherwise, that is fine with me. And I must say here and highlight this: I do not care what you and anyone else believes or does not believe or what faith you have or don't have; or if you believe in nothing. This is irrelevant at this juncture in Earth's history and destiny. And I do respect what others believe as long as it is good. What is definitely 100% true is that we are all living on this planet together, and right now this

IS the only planet we have and can live on. If we mess it up now and do not take the right and proper actions to secure a future that is **good for us**; then we may never get the chance again. Even if you do not care a damn about anyone else on the entire planet except yourself, not even your children (terrible to say but some do not!) or the planets, animals, Mother Nature or anyone or anything else (luckily some do!!!), this does not matter. Why? Because if we do not act now and deal with and handle these Lords of Darkness (I will go into full detail of these people and their families later, I promise); then the potential future of this planet will be like your worst nightmare and worse! Like George Orwell's 1984 and how-it-would-have-been-if Hitler-had-of-won. This kind of future is what I am taking about. Do you get me? Even if you don't and just say' Toot! What a load codswallop or bullshit,' that does not mean that things will all be fine and this is all just fancy and me spouting off my imagination. I can assure it is not! I have conducted lots of investigation and research into this; read lots of books; and I have been allowed to see some 'light' with the help of some friends of mine, who are privy to some interesting facts. So I am not speaking out through my asshole on this and the other topics I have written in this book. I can assure you that what I say is true. NOT conspiracy theories!!! But you check them out yourself and make up your own mind. For the moment, you and I are free to do this. But for how long more?

It will make little difference, actually, what you believe or think – because they will just keep going on with their evil Master Plan until they either achieve it or we take them out or stop them or the planet goes kaboom! These are the hard facts of it and we MUST wake up to these facts: confront them (and **_THEM_** and their servants and cohorts) and take the necessary steps and actions to handle it. Not just for ourselves but for our children; their future and the future of **ALL** life on this lovely blue planet we inhabit.

Some more stats on Drugs and Alcohol:

According to the: National Council on Alcoholism and Drug Dependence, Inc. there are:
2.5 Million Alcohol-Related Deaths Worldwide- Annually!!!!!!!
Fact: Alcohol and drugs are the leading causes of crime among youth.

Fact: Alcohol and drugs are the leading factors in teenage suicide.

Fact: More than 23 million people over the age of 12 are addicted to alcohol and other drugs, affecting millions more people ....

And webmd.com says:

Worldwide Illegal Drug Use Estimated at 200 Million People a Year!!!

And from www.livescience.com:

THEY SAY: Illegal Drugs Cause 250,000 Global Deaths Yearly

In 2009, between 149 million and 271 million people worldwide used an illicit drug at least once and this is an underestimate as some users may not admit their usage and data from poor countries is limited.

Marijuana and hashish (cannabis) topped the list. With these being used most in North America, Western Europe, Australia, and New Zealand.

Cocaine use was highest in North America with 14 million to 21 million users worldwide.

Opioid use, including heroin, was estimated to have 12 million to 21 million users globally.

FROM: **The Irish Examiner** newspaper article By Cormac O'Keeffe Dec 16, 2014

Legal drugs, including prescription medication and alcohol, account for three quarters of all deaths.

Tranquillisers known as benzodiazepines, methadone and anti-depressant medication, along with alcohol, accounted for 262 of the 350 deaths from poisoning in 2012.

There were 86 deaths involving methadone, the second highest number of deaths since 2004, but a drop from a high of 118 in 2011.

Between 2004 – 2012 drug related deaths (which includes Alcohol) have increased by 50%, with half of those who died aged 40 years or younger.

This is just in Ireland, which has a small population!

In the UK:

From: The Office of National Statistics (www.ons.gov.uk) the stats say:

Key Findings (for drug related deaths)

2,955 drug poisoning deaths (involving both legal and illegal drugs) were registered in 2013 in England and Wales (2,032 male and 923 female deaths).

Male drug poisoning deaths increased by 19% compared with 2012. Female drug poisoning deaths have increased every year since 2009.

Male drug misuse deaths (involving illegal drugs) increased by 23%, from 1,177 in 2012 to 1,444 in 2013. Female drug misuse deaths increased by 12%, from 459 in 2012 to 513 in 2013.

765 deaths involved heroin/morphine in 2013; a sharp rise of 32% from 579 deaths in 2012.

Deaths involving tramadol have continued to rise, with 220 deaths in 2013.

There was a sharp increase of 21% in the number of drug misuse deaths in England in 2013, with no change to the number of these deaths in Wales. The mortality rates were still significantly higher in Wales than in England.

Male mortality rates significantly increased in three substance categories: heroin/morphine, benzodiazepines and paracetamol. Conversely female mortality rates remained relatively stable except for a sharp increase in the cocaine-related death rate. In England, the North East had the highest mortality rate from drug misuse in 2013 (52.0 deaths per million population), and London had the lowest (23.0 deaths per million population).

In 2012 there were 8,367 alcohol-related deaths in the UK, 381 fewer than in 2011 (8,748).

Males accounted for approximately 65% of all alcohol-related deaths in the UK in 2012.

In the USA:

From: The National Institute of Alcohol Abuse and Alcoholism

Alcohol Use Disorders (AUDs) in the United States:
Approximately 17 million adults aged 18 and older had an AUD in 2012.

About 1.4 million adults received treatment for an AUD at a specialized facility in 2012.

In 2012, an estimated 855,000 adolescents aged 12–17 had an AUD.

An estimated 76,000 adolescents received treatment for an AUD at a specialized facility in 2012 (8.9 percent of adolescents in need). This included 28,000 females (6.3 percent of adolescent females in need) and 48,000 males (11.7 percent of adolescent males in need).[6]

Alcohol-Related Deaths:

Nearly 88,000 people die from alcohol related causes annually, making it the third leading preventable cause of death in the United States.

In 2012, alcohol-impaired-driving fatalities accounted for 10,322 deaths (31 percent of overall driving fatalities)[9]

Economic Burden:

In 2006, alcohol misuse problems cost the United States $223.5 billion.

Global Burden:

In 2012, 3.3 million deaths, or 5.9 percent of all global deaths were attributable to alcohol consumption.

Alcohol contributes to over 200 diseases and injury-related health conditions.

Globally, alcohol misuse is the fifth leading risk factor for premature death and disability; among people between the ages of 15 and 49, it is the first.

From: Centers for Disease Control and Prevention (www.cdc.gov):

Drug overdose was the leading cause of injury death in 2012. Among people 25 to 64 years old, drug overdose caused more deaths than motor vehicle traffic crashes.

Drug overdose death rates have been rising steadily since 1992 with a 117% increase from 1999 to 2012 alone.

Between 2004 and 2005, an estimated 71,000 children (18 or younger) were seen in EDs each year because of medication overdose (excluding self-harm, abuse and recreational drug use).

Among children under age 6, pharmaceuticals account for about 40% of all exposures reported to poison centers.5

Health care providers wrote 259 million prescriptions for painkillers in 2012, enough for every American adult to have a bottle of pills! In the United States, prescription opioid abuse costs were about $55.7 billion in 2007.

And, just to finish off, if you go to the link below, you can see the percentage of drug and alcohol deaths every 100,000 people, for every country in the world:

http://www.worldlifeexpectancy.com/cause-of-death/drug-use/by-country/
El Salvador has the highest Alcohol caused death rate at 25.1%

Afghanistan has the highest Drug caused death rate at 29.1%

So, as you can see from the above, many deaths each year are caused by Alcohol, Street drugs and Psychiatric Drugs. This is all so unnecessary!!!

HOW ONE SHOULD LIVE!

It is funny these days that, despite having so many good books, religions and philosophies around on how we should behave and lead good, moral lives- mankind still has dealings with and shares in dishonesty, immorality, stupidity, sins, crimes, sleeping around with and shagging anyone that comes along despite being married or in a relationship, maybe even with kids; tax evasion (I don't agree with this but some taxes are too high and some are suppressive and not needed at all!) and how many children, teenagers and adults are incompetent at their hobbies, jobs, and other fields. How many leaders and governments are incompetent, commit crimes and are allowed usually to get away with it? It is a strange wonder that we and life is still on this planet in view of the above!

One may wonder why one is not happy? Well, one has an unconscious mind – that can make one unhappy all by itself, and, it can make one insane and do/say things you would never normally do if you did not have one. One can be living with or in a family that is not good for you and pulls one down or destroys or holds one back in life. One can also be living in a town, city, village or neighbourhood or country that is criminal, immoral, Fascist, Communist or just not good for whatever reason.

However; despite these: If you are doing all or some of the above in the first paragraph, no matter where you live; you will not be happy. You will usually not be successful or very successful in life and you will usually fail, be miserable and your time of this Earth will not be long. And some people – actually quite a few in this day and age - believe me on this point, despite what they say or do; want to die anyway because of how the unconscious mind affects them. But you and your life will be even worse if you are doing things you should not be doing; whether it is written in some bible or moral book or not.

And don't get me wrong. The bible and many other good books and moral codes and some parents, do help and teach people and children/ teenagers how to lead good, happy and prosperous lives. But how many read these books, whether they go to church or not but claim to be good, moral people and yet they are not? They are liars and deceivers and cheaters; some are even killers or rapists. Some are even politicians!

If a person, right now, were to look at their entire life, in every aspect and in every detail; and see what needed to be corrected and put right or stopped, or; one could NOT be doing something that one should. If we all did this, and did it in such a manner as to not to have to justify or come up with excuses or reasons for what one is doing/not doing or that one should be doing- but just looks at it honestly by oneself.

>And one can do this for bad deeds one has done in the past; one can take responsibility for them and resolve them and put matters right regardless of what you did or did not do <

A person, no matter who they are, knows when they are doing wrong; or if it is a legal issue or tax issue or something of this ilk, then they can always get some advice on the matter. Well, if one made up a list from doing this and then decided to put right or correct all of these and then did actually do it. One would find enjoyment and happiness in life again or more of it if some was present before.

This also includes many spheres of life. If one wants to be a golfer; writer, artist of any kind; an engineer; businessman/entrepreneur or whatever it is one wants to do or be, which includes hobbies: one should do it in a competent or professional manner. Obviously when you begin, you will be an amateur or dilettante but don't remain one. One should not be second best to oneself and to others. You go see a lawyer or a doctor and one expects to be treated in a fully professional and honest manner; one pays for this and usually this is what one gets. Well, we all can and should be like this in every aspect of our lives; no matter what it is: being a great lover in bed (or a good kisser);

making dinner or breakfast; washing clothes; building a dam or a bridge; playing games; discoursing, bantering or conversing with someone; mowing the lawn; sports; knitting/sowing; skiing/camping/fishing – no matter what it is, one should do it as a pro or learn to do it as a pro. Get the books/handbooks/ guides; find out the meanings of the words/terminology in good, simple dictionaries; do some classes, ask questions; or learn from Pros/experts. No matter what it takes to do this, it should be done. And that means also knowing about one's body; where its parts are and what they do; what food they need; what vits, minerals and herbs are good for it and in what quantity and how to cure physical ailments naturally if possible, without drugs. And the one should know something cars and the machines/devices one uses whether in work or at home. Why be ignorant of these areas and fields? I know am not saying you have to do a degree in everything but if some course, qualification or training is needed, then do it. You will also save yourself money but you will also have more knowledge; and you and others you deal with will feel good about you knowing how to do things and that they CAN trust you in a personal matter or in some business deal and; your partner, wife/husband or lover can trust you too and you trust them. And we could trust – God help us all if this ever happened – we could trust our governments and its politicians. Now that would be some miracle!!!!

And the day that this happens; and that criminals see the harm they are doing and reform; and bad businessmen and politicians the same; then, and only then will we have a more happier, knowledgeable, efficient, prosperous and loving planet. All that would be left would be to handle and get rid of our unconscious minds; but I know one new group that is starting to deal with this rather large problem. If anyone cares to contact me about this; I will let them know and point them in the right direction and they can decide for themselves what they want to do. And, at the end of the day; that is all one can do: Ask people to change and point them in the right direction. It is THEIR choice and so too, in this matter, it is Mankind's choice what he does with or too himself and this planet we live on. I think you have gathered this by now that this is what I am asking from you, the reader of this book?

CHILDREN: I do have to quickly mention our children, who are the future of Mankind whether we like or want it or not. They should be treated with more respect and love than they are! They are young adults in small bodies. They are NOT stupid. Father beats mother in front of child. Unless the child is a sadist or a future criminal, rapist or murderer or dare I say, a Hitler, then any child is not going to like seeing this. You do not have to shout at, abuse or beat up children. Sometimes you do; if the circumstances require it. But not all the time and not again and again. Usually once or twice is enough throughout that child's life and they usually will not forget. They also are not animals, as some would like you to believe. They are usually, in fact, more humane and human and loving that their own parents – which is not saying about our modern society. And couples, women and men, if you can not a look after yourself then how can you look after a child or children! Some people should be banned from having children as they are nuts or just would not be justice to rearing and looking after children as they should be. A child wants to have its own space, belongings and some money to spend just like adults. Parents should not try and mould or shape the child as to what they want. If they do not want to be a doctor or lawyer or whatever; then let them be for heaven's sake. And let your children speak to you about things, without telling them to shut up or go to bed or punish them for asking you something. You may laugh at what they say sometimes but for them it could be serious. Yes you need to control them but not 100% in everything they do. Some control yes; but they need freedom too, just like parents and adults have. Obviously one needs to protect them and teach them about possible dangers, etc. But one needs to have faith and trust in them too. And giving them sweets and chocolate and fizzy drinks all the time, is not right and not good for the child. Sometimes yes or some ice-cream once a week or something – a treat – this is fine. But these should be not a diet for the child. And neither should they be watching TV, playing computer games or on their computers, laptops or mobile phones all the time. These are not a substitute for direct face-to-face communication, which IS a skill every child needs: how to communicate correctly, confidently, and effectively. And they should be encouraged to solve and work things out for themselves, and defend themselves outside in the playground or whatever the case may be. I don't think we need grown adults who are still behaving like babies or children: but that is not to say that an adult should lose their imagination (that amazing talent or gift most or all of us have!) and their spirit-of-play (which most children have; you know pretending games and creating a whole world in their room or garden which only they can see –but they usually can see if in such a vivid, clear way and for them it is real; because they have created it) and that life-is-good feelings, and having fun and playing games and not being too serious. Yes sometimes everyone has to be serious some point in their lives or in work, even children have to be serious sometimes –but they do not need to serious all the time and, in face non-one should be serious all the time!

And, usually if you are having problems with your child, it could be many things causing this. But shouting at them or punishing them or beating them up or not loving them anymore is NOT the solution. Get in communication with them and see if you can find out what is wrong or going on with them or their lives. Maybe they need some more exercise or an improvement in their diet; maybe they are bored; maybe they are being bullied; maybe they don't know what to say to the boy or girl they have fallen in love with in school. Maybe they want something but are afraid to ask. We are all different, children are the same. Try and bring out the best in our children and encourage them in whatever they want to do, be, make, create or have – as long as it is good of course. And if you find you have a Hitler or a criminal on your hands, then giving them and good hiding and saying, 'NO!!!!' is probably the best action to take as if you let them away with doing bad things at a young age; then it will be hard to stop them when they are older. But if one or both of their parent's is already a criminal, rapist, psychiatrist, murderer or paedophile, etc. then it will be VERY hard on the child or children indeed and they may end up like their parent/parents or be put in to care or end up dead; and that is no joke!

But apart this, most children want to help their parents and do things about the house or in school or their community; they want to help other people; help other children; help the animals and nature, help the planet – you know they are usually so kind-hearted, loving, honest, bubbly and cheerful and they have emotions and feelings just like adults. And just because they are young does not mean that they are ignorant and parents always know better than them. Just because they do not have a big vocabulary is no reason to not listen to what they have to say. It is usually when the parents impose their will on the child and the knocks, shocks and impacts (physical and mental) of just growing up and learning how to be human and how to all serious like most of the adults and their parents; it is usually only then that they do down and become more solid and more serious as they grow up and go through life. It does NOT have to be like this. And, as I said and this is something we all know: the children are our future. So it is up to you, the reader of this book, to decide how you want to treat your children to be and how you want the future of Mankind to be, because nearly everything we do or say or don't do or say has some effect, good or bad on our children. Thank you for listening to me on this point: as it is SO important!

MONEY

No other subject - apart from LOVE maybe - has got more type, hype, exposure and been written and talked about than Money. It is now a product all by itself as it is now traded on the Foreign Exchange of currencies and people gamble their money on it every day; and just like shares: it is bought and sold just like any other commodity, i.e. Gold and Silver. Wars have been fought over it, people have killed and been killed over it and marriages have broken up over not having enough of it.

To be honest, it is only pieces of metal and paper and we all agree and accept it in exchange for products and services. That is all it is and there is FAR too much emphasis on it!!! It is a shame really. I do not think you can have sex with money, eat it and elicit any kind of love, communication or emotional response from it. It has no feelings and does not care who owns it. It is lifeless really, dead and not alive. A nice dog or pet gives you far more enjoyment. We only grant so much importance to it because with inflation at the high rate it is worldwide, and with taxes and bills going up and up (not down as you would expect a rich, prosperous country to be doing?) you need more and more of it to buy what you need, just to survive. Not to be rich. Just to survive and lead an average life.

In January 1913, the CPI (Consumer Price Index: how much people are paying for certain pre-chosen goods and services) for America was 9.8% (up on the base cost for when the CPI was first started) and inflation was 0.0204%. In April 2012, the CPI was 230.085 and inflation (which is calculated yearly) has been, during most of this time, been going up and up. Deflation occurred during times of Recession and War. As inflation is linked with and worked out from the CPI, then one can see that inflation is at about 220% as compared to the CPI in 1914

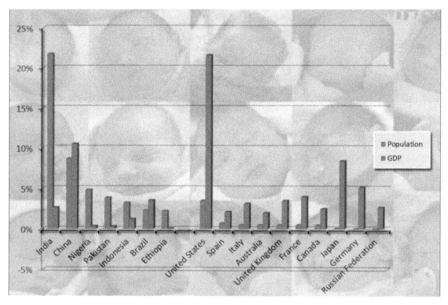

http://www.sodahead.com/united-states/does-anyone-seriously-want-to-see-the-clintons-back-in-the-white-house-in-2016/question-3682669/?link=ibaf&q=&esrc=s I cannot find out if this is copywritten or not or who owns it?

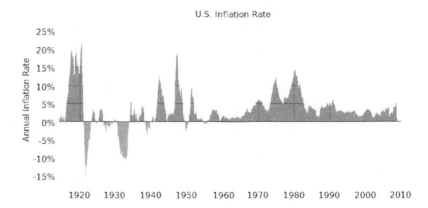

http://commons.wikimedia.org/wiki/File:US_Historical_Inflation.svg from US Department of Labor / Bureau of Labor Statistics

For Japan, the annual CPI in 1970 was 32.533%, and in April 2012 it was 100.4%.

For Australia, its annual CPI was 6.75% in 1948. In 2012, it was 179.5%.

For the UK (which used to have the Retail Price Index, but now has the CPI and would you believe, this is linked to the Bank of England, which uses these interest rates to control or raise inflation rates. And the Bank of England is or was owned and run by the Rothschilds, who minted the Gold there too, with their name on it. Strange that? I wonder if the Queen and the Government knew about that? Hmm. I do not think they are so innocent – are they? Come on. Get real. The plot thickens?) in June 1948, the annual RPI was 9.7%. Then in January 1989, the CPI came in and it was 4.9% and would you believe, the UK has had almost continuous inflation from 1948 up until 2012. From 1921-1933, there was deflation. But apart from this period of time, the UK has pretty much had inflation since its wars with France in 1793. That's nice. In 1900, 100 UK pounds would be worth about 10,115 UK pounds based on 2012 prices. That is a lot of inflation since today 100 UK pounds buys you very little.

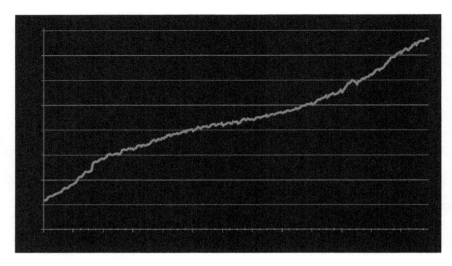

UK CPI 1988 – PRESENT (Look the hell at this wonderful UK inflation which is pretty much non-stop! Who is paying for all this inflation and borrowing. Oh, it is YOU and I. Nice!)

When you have wars, you have inflation, because the countries borrow money (from the Lords of Darkness) to fight the war (they buy arms from the companies owned by the Dark Lords) or if not, they borrow money to rebuild their country after the war. And they borrow their money from the Lords of Darkness (or from one of their vastly complex but interlinked Banking & Finance houses and empires), who own and control most if not all of the major Banks in the world, either directly or indirectly. And they charge interest rates, of course, on all they lend.) And this gives them power over the people (US – when you borrow money you borrow from them and it is the same for a business or country. Fact!!!) or a country/business and in particular, the countries and Royalty they lend it too. They do not produce anything like a table or a chair. No. They just cause wars, trouble, destabilization, inflation, depressions, recessions, pollution, drug addiction, crime, illiteracy and all the rest of their dirty devil work; and they lend VAST amounts of money and get the interest paid back like the good Jews they are (yes, they are Jews but insane ones as they think they are above normal Jews and are God's chosen to rule Earth or they even think they are Gods themselves) – and they get the control and power over us, business and nations. They have been doing this for many, many years. And they say, 'Oh banking is very complicated. Not many people know how they are run. Leave them to it. They know what they are doing.' Yes, they know how to bankrupt us all, cause inflation, recessions and depressions; put us all into debt and suppress us so much that the majority of us now are just working to pay bills, debts and taxes (kindly provided to us by 'our' own Governments, who are controlled by *THEM* and who work with them.) Oil prices go up (which the Rockefellers control and which our governments are in collusion with – they make billions or trillions in the taxes they add on to the price of oil) then inflation occurs. Governments put taxes up on fuel, oil, gas, cigarettes, alcohol and whatever else they want, then inflation occurs. Banks put their interest rates up (which the Rothschilds and Rockefellers own) and inflation occurs. Many train, rail, London Underground, Supermarket Chains, bus companies and many other companies AUTOMATICALLY put their prices up every January for the New Year – and sometimes later on in the year too. It is so kind of them. They are making sure that their profits stay or go up – while our free spending money [if we have any left that is] goes down). Oh no. We cannot make a loss or have our profits go down. They are just passing on future expense to US the consumers and we are paying for their new developments and projects (or wage increases for their staff – but little or no wage/pay increase for us the majority taxpayers and workers!!!) – which they should be paying for out of their *own* savings/profits. And the Governments, Banks, big businesses/ multi-nationals, etc. they are just milking a big giant cow (us) that is already or nearly dry. If they would only let that giant cow have some free extra milk to save and put aside, then the current world economy would be kickstarted again. But hey, they already know that. Their plans are NOT to kickstart the economy but to crash it further and further, then the rich and powerful and all the rest of them, including the Royal families and the Dark Lords can (and are) buy up everything they can at far-below-market-prices and take over the world; while we live off of cheap food/bargains from pound shops and other cheap supermarkets and stores. It is really a VERY nice state of affairs, is it not?

A person might start to wonder what the hell am I working for? Or who the hell am I working for? And the governments and their leaders – most of them – do not give a shit. Why; because they are looked after by the Powers-That-Be for doing their dirty work. And the Royal

Families (including the Queen of England) are in with them too as well as many other big industry and business leaders and owners: the Bilderbergers included. Nothing much happens on planet Earth today (the big or important stuff anyway) without the Dark Lords giving the OK They pretty much run it all, with help of the J.P. Morgans, Warburgs, et al. Interesting, but if you traced all of what is happening today, all the bad stuff and apparently the not-so-bad stuff (which is a lie because below the surface, if you investigate, it is bad; but they say they are helping us. And the Media generally portrays things as fine unless they want to cause a Recession or Depression or cause the price of Gold to rise or fall ... See?), you will find: death, suffering, murder, pollution, bribes, starvation, mass killings, ethnic cleansing, higher crime rates, inflation, higher taxes, lower literacy and educational standards, wars, drugs, prostitution, all these swine flu and other sudden virus outbreaks (O they just appeared from nowhere. How strange?), AIDS, increases in number gays and lesbians, sex changes, less or the same pay per hour (but prices keep going up and up) for more and more work and if you don't like-it-then-leave attitude: We'll find someone else or some Eastern Europeans or other Foreigners to do the work; fixed price rigging from various cartels/multi-nationals and from various countries like the USA and Europe: keeping the prices up for more and more profit; additives and preservatives to/in foods, meat, fruit and vegetables, drinks, our water and dairy products; nuclear bomb testing in the sea (this is so good for the fish, marine life and for all life on planet. Any nuclear detonation spreads its harmful effects around the entire planet and the entire population of Earth, as these are the properties of nuclear radiation, despite what the experts say to the contrary) and this list here barely has an end.

Your/Our money buys you/us far less than it used to and it has all been planned that way. Their motto is: Keep them down and out for they cannot find out who they really are and then they will not have the time, money or intelligence to be able to think for themselves, question things and they will not find out about us or be able to stop us until it is too late.

Check out some of this insanity below:

http://commons.wikimedia.org/wiki/File:Crude_oil_prices_since_1861_%28log%29.png data from BP workbook of historical data

According to The Sun, in 2008, **Venezuela had petrol prices of 1.6 pence per liter**; Iran 5p a liter; Saudi Arabia 6p a liter. Most expensive in 2008 was Sierra Leone at 244p a liter (probably imported or with high taxes added on, just like in the UK!). It is not OPEC or the Oil Companies that make the price of petrol and diesel high in the UK – it is the Government which keeps adding tax duties on top of it and one pays VAT too on top of this. Nice. Thank you for very much UK Government! You really help and like your people so much. That is why you get voted back in so much and why so many different parties go out of favour and why so many PMs leave. I suppose some scapegoats, namely the people of the UK have to pay for all the wars you have fought over the years and all the money you have borrowed. The same with the USA and other countries.

Governments like the UK and many others, say they have to keep the fuel taxes on petrol and diesel up and above inflation to cut down on global warming and pollution and cut down on the number of cars on the road and all this bullshit they feed us. But since 1993 and with Tony Blair in power, tax duty has just gone up and up. We now pay about 60% in tax duty and VAT on petrol and about 58% on diesel, as off February, 2012. In the 1960s the UK paid about 25p per gallon, which is about 5.5p per liter. And Italy, Germany and France are not far behind. So like I said, more than half of what we pay is in taxes to the governments. But apparently they can do nothing about the prices. Why not? We are in a recession and they cannot lower prices? But the USA, the UK and the EEC just do what they are told and so do most of the rest of the world. If they do not do what *they* say, they get put out of office or get killed but it is made to look like a suicide or an accident, like in the airplane crash of the Polish Present Lech and his government officials and ministers. Funny that. I wonder why?

But getting back to money. Most people are forced to think and dream about it because they do not have enough of it: they are poor, hungry or are in the working class band or a little above it. But even the middle income earners and the high earners are all feeling the pinch now. Why? Because their money does not go as far as it used too because of inflation, higher income taxes and all the other increases in the costs of living. The Hollywood films, newspapers and magazines and the wonderful media in general (all or mostly all are owned, run or controller by the Lords of Darkness by the way - fact!) all portray how great it is to have money. They don't really say how to get it except to rob, steal, cheat, con, swindle or be a prostitute or sell drugs. The rest, who have money, don't usually give a damn about anyone else, except they maybe help a charity or two (and some rich people are very good people – do not get me wrong on this please and their hearts are in the right place but some are a bit naive or they just do it for show or they leave their money to a cat and dog home or to a charity). And who knows where that charity money actually goes to (into some Swiss Bank account of some African black leader or some politician or wherever). Apparently we are all dogs and we are meant to eat each other: Dog-eat-dog-world and all the other sayings which really mean: fuck everyone else and just think about NUMBER One – I only care about myself. Now that is money. And sadly, that is the attitude that a fair number of people on planet Earth today have: from the top to the bottom, not the very top but up to about 70% or %80 of the way. Those above that are in a different league and they (the bad ones that is) want to keep it that way and they do not want anyone else to get a slice of the big cake or even a few crumbs. NO. They want it all for themselves. And when they die, they pass it (their vast billions and trillions) on to the next-of-ken in their wills when they die (who usually do not work anyway because they are above that) and they just hoard it and make more money or throw it away or misspend it. And we suffer because of this. We cannot all be millionaires; this is true – but there is enough money to go round so we can ALL have a nice, comfortable, decent life: whether we be a Cleaner, Rubbish Collector or a Waiter, etc.

And now check out the super-rich:

SOURCE: https://www.statista.com/statistics/272047/top-25-global-billionaires/

The world's top 25 billionaires in 2017 based on assets (in billion U.S. dollars)

Bill Gates (USA) 86
Warren Buffett (USA) 75.6
Jeff Bezos (USA) 72.8
Armanico Ortega (Spain) 71.3
Mark Zuckerberg (United States) 56
Carlos Slim Helú (Mexico) 54.5
Larry Ellison (United States) 52.2
Charles Koch (United States) 48.3
David Koch (United States) 48.3
Michael Bloomberg (United States) 47.5
Bernard Arnault (France) 41.5
Larry Page (United States) 40.7
Sergey Brin (United States) 39.8
Liliane Bettencourt (France) 39.5
S. Robson Walton (United States) 34.1
Jim Walton (United States) 34
Alice Walton (United States) 33.8
Wang Jianlin (China) 31.3
Li Ka-shing (China) 31.2
Sheldon Adelson (United States) 30.4
Steve Ballmer (United States) 30
Jorge Paulo Lemann (Brazil) 29.2
Beate Heister & Karl Albrecht Jr.(Germany) 27.2
David Thomson (Canada) 27.2
Jacqueline Mars (United States) 27

Also, according to the Mail Online:

There were 1,826 billionaires in 2015 - up from 1,645 in 2014

Read more: http://www.dailymail.co.uk/news/article-2975699/Bill-Gates-repeats-Forbes-list-billionaires.html#ixzz3nPD4Ld6O
Follow us: @MailOnline on Twitter | DailyMail on Facebook

SOURCE: https://www.statista.com/statistics/620926/global-billionaire-population-by-region/

Number of billionaires worldwide in 2016, by region

Asia-Pacific – 590
USA – 540
Europe – 489
The Americas (excluding USA) – 101
Middle East & Africa – 90 © Statista 2017
If you go to: https://en.wikipedia.org/wiki/List_of_countries_by_the_number_
of_US_dollar_billionaires
You can find your own country in the list by wealth
And, as mentioned in an earlier chapter, Credit Suisse says 29.7 million people in the world with household net worths of $1 million (representing less than **1% of the world's population**) control about **$89 trillion of the world's wealth**. That's up from a share of 35.6% in 2010, and their wealth increased by about $20 trillion.
WOW!
The wealth of the millionaires grew 29% — about twice as fast as the wealth in the world as a whole, which now has approx **$231 trillion in wealth**.
Can anyone please tell me what the hell is going on with the above stats and figures? People are trying to live on crap minimum wages; people are starving or doing slave labour work or anything they can so they can JUST pay their ever-increasing bills and have some food on the table.
IS THIS FAIR? And some of these people are skilled workers or even engineers, doctors, lawyers like in Eastern Europe and Russia, etc. The disparity between the Super Rich, the Rich and the working class and the poor is huge and growing bigger every year. And the Middle-Income earners are not escaping either, as inflation and bills keep mounting up.

What I cannot understand is why it is OK with these rich people that they pay their workers (or most of them) such low or not enough wages, so they can add more millions or billions on to their already inflated bank accounts, off-shore tax-free accounts or Swiss accounts at the expense of those below them. I just cannot think with this. Can you? What do you think God or the Supreme Being must be thinking when he looks down and sees how things are on this planet? And if there are aliens out there (which I am sure there are) what must they be thinking about us? In fact, let's take this to the limit and beyond: what does Man think about Man when he looks around and sees what is going on? They must think we are all either nuts, evil or savages or all three. And very callous. What do you think about all this - the person reading this book?

How much does any human being need before he has enough money? Obviously some do not care about others and just want more and more or to be the richest or one of the richest people in the world at the expense of others. They will probably say: I've worked hard and earned it. Well others have and do work hard but they are not earning it. And they are being intentionally kept that way as slaves to a system set up by others, not us. But we have also allowed these financial, economic and political systems to remain in place and we allow our governments to get away with fixing such a low minimum wage; and of course they are in cahoots with the big businesses.

I cannot see why these rich people and companies cannot pay their workers better wages? Does anyone know why?

And so what if these people or companies made less money or profits? Would this be a bad thing? Would they not feel good and sleep better at night knowing that the rest of the peoples on Earth were living better lives because of their help in giving them higher wages?

Something is drastically wrong about all of this and something must be done about it. Either by those who have the money or by Government or, failing this, the working classes and poor take it into their own hands and join together and do something effective about it. I don't think the Middle Class people (not the Middle Income Earning Class – there is distinction here but sometimes they are the same breed) will do anything about this as they look down on the working class and the poor (and want to keep them down), and see them as servants to them or beneath them. Why I do not know. Some kind of mental or spiritual aberration or something out-ethics or immoral in them. But then again, those who are amassing vast sums of money (they are not all bad though as some do pay good wages and help others. But sadly not many!) and this applies to big companies and multi-nationals too, must have something wrong with their mentality and ethics too. As the imbalance, which they are obviously supporting, is wrong purely on an ethical, moral and humane basis. And some of these leave millions or billions, plus land and properties to say just one heir or heiress or to a few brothers and sisters. And then they too may want to buy more and make more and more money too. And it goes on and on. And the working class and the poor never really get much of chance with all this going on all the time.

I am not against being successful, making it to the top and being number one and having a few million and being powerful and having status. But there is or there must be point where on draws the line and says: I have enough now; let's help others have a good life too and help them get some success. Is there something wrong with this 'think' or am I missing something here? Well, I do not think there is anything wrong with my philosophy, logic and think on this important matter. If there is, then do let me know?

I think, by the time everyone has read this book, they should then reflect - by themselves - on all I have said; take a good look inside themselves and at their own lives and then the lives and condition of those around them, AND this planet, and then see if they are OK with how it all is? If not, then they should decide what they are going to do about it. If they are happy about how everything is, then fine. But if they do fall into the various categories

I have mentioned above and in this book, and they are still not prepared to do nothing about it, then there is nothing more that need be said about and too these kind of people. They have made their choice; they have made their stand. And so the rest of us good, sane (relatively), moral and ethical people, with good hearts, will have to make our stand too and do whatever it takes to make this world and planet a better place for all, and handle, remove, imprison or defeat those who get in our way. There is no other way that I can see of dealing with this inequality matter and all the others important matters I have raised and will raise in this book. I am telling you how it really is. not fiction, hearsay, gossip, lies or bullshit: but how things really are on this planet.

I wrote this book for you, and myself and all others, so that we can all help one another and do our share of what has to be done to make this planet fairer and better for all, not just the few. If you like how it all is, then do nothing. So the question is: what are YOU going to do about it? Well?

Let's continue.

Funny, but I never heard of anyone coming into the world with money or departing their bodies (dying) with money, no matter how much they have. Fact!

If it was actually shared around a bit more and people in all countries were actually paid a good decent wage (can you or any politician survive on 6 or 7 or maybe even 8 (wow!) pounds or Euros an hour or 10 bucks an hour (or whatever the currency may be): buy a car, buy a house, bring up, feed, clothe and send children to school and have a nice holiday every year on this?) I think not, yet the minimum wage in the UK is just over 6 pounds an hour. The USA is about $7.25 an hour (2011) and China, India, Brazil, etc. is far less, with people even being kept and worked as slaves with no wage at all and some unfortunate young girls (and boys), who should be in school, are actually being forced as sex slaves for some rich men or they are worked as prostitutes. Some children are also kidnapped or Jesus (forgive me!) dare I say are also kept as sex slaves or used as child prostitutes to satisfy mentally deranged men (or beasts) and they rape them and take photos and make illegal videos and films of them (some just do it for money as do those who make porno films and run porno websites): and these slaves do not even get paid. And some parents even sell their children into slavery (their own young sons and daughters) or they even abuse them themselves (this is terrible and so shocking!) sexually and with dogs and animals. And some women, desperate for money to feed themselves and their children are actually forced into prostitution just to survive. Some also sell their own body parts for money (Kidneys). Some are forced into criminality because they cannot get work or they are starving and it all ends up a vicious circle. And the rest of the poor and homeless can just beg or become criminals: or they die! The same applies to drug addicts and alcoholics, who MUST get their next fix or drink, somehow. This all revolves around and is caused to some extent by money not being shared out fairly and by the Richer (and the rich, the rich landowners, plantation/farm/ranch owners, business tycoons, bankers, multi-national businesses, etc. who pay their workers crap [some do pay good wages, true, but not many) and low wages and they know it?) countries of planet Earth (G8, G20, G60 countries) are using, abusing and FORCING the poorer countries to do and accept what they want and on their terms (World Bank, IMF); and they arrange and do these deals with the political or ruling/ rich families in the poor countries, which benefit THEM but not the peoples in these countries. And it benefits BUSINESS in the richer countries (they can make such huge profits and have such huge markups on their products) and it benefits CAPITALISM: there is nothing wrong with Capitalism; but such huge profits are not needed and not fair and it causes inflation (just the same as the banks and the oil companies cause inflation by keep increasing their prices and interest rates; and the Governments keep raising taxes in their budgets!!!!). Anyone can and should make a profit (to pay bills, wages, rent, etc.) but not as much as some businesses and Capitalists are making. How some of these people can sleep at night- I do not know? Do they not have a conscience? How can they be so callous? And some of these people came from poor or working class backgrounds! I am not saying all businesses, Capitalists, businessmen are bad or corrupt; and some do try and some do DO some good – but how many? And the banks, huh – more on these assholes later.

Multi-billion-dollar companies and multi-national companies make so much money that they can only afford (they are so poor, god what a shame!) to pay their lowly workers (down at the bottom of the food chain) about 6 pounds an hour: Petrol Stations (Shell, BP), Food Chains, Supermarkets, etc. The rest goes to the bosses in pay and commissions; and to the shareholders. Nice for *them;* but what about the rest of us??????

So money is JUST money. That is true. But what is important is how you make it and how much you have of it. But what is MORE important than money is how you live your life; how your family and friends are and ARE YOU REALLY HAPPY? And are you doing anything good to help others or anything helpful, creative or productive for other people, other countries, and life in general (including the plants, animals and Earth and Mother Nature herself)? So money is not a substitute for living and enjoying your life; talking to people in a genuine and sincere manner, with a nice genuine smile and a good handshake. It cannot replace inviting your friends or neighbours (how many people actually know their neighbours and their names and REALLY care about them? Rare these days, huh?) around for a coffee or nice meal or party. How many people actually really know who they work with, know their names, care about them and care about their jobs or the company they work for? Not too many in this day and age. No. They just want or have a job to make MONEY and usually that is ALL they want; and some do not care about anything or anyone else except money. I am not saying everyone is like this but it is getting that way, sadly. Surely there is more to life than this? Surely? I would like to make an additional point here: computers, internet, text messages, Facebook, Twitter and all the rest are no substitute for meeting people and having a real face-to-face conversation. Ok granted they are good for fast communication and all that but on a human relationship and human being level: all this technology and electronic wizardry is no substitute for REALLY living and having fun with real people, not virtual people or a virtual world or virtual family – as families seem to be turning into these days. Money and Technology cannot replace people and livingness: good communication and having real fun: they never will never be alive. It is US, the Human Beings of planet Earth that are alive; and the plants and animals. And actually, only the Spiritual Being, which we all are; is actually truly alive and able to cause things, think, rationalize and communicate; and all the rest. Nothing else is more important than that: except being FREE and having a return of our native powers and abilities as free Spirits again. Having **enough** Money is needed too because we have bodies, children, and have to eat, pay bills, mortgages, etc. and we live on a planet like this: which WE have all helped create and make (we are all participating in life and are all part of Mankind, yes?) it is the way it is (except for the effects and bad influences of the Powers-That-be and their bad apples and minions have caused- without this and them, Mankind would be FAR much happier, freer and less money-strapped and worried about money than he currently is......?). They, the current economic climate and recession and huge world Debt to the Powers-That-Be; and automatic inflation; increased taxes; more new taxes; decreased wages, etc, all force us **WRONGLY** to focus more and more on money. It is wrong!

So we all need to make and earn money and have a nice lifestyle: but it should be much fairer than what it currently is on this lovely planet, and the pay/wages should be better and higher for all; profits shared out and the rich people; ruling/elite/royal families; tycoons, banks, governments, oil companies, OPEC countries, Leaders, Despots, Sheikhs, Premiers, Presidents, Managers, Bosses, Directors, et al, SHOULD be fairer and nicer to their workers, peoples and to all mankind (including all other countries and races) as a whole and REALLY care about him and not say just they do but actually do (and really show it by their actions); and share the money, wealth and power around: not just hoard it all and keep it to themselves! We should be all nicer to each other really and actually helping each other far more than what we presently are (not having some countries and people looking down on us as if we are sheep or dogs [I do not know who some people they think they are because we are all human and having a title and/or money or power or 'I am above you' attitude does not put one above the rest of Mankind or ones fellow Human Beings] and being condescending to others; and treating them as inferior or beneath one: this is not right! The countries and people behaving like this, including the Middle Classes [not middle-income earners; I am talking about the mental attitudes here of the real Middle Class], would not like to be treated like this themselves, so why do they treat other people like this, well?) More emphasis should be put on the SPIRITUAL side of life and on the problems the MIND (Please: not Psychology and Psychiatry because they do NOT and will not EVER work despite what the experts, politicians, doctors, drug companies, the criminals, anti-socials and the Lords of Darkness might say) and our GOOD religions and other groups. They should not be attacked as they are. We should not put so much attention on the body, brain, DNA, genes, sex, food, money, technology, electronics, computers ('I AM PC' – what is that all about? I Robot? I ROBOTIC HUMAN. ME KNOW THINKY FOR MY SELFY and all that), Science and worshipping and praising the materialistic and Physical Universe to such an extent. These can all be fun of course and don't get me wrong on this. However; YOU – as a Spiritual Being and the Spiritual World – are FAR more important than all of the above aforementioned…far more!!!!! Have I emphasized that enough?

And as the Unconscious Mind affects us Spiritually and physically, then this has to be fully handled too.

> Note: You handle the problems of the Unconscious Mind first and while doing this, you will also handle the problems of the Spiritual Being and then, once that is done, one is then able to concentrate on and further enhance the powers, abilities and knowledge of the Spiritual Being (which is you right there reading this book, by the way!), which are not related or fully dependent upon handling or erasing the Unconscious Mind – the Unconscious Mind would be gone at this point! <

And you may ask: what am I or what is a Spiritual Being, well you can check this out and research this for yourself and maybe you already know or have you own ideas about it? But I will give you a clue- combine what you know about Ghosts, God, gods (Norse, Greek, Roman, Indian (India) and others), spirits, souls, angels, demons, fairies, deities, demi-gods, genies, magic, mysticism, the mind, superheroes (like the ones you see in the comic books and films); myths and legends of old, and religions, and you are very close or even have the answer? But there are degrees and levels of this and we are all not equal in this. I am certain that there are a number of people on this planet right now who do know who and what they are and can leave their bodies at will and go off and do things without a body; and who have spiritual knowledge and are enlightened. But sadly we are all different and not everyone – the vast majority - is like this or can easily attain this state at this time: however I fully believe that will change VERY soon! Sadly an ever more increasing number of people believe they are only a body and when it dies, that is the end of them and it is all chemicals and neurons. And the sooner the planet is blown up the better. This is so FAR from truth that it is almost light years away from the truth of who we really are and what we are capable off. Most people do not even believe in past lives, of which there is much evidence. The problem is, people only believe what they want to believe dependent on the current state they are in as a Human/Spiritual Being. Most Souls or Spirits or Spiritual Beings are sadly unconscious as Beings, and therefore the body and the Physical Universe is everything and all powerful.

THE BANKING/FINANCE/LOAN SYSTEMS

http://www.clipartpanda.com/clipart_images/royalty-free-vector-clip-art-32415311 Can I use this?

My god! What we are confronted with here is the BIGGEST scam, con and downright DIRTY TRAP of all time: I lend you blah amount and in return you pay me 3 or 4 hundred percent (and even much higher: this is called usury) back in return (or whatever the case may be?) Oh, and the said lender may sometimes request security of some sort (you know, we take your house, car, your company or something else if you cannot pay back the loan.) If you default, you credit history is shagged or you could even go to jail. And if you have to borrow money to buy a house or apartment: the lovely and sometimes dreaded MORTGAGE is the wonderful answer; and if you default, they take your house/apartment back and you are homeless or something – and once again you credit history is fucked and you most probably have lost some or a lot of money from this experience. And how much worry goes with all this: can I repay the loan, credit card or mortgage, or dare I say, business loan (which usually has to be supported by some kind of security or collateral – how nice and kind of them!). What if I lose my job? What if my partner or wife loses her job or leaves me? What if my business's sales go down? What if the value of my house decreases? What about our children? What will our friends and neighbours say if we lose our house. And the list of angst, worries and mental sufferings goes on and on.

Firstly, can I ask the big number one question: Why are we not ALL earning good enough wages? (I say all because all levels of society have to be considered: how can the poor and working class have a nice life for themselves and their children, by being paid such a low minimum wage? NOT I say!!!! Shame on those who set this amount. I would love to see any politician, leader or Middle or Upper Class person live on the minimum wage THEY set and support? Actually, I think they do this on PURPOSE just to keep those below them down. How nice of them!) We should be able to save or earn enough money ourselves WITHOUT having to borrow from these lovely wonderful banks, finance houses, mortgage &credit companies and all the rest. Now that is the most relevant question on finance and banking. The other valid questions are: what do the banks do with all their dishonestly earned money and what do our governments (who are in cahoots with them and the Big Businesses) do with all of our countries' money too?

And it is all these terms and conditions they set. Well, who is the 'THEY' I have been talking about for some time? THEY are: The Rothschild family, The Rockefeller Family and the rest who work with/for them. They run and pretty much own the Bank of England (now run by a Canadian – why is this?); the Federal Reserve Bank of America (run, owned and controlled by the Rockefellers, the Rothschilds and others [cohorts]) and all the other HUGE-NAMED BIG banks they own, run or control either directly, secretly, indirectly or via minions, family members and those on the board of directors (bought and paid for).

It is a VERY sad affair! Which it does NOT need to be. And how did this state of affairs on finance and banking come about? Profit, more profit and profit on top of profit. How much money, power and profit do these assholes want to have/make? So much so that they will never be able to use or spend in their lives (nor their children)? How can they sleep at night knowing all the misery and suffering they are causing around the planet? I know some businesses need a lot of money upfront to achieve their goals and objectives – but some of the rates and conditions *their* banks charge and their terms are unbelievable!

[Mankind is strange in many ways. As long as he has some money, some food, a job or business and a place to live and some entertainment – he can just accept his fate and get used to it. Mankind has been getting so used to it for hundreds and thousands of years; that now he just takes it all as a normal and has this dejected: 'What can be done about it all anyway' kind of attitude. No matter how terrible things get, he can endure and put up with almost anything and history has shown this to be true. He only revolts – normally blindly and unconsciously (with little logic or rational thought) - when 'THEY' go too far; however **NOW** they have gone way too far! But you just don't know it yet. Read on...]

Why don't these nice banks - and the people who own them - take a more active, compassionate and interested role in the lives of their fellow human beings and businesses AND countries; listen to their problems and change of circumstances; and instead of calling in on the terms and conditions – actually try and HELP (dare I say) them and work out a solution?

Life is about achieving ones goals and purposes (hopefully good ones?); helping others achieve theirs and being moral, ethical, and honest: honouring ones obligations, whether one is aware of them or not – and NOT just thinking about oneself only and how many people can I stab in the back, et al. It should be more about love, being kind, friendly and in good, nice and honest communication with one's family; ones friends; business associates/colleagues; owns neighbours; owns village/town/city – ones country and the REST of the other countries and Mankind as a whole. And looking after the plants and animals. It is, and SHOULD not be all about money and profit and fuck everyone else. I know this may seem naive and innocent – but life, including banking, finance and business (including family life) should not be the way it is currently. It is sad, a big shame and should not be. But I cannot change it by myself. No. It can only be done by the whole of mankind collectively as a group, not a crazy or unconscious mob. Mankind personally – which means each and every person! -

NEEDS to change his ways very much if he is to survive at all. And just because 'everyone' may agree and accept things as they currently are, does not mean this is right. Something CAN be done about oneself, one's condition and the various states and parts of life on Earth, and on Earth itself.

And these banks, they claim, have all their formulas, charts, matrices, and theories, which ONLY they can understand. Bollix! This façade just allows them to do whatever they damn well want and do their probability, profit and loss and risk analysis and lending via complex vias and multiples and shaft us all up the ass; and they make all the money and profit; and we do not even see their accounts and inside workings: their innards and books down on the table to be analysed. Our Governments and Multi-National Corporations do the same.

These banks and financial bodies should be HELPING us, just like all aspects, forms and echelons of life and business should be!!!! They use a lot of our own personal and business money anyway to fund their ventures and evil plots and secret hidden funds to start wars and to cause wars or cause the downfall of Leaders or Governments by using covert ops and/or Black Propaganda, Public Relations and the various Medias.

The power has and always will be with the people, the majority of the good peoples of planet Earth but that may not be the case forever as it is always possible for a few to get so powerful and technology-wise, so advanced, that they can and would control ALL people on this planet and their minds, bodies and thoughts too – but by then it is too late! Isn't it about time we used the power we still have and begin shaping/ changing this planet - in a rational and logical way I must interject – to how it would best suit and help US; not just them and **not** allow the few Others and the vested Interests and the Lords of Darkness to do what the hell they want and keep messing this planet up and messing up/interfering with our lives?????

Check this out:

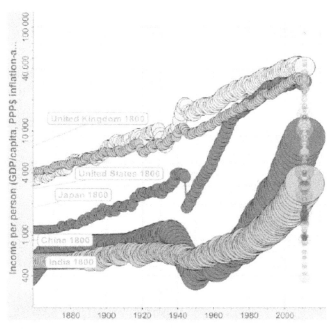

http://commons.wikimedia.org/wiki/File:Globalization-5.png AUTHOR: Globalizr Adapted from gapminder.org

And according to The Economist.com World debt comparison Current Global World Public Debt is:

(date: 24/10/2017) **$059,939.186,229,581** (approximate as it is increasing every few seconds. I wonder who this world debt is owed to?)

In 2014 Global Public Debt was $054,774,851,445,786

In 2013 Global Debt was $052,099,607,390,000 (approx)

Government debt
In the red

Source: Nov 10th 2010, 12:25 by The Economist online

According to the graphs at:

http://www.economist.com/blogs/dailychart/2010/11/government_debt SOURCE IMF

In 1932, most world debt, as a percentage of GDP, was in Europe, Canada, Australia, America and Brazil. US debt was 33% of GDP.

In 2009, world debt has spread to nearly every country in the world. With the USA having 84% of GDP.

Funny, that data came from the IMF, which is responsible for a large amount of this debt, so it must be accurate. And guess who owns and runs the IMF? Look at how much red there is on this second chart compared to the first one?

And people wonder what causes inflation and low wages generally worldwide?

List of countries by external debt

From Wikipedia, the free encyclopedia

https://en.wikipedia.org/wiki/List_of_countries_by_external_debt

Rank	Country	External debt[2] US dollars	Date	Per capita[3] [4][5][6] US dollars	% of GDP[7] [8][9]
1	United States	18,540,448,667,000	20 June 2015	58,437	106
2	United Kingdom	9,590,995,000,000	31 March 2014	160,158	406
3	France	5,750,152,000,000	31 March 2014	86,317	222
4	Germany	5,546,869,000,000	31 March 2014	68,720	145
5	Luxembourg[note 1]	3,472,282,000,000	31 March 2014	3,696,467	3,443
6	China	3,000,000,000,000	31 December 2013[10]	2,220.57	37.5
7	Japan	2,861,488,000,000	31 March 2014	24,000	60
8	Italy	2,651,413,000,000	31 March 2014 est.	43,621	124
9	Netherlands	2,526,895,000,000	31 March 2014	226,503	316
10	Spain	2,305,648,000,000	31 March 2014	52,045	167
11	Singapore	1,813,650,200,000	2015 1Q		[11]
12	Switzerland	1,610,897,000,000	31 March 2014	154,063	229

Rank	Country	External debt[2] US dollars	Date	Per capita[3][4][5][6] US dollars	% of GDP[7][8][9]
13	Australia	1,395,638,000,000	31 March 2014 est.	52,596	95
14	Canada	1,337,445,000,000	31 March 2014 est.	29,625	92
15	Belgium	1,286,918,000,000	31 March 2014	113,603	266
16	Hong Kong	1,231,233,000,000	31 March 2014 est.	105,420	334
17	Sweden	1,145,785,000,000	31 March 2014	91,487	187
18	Austria	820,010,000,000	31 March 2014	90,128	200
19	Norway	737,118,000,000	31 March 2014	131,220	141
20	Russian Federation	599,819,000,000	31 March 2014	3,634	23
21	Denmark	593,221,000,000	31 March 2014	101,084	180
22	Portugal	548,800,000,000	30 June 2011	47,835	223
23	India	455,900,000,000	31 September 2014 est.	364	22.795
24	Brazil	428,300,000,000	31 December 2012 est.	1,608	15

NOTE: The rest of the World's countries in debt are shown in the link above.

This is a lot of official debt (but you will find that our governments also have unofficial debt and money stashed here and there and special secret funds hidden all over the place even though it is OUR money?) and you can be sure that pretty much most of it is owed to the Lords of Darkness – those who the run this planet. This is NOT a conspiracy theory but a FACT. This is in trillions – as you can see. This is HUGE and way too high; which would explain why taxes are so high and why it is hard to find good paid jobs and why a fair percentage of those leaving University and College can find it hard to find a good paid job. And it goes on and on as WE, the peoples of this planet, have to cope and contend with this and also it is US who are paying it back in one form or another. Now is that not the biggest joke of all? We are paying it back to our Governments, who kindly and loyally pay it back to the World Bank, IMF, European Central Bank and all the rest of these finance organizations. Thus, we have inflation going up and up and our wages/pay stays the same or goes down. And our money buys less and less – less buying power. So how are we to cope with or handle all this I ask you? Is there not a solution?

ASYLUM SEEKERS/ILLEGAL IMMIGRANTS

http://www.clipartpanda.com/clipart_images/peace-coloring-pages-34713913 I think I may have to pay to use this image?

I have nothing against valid, genuine and legitimate Asylum seekers and migrant workers; as some countries are corrupt or at war or their work skills are needed. However; there just seems to be so many these days. They seem to be everywhere and I don't know how many of them work or not or just claim benefits (or both) and bring over the rest of their families. It does seem strange that there are so many – especially now in the EEC (Europe) and the USA. Why can't the EEC and the USA be like Australia? Why can't there be more tougher measures in place to control and no one really knows how many illegal immigrants and workers there are around the world. I also see no point in people running away or leaving there own countries because they can't get work or a good job or because their government or that countries leader is corrupt or tyrannical. The solution is for the people in these countries to join together and do something about it; not just leave and go somewhere else. There countries will still have the same problems and they may even get worse. And if they later return back to their countries (now they have money to buy a house or pay off their mortgage) their country will still be in the same state it was in when they left or even worse. So what is the point of that?

No, I feel there is more to this Asylum Seeking, Refugee and Illegal Immigrant workers' problem than meets the eye. I think it is being done and allowed intentionally. Why? Because the CIA and those secret organizations that cause terrorism and wars, etc. around the world, can then more easily place their people (probably brainwashed and mentally programmed for some mission [this is happening in many countries now but it also seems that a lot of them are also Muslim {I have nothing against Muslims by the way!} and they are being turned into killers and assassins?]) in every country and have them ready to carry out their evil deeds (and they fund all this by the Global Security Fund, a name actually meaning in the secret cult's language Global Terrorist Fund. In simple terms, it's a gigantic illegal trust fund, estimated by undercover overseas financial investigators at 65 trillion dollars, set-up for "Illuminati rainy days" and established when it is desperately needed in a pinch for bribery, assassinations and sponsoring Worldwide terrorist activities to divert attention from their banking mafia.)

Also, as I said before, this mixes up all the races of Earth (I mean look at Europe! Nearly everyone wants to go there now and they just let them in? It is turning into a mess for the natives of Europe. Oh but the business will like it because of cheap labour. Nice for them. But what about our future children and what about the rest of us who are and will suffer for this. Well? And these people seem to have more rights than the rest of us and it is not happening by accident; I can tell you that. I think countries should look after their own people first!) so we end up with no race and little culture, ready for the New World Order to take over and rule. It also creates a lot of hostility, friction, racism and financial troubles and unfairness in the countries they end up in and less jobs/less pay for the natives of that country, etc. And most of them do not speak English or the language of that country and they do not mix well and some try and form their own state or mini-country within the country they are in and all the other problems and rubbish caused by them being allowed or let in. This is NOT happening by accident. I can assure you that. Those in power in all the major countries and governments of Earth know exactly what they are doing. That is why they have G 8 and G 20 meetings all the time and the Bilderburg agendas. They know what they are doing and it is all pre-planned. I also do not know why these Asylum Seekers cannot go back to their own country once and if matters have been resolved on why they were seeking asylum in the first go-off? And Illegal Immigration and Illegal People and Workers getting in to countries needs to be stopped as it also affects those people who legally live in that country or were born there. Furthermore, what is the UN and all these other supposedly wonderful European and World organizations that are meant to be helping mankind – what are they doing to solve the problems in this countries that cause Illegal Immigration and Asylum Seekers in the first go off? Nothing effective that I can see and that is because they are owned, funded and controlled and ordered by the ruling families and people of Earth. It is really a nice state of affairs we are all in because of these people and their wonderful organizations and those Governments and their leaders that serve/collude with them???!!!!

And if the wealth of the world was shared out; and big companies and multi-nationals paid decent wages and there was a high or good minimum in every country around the planet; then people would not want or have to leave their own country to seek jobs and money elsewhere.

I do not blame the Asylum Seekers and Illegal Immigrants for this. And if there were not so many wars in particular; and droughts and famines, then there would be little or no refugees. No; I blame their own governments for allowing their countries to fall into a bad condition; I blame big multi-nationals; I blame corrupt government leaders, officials and governments; I blame mis-management of countries; I blame those countries that take advantage of weaker and poorer countries; and most of all: I blame the ruling families of this world – which we will cover in detail later!

Some data on Asylum Seekers and Illegal Immigrants. I am sure these figures are not 100% accurate as it would only include those they know about:

SOURCE: Migration Policy Institute

Annual Number of New Asylum Applications in Select OECD Countries (The Organisation for Economic Co-operation and Development) 1980-2010

Countries of destination	2003	2004	2005	2006	2007	2008	2009	2010
Australia	4,295	3,201	3,204	3,515	3,980	4,771	6,206	8,250
Austria	32,359	24,634	22,461	13,349	11,921	12,841	15,821	11,020
Belgium	16,940	15,357	15,957	11,587	11,115	12,252	17,186	19,940
Canada	31,937	25,750	20,786	22,873	28,342	34,800	33,970	23,160
Denmark	4,593	3,235	2,260	1,918	1,852	2,360	3,819	4,970
Finland	3,221	3,861	3,574	2,331	1,434	4,016	5,910	4,020
France	59,768	58,545	49,733	30,748	29,387	35,404	42,118	47,790
Germany	50,563	35,607	28,914	21,029	19,164	22,085	27,649	41,330
Greece	8,178	4,469	9,050	12,267	25,113	19,884	15,928	10,270
Ireland	7,900	4,769	4,324	4,314	3,988	3,866	2,689	1,940
Italy	13,455	9,722	9,548	10,348	14,053	30,324	17,603	8,190
Netherlands	13,402	9,782	12,347	14,465	7,102	13,399	14,905	13,330
Norway	15,959	7,945	5,402	5,320	6,528	14,431	17,226	10,060
Spain	5,918	5,535	5,254	5,297	7,662	4,517	3,007	2,740
Sweden	31,348	23,161	17,530	24,322	36,370	24,353	24,194	31,820
United Kingdom	60,050	40,625	30,840	28,320	28,300	31,315	30,675	22,090
United States	43,338	44,972	39,240	41,101	40,449	39,362	38,080	41,005

SOURCE: **EXPRESS** Newspaper

Scandal of UK's 863,000 illegal immigrants...one in four of the EU's total BRITAIN's illegal immigrant population is the highest in Europe, official figures have revealed.

By: Anil Dawar
Published: Tue, December 18, 2012

In this article it says that there could be as many as 900,000 "irregular migrants" in the UK.

It's no surprise that after years of uncontrolled immigration, we have a sizeable illegal immigrant population in Britain

The European Commission study, Clandestino, calculated there were between 1.9 million and 3.8 million irregular migrants in the EU in 2008.

And now we have Syrians and many other people from other countries coming in to Europe. Where is it all going to end?

SOURCE: **MAIL ONLINE** (newspaper)

The foreigners being paid £2billion in benefits a year including 371,000 on the dole (and 5,000 claiming £42m in illegal hand-outs)

>   **DWP fraud probe after 5,000 illegal immigrants claim £42m in hand-outs to which they are not entitled**
>   **371,000 foreign nationals on out-of-work benefits**
>   **6% of all benefit claimants are foreigners, study finds**

By TIM SHIPMAN
UPDATED: 16:31, 20 January 2012

And in this same article is says:

A Somali asylum seeker was given a £2 million pound house, at taxpayer's expense and was granted £8,000 a month in housing benefits, for himself, his wife and kids.

Read more: http://www.dailymail.co.uk/news/article-2089118/Benefits-Foreigners-paid-2bn-year-5-000-claiming-42m-illegal-handouts.html#ixzz2XiA7G7wQ
Follow us: @MailOnline on Twitter | DailyMail on Facebook
Writer: A recent newspaper article has said that 1 in 4 new-born babies in the UK are now being born to foreign migrant workers (mainly Polish and Indian). I have nothing against these people, as they are just using the system but they are also very clever even though they are doing nothing illegal. Because the wonderful Brussels and the UK (its Commonwealth policy) allows them to come in and pretty much do what they want. And then these foreign people have to get housed

(why can't I get housed? Surely a country should look after its own first? If we go to Poland or Romania, or some such country or India, do we get housed or get benefits) because of their new-born babies and children and if they are not earning enough, then they claim Housing Benefits and the UK Government (which is in cahoots with Brussels and the USA on their master plan for a New world Order and New World Government, which already exists in the G8 and now the G20. And what do the UK, German Spanish, French, Irish and other richer Western countries in the EEC do about this and other rubbish laws, rules and policies coming from Brussels – NOTHING!!!!! The UK and the other countries, don't really give a shit anymore as long as everyone works, obeys the laws and pays their taxes. You MUST pay your taxes! And the medium to rich landlords and other wealthy people are laughing all the way to the bank and this is not just in the UK but all over the world. Those in the know and those who are rich and wealthy nearly ALWAYS (unless their business is directly hit by a recession or a market slump or some such disaster) win in times of recession and growth or boom. And do they (most of them anyway) do not give a fuck about the working class and the poor – no they do not - and most of them never really have, except for a few exceptions - the good ones. And the Middle Classes are just as happy, as are the rich and the business owners and PLCs: so happy to get cheap labour and cheaper products and services from these foreign migrant and Eastern European workers. Oh, don't we all love and care about each other so much on this wonderful planet, huh? I don't think so. Some love themselves only and do not give a fuck about anyone else, except maybe their close friends and family. What a wonderful planet we live on?

Markets December 27, 2013

Immigration fears spark political firestorm in UK

LONDON (AP) — They're portrayed as pickpockets who will steal British jobs. There are predictions they will beg, the unruly young ones will stir up riots, and some will even try to sell babies.

From this story is says 100,000 migrants from Romania and Bulgaria now work in Britain.

And since 2004, over I million Polish people have moved over here.

How come we do not get to vote on who joins the EEC or even who should leave? Oh no, you cannot ever leave the EEC once you are in; that's what they keep telling us – why? No referendums? Maybe I don't want Germany or Poland to be in the EEC or other Eastern European countries? Maybe I don't want the UK to be in the EEC? Maybe I don't want an EEC? And what all these legal, automatic quotas that every country in the EEC has for the number of Asylum Seekers, etc. they must take every year? Quotas for this, rules for that, laws for god knows what else and we have no say in any of it because our wonderful MEPs and heads of state take care of all this and they know it all anyway. Yeah, right they do. That's why the EEC is in a ruddy mess and the Euro is worth nothing!

The EEC is now a Super Slave state, where we know not what they are doing in Brussels?

Recently, just this month, in July 2015, Greece has voted to not get any more bailouts or to have more austerity measures. Well, I hope Greece leaves the EEC and the Euro; and then I would other countries will follow suit. Great I say!!!!!

Writer: I have included some worldwide graphs on Asylum Seekers, Refuges and Illegal Immigrants below. For a full detailed report on immigration in the United Kingdom go to:

http://en.wikipedia.org/wiki/Modern_immigration_to_the_United_Kingdom

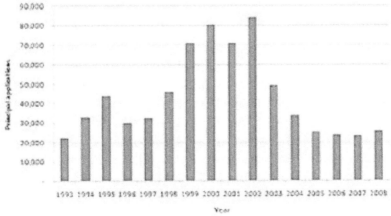

http://commons.wikimedia.org/wiki/File:Asylumapplicants.jpg Cordless Larry at the English language Wikipedia

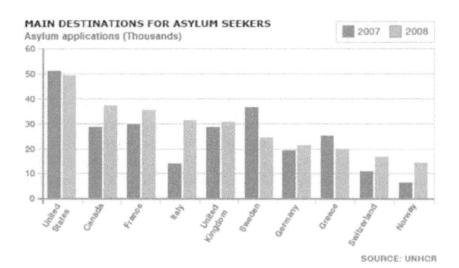

These are only the Asylum Seekers, Refugees and Illegal Immigrants that are officially known about and recorded! I have nothing against these people as they are just looking for a better life. But there is just too many and why can't the richer countries help the poorer countries and why can't the people in the poor countries solve their own problems and sort out their own economies, business and political issues so they can live and work in their own countries instead of coming over to Europe, the USA, etc.? Now this is the real issue at hand and which needs to be dealt with. And then we have the fact that the richer countries have been dominating, taking advantage of the poorer countries and actually keeping them down for their own benefit and gain. And this is a matter of morals, justice and ethics!

FROM: http://en.wikipedia.org/wiki/Modern_immigration_to_the_United_Kingdom
According to Eurostat 47.3 million people lived in the European Union in 2010 who were born outside their resident country. This corresponds to 9.4% of the total EU population. Of these, 31.4 million (6.3%) were born outside the EU and 16.0 million (3.2%) were born in another EU member state. The largest absolute numbers of people born outside the EU were in Germany (6.4 million), France (5.1 million), the United Kingdom (4.7 million), Spain (4.1 million), Italy (3.2 million), and the Netherlands (1.4 million).[86] Expulsions[**edit**]
Expulsions of immigrants who have committed crimes varied between 4000–5000 a year between 2007 and 2010.[87][88]

WRITER: It is also strange that the businesses in the EEC don't mind all these foreign and Eastern European people coming over to work here. No, they are usually quite happy and they can then not have to give the natives of their own country a payrise or something like this; and they can get them to work part-time, which many employers are now doing with both native and foreign workers. Obviously they must be saving money by doing it this way. And then we have 'zero' hour contracts. Business, especially big business and multi-national companies MUST keep making profits at the expense of their own native workers; their own country and the planet. I think they should teach something about the Humanities to people in business or to the world at large: as this 'dog eat dog' and 'look after number one' attitude is destroying us all, even those practising it. I also think too many people have become individuated and even super individuated, and most tend to ONLY think about themselves and most do not even know what 'self' is. I mean, I walk down the street in some parts of the world (I won't mention any names) and no-one talks to each other. Only if you want directions or help; otherwise they do not even look or see other people and then one cannot look at people in the eye. No they might eat or attack or rob you or something: they are afraid or something or have something to hide or they are racist – who knows because they don't say. And in traffic the attitude is: get out of my way and fuck everyone else on the road. Well it seems this attitude is becoming too prevalent now on this planet. Oh, I've got my family and friends, and my wife or girlfriend and kids. I don't need to know or help or pay attention to anyone else. So how is a single man or woman, who have moved to a new town or country: how are they meant to find new friends or find a partner if most people do not talk or do not want to be friends? I know in Ireland it is different and in America; they would talk to anyone I think and help if they could. I am sure some other countries are the same. But it is not good. Mankind is generally out of communication with himself and this is not good!

God help us all if Russia, India and Turkey join the EEC! What would the economic impact be? How much would we be paid an hour with all this cheap labour on the market. Insane! But this is how the EEC is going to go if we let it?

CLASS/CASTE/SOCIAL SYSTEMS

Last time I checked and looked in the mirror – I was born as a human being and I look like a human being. Now I thought I had the same rights as everyone else; and we are all equal as humans; and have the right to happiness and a good life? We are all human beings living on planet Earth together right? Now, what I am getting at here, is that I know the humans on this planet are a mixed bag, with different abilities and talents, and goals and purposes. Some have the great ability to lead or manage others; some can do amazing works of art; some just have the Midas touch and everything they want to do or achieve happens; others are always making mistakes and nothing ever goes the way they planned: failures and disasters (one after the other); some are born rich or super rich; others inherit farms, businesses, land, property, wealth, titles, etc. and others just are poor all the time; never knowing where their next meal is coming from; and some just cannot get above being working class; and some do not even want to work and claim benefits. The list is nearly endless. However, something is amiss here, and wrong. Some people on Earth think they are above others and patronize, mistreat and look down on the rest of us (the Working Class for example). I am talking especially about the Middle Classes and some of the Upper Classes and some with money, power and authority: not all but some, thank God! They even mistreat and will not hire or talk with equality and respect to those people (they think) who are not like them and who do not have the same lovely mindset as *THEM*. I am not talking about people who are confident, cocky or think a lot about themselves. No. This is different. I am talking about people who look down on other human beings as scum and beneath them for some reason; as if they are their slaves or inferiors or something. This is what I am talking about. It is a spiritual and mental flaw in these people. And it is also their attitude to others.

Some have their heads so far up their own asses and/or someone else's; that it is beyond a joke!

This is wrong and they know it! Just because we do not speak POSH or we were not born into the right family; or did not go to the right school or University and hang out with the right friends; does not make a human being inferior to others; or anyone else on this planet, including the Queen of England; the Sultan of Brunei; or anyone else of high rank, wealth, title or power. This is unjust and unfair and it is a MENTAL and SPIRITUAL flaw in them not US that they look down on or mistreat the lower classes and they really consider that we are their slaves and servants: their sheep: their animals to be ruled, controlled, abused and kept in the dark and kept in a low status educationally and financially in life. 'Keep them down, do not let them up,' is their motto. Nice, huh?

Well let's put the record straight: We are ALL equally important and should think of and treat each other as equal and as best we can. I am not taking about having equal money. I am talking about how we treat one another and have respect for each other. We are not sheep or cattle to be herded into corals and done with as they decree, direct or command. We are not animals anyway, which I said before. I am not saying that all rich people are bad or that all Upper Class or powerful ruling class people are bad and look down on the rest us; NO I am not saying that. And I am not talking about the Middle-Income classes either. This is not about money. These special kind or breed of humans, think this way and look down on the lower classes regardless of if they have a lot of money or not or if they have a high or lowly job or not. They seem to look up to the Upper Classes and the Rich and Powerful, and to be honest, I think a good percentage of the Rich, Upper and Ruling Classes are actually good. And some do like and do help the working and lower classes (except they have more money, power and have had more success) more than these Middle Classes (not Middle Income classes, get the difference?) help the Working Class and Poor.

Some of us cannot study or learn very well (this can be handled by the way, if one can learn how to correctly study and this is the first thing any student should be thought once they learn their own language well), so we cannot pass the exams and get a good job and go to the so-amazing UNIVERSITY (University is not everything and getting a degree does not put you above those who don't have a degree. How many people in school and university just memorize everything JUST to pass the exams; and they do not even understand what they have studied and cannot even apply it? Luckily some do understand what they have learnt in school and university and they probably knew if from before, say in a past life or something like this or they just have it well in that field as a natural, intuitive ability or talent.)

Some people are born poor; into poverty or the working class. Some have flaws in themselves which they may already know about; but do not know how to handle them; i.e. they stammer; cannot speak or perform in front of people; keep making wrong decisions; keep being sick or having accidents; cannot read or learn well (dyslexia); nothing ever goes right for them and they never make it big or do well anywhere in life.

Some are born very poor or into poverty or are working class and they still make it big or HUGE in life and become multi-millionaires and are super- successful. Explain that? So, as you see can see, we all have different talents, flaws, mental/ spiritual; problems, abilities and all the rest.

But, no matter who you are in life, where you live or what job you do and how much money you have in the bank; title, rank, social class – it makes no difference to the fact that we are all humans and all living on the same planet, which is called Earth: and we should treat; help and think of each other on the same level, not I am above you and do not speak to me and I cannot associate with you or be your friend and you are my slave or are beneath me and all this rubbish. I mean some people threat their dogs and cats better than the cleaners or servants they employ. What is this all about? I think some people should get a taste of their own medicine and see how they like being treated in this manner, hum?

A good example of this is James Cameron's 'Titanic' (I really like James Cameron and his films! He is truly a very able, creative and causative guy! We need more people like him in the arts!) which portrays how most of the Upper and Middle Classes threat the working class and poor. And of course we have Charles Dickens' books on the subject and 'Slumdog Millionaire' and many others fighting for the cause.

Every level of society is important and every job in all business ranks are important. When your office or toilet is dirty, who do you call? The cleaner. When your food is not cooked and ready when you go to café or restaurant to eat at lunch or dinner time, then who do you need? A cook? We all different in many ways; but we are **ALL** important and we should be treating everyone: from the top to the bottom, with love and respect, kindness and sincerity. And as I said before the peoples of Africa, parts of South America and Asia should NOT be treated like animals, slaves or shitty low-life worthless factory workers, et al. These people should be paid more by their employers and the leaders of these countries SHOULD be helping them and looking after them, not leave them in the gutter or on the street or with hardly any food to eat – what is this all about? The rich, and I am not against the rich, the big multi-nationals, the Royal Families and the Ruling and Upper Classes and all the rest, however; they should be sharing the money and wealth around so it gets to the bottom too. And shareholders do not need to get so much money and profit. Something is VERY drastically wrong with the entire social and economic systems on this planet and they need to be changed. Communism and Capitalism and all the rest have not worked. So some system, which is fairer for all is needed so all echelons, classes and levels of society can have a good, happy and successful life, not just the elite!

Furthermore; I have seen on TV these wonderful programmes in which millionaires or famous people go undercover or spend a few days or a week in the lives of a lowly or low-paid person or family, which *THEY* employ. O yes, they can get to feel and understand how these people live, like those in the shanty towns of Manila in the Philippines and those in Brazil and India. They do get to empathise with them; but they know they will be back in their own rich lives very soon. Some do help when they see and feel how these people's lives are; but they have no real and full reality of how it is to live in this manner and to be born into it; and to try and survive in it and to have to find a way to get out of it. It is like journalists shooting the news on people being shot dead in front of them or dying of starvation. They are detached from the situation and are just spectators, and some do not even care – it is just news and of course they are just doing their wonderful jobs. Amazing!

Check out this article:

CLASS BACK IN RISE IN UK BUT ELITE DIFFERENT

LONDON (AP) — For the past three decades, many Britons had hoped the rigid class system that defined their country from Dickens to "Downton Abbey" was finally dying. Now they fear that class, their old bugbear, is back on the rise. (excerpts off) http://www.dailymail.co.uk/wires/ap/article-2555661/Class-rise-UK-_-elite-different.html

POLLUTION

Earth

Modern farming chemicals, which make such huge profits for the Capitalist' companies, but give us food (especially in the Western world) that tastes shit. It looks good but tastes crap, with not much goodness in it. But all these farming chemicals have to go somewhere and that is into the soil, rivers, valleys, lakes and finally into the sea and into the air. But they also go into plants and plants, which are eaten by us and by other animals, which we eat too. So it is a cycle and a system. Then we have all the pollution from all the various carbon-based fuels and other chemicals/gases. They were all in the ground and under the sea before – now they are in the air, water and soil. And Mankind's population is growing exponentially such that there is less and less land for wild animals to live on and plants to grow on. Plants are being poisoned too, as well as people by drinking the polluted water. And then we have poachers who sell endangered species to people who don't give a f*** about the consequences of their actions, which sadly is a very common state among people on this planet.

Farmers and the food Processing industries use so many chemicals. They feed the chickens colouring agents to make the eggs more yellow; the same for beef to make the meat more red. This does NOT make these products taste better! Then they feed them super hormones to make them fatter and grow super quick. Then in processing, they inject 'water' in to the meat, and we pay for the extra weight; which is why when you cook it, it cooks down to almost nothing. And who knows what else these farmers and food processing industries are doing to the food we eat. I vividly remember when I was growing up in the 1970s and 1980s – which is not that long ago – that the eggs, meat and veg, milk, bread, etc. tasted so much nicer, being more natural; I felt healthier and got more energy out of the food I ate. This has all changed now. Even 100% organic food and meat cannot be guaranteed to be 100% natural with cross-contamination and other pollutants in the air, water and soil. And then we have GM crops, food and meat; how far is this going to go? And what will they come up with next: Genetically Modified Alien food? We all – each and every one of us – reap what we sow and sow what we reap! Isn't it about time we sowed or caused something good and then we can reap something even better? What I am saying, and what I have been saying throughout this book, and I will probably say it again many times, is: We cannot go blaming God or the Devil or some other Higher Being or force for the harm and wrongdoing we are doing to ourselves, others and to this planet. If you find a large mirror and take a nice, long look in it, you should get the idea? *You* are responsible for everything you have done, are doing and will do – good or bad! Now, if we got a huge magic mirror, that would allow 7 billion people to look in it all at the same time and each be able to see everyone else in the same mirror, all at the same time; then we would have 7 billion people who are responsible (whether they know it or not) for their own lives, everyone else's life and all life on this planet, including inanimate objects. Now that is a lot of people and a lot of responsibility! But, if we all took it, a little tiny piece of it each, and shared it, then the job of sorting this planet and ourselves out, would be so much easier and less lonely; and, the job would be done so much faster, and a very small few would not have to do it all. Onward-bound on this journey of responsibility…

Some info on Farming chemicals and Pesticides (this is just tip of the iceberg. You can find gazillions of data on what farmers and food suppliers/processors do to our food before we get to consume it. And WE are paying for this! MY god!):

FROM: Grace Communications Foundation website

Pesticides

It details that: The US Environmental Protection Agency (EPA) from 2007, reported that over 1 billion tons of pesticides were used in the US every year. This is 22% of the estimated **5.2 billion** pounds of pesticides used worldwide! Agricultural use accounted for 80% of pesticide use in the US.

They say there are over 350,000 current and historic pesticide products registered in the United States alone, and the pesticide business is a 12.5 billion dollar industry!

This has resulted in:

Decrease in biodiversity
Loss or dwindling numbers of some species (bees[**responsible of 80% of pollination worldwide!**], wasps, etc.)
Water pollution
Soil contamination
And pest resistance means increased doses of pesticides are needed or formulation of alternate ones.

Pesticides and Public Health

Everyone, including children and farmers are highly vulnerable to the harmful effects of pesticides.
This also includes other animals, insects and plantlife.

These chemicals can get and end up anywhere!

And having organic crops is fine but if you have GM crops nearby and also a non-organic farm nearby, then you will get cross contamination. You will also get pollution from the air and water. So this is not a proper solution really and then at what cost do we have to eat organic food and vegetables.

And from: http://ecowatch.com/2013/06/11/worldwide-honey-bee-collapse-a-lesson-in-ecology/ in an article called Greenpeace by Rex Weyler Biologists have found over 150 different chemical residues in bee pollen!

A single bee colony can pollinate 300 million flowers each day!

Seventy out of the top 100 human food crops, which supply about 90 percent of the world's nutrition, are pollinated by bees!!!!!

And in this same article, bees "contribute more than **€22 billion ($30 billion U.S. dollars) annually** to European agriculture." And Worldwide, bees pollinate human food valued at more than **€265 billion ($350 billion)!!!!!!!!**

WOW!

You should read this above article in full. Worldwide, the honey bee is disappearing. This year, I did not see many bees at all myself. And it has been like this for at least 6 years or more. I remember when I was growing up; I used to see bees everywhere, and wasps too. Now? This is already having huge side-effects worldwide, and it is going to get worse as regards our food crops and plants; and on flower populations, etc., not to mention the bees and all those other creatures and insects that depend on this symbiotic relationship in nature.

In the same article:

A European Food Safety Authority scientific report determined that three widely used pesticides—nicotine-based clothianidin, imidacloprid and thiametoxam— are the main toxic pesticides found in bee hives.

And a Greenpeace scientific report identifies seven priority bee-killer pesticides—including the three nicotine culprits—plus clorpyriphos, cypermethrin, deltamethrin and fipronil. The three neonicotinoids act on insect nervous systems.

And now President Obama, has signed the now infamous "Monsanto Protection Act"—written by Monsanto lobbyists. This gives biotech companies immunity in federal U.S. courts from damages caused to people and the environment. Thanks Obama!

Come on! This makes me sick! I wonder whose side Obama is on? Definitely not ours! We, and a lot of other plants and life are all, directly or indirectly affected by honey bees. I wonder what will come next: human mutations or extinction?

How are 7 billion people going to be fed if no bees are around and how will they get watered if the water is full of crap? And what about the pollutants we breathe in every day and the Oxygen content of the air? If the world gets too polluted, which it is coming real close to, then how will we and all life survive? We all will be eating contaminated food and meat? Contaminated plants and animals will all be eating, feeding on each other. And drinking contaminated water; breathing contaminated air. I don't want to keep going on about this – but I think you get my point, huh?

More from GRACE Communications Foundation website:

> In the US, about 40 percent of all chemical fertilizers eventually break down into ammonia and get released into the atmosphere.
>
> The waste generated by animal agriculture has polluted over 35,000 miles of river in 22 states.
>
> And the annual cost of environmental damage by industrial farming is $34.7 billion.
>
> And in the last 40 years about one third of the world's arable (farmable) land has been lost.

I remember that great English chief Jamie Oliver. I watched his show as he went to America, with real good intentions, to get all the people, and those in schools, colleges and Unis to start eating, good healthy honest food instead of processed rubbish: which is a multi-billion dollar industry, with many hospital and medical spin-offs from those who are obese, over-weight and sick. And from those who die from bad food or being over-weight. And this is no accident, I may add. But the amount of resistance he had was unbelievable! I mean, he was almost shot or thrown out of the country; or he would have been if he had of persisted. This is what we are up against and I really take my hat off to Jamie for having made a very good attempt, and at least got some success!

Here is some e-pollution facts from: **Greenpeace** International at:
http://www.greenpeace.org/international/en/

NOTE: I really admire and praise the work that Greenpeace does!!! At least they are doing something about the state of this planet; and not just discussing it or sitting on their backsides, which is what a lot of people are doing. Discuss matters yes; but then the right ACTION is needed to bring about the correct changes!

Where does e-waste end up?

Background - 24 February, 2009

Many old electronic goods gather dust in storage waiting to be reused, recycled or thrown away. The US Environmental Protection Agency (EPA) estimates that as much as three quarters of the computers sold in the US are stockpiled in garages and closets. When thrown away, they end up in landfills or incinerators or, more recently, are exported to Asia.

Landfill

According to the US EPA, more than 4.6 million tonnes of e-waste ended up in US landfills in 2000. Toxic chemicals in electronics products can leach into the land over time or are released into the atmosphere, impacting nearby communities and the environment. In many European countries, regulations have been introduced to prevent electronic waste being dumped in landfills due to its hazardous content. However, the practice still continues in many countries. In Hong Kong for example, it is estimated that 10-20 percent of discarded computers go to landfill.

Incineration

This releases heavy metals such as lead, cadmium and mercury into the air and ashes. Mercury released into the atmosphere can bio accumulate in the foodchain, particularly in fish - the major route of exposure for the general public. If the products contain PVC plastic, highly toxic dioxins and furans are also released. Brominated flame retardants generate brominated dioxins and furans when e-waste is burned.

Reuse

A good way to increase a product's lifespan. Many old products are exported to developing countries. Although the benefits of reusing electronics in this way are clear, the practice is causing serious problems because the old products are dumped after a short period of use in areas that are unlikely to have hazardous waste facilities.

Recycle

Although recycling can be a good way to reuse the raw materials in a product, the hazardous chemicals in e-waste mean that electronics can harm workers in the recycling yards, as well as their neighbouring communities and environment.

In developed countries, electronics recycling takes place in purpose-built recycling plants under controlled conditions. In many EU states for example, plastics from e-waste are not recycled to avoid brominated furans and dioxins being released into the atmosphere. In developing countries however, there are no such controls. Recycling is done by hand in scrap yards, often by children.

Export

E-waste is routinely exported by developed countries to developing ones, often in violation of the international law. Inspections of 18 European seaports in 2005 found as much as 47 percent of waste destined for export, including e-waste, was illegal. In the UK alone, at least 23,000 metric tonnes of undeclared or 'grey' market electronic waste was illegally shipped in 2003 to the Far East, India, Africa and China. In the US, it is estimated that 50-80 percent of the waste collected for recycling is being exported in this way. This practice is legal because the US has not ratified the Basel Convention.

Mainland China tried to prevent this trade by banning the import of e-waste in 2000. However, we have discovered that the laws are not working; e-waste is still arriving in Guiya of Guangdong Province, the main centre of e-waste scrapping in China.

We have also found a growing e-waste trade problem in India. 25,000 workers are employed at scrap yards in Delhi alone, where 10-20000 tonnes of e-waste is handled each year, 25 percent of this being computers. Other e-waste scrap yards have been found in Meerut, Ferozabad, Chennai, Bangalore and Mumbai.

How did the trade evolve?

In the 1990s, governments in the EU, Japan and some US states set up e-waste 'recycling' systems. But many countries did not have the capacity to deal with the sheer quantity of e-waste they generated or with its hazardous nature.

Therefore, they began exporting the problem to developing countries where laws to protect workers and the environment are inadequate or not enforced. It is also cheaper to 'recycle' waste in developing countries; the cost of glass-to-glass recycling of computer monitors in the US is ten times more than in China.

Demand in Asia for electronic waste began to grow when scrap yards found they could extract valuable substances such as copper, iron, silicon, nickel and gold, during the recycling process. A mobile phone, for example, is 19 percent copper and eight percent iron.

Writer: And what about Nuclear Power; it's risks and its toxic waste? I am sure; however that a more safer and better 'CLEAN' Nuclear form of power could be invented; whether fission or fusion. There is VASTS amounts of energy in matter. It is pretty much limitless if one could find a way to tap in to it or convert it to usable, safe energy? Personally I know this can be done! All those particles – Electrons, Protons and Neutrons in matter (and all these newly discovered ones [Neutrinos; Higgs boson; Anti-matter] at CERN [which is right beside the French-Switzerland boarder near Geneva. And it was at CERN, I may add, that the World Wide Web was invented in 1989 by CERN employee and British scientist Tim Berners-Lee. Why has it taken CERN so long to come up with new, cleaner and safer forms of Nuclear Energy? If indeed that is its purpose? Or maybe they have done it already?) can be broken down to provide unlimited energy. Whether this can be done chemically; using vibration or sound technologies or by using certain Light or Electro-magnetic frequencies, I do not know exactly – but I am certain it can be done and I am sure inventors have already developed technologies to provide clean and free energy; but it gets stopped by the Powers-That-Be; big corporations with vested interests and by Governments, who also have vested interests and taxes to be made.

We all know about the Chernobyl and Fukushima disasters. When will the next one be?

Here is some very interesting data on the USA's Nuclear Programme. And they are dictating to other countries what Nuclear Weapons and Power they can or cannot have? I think they should be taking care of their own backgarden before they start telling others what to do, huh?

FROM: The Brookings Institution
http://www.brookings.edu/about/projects/archive/nucweapons/50

50 Facts About U.S. Nuclear Weapons

*The **U.S. Nuclear Weapons Cost Study Project** was completed in August 1998 and resulted in the book* Atomic Audit: The Costs and Consequences of U.S. Nuclear Weapons Since 1940 *edited by Stephen I. Schwartz. These project pages should be considered historical.*
New research on arms control and nuclear weapons is being conducted by the Brookings Arms Control Initiative.
Except where noted all figures are in constant 1996 dollars -

1. Cost of the Manhattan Project (through August 1945):
$20,000,000,000
2. Total number of nuclear missiles built, 1951-present: **67,500**
34. Total number of nuclear bombers built, 1945-present: **4,680**
11. Largest and smallest nuclear bombs ever deployed: **B17/B24 (~42,000 lbs., 10-15 megatons);** W54 **(51 lbs., .01 kilotons, .02 kilotons-1 kiloton)**
13. Fissile material produced: **104 metric tons of plutonium** and **994 metric tons of highly-enriched uranium**
14. Amount of plutonium still in weapons: **43 metric tons**
17. States with the largest number of nuclear weapons (in 1999): **New Mexico (2,450), Georgia (2,000), Washington (1,685), Nevada (1,350), and North Dakota (1,140)**
20. Legal fees paid by the Department of Energy to fight lawsuits from workers and private citizens concerning nuclear weapons production and testing activities, from October 1990 through March 1995: **$97,000,000**
21. Money paid by the State Department to Japan following fallout from the 1954 "Bravo" test: **$15,300,000**
22. Money and non-monetary compensation paid by the United States to Marshallese Islanders since 1956 to redress damages from

nuclear testing: **at least $759,000,000**

23. Money paid to U.S. citizens under the Radiation Exposure and Compensation Act of 1990, as of January 13, 1998: **approximately $225,000,000 (6,336 claims approved; 3,156 denied)**

26. Number of secret Presidential Emergency Facilities built for use during and after a nuclear war: **more than 75**

27. Currency stored until 1988 by the Federal Reserve at its <u>Mount Pony facility</u> for use after a nuclear war: **more than $2,000,000,000**

29. <u>**Total number of U.S. nuclear weapons tests, 1945-1992: 1,030 (1,125 nuclear devices detonated; 24 additional joint tests with Great Britain)**</u>

33. Largest U.S. explosion/date: **15 Megatons/March 1, 1954 ("Bravo")**

35. Number of nuclear tests in the Pacific: **106**

36. Number of U.S. nuclear tests in Nevada: **911**

37. Number of nuclear weapons tests in Alaska [1, 2, and 3], Colorado [1 and 2], Mississippi and New Mexico [1, 2 and 3]: **10**

41. Volume in cubic meters of radioactive waste resulting from weapons activities: **104,000,000**

44. Number of U.S. nuclear bombs lost in accidents and never recovered: **11**

47. Minimum number of classified pages estimated to be in the Department of Energy's possession (1995): **280 million**

50. Estimated 1998 spending on all U.S. nuclear weapons and weapons-related programs: <u>**$35,100,000,000**</u>

And from: Reaching Critical Will website we have this:

http://www.reachingcriticalwill.org/resources/fact-sheets/critical-issues/4734-environment-and-nuclear-weapons

Under: Environment and nuclear weapons

New technologies will have to be developed to retrieve radioactive materials which have already been released or dumped into the environment. This is about the dumping of nuclear wastes into bodies of water as well as the burial of radioactive materials. Some has been put in concrete and dumped in the sea. Nice!

In the US, from 1945 until 1970, coolant waters from nuclear reactors at the Hanford Reservation in Washington State were routinely discharged into the Columbia River. In 1991, the General Accounting

Office stated that 444 billion gallons of liquid radioactive wastes, from coolant waters to radioactive liquids, were discharged into the environment from the Hanford site alone.

In Russia, some Nuclear submarines, still armed with nuclear warheads, are rusting away in the fjords of Murmansk.

In the United States alone, more than $44 billion has been spent on the production of nuclear weapons as of 1996. 'Clean up' is projected to cost more than $300 billion through to 2070!

This is just in the US – what about the rest of the world?

Radioactive wastes created in the manufacture of a single nuclear bomb containing 4 kg of plutonium-239 and 20 kg of uranium-235 include: 2,000 metric tons of uranium mining waste, 4 metric tons of depleted uranium, 12,000 curies of strontium-90, 12,000 curies of cesium-137, 50 cubic meters of 'low-level' waste and 7 cubic meters of transuranic waste. Multiply the above by the estimated **70,000 nuclear warheads** that have been produced on a worldwide scale.

My god!!!!!

At the Waste Isolation Pilot Plant, in Carlsbad, New Mexico, plutonium contaminated waste and plutonium residues are being buried in a salt flat formation, more than 2000 feet beneath the surface of the Earth. The population surrounding the area are mainly Hispanic and Native American, who have little or no political power in the USA. This environmental racism also applies to the High-Level Radioactive Waste dump in Yucca Mountain, Nevada.

I also wanted to mention China here, as it is a main cause of pollution on this planet; but how many other countries are also burning coal? Why can they not use Carbon filters, then they can burn all the coal they want? Why can't all our household and commercial rubbish be burned to make electricity or chemically processed/converted to other forms of power or turned into products/compounds we can use instead of dumping them in the sea or burying them in huge landfill sites. This will only cost us MORE money and more pollution in the future if we do not handle this NOW! Mankind has NO excuses on this matter!

From: Wikipedia
CHINA'S POLLUTION:

Coal Power Plants:

http://www.china-mike.com/facts-about-china/facts-pollution-environment-energy/

Linfen: most polluted city in China and the World (below)

http://globe-net.com/the-environmental-side-benefits-to-climate-change-mitigation/ source?

Pollution in China and the price they pay for profit (for the few) and _we_ pay for Cheaper Products for Capitalism

(From Wikipedia, the free encyclopedia)

Pollution in **China** is one aspect of the broader topic of environmental issues in China. Various forms of pollution have increased as China has industrialized, which has caused widespread environmental and health problems. Sixteen of the 20 world's most polluted cities are in China.

In 2011, China produced 2.3 million tonnes of electronic waste, second largest in the world

Air pollution caused by industrial plants according to the Chinese Ministry of Health, industrial pollution has made cancer China's leading cause of death.

> Every year, ambient air pollution alone killed hundreds of thousands of citizens.

500 million people in China are without safe and clean drinking water. Only 1% of the country's 560 million city dwellers breathe air considered safe by the European Union, because all the China's major cities are constantly covered in a "toxic grey shroud". Before and during the 2008 Summer Olympics, Beijing was "frantically searching for a magic formula, a meteorological deus ex machina, to clear its skies for the 2008 Olympics."

Lead poisoning or other types of local pollution continue to kill many Chinese children.

A large section of the ocean is without marine life because of massive algal blooms caused by the high nutrients in the water.

The pollution has spread internationally: sulfur dioxide and nitrogen oxides fall as acid rain on Seoul, South Korea, and Tokyo; and according to the Journal of Geophysical Research, the pollution even reaches Los Angeles in the USA.

The Chinese Academy of Environmental Planning in 2003 had an internal and unpublished report which estimated that 300,000 people die each year from ambient air pollution, mostly of heart disease and lung cancer.

Chinese environmental experts in 2005 issued another report, estimating that annual premature deaths attributable to outdoor air pollution were likely to reach 380,000 in 2010 and 550,000 in 2020.

A 2007 World Bank report conducted with China's national

environmental agency found that "...outdoor air pollution was already causing 350,000 to 400,000 premature deaths a year. Indoor pollution contributed to the deaths of an additional 300,000 people, while 60,000 died from diarrhea, bladder and stomach cancer and other diseases that can be caused by water-borne pollution." World Bank officials said "China's environmental agency insisted that the health statistics be removed from the published version of the report, citing the possible impact on 'social stability'".[10]

A draft of a 2007 combined World Bank and SEPA report stated that up to 760,000 people died prematurely each year in China because of air and water pollution. High levels of air pollution in China's cities caused to 350,000-400,000 premature deaths. Another 300,000 died because of indoor air of poor quality. There were 60,000 premature deaths each year because of water of poor quality. Chinese officials asked that some of results should not be published in order to avoid social unrest.[11]

WRITER: Pollution sucks. I hate it. There must be some sane, logical ways to sort it out and to stop it getting worse and to reduce it? Surely out of all the top companies and top scientists and geniuses on Earth, there could be found better ways to handle this?

This all sucks!!!!!!

NATURE

http://alexandriaruthk.hubpages.com/hub/The-Symbols-and-Emblems-of-Ireland#slide2636331 source?

I really love nature and the plants and animals of this planet. Why does man do what he does to them? Because what we do to them directly affects us! What will the future hold for all plants and animals when the population of this planet grows to ten or fifteen billion people? I think it is sad what is going on around the world;)

Some stats and articles below:

International Union for Conservation of Nature and Natural Resources
http://www.iucnredlist.org

IUCN Red List:

The Siberian tiger is a subspecies of tiger that is endangered; three subspecies of tiger are already extinct
IUCN categories include:
Extinct: Examples: Atlas bear, Aurochs, Bali Tiger, Blackfin Cisco, Caribbean Monk Seal, Carolina Parakeet, Caspian Tiger, Dinosaurs, Dodo, Dusky Seaside Sparrow, Eastern Cougar, Elephant Bird, Golden Toad, Great Auk, Haast's Eagle, Japanese Sea Lion, Javan Tiger, Labrador Duck, Moa, Passenger Pigeon, Pterosaurs, Saber-toothed cat, Schomburgk's deer, Short-faced bear, Steller's Sea Cow, Thylacine, Toolache Wallaby, Western Black Rhinoceros, Woolly Mammoth, Woolly Rhinoceros.
Extinct in the wild: captive individuals survive, but there is no free-living, natural population. Examples: Barbary Lion (maybe extinct), Catarina Pupfish, Hawaiian Crow, Northern White Rhinoceros, Scimitar Oryx, Socorro Dove, Wyoming Toad
Critically endangered: faces an extremely high risk of extinction in the immediate future. Examples: Addax, African Wild Ass, Alabama Cavefish, Amur Leopard, Arakan Forest Turtle, Asiatic Cheetah, Axolotl, Bactrian Camel, Brazilian Merganser, Brown Spider Monkey, California Condor, Chinese Alligator, Chinese Giant Salamander, Gharial, Hawaiian Monk Seal, Iberian Lynx, Island Fox, Javan Rhino, Kakapo, Leatherback Sea Turtle, Mediterranean Monk Seal, Mexican Wolf, Mountain Gorilla, Philippine Eagle, Red Wolf, Saiga, Siamese Crocodile, Spix's Macaw, Southern bluefin tuna, Sumatran Orangutan, Sumatran Rhinoceros, Vaquita, Yangtze River Dolphin
Endangered: faces a very high risk of extinction in the near future.

Examples: African Penguin, African Wild Dog, Asian Elephant, Asiatic Lion, Blue Whale, Bonobo, Bornean Orangutan, Chimpanzees, Dhole, Ethiopian Wolf, Hispid Hare, Giant Otter, Giant Panda, Goliath Frog, Gorillas, Green Sea Turtle, Grevy's Zebra, Hyacinth Macaw, Japanese Crane, Lear's Macaw, Malayan Tapir, Markhor, Persian Leopard, Proboscis Monkey, Pygmy Hippopotamus, Red-breasted Goose, Rothschild Giraffe, Snow Leopard, Steller's Sea Lion, Scopas tang, Takhi, Tiger, Vietnamese Pheasant, Volcano Rabbit, Wild Water Buffalo
    United States

Currently, **1,556 known species in the world have been identified as endangered, or near extinction**, and are under protection by government law.

http://commons.wikimedia.org/wiki/File:Dhole.jpg Julielangford

The most endangered Asiatic top predator, the dhole, is on the edge of extinction.

315

Statistic Verification
Source: World Wildlife Fund
Research Date: July 13th, 2014

Animal Species Extinction Statistics	Number of Species
Number of Animal species that have gone extinct	801
Number of Animals that are extinct in the wild	64
Number of Animals that are critically endangered	3,879
Number of Animals that are endangered	5,689
Number of Animals that are vulnerable	10,002
Number of Animals that are near threatened	4,389
Number of Animals that are least concern	27,124
Top Endangered Animals (select few)	**Number Left**
Amur Leopard	40
Javan Rhinoceros	60
Panther	80
Red Wolf	100
California Condor	130
Sumatran Rhinoceros	300
Cross River Gorilla	300
Asiatic Lion	350
Northern Right Whale	350
Indochinese Tiger	500

Malayan Tiger	500
Sumatran Tiger	500
Grizzly Bear	500
Eastern Gorilla	700
Camels	950
Giant Panda	1,000
South Asian River Dolphin	1,000
North Pacific Right Whale	1,000
Cape Mountain Zebra	1,500
Bengal Tiger	2,000
Indian Rhinoceros	2,500
Grevy's Zebra	2,000
Snow Leopard	4,000
Gray Wolf	6,600
Sumatran Orangutan	7,000
Cheetah	7,000
Blue Whale	10,000
Polar Bears	20,000
American Bison	30,000
Bonobo	30,000
Borneo Orangutan	40,000
Tasmanian Devil	80,000
Narwhal	80,000
Beluga Whale	150,000
Chimpanzee	150,000
Sperm Whale	400,000
Asian Elephant	470,000

http://commons.wikimedia.org/wiki/File:Panthera_tigris_altaica_13_-_Buffalo_Zoo.jpg Dave Pape

And then we have this article:

IVORY TRADE:

THE INDEPENDENT Sunday 9 February 2014
By *MICHAEL MCCARTHY*

London conference 2014: The world wakes up at elephants' eleventh hour

Delegates from about 50 countries will meet in London this week to try to end the slaughter that feeds the illegal market in ivory and Rhino horn

Illegal wildlife trade is making an estimated $19 billion a year. 50,000 Elephants are being shot every year to meet the Chinese market for ivory; while Rhino are being killed too for their horns.

Both animals are on the road to extinction in the wild. While more than 1,000 wildlife rangers have been killed trying to stop the poachers.

In Vietnam, Rhino horn sells for $65,000 a kilo!

And the typical price for Ivory worldwide is about $3,000 a kilo.

This is insane!

This is so sad, as these animals could be knocked out with darts or drugs, their horns/tusks cut off and the animal would still be alive and so would their young. Or, why not set up Breeding/ Poaching farms, parks or ranches where the animals are breed just for their horns and tusks? Plus, there must be some other substitute for those that buy/use the horns and tusks; and people must be educated about what harm they are causing by supporting and buying them. Plus, the world as a whole, which means all the major countries in the world. must join together financially and otherwise, to help police and protect these animals before they become extinct. What else can be done to stop this, I don't know? Anyone else got some good, bright practical ideas on this? Some more stats:

Ivory-Billed Woodpecker: A North American bird so endangered it may actually be extinct
Amur Leopard: The world's rarest cat: Only 40 left in Russia's Far East
Javan Rhinoceros: No more than 60 of these swamp-dwelling Asian rhinos exist
Northern Sportive Lemur: Here's the scarcest of Madagascar's fast-dwindling lemur species
Northern Right Whale: Hunted to near extinction, 350 right whales still swim the Atlantic
Western Lowland Gorilla:Disease and illegal hunting are taking an alarming toll on this gentle giant of a primate
Leatherback Sea Turtle:The population of the world's largest turtle is dropping at an alarming rate
Siberian (or Amur) Tiger: The world's biggest cat weighs as much as 300 kilos (660 pounds)
Chinese Giant Salamander:Humans are eating the world's largest amphibian into extinction
The Little Dodo Bird:Samoa's little dodo bird is in imminent danger of following the large dodo into extinction.
Plus . . . Four Important Species From Our Previous Lists
Kakapo Parrot: These flightless New Zealand birds are so rare they all have names
Greater Bamboo Lemur: Fewer than 100 of these Critically Endangered animals remain
Mountain Gorilla: Their habitat is shrinking, and fewer than 700 remain
Hawaiian Monk Seal: Scientists don't know why this seal's population keeps declining

Look, this world and nature; this entire planet and everything in and on it, from the plants, insects and animals to the inner and outer cores and the plates and lava, to the entire human species and all its races, are ALL part of a huge interactive system. This system is vast and is composed of hundreds and thousands of other sub-systems. And this planet is also part of the Solar System, this galaxy and on and on. It has closed systems (apparently but very few of these) but most are open and interconnected systems (not all visible to human eyes, perception and to man's instruments at present.)

Our bodies are a system. So are the plants and animals, each and every one of them and their development, evolution and procreation. Plate tectonics. The weather, the mountains, lakes, valleys, rivers, seas, light, heat, gravity, light, atomic particles, all power and nuclear power, electricity and so on. They are all interactive systems, not closed, which means they all affect each other.

If you alter or change one – depending which one and by how much – it usually has an effect on some or all of the rest, and on itself. Some, like blocking out the Sun or lowering the temperature have catastrophic effects for all the other systems and other forms of life on this planet.

As nothing is really disappearing, even though it appears that they do, everything is actually just changing either very, very slowly or very, very quickly or at a varying or medium speed. So, if you pour Uranium waste into the sea or blow up a nuclear bomb to see if it works (and to show your neighbours and the rest of the world that you have deadly weapons too); this has repercussions for all life on this planet, including the planet itself, and more so to the areas closer to the explosion. Pollution and Nuclear Waste or Nuclear Explosions, and all the gazillions of pollution from petrol, jet and diesel engines, all have to go somewhere and where they go or end up deposited; has to have effects and side-effects all over the place, and some can go on for hundreds of years or longer. Some effect our bodies, food, plants, animals, water and all the rest. All the pollution has to go somewhere and it has to cause something. Newton's laws do apply, as do many others. There are also mental and spiritual side-effects in all this too. It is all linked and we all linked to it to. Oh yes!

It is getting that bad we have acid rain in many parts of the world. And the air we breathe in some cities and towns, including our children, is getting worse and worse (skin and breathing disorders, allergies, etc.), with the air not giving as much energy as it used to to our chemical bodies. It would be nice to see the test results for the composition of the air we breathe now and to say fifty years ago? We are even getting freaky animals: two headed dogs and fish. The food we eat now does not even taste like it did say twenty or thirty years ago, especially in the Western Hemisphere. People are getting fat and going around with skin disorders and look not very healthy or are overweight. Some look weak, pale, low energy levels and poorly. Nice, huh. But does anyone really care? Do you, the person reading this book care? If yes, then what are you going to do about it?

This lovely planet Earth can only cope and recycle so much. The same is true for Nature and its systems; and our fragile bodies, with its tolerances, needs and demands. And yet the Lords of Darkness, those lovely Powers-That-Be, whether they be alien, devils or not; or whatever kind of callous human trash they are; THEY are the ones causing it all and they are the ones keeping it going – and those who collude, profit and work with them. And WE are the ones agreeing with it and them and NOT doing anything or not enough about it and them!!! Why is that? Is it not time to change this? Well? I say 'YES!!!!!'

We let them sell more and more cars and trucks and jet planes on the planet now than there ever was. Why is there no filter that 100% eradicates all the pollution from all these toxic fuels, which can be attached to our exhausts; taking the catalytic converter to the next level? What are our wonderful leaders and Governments doing about it? Nothing really as they get very, very, VERY well looked after. Look at Tony Blair and all the other ex-Prime Ministers and ex-Presidents and all the rest of them around the planet. I never see or hear of any of them being poor. No, they are all rewarded for their crimes against their country, the people they are meant to serve (what a big joke) and against Humanity. How they can sleep at night or live with themselves, I am truly mystified by this? You do a deal with the Devil or sleep with him and you have to pay the price. And there is the law of Karma also. Their days are number, I can tell you that. Oh yes, they are going to get their comeuppance very soon!

And what the hell is our wonderful Brussels in Europe doing about all this pollution? FUCK ALL I tell you!!! And do the Lords of Darkness want to do anything about it – no! And what about our wonderful MEPs, Ministers, Leaders, Ruling Families, Royal Families and Politicians? NOTHING! No, they all have their heads stuck up their own asses, or someone else's. And they have their own vested interests, their vast lands and wealth, power and they do not even care about themselves – as if they did – they would not allow all this to happen. They seem to think that when one dies that is the end of one. Little do they know. And what about our future generations and children – what future will they have – well?

No, all of these assholes will do is raise taxes or bring in a new pollution tax or some such ploy, why - I don't know because that will not handle and cure the vast amounts of pollution seeping and flowing around Earth. And where are all the geniuses and Science gurus, experts and top guys? No, they are all pretty much controlled by the Powers-That-Be or by their millions of subsidiary companies (owned by them and their affiliates and Minions) or they are scared. Wussies! Some, a very few ARE doing their utmost to bring in new technology that will sort out our worldwide pollution and fuel problems, but they are underfunded and hounded like hell (or even killed) and are blocked at every turn when they go to get the technology out to the world. Believe me, this IS fact! And so many people today will accept large payments and large pay packets, bribes, commissions and all the rest, just to look after themselves, make a profit and lot of money and to hell with the rest of the planet and its peoples. Nice people – NOT!!!! Just like the politicians, how these Science gurus and geniuses can sleep at night is beyond me!? Witness those geniuses worked on the Manhattan Project to build and test the first atomic bombs. Most were dead within a few years after the project and when they saw what they had created, I don't think they slept to well and could live with themselves, despite maybe getting some radiation poisoning.

And what about all this gas fracking which is being done in the USA and has been Oked to be carried out in the UK. And, they also want to start oil exploration and drilling in the Artic. What is going on with these people and oil companies? Why don't we work out a way to burn or consume physical matter and then we can burn the entire planet and leave it dead and Carbon black and we can then go live on the Moon or on another planet and do the same there! We need NEW, limitless (or almost) and non-pollutive forms of energy and power. And we need them like yesterday!!!???

Now onto something I really adore and will ALWAYS support and help all I can:

ART

Well, people say that money makes the world go around; but I would say ART does too. It is everywhere, in pretty much everything we do, see and perceive. It may not seem that way to you but it is. It is an integral part of life and one which must be mentioned.

If one opens one's eyes, and looks around and perceives what is around one on this planet and in the environment we are in, you will see art almost everywhere: the cars we drive, clothes we wear; make-up for women (and men these days); the houses and apartments we live in were all designed by architects or builders; how we dress; a woman dressing up for her man; a man dressing up for his woman; a cook preparing some tasty, nice-looking food; a hairdresser; how the interior and exterior of our abodes are; our gardens; how we dress our children; clothes and fashion designers; Feng Shui; how farmers and civil engineers and town planners shape our land, roads and cities; how mother nature shapes the environment and how grows things; how DNA scientists now alter lifeforms (which needs to be done ethically and correctly by the way!); landscape gardeners and designers; the look and presentation of the foods we buy and eat; and the beverages we drink; play and adventure worlds like Disney: it is all different forms of art, with different purposes and goals behind them.

Look to the stars and planets spinning out there in the vast distances from Earth. Look at those amazing pictures taken with the Hubble telescope? WOW! It is pretty much all art in some form or another. It is playdough, or Mechano or Lego for us as Human Beings and playdough for the demi-gods, gods and GOD, GODS and SUPREME BEINGS!

Life is an art form!

So this is all fine and great and I love art too! Where would we all be without it and that includes inventors?

But, in this our modern age, how many artists are setting a good example for themselves and the rest of us; and our future children, teenagers and generations? Our morals and ethics, as well as those of the artist, are highly involved in this too; as well as our Unconscious Minds. Children see how their parents behave, and the rock and pop stars, actors and actresses, and the rich and famous. They see the movies, where it is OK to do drugs, drink, shag any man or woman when one wants, steal, murder, rape. The novels too. Not everyone is affected by these, but some are.

ART and its artists **SHOULD** be more responsible for what they create and the messages they are communicating! They should be setting good examples and they should be helping Mankind lead better, more happier, moral and ethical lives, where genuine love, honesty, truth, respect for one's fellow human beings are paramount – for without these – Mankind is dead and will head in the wrong direction; which is down. They – the artists – and our leaders, educators and scientists too; need to sending/guiding us upwards and helping us to rise up in our morals, ethics, our knowledge; our wisdom; our abilities; our cultures and how we treat each other and other lifeforms, and plants and animals and our planet.

This should be the main purpose of art! But, at the end of the day; it is ultimately down to the artist what he does with his art and what his/her message is; and what example he/she sets?

Not to just have sex with any nice girl or man that one sees; drink and do drugs to excess; give the message that it is OK to do whatever you want; without any repercussions or side-effects. This is art which is pandering in to the psychotic needs and desires of the Unconscious Mind and just creates an immoral and unbalanced life for all: where one does not take or have enough responsibility for his actions.

ART and ARTISTS, and all those involved in nourishing or teaching/

helping those who creative and artistic; need to be more responsible for what they create, and think what is the purpose or message of what they are creating. And those in power, in government, our leaders, our scientists, the rich and famous, big company owners, etc., all of us actually, but more so these people, as they have more of a direct influence over our lives than anyone else. They all need to wake up as to what they are doing and causing in their lives; and more importantly, what they are doing and causing to others, including this planet, and all that is on it.

Man should not just be wondering around aimlessly from life to life; not really knowing what is going to happen next or what state the planet and his fellow human beings are going to be in. All of Mankind, which includes everyone! needs to start taking control of his destiny. The artist, and those connected to him, can be so effective in bringing about a new, better culture and a much brighter and happier for future for all!!!!!

Sure look at some of the amazing talent we have around this planet: Michael Flatly and his Riverdance, Lord of the Dance and Feet of Flames. Now this man is a genius. I think his message is one of love, happiness, feeling more alive and feeling better inside, with maybe a little bit more love inside oneself for one's fellow human beings. I mean his shows, could bring the dead alive and reform the Devil and make him want to join in! Then, what about 'Harry Potter' by J.K. Rowling and his war against Voldemort. Harry died, went to Heaven and still defeated Evil. Maybe Michael Flatley and J.K. Rowling did not know their creative works would be so huge? But the essence of these is: magic, love and determination (never give up!). Real magic is the essence of Man. Real magic is not tricks or getting spirits or demons to do one's bidding as they used to do in the ancient days of Kubla Khan. No. Real magic is being able to make anything happen or appear either by a wave or gesture of one's hand; but senior to this is by just **thinking** something, and 'Hey Presto!' it happens or appears. This is real magic. And most probably Man's true origins rest along this line, and that is why Magic is so popular today, and super heroes and all that. This is also linked to Man's belief and attraction to Divinity and attraction/interest/belief in deities, gods, GOD and SUPREME BEINGS: as they can do this magic. And then we have LOVE; which I think could be said to be the most powerful Magic there is! They are linked. And then nothing can be done or achieved unless one has determination and is not a coward. Irish culture, for example, is very strongly based on Magic, Art and Love. And strong determination. And one also needs Power; be able to wield a sword or an axe; or let off bolts of lightning or electricity like Thor or Zeus. Or defend oneself and one's loved ones. And with Power comes responsibility. And one needs knowledge too. The correct, true knowledge. Michael Flatley and J.K. Rowling did not create their works of art without knowledge. You try doing your job without some knowledge? You will find too that a lot of cultures – usually good ones - were founded on these qualities/abilities too, if you care to trace them: Arabian Knights; Genies; Dragons; Hans Christian Anderson tales; Merlin and Excalibur; Viking, Greek and Roman gods; Leprechauns, Fairies, Wizards, etc...

And we have (in no particular order) U2, Elvis Presley, The Beatles, Pink Floyd, Michael Jackson, Frank Sinatra, Righteous Brothers, Neil Diamond, Van Morrison, Simon and Garfunkel, Foreigner, Abba, Roy Orbison, Clannad, Enya, Bee Gees, Celine Dion, Dolly Parton, etc., etc., and all those other great writers, film makers and painters out there – past and present – who caused and are causing **good** effects for Mankind with their art. WOW!

To be honest, I truly think there is an artist in all of us, deep down inside, as life is all about causing and creating things, good or bad. It is also about being effect. One can be causative Cause, and causative Effect or not. Isn't it time we **_all_** started causing and creating some good stuff? I think now is a good time to start doing this! Each and everyone one of us. I think Jesus, Mohammed, Buddha, Vishnu, Moses, etc. we all trying to teach us this in one form or another. Isn't about time we returned the favour? And there does not always have to be Evil or a villain in stories, films, art or life. There can be just good too? So why not bring out the real Magic, Love and determination in all of us and make this planet are a better place? And let's also defeat or stop the real Evil People who are keeping us down and preventing us from getting back this real, special Magic which resides in all of us; and this Love and determination too?

But none of this means you can do whatever you like, whenever you like. That is why we have laws. And that is also why Mankind is in the condition he is in today; because he lacks the above and art has let him down to some extent; and some people with power and money abuse it to the detriment of us all but to the benefit of the few. All parts of life are linked. Art and the above, can help bring Mankind back to where he should be; and thus, we can have a Second Renaissance. The one that will bring Man back to his natural state as a Spiritual Being; and also to the Stars and beyond. I know this may seem unbelievable, or even a load of rubbish; but that does mean it is not possible to attain. At the very least, we need to stop a certain number of individuals who are quite busy suppressing and pulling and keeping Man down as an animal; and destroying our lovely planet.

ALTERNATIVE ENERGY

http://commons.wikimedia.org/wiki/File:Tesla_circa_1890.jpeg circa 1890 Photo By D.C. Martin

'If you wish to understand the Universe, think of energy, frequency and vibration.' Nikola Tesla

One of my all-time heroes Tesla, who took on [or threatened] the Powers-That-be, maybe without even knowing it or knowing who they were and what they were up to - and he died haggard looking, almost penniless, all alone in a hotel. And then they went in and stole his papers and inventions. I would say 100%, he was the greatest genius in terms of inventions and in particular Alternative Energy/Power production this planet has ever known (with Faraday and a few others not far behind.) And I take my hat off to him – and I thank him for being/coming here and for what he did invent, create and accomplish. His legacy still lives on in almost every electrical and energy sphere/field on this planet, including what the military in the US are up to and also in what the Powers-That-Be are up too technology wise. And I must add, he revealed too much of his inventions to the world and created inventions and technology, without thinking of the implications and what if they fell in to the wrong hands – which they did. But he was a good guy too – way ahead of his time, even by today's standards. And, regardless of all this, I very much thank you my friend: Nikola Tesla!

NOTE: you can know a person and their behaviour by their eyes. The eyes do mirror the soul or being (if you care to look), as well as their tone of voice, facial expression and bodily characteristics (although sometimes they fake it or pretend and put on a false smile or personality. One can usually detect this by spending time with that person and by asking them more personal questions instead of the ordinary, everyday stuff like 'How is the weather?') Look at Tesla's eyes! WOW!

Other great Alternative Energy inventors have been:

MICHAEL FARADAY and his HOMOPOLAR DC GENERATOR; BRUCE DE PALMA and the 'N' MACHINE; STANLEY MEYER; OTIS T. CARR; JOSEPH NEWMAN; JOHN BEDINI; LESTER JENNINGS HENDERSHOT; VICTOR CHAUBERGER; STELLELETTER, THOMAS T. BROWN; ROBERT ADAMS; SCOTT McKIE; PROF. JOHN SEARL (who I met in person a few years ago) AND HIS FLYING SAUCER; DR. THOMAS HENRY MORAY; BILL MULLER; BERT WERJEFELT'S MAGNETIC BATTERY; KARL SCHAPPELLER AND MANY MORE. Heroes the lot of them!

Welcome to the REAL technology that WILL save Mankind, Nature, the animals and plants and our so beautiful planet Earth; and sort out his energy, power, pollution and fuel problems; so that we can pay lower fuel prices (which would be lower too if the Governments lowered their lovely taxes on them, on which they make their vast sums of money and which they say they can do nothing about: bollix I say!!! They are all in cahoots with the Lords of Darkness, who control all the oil, gas and power on this planet. No diesel and petrol and the countries and their industries come to a standstill - fact! With lower taxes and lower fuel and power bills; and freer industry and uncontrolled Education, Science and Physics; and with, in particular, freer inventiveness for inventors (especially Alternative Energy inventors!) then Man would be able to rise to higher heights: the heights which we have dreamed about since we first saw Star Trek, Star Wars and all the rest of those great movies. Unlimited power, unlimited speed (beyond the speed of light – which is not a constant and never will be – and on to hyper-light speeds, space warping and all the rest), unlimited fuel, power and energy for every mode of transport on the planet, very household, every business, every country and it would be all free, safe and non-pollutive. Now that is my dream!!!!! And we could pay a small tax on this type of energy, just to keep our Governments happy; but then all the rest of these other rates, duties, VATs and other taxes, would have to go or at least be vastly reduced. As they are way to high!

I listed about some of these inventors and you can check them out for yourself and on the internet, etc. and get a good view, understanding and picture of who they were and what they were about, and what happened to them. Great guys! I love them all!!! Nicola Tesla being, for me, the greatest of them all, and from whom so much technology we have today actually came from in one way or another.

Furthermore, Science, Physics, Maths, English, Astronomy, and all the rest of these wonderful subjects; have all been altered and changed over the years to make students and learners unable to comprehend them, think with them, and more importantly be unable to 'THINK' for themselves on them and be unable to be creative in these fields. Most students and people now – sadly – are only able to memorize the data, laws, theories, formulas, equations and all the rest: but they (not all but most, and those who do not do this, already understood them anyway and knew them without being actually 'thought' or educated in these subjects. And you always get geniuses: a complete genius at pretty much everything – is VERY rare; and also specialized ones [genius in only one field) do not really and actually understand and comprehend the subjects they are being 'educated' in. This is sad because most students will be confused about their subjects – some more than others. But, more seriously, this is actually being done intentionally. Why? Because then it will be harder for Mankind to rise to greater heights and for him to invent, solve and create better technology, inventions and solutions to his now many problems. Especially with the population of Earth now at about 7 billion human beings and all the resultant and associated problems that this incurs and produces.

Man *IS* being INTENTIONALLY kept ignorant! Now just Africa, Asia, South America and all those other poorer Third World countries around our planet. But EVERYONE! If man really knew who he was, what he is, what he is truly capable of, where he came from, and what his actual and true history IS; and more importantly WHO has been denying him this data and truth, then, I think he would become VERY angry and would kill or jail those who are responsible. The history of mankind that you read in our school books, is to a large extent, inaccurate and more importantly, they do not divulge WHO has been controlling, influencing us (in a bad way) and keeping us DOWN in more ways than one. It is all about power, control, money, slavery, ignorance and freedom. It is basically and intrinsically a war between Good (majority) and Evil (very small minority). We want, most of us anyway, to be happy, free and able to do what we want (to within reason and not to the harm and detriment of others and planet); have what we want and be what we want. They, on the other hand, are against us on this and THEY want us to be HOW they us, which is: ignorant, stupid, unable to think, reason, deduce, be logical and solve problems for ourselves; not free both as humans AND as Spiritual Beings; trapped and unfree mentally (with an unconscious and growing Unconscious Mind – which they use and take advantage of to get is to react the way they want and therefore be controlled); trapped and unfree FINANCIALLY, i.e. higher taxes, bills, rates, loan repayment amounts and all the rest of the rubbish our wonderful Governments, The Vested Interests, Royal and Ruling Families, Banks, Oil/Gas/Energy Companies; Drugs Companies and all the rest of the big Multi-nationals, who force us to live how they want, earn what they want, pay what they want, die how they want and all the rest of the crap. And we allow and pay them to do it!!! That's a nice state-of-affairs, isn't it, hmm?

And if THEY keep putting everything up; then INFLATION (that lovely word we all like to here – NOT!) goes up, our wages and living expenses go down, and like I said before if there is less money in circulation and freely available to the majority masses of people on

334

Earth – and it has to be available to the majority of the people, which is the Working Class, the poor and so some extent the Middle Class earners and by that I mean the Middle Income earners (not the mental attitude.) The Middle & High Income earners, and the Upper and Rich classes, they already have the money. And those above them: the multi-millionaires, billionaires and the handful of trillionaires are making more and more every day, to the detriment of us. But some people just want more and more money and power, and they want a system on this plant whereby THEY keep those below down but are still making money from them and still taking advantage of them to fill and line their own pockets (and governments and large companies use US to pay their bills, debts and future investments in their companies, and give themselves huge salaries, pensions and bonuses). There is plenty of money on this planet, yet a small minority are amassing and hording it all and actively preventing, suppressing and stopping us from getting enough of it, without having to borrow it I must add, so we can have a lead a nice, pleasant, worry-free life. Extreme Capitalism and these Vested Interests' People are the ones to blame, and SO are WE for being scared, ignorant and ALLOWING them to get away with it and believing all the bullshit and crap that our Government and Leaders and the Media have been telling us for many years!!!

I keep saying this, but it is a law of Finance and Economics: if the majority of people (us) do not have enough extra free money, in excess of what we need to live and support ourselves and our families: just the BASICS of what we need to survive; if people do not have a little to a good bit more than this, then the rest of the Business World suffers (except businesses that sell food and provide power, fuel and electricity, etc. as we all need to eat and have power and electricity [but their sales will go down too as people buy less or go elsewhere for cheaper products); businesses close down or pay their workers less pay (which makes it snowball); governments get less money from taxes, VAT and their litany of rubbish other taxes and rates and levies; councils put Business Rates and other fees up and this, once again, makes the whole situation worse. And the economy does not expand but actually gets worse.

Another point is: money needs to be backed up by something of value. Not just be a credit blip on the screen of some bank somewhere. And not have written on it: 'This Money is of value because we, your

Government, say it is and I promise to pay the bearer of this…blah, blah, blah…' This is not real money of value; but trash or rubbish money. I can shortly see them doing away with paper and metal money very soon and it will all be computer credits and digital money: what value will that have? And part of a country's value of its money comes from its Culture, Economy, Business and Banking condition, Education, its Art and Creativity, local fate in it and international fate and trust in it by other countries. It's a whole package! And it also needs to be supported and backed up by something of REAL value, for example Gold or Silver; or, in this day and age: Oil, Gas, Nuclear Power; or even water and Oxygen (items like this will become more and more valuable as this planet goes more downhill and gets closer and close to destroying itself).

Literally hundreds of inventors and geniuses, over the, say last two hundred years (in particular the last one hundred) have been killed, assassinated, blackmailed, threatened, gotten into huge debt which they can never pay back and are thus ruined; they commit suicide which is not actually suicide but it is made to look it is (and some do actually commit suicide because are connected with unsavoury people who claim they want or are helping them but they ARE not and the inventor does not see this and is thus destroyed)' or they are bought out: and their invention, chemical formula or new discovery is locked away in some secret, hidden vault somewhere that belongs to one of the Lords of Darkness. O this is a fact my reader. Not fully known about and not made publicly know – but true none the less.

Alternative Energy, in ALL its VERY broad spectrums and spheres, can and WILL solve getting Mankind out into space and inhabiting the other trillions and trillions of planets out there and it can get our spaceships to go up to the speed of light and beyond! O yes!!!! It can do everything which is the opposite of what those in the current Scientific, Physics, Mathematic and engineering worlds tell us is impossible. Funny that. I wonder who pays the wages of these so-called 'EXPERTS' and wonderful 'PROFESSORS' who are either one-minded (with blinkers on) and do not have a clue what they are doing, saying and working on; or they are fools and are just very easily bought off. Or they are afraid to speaketh the truth and reveal the truth, if they know it. Or they do not know the truth. And some are idiots too. No other possibilities are possible. I know that.

Alternative Energy can and **will** fully solve Man's energy problems by having lots of various different perpetual energy, power and fuel sources/devices and machines, and SPECIAL chemical formulas too. Or just taking energy straight out of the air, environment or from outer space, as Nicola Tesla (he tried to go it and do it all alone and he failed and died all alone) could do. What a genius! I love him! You look at a photo of him and you see a true genius and a very good and decent man! Our worldwide communication and mobile networks all came from him in around the year 1900 – WOW!!! He was working on stuff which they, maybe are only now, starting to understand. I believe Tesla was working on technology which could control weather and also cause earthquakes, tornadoes, hurricanes, and even electric explosions. He was the man who could have freed mankind from his fuel bill and every crisis and he died alone, almost penniless, in a hotel and his papers, theories/ papers and inventions were stolen (those secret agents or men-in-black and all those 'created' assassins and spies are all real, you know.) This was thanks to J.P. Morgan Senior, who was also responsible for the 1920s Wall Street crash, so he could take over the power and fuel companies he wanted. And he was funded and backed by the Rockefeller and Rothschild Family Empires, and their other interlinked worldwide families, which the Royal and Ruling Families of the world know full well who they are; and who our wonderful loyal and faithful (NOT!) Government and World Leaders also know who they are – because they work for them and are bought and paid and controlled by them via threats and also via Psychiatry and Deep Sleep or Hypnosis Therapy – which turns them into OH-SO-WILLING-SLAVES and willing slaves to their will, and they probably do not even know it. Or they are just bad, evil-intentioned-mother-fuckers themselves and totally agree their agenda to squash, control and suppress Mankind. And they are rewarded for their endeavors. Witness Tony Blair, Bush and all the rest of the leaders of the G 20 countries and those who came before them, including the USA (some presidents knew what was going on and who they were but were made to surrender to their will because they had them by the balls and controlled most of the finance, banking and oil and gas on the planet; and today they DO control it all: which includes the World Bank, the IMF, ECB and all the rest of it. Hey, you think I jest. You can verify and check all of this data for yourself if you want and care to.

You WILL find it to be true.

These ruling families, who run plant Earth today, have the most complex and intricate and confusing corporate, financial and banking set-up that has ever existed on Earth today. It would take a group of experts at least six months to work it all out and find out who owns what, who gets what and the sum total of their profits; and their total monitory worth. This would be in terms of trillions or even quadrillions; and they are not on the top worldwide richest list because they want to remain unknown, secret and working in the background – undetected. Why so WE will not be able to detect and identify them and be able to find out who the fuck is fucking us up the ass and fucking up this lovely planet we live on.

Personally, I do not give a fuck if they kill me for writing this book or not! They brought what they ARE going to get in retribution on themselves. And they ARE 1000% going to get it!!! That I promise you! They know it. Greece, Ireland and the rest of the good people in the EEC countries know it (well they do now! And so does the rest of the world!) The USA knows it. And so do many other countries. They can kill me and if they do, I will come back and haunt the mother fuckers and make sure their lives are Hell and they DO NOT achieve their goals: which is either all Mankind in slavery to them or a Mankind that does not exist anymore and has been wiped out and so has planet Earth with it. You think I am joking – I am not. This is what is at stake and how far I am willing to go. How far are YOU, the person reading my little big book here, willing to go for freedom, happiness and a new world and a new tomorrow for yourselves and your children? Well that is what is at stake here and that is the trillion-dollar question which every single one of us has to answer right now? Not next year but ***NOW***!!!!!????

We CAN put them down or put them in jail; or force them to change and be good to us – if that is at all possible? But, we have to act NOW and get this job done or we are done. They mean business and have done so for hundreds if not thousands of years. And now, I think, it is OUR TIME to take the reins of our own destiny into our own hands – NOT theirs!!!! Now I think that sounds like a good idea. And, it is not just something to consider lightly or to shove under the carpet or ignore (at yours and everyone else's peril). It is yours and all of Mankind's future and destiny that is at stake here. I AM NOT JOKING with you on this. Please believe and trust me on this. I am on your side and with YOU on this – not them. It is US against THEM, and that is how it is. The endless tail and battle of Good Vs Evil. Our Spirits, Souls, Minds and Bodies and our future Eternity and happiness are all at risk. No farce. Not fiction. No Sunday matinee. I give it to you straight. Question is: can you take it, accept it, understand it and believe in, have faith in and trust what I am communicating? And can you handle it and decide to do WHATEVER it takes to get the job done. Now, that IS where it is at, right here, right now, on planet Earth today. Are you in or are you out?

Even if you just want to do whatever it takes to just look after yourself and number one only and not give a damn about anyone else; I don't care. Whatever reasons you may have for coming on board, I don't really care, just as long as you are on board, on the right side and helping us and our new cause to make a difference and to get and keep us free and to make this world and planet a much better place than what it presently is!? If you and we can do and achieve that, then I will be happy, and so will you: and we will be free and so will our children and their future children:)

Some pictures for you:

http://en.wikipedia.org/wiki/Nikola_Tesla#mediaviewer/File:Tesla_colorado_adjusted.jpg in public domain as published before 1923

Tesla at work

http://en.wikipedia.org/wiki/Nikola_Tesla#mediaviewer/File:Tesla_Broadcast_Tower_1904.jpeg in public domain as published before 1923

Tesla's **wireless electricity transmission** tower: 1904
You should check out some of Tesla's free patents online: here are some:

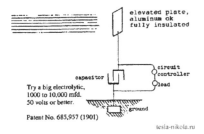

Was a patent, now in public domain.
Free energy from space with this!
No copyright. Now in public domain.

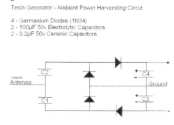

John Searl's free energy generator

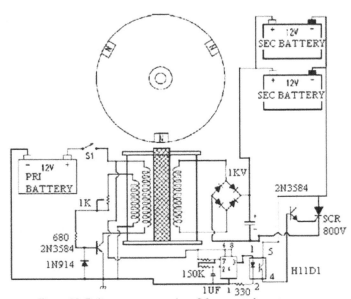

Figure. 18. Radiant energy powering of the monopole motor.

from patent in public domain

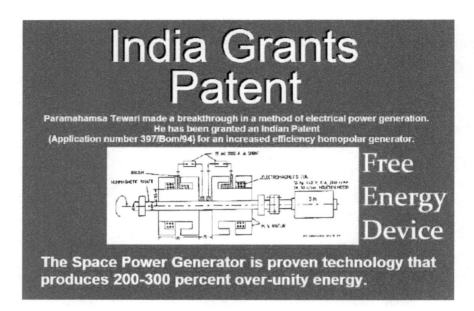

Tewari

Interior of Searl Levity Disc, showing magnetic rings and rods.

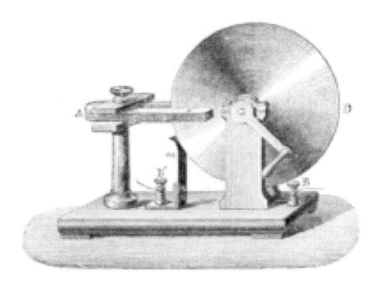

Howard Johnson: U.S. Patent No. 4,151,431 in public domain

http://commons.wikimedia.org/wiki/File:Faraday_disk_generator.jpg In Public Domain as published prior to 1923 copyright expired

Michael Faraday's DC Generating Disk which led to Bruce DePalma's 'N' Machine and others.

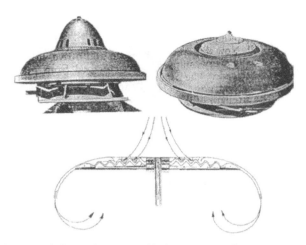

http://www.sciencebadger.com/hollow-earth-cover/ in public domain no copyright

Viktor Schauberger's Flying Saucer Model (using Vortex Air power)

All of these inventors and their inventions, plus many many more are all out there and on the internet, plus there are many books and patents available for anyone to check. Please check these out for yourself. We all need to know this data and be able to think with it to some extent. Why? So someone or a special few (our children or some college or Uni student) can come along and develop, create, invent this new free, safe energy technology and super-faster-than-speed of light speeds for space travel!

Sure Tesla and others were capturing totally free energy from outer space and/or from planet Earth itself (magnetic flux forces, etc.) and they were hellbent on giving it all to Mankind for free or at least for a one-off price, with a manual, spare parts and maintenance. And sadly, they were all either stopped, murdered or bought off. And so we all drive slow vehicles, powered by diesel (he was murdered for inventing the diesel engine!), petrol/gas or other forms: Ethanol, Hydrogen, Electric, gas, etc. And meanwhile the Mother Fuckers running this planet laugh all the way to their own banks and keep us all down, held back and suppressed. How nice of them. Their time is coming! I promise you that my friends. And I promise that to them too. Why because they need help too. Much more than you or I. They are the ones who should be in the mental asylums; getting their own Electric Shock treatment, Psychiatric Drugs and all the rest of their so-called mental treatments they sell or enforce on us. But, whatever the method – they need and MUST be stopped for their and our sakes. This I promise. And so must you. (do you see that I am inviting you to participate in something more than just: bills, mortgage, sex, food, cars, holidays, shopping and all of those regular, mundane stuff we are involved in every day: whether we like it or not. They are a part of life yes. But they are not number one. No! I am asking you to think beyond these transient and less important issues. I am asking you to think of ALL of Mankind, think of yourself, think of others, think of ALL life on planet Earth; think of your soul, your future [Oh you maybe do not believe in it. But YOU exist after your body dies. I promise you that with both hands on my heart. Look at those people on their deathbeds or waiting to die. Do they want to die. No they don't. And most would give up all their wealth and material possessions to live another 10 or 20 years in relatively good health so they continue to exist and be with their friends, families, loved ones; and achieve maybe more of their goals and purposes. Look at all those Rock/Pop stars and actors/actresses – they know they are getting old and do not look as good as they used to. They, most of them anyway, unless they have a secret death wish (which they do not even know about themselves), would give anything to look younger and at least be able to live longer so to be able to at least have an OK and functional body with which they can continue to create and do their arts. But if they and everyone else on this planet knew for real that _**only**_ the body dies then no-one would be worried about dying. But most are. **YOU** do not die as a spiritual being or soul! I know lots of people believe and have faith in this but they do not 100% know it is true and have not experienced it for themselves before they die. Hence, this is an unknown and a trap for all. This is not a good state of affairs to be in and it is something which needs to be addressed and resolved ASAP, as along as everything else in this book, this can be a factor which keeps man down and could be his downfall. As, if one thinks one is only a body and when it dies, that is the end of one: then one could feel inclined to do and think whatever one wants; without any risk or liabilities. And one would not believe in God or anything else in the afterlife. But, sadly, then one can be controlled and made eternally a slave, and also, because one is just an individual, not really caring too much about the other parts of life; but mainly thinking of oneself most or all of the time. That, sadly, _**IS**_ the state Man is in today whether he knows it or not. But I am sure, deepdown, he does know this to be true!)

Isn't it about time we got a new super breed of inventor to come along - another Tesla or two - and propel Mankind into the Star Age; Free Power and Energy age - but that will only happen if we sort out the Powers-That-Be, as they do not want this technology to come out (except for the Military, which has, I am certain, been using this technology for many years? I heard a story once, that when they first landed on the Moon, people were already there and they had super spacecraft. This was probably on the dark side of the Moon. And the dark side of Moon was all blown up eons ago, which is why the same side of the Moon always faces Earth) And, our educational systems need to corrected too, with proper study and teaching methods and the 'correct' factual data being thought.

THE THEORY OF ALL

I recently saw this film and I wrote this straight after.

The Theory of all:

Hawkings, Einstein, etc.: they have all TRIED to find the answer to the allness of all and have, for the most part, failed. Why? Because they, and most of the mathematicians and Physicists, etc., have failed to embrace the laws, truths and facts of the Spiritual Universe: or that of Gods, gods and Spiritual Beings. They exclude this in all of their formulas and equations and the zero symbol has been sitting right there in front of their faces all this time and they have been using it all this time but for different reasons. The zero symbol also happens to be a circle. Folly really. It has always been: WHO, WHY, WHEN and HOW? This is the ultimate age old question and puzzle to be solved. But it is an easy solvable question if one thinks beyond formulas, equations and trying to solve things only in terms of the Physical Universe, mathematics, Physics and symbiology.

Pure simplicity but also other quite esoteric knowledge and personal experience were the key to solving this ultimate truth. To try and make it more complicated than what it is, is folly and stupidity and will lead one down the wrong path.

So, the Ultimate truth - which _IS_ the supreme fact and law of all – the truth of all truths, the highest one there is: it has no senior or equal: is =>

O -----> ●

The black dot represents everything and anything which is outside of or not part of the O.

O means a nothingness which is not a somethingness in terms of the Physical Universe. It means God/s or god/s or Spiritual Being/s and anything connected with it which is not Physical. It also means that which is at Cause and that which is not physical but which exists independent of the physical universe or any universe (there is quite probably more than one universe. This is just the one that we are in at this time and we may actually be in many at the same time without even being aware of it. But this I cannot confirm or prove at this time as I am in this Physical Universe now too, just as you are. Not I am not nuts; but this is just food for thought.

One cannot say: O = Everything Physical. This is not correct. But everything Physical or non-physical (which includes any other type of Universe including the Spiritual Universe) all come from this source, which is O. Basically anything outside of oneself as a Spiritual Being is created and caused by oneself or another or other Spiritual Beings. This is done by thought or thinking or postulating (self-created truth) something and then it is so. You make it so. Anything inside oneself is O.

Most of us cannot do this now but in the past we could. But we are still at Cause in our lives and we cause things in this and other ways. But many people have just decided to win the lottery; they buy one or a few tickets; and they win. This is almost instant. Or a man sees a woman, decides there and then that he wants her as his girlfriend or wife. And next thing you know, he is talking to her or she to him or he bumps into her sometime again in the near future and Wham-Bam, he gets the girl and hopefully lives happily ever after. So there are gradient scales of this CAUSATION, just like a thermometer. There are gradient scales of anything really. Another example of this is what you cause in your mind – your thoughts, the pictures you see. You are creating them. Did you know that? Well this is an example of a Spiritual Being O (which is you) creating something Physical ● or something non-physical, which can be shown as O ----> O (this represents your mental thoughts or pictures or something you create which is not physical).

O is that which is CAUSE; that which produces EFFECTS and that which also receives EFFECTS. It is that ENTITY or SPIRIT which is aware of itself and can cause things by thought, action, energy or force. And its abilities and powers have no limits (but they can and do decrease). O is not made of anything physical which is why Spirits or ghosts can go through walls.

O -------> ● is a precise and unlimited definition.

O means CAUSE. ● means EFFECT or anything caused or created by O, good or bad. As you can see ● comes from O which is quite amazing!!!

Then we can have the EFFECT becoming a CAUSE to the first CAUSE, which is:

O <-----------> ●

This is causing something or something being caused which then causes something to or on oneself; another; others or to something else.

And one can have:

O <-----------> O and ● <-----------> ●

These various interactions thus become the LIFE and Universe we have. If one looks in the mirror, then one will see that YOU are the CAUSE (maybe not of everything but most of it. But one is obviously being affected by other causes too: for example, a government creates a new tax and there is no referendum on this tax and if you don't pay the tax, you go to jail. A nice EFFECT being imposed on us. We did not cause this ourselves but in another way we did; because we allowed a government to be set up which we have little control over) and one causes EFFECTS and then one has these EFFECTS become a CAUSE on oneself, which one usually wants, as they are perceived as being good and desirable: for example: eating food, sex, love, possessions, money, etc... YOU are not your body or your mind even though you may feel that you are!

This is the equation or formula or more correctly the EXPLANATION of <u>ALL</u> life and all possible Universes that may or will exist. Even that which is not of this Physical Universe. One cannot just be a ONE or a O and have, be and do nothing else and be all alone. NO, this is the acceptable theory and equation of life and living whether one has a body or not. Just being ONE does not suffice. There ALWAYS must be at least TWO of anything, something (alive or not) or another Spiritual Being; otherwise one is alone and eventually one goes insane or becomes sad or just ceases to exist anymore: which is possible.

O is also ∞, which is infinity but this is conditional as a GOD, Supreme Being or a Spiritual Being can descend down so low as to almost not exist or be aware any more. It most probably is also possible for one to be completely destroyed or made to not exist anymore either by oneself or by another. This rarely happens but I believe it is possible. So apart from this conditional point, O is infinite and has infinity. Question: What is one going to do with it?

This is **_NOT_** a theory like the one Einstein and Hawkings tried to prove or formulate. This is fact. This is the Ultimate Truth! There is no other higher truth than what I have told you above. This solves the allness of all. It solves every question you may have and it solves every theory, problem, equation and formulae. It is senior to everything and anything! You add this O in to any formula, equation, problem or theory or question that can be posed, and it can be solved. Maybe not straight away: as this depends on the person (O) trying to solve these or the available data. This – that which I have given you above has no senior laws or truths, formulas or equations. This is the NUMBER ONE truth in existence. You can try and find a more senior one and you will not. This also equates to that age old saying of: take a look in the mirror and see who is there and who is at cause: it is YOU! O is you and every one of us; not our bodies or minds.

The only unanswerable question I have not fully 1000% found an answer to is: Was there a first GOD/s or Supreme Being/s or Spiritual Beings or have we, as Spiritual Beings, always been in existence since before the beginning of time or was there just one big Supreme Being who was lonely and then decided to make other GODS or Supreme Beings, who could then make other spiritual beings like us (with or without bodies) and thus, the entire Spiritual Universe and Physical Universe become populated too (we are not alone: there are many, many other races and alien forms out there despite what you may think. It is NOT fiction, I promise you that but we don't need to concern ourselves about this at this time) and thus the allness of all came to be created.

The answer to the above question does not need to be answered at this point in time, as it does not change the fact of what is and that we are what we are.

No big bang made us all and everything in this Universe. Maybe a part of this Universe, say a galaxy was made like this but not all of it. And, as I said before, even if this was the case; there must have been something created in order for it to be exploded and thus there was an ENTITY or ENTITIES or a O in existence first in order to make that something => Somethingness does not just appear from nothingness or out of thin air or from empty space. A CAUSE had to create it. And since O is not physical or a somethingness; it cannot be created by something physical or otherwise. I know this is hard to comprehend when one has a body all the time and when one is told lies and fed crap from various sources from when one is born. But trust me: the above is TRUTH!

The above data answers and solves any and all questions, formulas, puzzles, equations and theories that have, do and will ever exist. It answers, solves and explains the past, present and future. It also solves and explains and delivers power and knowledge to YOU as Spiritual Being, with or without a body.

This resolves **YOU**. It resolves **LIFE**. It resolves the Physical Universes and any other possible Universes. It solves all those imponderable questions those scientists, physicists, mathematicians and philosophers have asked since the beginning of time, and I do not just mean just this planet. I do not think we are native to this planet. DO you think 'Stargate, Star Wars and Star Trek' are 100% entirely fiction? They are not! We come from somewhere else. And those black holes out there go to and from different places – different parts of the Physical Universe – or even to other Universes. I will not say any more on this than that. This is hard to believe or understand when one has a body and has forgotten one's past lives. Mankind needs to broaden his knowledge and point of view. It is TOO limited. He needs to take his blinkers off! Mankind has descended so far down that he does not realize he is **O** anymore. People say 'I' but most do not know what 'I' is. And most people who do believe they are a spirit or soul, still do not know what it is.

But then Mankind always wants proof. Well, sometimes there isn't any or at least any that can be provided at this point in time. But if you look deep inside yourself, you will know that the above IS true! People believe in God and other things and they have had little or no proof, right? The only way one would know this truth would be to be able to be outside of one's body. And I don't mean astral projection or mind games but be spiritually 100% outside of one's body and able to perceive and sense one's body and other things around one. Then one would know and not just have blind faith. And when one has done this one would never be the same again. And it is nothing to be scared about.

I hope this knowledge will help you all and those who look for the answers and truth. There is no more higher truth than this. If you find one, then let me know. And Prof. Hawkings, Prof. Brian Cox and any anyone else can contact or question me about this. But the other major problem Mankind has, is that he is only aware of and can usually only accept that which is acceptable to him and that which he can comprehend and understand at any given time. Anything outside of his comfort zone is usually rejected and attacked even if it is true: witness Galileo, Darwin, Jesus and many more. But now their beliefs, discoveries and findings are broadly accepted around the world. Sometimes there is not always proof or immediate proof. And if one was able to exist without a body or be outside one's body, with full perception, then one would at least know that one was a Spiritual Being, which is worth more than all the money and wealth in existence.

I hope this helps YOU and it is for you to use as you wish. I give it freely. It WILL set Man free. And it doesn't mean either, that one can do as one wishes as one knows one is immortal and cannot die. There are repercussions, good and bad, to everything we do! And this could set you free too if one can see beyond the limitations of the body you now have; and the knowledge you now possess. I wish the scientists, mathematicians and Physicists would stop ignoring this truth as there is nothing senior to it and it resolves all that they want to solve!!!!!!?????

WHO ARE THE POWERS-THAT-BE AND WHO REALLY RUNS THIS PLANET?

http://fellowshipoftheminds.com/2011/02/19/the-satanic-rothschild/ in public domain

Oh, we have drug dealers and criminals; but they are very, very petty and VERY small compared to the really sick assholes who are running, ruining and guiding Mankind to either total destruction, or total slavery, domination and control by THEM, their Minions (Government and Country leaders, Presidents, Prime Ministers, Ruling and Royal Families, including those in Russia and China) and their Technocrats, Scientists, wonderful Psychiatrists and Psychologists; CIA, FBI, NSA, FDA, Bank of England (which used to be privately owned by the Rothschilds [can you believe this?]) is now part composed of a limited company of which the shareholders are secret: Bank of England Nominees Limited), Federal Reserve Bank of the USA (which also used to be privately owned by the Rockefeller Family, is now still run by them and from which they get their commissions and all the rest of their underhanded dealings); the IMF, G8 & G20, ECB, [NOTE: the Rothschilds financed and got Communism in; they got Israel given to the Jews (even though they really do not give a damn about the Jews: but just want to finance the arms and war and take over the world] by the British and the UN. I have nothing against Jews but it was nice of them to take or be given land which was not theirs (which they lost a very long time ago in biblical times), and which actually belongs to Palestine, and give it to Jews who did not legally own it?], Global Security Fund, The World Bank, most (if not all) of the Banks and Finance Houses on the planet, Drug Companies, Street Drug Supply & Operations (run by the CIA/FBI and other covert Op groups), all the Oil and Gas Companies, Arms Manufacturing Companies and all the rest of the agencies, Foundations, Charities (do you think all this charity money and International Aid goes to where it is meant to go? Ha!), Organizations, companies and Multi-nationals they own and control (either openly or secretly); and of course our GPs and Doctors have a hand in this too, because they prescribe their wonderful cure-all drugs after being fed false data by their salesmen for years.

Well, who are these big, super-powerful, super-rich, super-evil and ultra-callous people and their families, who have been operating – unbeknown to most of us for hundreds, if not thousands of years (since before the times of the Bible?)

I will tell you.

Maybe you have already guessed who they are? Or you have read or heard about them? Or you already know who they are. But factually and truthfully (you don't need to wonder if it is true or not any more) the **_real_** enemies of Mankind factually are: and this **_IS_** fact, not fiction or a theory:

The Rockefellers and the Rothschilds!

And the rest who work with or for them.
Source: http://theglobalelite.org/globalists/

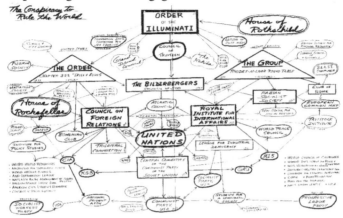

http://www.navigate3d.no/mbbs22/forums/thread-view.asp?tid=1762 no copyright

The Families
(In order of importance)
Rothschild family (writer: second place now)
Warburg family
Schiff family
Oppenheimer family
Royal Family of England
Saxe-Coburg-Gotha family
Rockefeller family (Writer: first place now!)
Morgan family
Harriman family
Carnegie family
Owners of the Federal Reserve –

Rothschild Banks of London and Berlin
Lazard Brothers Bank of Paris
Israel Moses Sieff Bank of Italy
Warburg Batiks of Hamburg and Amsterdam
Lehman Brothers Bank of New York
Kuhn Loeb Bank of New York

Chase Manhattan Bank of New York (controlled by the Rockefellers)
Goldman Sachs Bank of New York

Bilderberg Group

This list of Bilderberg Group members is according to the country of origin of the individual member, in order of the country with the most participants. Note the last "country", which is actually "all countries" as it is International, which includes members/participants that cannot be assigned to just one country. Also note, the very last entry, as he is perhaps the most influential of all, considering he represents of the influence of the Rothschilds, Rockefellers and other international banking moguls. His name is, Robert B. Zoellick, President of The World Bank, representing the interests of Group Rothschild Banks of London and Berlin, Lazard Brothers Bank of Paris, Israel Moses Sieff Bank of Italy, Warburg Batiks of Hamburg and Amsterdam, Lehman Brothers Bank of New York, Kuhn Loeb Bank of New York, Chase Manhattan Bank of New York (controlled by the Rockefellers), Goldman Sachs Bank of New York. Notice, there are no participants from China Japan or Korea, which are some of the most economically powerful nations on earth. Could it be that the Bilderberg Group is prejudice? Or is it, that they are planning something meant only for people of a certain ethnic background? Or of a certain religion?

SOURCE: https://www.infowars.com/bilderberg-2017-agenda-participants-revealed/

Bilderberg 2017 (June 1-4) Attendee List at Chantilly, Virginia

CHAIRMAN
Castries, Henri de (FRA), Former Chairman and CEO, AXA; President of Institut Montaigne

PARTICIPANTS
Achleitner, Paul M. (DEU), Chairman of the Supervisory Board, Deutsche Bank AG
Adonis, Andrew (GBR), Chair, National Infrastructure Commission
Agius, Marcus (GBR), Chairman, PA Consulting Group
Akyol, Mustafa (TUR), Senior Visiting Fellow, Freedom Project at Wellesley College

Alstadheim, Kjetil B. (NOR), Political Editor, Dagens Næringsliv
Altman, Roger C. (USA), Founder and Senior Chairman, Evercore
Arnaut, José Luis (PRT), Managing Partner, CMS Rui Pena & Arnaut
Barroso, José M. Durão (PRT), Chairman, Goldman Sachs International
Bäte, Oliver (DEU), CEO, Allianz SE
Baumann, Werner (DEU), Chairman, Bayer AG
Baverez, Nicolas (FRA), Partner, Gibson, Dunn & Crutcher
Benko, René (AUT), Founder and Chairman of the Advisory Board, SIGNA Holding GmbH
Berner, Anne-Catherine (FIN), Minister of Transport and Communications
Botín, Ana P. (ESP), Executive Chairman, Banco Santander
Brandtzæg, Svein Richard (NOR), President and CEO, Norsk Hydro ASA
Brennan, John O. (USA), Senior Advisor, Kissinger Associates Inc.
Bsirske, Frank (DEU), Chairman, United Services Union
Buberl, Thomas (FRA), CEO, AXA
Bunn, M. Elaine (USA), Former Deputy Assistant Secretary of Defense
Burns, William J. (USA), President, Carnegie Endowment for International Peace
Çakiroglu, Levent (TUR), CEO, Koç Holding A.S.
Çamlibel, Cansu (TUR), Washington DC Bureau Chief, Hürriyet Newspaper
Cebrián, Juan Luis (ESP), Executive Chairman, PRISA and El País
Clemet, Kristin (NOR), CEO, Civita
Cohen, David S. (USA), Former Deputy Director, CIA
Collison, Patrick (USA), CEO, Stripe
Cotton, Tom (USA), Senator
Cui, Tiankai (CHN), Ambassador to the US
Döpfner, Mathias (DEU), CEO, Axel Springer SE
Elkann, John (ITA), Chairman, Fiat Chrysler Automobiles
Enders, Thomas (DEU), CEO, Airbus SE
Federspiel, Ulrik (DNK), Group Executive, Haldor Topsøe Holding A/S
Ferguson, Jr., Roger W. (USA), President and CEO, TIAA
Ferguson, Niall (USA), Senior Fellow, Hoover Institution, Stanford University
Gianotti, Fabiola (ITA), Director General, CERN
Gozi, Sandro (ITA), State Secretary for European Affairs

Graham, Lindsey (USA), Senator

Greenberg, Evan G. (USA), Chairman and CEO, Chubb Group

Griffin, Kenneth (USA), Founder and CEO, Citadel Investment Group, LLC

Gruber, Lilli (ITA), Editor-in-Chief and Anchor "Otto e mezzo", La7 TV

Guindos, Luis de (ESP), Minister of Economy, Industry and Competiveness

Haines, Avril D. (USA), Former Deputy National Security Advisor

Halberstadt, Victor (NLD), Professor of Economics, Leiden University

Hamers, Ralph (NLD), Chairman, ING Group

Hedegaard, Connie (DNK), Chair, KR Foundation

Hennis-Plasschaert, Jeanine (NLD), Minister of Defence, The Netherlands

Hobson, Mellody (USA), President, Ariel Investments LLC

Hoffman, Reid (USA), Co-Founder, LinkedIn and Partner, Greylock

Houghton, Nicholas (GBR), Former Chief of Defence

Ischinger, Wolfgang (INT), Chairman, Munich Security Conference

Jacobs, Kenneth M. (USA), Chairman and CEO, Lazard

Johnson, James A. (USA), Chairman, Johnson Capital Partners

Jordan, Jr., Vernon E. (USA), Senior Managing Director, Lazard Frères & Co. LLC

Karp, Alex (USA), CEO, Palantir Technologies

Kengeter, Carsten (DEU), CEO, Deutsche Börse AG

Kissinger, Henry A. (USA), Chairman, Kissinger Associates Inc.

Klatten, Susanne (DEU), Managing Director, SKion GmbH

Kleinfeld, Klaus (USA), Former Chairman and CEO, Arconic

Knot, Klaas H.W. (NLD), President, De Nederlandsche Bank

Koç, Ömer M. (TUR), Chairman, Koç Holding A.S.

Kotkin, Stephen (USA), Professor in History and International Affairs, Princeton University

Kravis, Henry R. (USA), Co-Chairman and Co-CEO, KKR

Kravis, Marie-Josée (USA), Senior Fellow, Hudson Institute

Kudelski, André (CHE), Chairman and CEO, Kudelski Group

Lagarde, Christine (INT), Managing Director, International Monetary Fund

Lenglet, François (FRA), Chief Economics Commentator, France 2

Leysen, Thomas (BEL), Chairman, KBC Group

Liddell, Christopher (USA), Assistant to the President and Director of

Strategic Initiatives
Lööf, Annie (SWE), Party Leader, Centre Party
Mathews, Jessica T. (USA), Distinguished Fellow, Carnegie Endowment for International Peace
McAuliffe, Terence (USA), Governor of Virginia
McKay, David I. (CAN), President and CEO, Royal Bank of Canada
McMaster, H.R. (USA), National Security Advisor
Mexia, António Luís Guerra Nunes (PRT), President, Eurelectric and CEO, EDP Energias de Portugal
Micklethwait, John (INT), Editor-in-Chief, Bloomberg LP
Minton Beddoes, Zanny (INT), Editor-in-Chief, The Economist
Molinari, Maurizio (ITA), Editor-in-Chief, La Stampa
Monaco, Lisa (USA), Former Homeland Security Officer
Morneau, Bill (CAN), Minister of Finance
Mundie, Craig J. (USA), President, Mundie & Associates
Murtagh, Gene M. (IRL), CEO, Kingspan Group plc
Netherlands, H.M. the King of the (NLD)
Noonan, Peggy (USA), Author and Columnist, The Wall Street Journal
O'Leary, Michael (IRL), CEO, Ryanair D.A.C.
Osborne, George (GBR), Editor, London Evening Standard
Papahelas, Alexis (GRC), Executive Editor, Kathimerini Newspaper
Papalexopoulos, Dimitri (GRC), CEO, Titan Cement Co.
Petraeus, David H. (USA), Chairman, KKR Global Institute
Pind, Søren (DNK), Minister for Higher Education and Science
Puga, Benoît (FRA), Grand Chancellor of the Legion of Honor and Chancellor of the National Order of Merit
Rachman, Gideon (GBR), Chief Foreign Affairs Commentator, The Financial Times
Reisman, Heather M. (CAN), Chair and CEO, Indigo Books & Music Inc.
Rivera Díaz, Albert (ESP), President, Ciudadanos Party
Rosén, Johanna (SWE), Professor in Materials Physics, Linköping University
Ross, Wilbur L. (USA), Secretary of Commerce
Rubenstein, David M. (USA), Co-Founder and Co-CEO, The Carlyle Group
Rubin, Robert E. (USA), Co-Chair, Council on Foreign Relations and Former Treasury Secretary

Ruoff, Susanne (CHE), CEO, Swiss Post
Rutten, Gwendolyn (BEL), Chair, Open VLD
Sabia, Michael (CAN), CEO, Caisse de dépôt et placement du Québec
Sawers, John (GBR), Chairman and Partner, Macro Advisory Partners
Schadlow, Nadia (USA), Deputy Assistant to the President, National Security Council
Schmidt, Eric E. (USA), Executive Chairman, Alphabet Inc.
Schneider-Ammann, Johann N. (CHE), Federal Councillor, Swiss Confederation
Scholten, Rudolf (AUT), President, Bruno Kreisky Forum for International Dialogue
Severgnini, Beppe (ITA), Editor-in-Chief, 7-Corriere della Sera
Sikorski, Radoslaw (POL), Senior Fellow, Harvard University
Slat, Boyan (NLD), CEO and Founder, The Ocean Cleanup
Spahn, Jens (DEU), Parliamentary State Secretary and Federal Ministry of Finance
Stephenson, Randall L. (USA), Chairman and CEO, AT&T
Stern, Andrew (USA), President Emeritus, SEIU and Senior Fellow, Economic Security Project
Stoltenberg, Jens (INT), Secretary General, NATO
Summers, Lawrence H. (USA), Charles W. Eliot University Professor, Harvard University
Tertrais, Bruno (FRA), Deputy Director, Fondation pour la recherche stratégique
Thiel, Peter (USA), President, Thiel Capital
Topsøe, Jakob Haldor (DNK), Chairman, Haldor Topsøe Holding A/S
Ülgen, Sinan (TUR), Founding and Partner, Istanbul Economics
Vance, J.D. (USA), Author and Partner, Mithril
Wahlroos, Björn (FIN), Chairman, Sampo Group, Nordea Bank, UPM-Kymmene Corporation
Wallenberg, Marcus (SWE), Chairman, Skandinaviska Enskilda Banken AB
Walter, Amy (USA), Editor, The Cook Political Report
Weston, Galen G. (CAN), CEO and Executive Chairman, Loblaw Companies Ltd and George Weston Companies
White, Sharon (GBR), Chief Executive, Ofcom
Wieseltier, Leon (USA), Isaiah Berlin Senior Fellow in Culture and Policy, The Brookings Institution

Wolf, Martin H. (INT), Chief Economics Commentator, Financial Times
Wolfensohn, James D. (USA), Chairman and CEO, Wolfensohn &
Company
Wunsch, Pierre (BEL), Vice-Governor, National Bank of Belgium
Zeiler, Gerhard (AUT), President, Turner International
Zients, Jeffrey D. (USA), Former Director, National Economic Council
Zoellick, Robert B. (USA), Non-Executive Chairman, AllianceBernstein

Now we have: The **Rockefeller** Family (multi-trillionaires), led by **David Rockefeller**, the patriarch of the family that runs the world, with the other leading families: The Rothschilds being the other main one. David Rockefeller Jr; is heir.

As far as I know, David Rockefeller had his other brothers killed or murdered: Winthrop in 1973, John D. III in 1978, Nelson in 1979, and Laurence in 2004, so there was no competition. He is basically supreme leader of Earth, and with the help of the Rothschilds and all the other connected families, runs the show and pulls all the strings behind the scenes in all or most countries around the planet – FACT!!! Jim Marr's book 'Rule by Secrecy' gives plenty more info and data on the Rockefellers and the other ruling families.

I did mention before that the USA was an experiment orchestrated many years ago [going back to colonial times]; so was Communism in Russia and China. Now he/they want the world to be all of the same blueprint; which will pave the way for a New World Order (and one of their order not ours, I must add) – and a New World that we will either be forced to accept or we will be duped into accepting it but later we will see we were wrong for supporting and accepting it. And it will not be the New World that we want: NO! It will be how He above and the rest of his cohorts and families want it.

If you check out or read: The book: **13 Bloodlines of the Illuminati by Freitz Springmeier** you will get a very good idea of what I am talking about.

In his book you will learn about the Illuminati dynasties and:

Who really controls world events from behind-the-scene?

And the secretive, Chinese Li family, which operates with impunity in the U.S.A. and around the world.

Along the way you'll find out:

why President John F. Kennedy and actress Grace Kelly were killed
who created the United Nations
who controls the two major U.S. political parties
how the Rothschilds invented and control modern-day Israel
who secretly founded false religions such as the Jehovah's Witnesses

Etc....

You will discover the amazing role these bloodlines have played - and are now wielding - in human history, with family names such as:

The Contents are:

The Astor Bloodline
The Bundy Bloodline
The Collins Bloodline
The DuPont Bloodline
The Freeman Bloodline
The Kennedy Bloodline
The Li Bloodline
The Onassis Bloodline
The Reynolds Bloodline
The Rockefeller Bloodline
The Rothschild Bloodline
The Russell Bloodline
The Van Duyn Bloodline
Merovingian (European Royal Families)
The Top 13 Families & The Mormon Leadership (Moriah & The Mormon Leadership)

Interconnected families:

Disney - Uno de Los Mayores Engaños de Todos los Tiempos
The Disney Bloodline
The Krupp Bloodline

362

The McDonald Bloodline

Related Reports

13 Illuminati Bloodlines and Mind Control
Alex Jones' Interview "Bloodlines of The Illuminati" Author Fritz
Springmeier - **2011**
CFR - Council on Foreign Relations
Estos Mataron a Kennedy! - Reportaje, A Un Golpe De Estado
Kennedy and The Nazis
Merovingios - Los Reyes Perdidos
New World Order
Rockefeller Internationalism
Teflón - 'Only by DuPont' **(Solo por DuPont)**
The Biggest Secret - **The Book**
The Bilderberg Group
The Biological Basis of Elitism and "The Divine Right" Rule
The House of Rothschild
The Majestic Project / MJ-12
The Illuminati Formula to Create an Undetectable Total Mind Control Slave
The Trilateral Commission
Basically, there are 13 Satanic bloodlines that rule the world. The Rockefeller bloodline is one of them.

I would strongly advise anyone to read this book and the other books that I have mentioned in my book as you will get tons of data and you will be amazed and shocked at what has been going on behind the scenes and closed doors for many years!

Rockefeller's principal residence is at "Hudson Pines", on the family estate in Westchester County, New York. He also has a Manhattan residence at East 65th Street, as well as a country residence (known as "Four Winds") at a farm in Livingston, New York (Columbia County). He also maintains a summer home on Mount Desert Island off the Maine coast.

As you now know, The Rockefellers own/control most, if not all of the Banks on Earth today – with the Rothschilds: (Chase Manhattan and many others); Drug Companies (worldwide including Psychiatric and Pharmaceutical drugs which they would love every human to be taking as they are so wonderful and cure everything and then everyone can be controlled and mentally and spiritually fucked-up); Street Drugs (they control all drug trafficking worldwide in collusion with the Mafia and the Governments) – check out the Harrison Act of 1914?; despite what the Media, Police and Governments say to the contrary [as they pretty much control every Government and country on the planet, their Leaders, NATO, United Nations and all the rest, including Armies and Arms Manufacturing]; Oil and Gas (they own and run nearly every Oil Company on the planet) and they do their secret deals with our wonderful Governments; our Leaders and Heads of State (who get commissions, backhanders and other favours and rewards for their dirty work: witness Tony Blair, Bush and Clinton for example; but they were already groomed and handpicked for their positions well before they even got elected. They were created just like Hitler).

> **Note: See appendix 1** at the end of this book to see how people like Hitler were created. This details the Project MK-Ultra and the Monarch Program – but this is not for the faint hearted! It is not for children or teenagers! This part of my book is just for adults and even then, I would be cautious! This could make you sick, so be warned! This is basically using Drug Hypnotics; Deep Sleep Therapy and Pain-Drug Hypnosis, which have been employed since World War II. But the data and facts on this are something everyone should know about as it has been in use and variations of it, and other similar human/ mind 'control' and 'adjustment' programs for many years. It is more common and widespread than you may think and sadly, most of those who have had it, do not even know it! And the extent of it I do not know, but I am sure it is far-reaching. It is also worth mentioning that L. Ron Hubbard was strongly attacked when he published Dianetics: The Modern Science of Mental Health to the world (after he did extensive and research into the mind and he discovered why Man was behaving the way he was and how to undo these problems of the Mind), in 1950. Why he was attacked, apart from providing the solutions to Man's Unconscious Mind (which affects us all and is working non-stop, 24 hours a day [it is never unconscious by the way), was because he provided a way to undo all of this Monarch, Cover Operations and Spy/Assassination 'mental' treatment brutality. I just

thought I would mention this, because there ARE solutions to Man's mental problems and they do not involve the use of Psychiatric Drugs; deep sleep therapy; shock treatment to the brain or operations on the brain or any other inhumane *'so-called'* cures and treatments. These discoveries of the source of Man's irrational and illogical behavior by L. Ron Hubbard, also lead L. Ron Hubbard to discover and prove the existence of the SOUL. Which, was no mean feat!<

And do not forget that all the money that goes into all of the world's business and personal bank accounts lines the pockets of the Rockefellers, the Rothschilds and the other ruling families that work with them and that also includes their control of most, if not all of the Central Banks in every country and the Bank of England and the Federal Reserve Bank in America. They may not fully own all of these but they either have a majority shareholding in their own names or via some company which they own. But directly or indirectly they are making gazillions every day out of the money we have in their banks! And when you fill your car with diesel or petrol you are also lining their pockets with even more money! How much money do you think these families and all of their companies are making every day, every week from just banking and fuel? That does not include all of their other ventures, crime, drugs and all the rest. People do not get the extent of these families wealth and power. It is immense: they run this planet! If you do not believe me or think this is all conspiracy then you may as well just forget everything I have said and forget you ever read this book and just continue on with your life and hope and pray that Destiny is favourable to us and kindly looking down, because that is all the help we may ever get. And that is a very slim chance indeed, and one I would not bet on. If you are a betting man or woman, then it is always clever to increase the odds of winning. THEY have the odds hugely stacked up in their favour so we need to do the same and change the odds around in OUR favour. More on this later.

Some other notable names involved in all this are:

1) Lord Jacob de Rothschild. 2) His son Nathaniel. 3) Baron John de Rothschild 4) Sir Evelyn de Rothschild 5) David Rockefeller 6) Nathan Warburg 7) Henry Kissinger 8) George Soros 9) Paul Volcker 10) Larry Summers 11) Lloyd Blankfein 12) Ben Shalom

And then we have all the rest who work with them: J.P. Morgan and co; the Warburgs; The Bilderberger Group (it's members and organizations); and those others who run and are in the Illuminati and all their secret other spin-off groups and orders (Freemasons, Brotherhoods, Lodges, etc.). Most of these are Jews or Jesuits (but they just have really invented what they really are at present to suit their own evil nefarious needs and they just take a piece of belief, data, fact, system, philosophy, scientific fact or law or a religion, etc., from here and there and just mould it to suit themselves and their black-hearted goals and intentions); but they even consider themselves above 'normal' Jews, and indeed, they even consider that they are somehow above the rest of Mankind: the chosen few, who are godlike (or even Gods) and the ones who must be and are destined to rule and control all of Mankind and planet Earth. With the sole purpose to rule, control, dominate and keep him enslaved – and they work with and vice versa, all the Royal, Aristocratic, Rich, Ruling, Powerful and wealthy families and individuals on this planet. This is a fact. Most do not get to the top and stay there, without going through them and getting their either OK or co-operation or approval or financial or other help. Fact. If their goals and intensions were good, then all would be well but sadly their intentions are VERY devil-like indeed. (I must add in here that just because a person or company has or can take over the world or country and amass gazillions of money and power, does not make them bad. It is how they got that wealth and power, and more importantly, what are they going to do with it: good or bad? No that is the BIG relevant question on Earth today. I am not against a World Government and World Order: however it must be good and have GOOD, PURE and KIND intentions, and not hoodwink people and the masses with lies and deceit; and keep about 60-70% of us in poverty or low-struggling conditions or suffering, when there is no need for this. And they keep us all ignorant and full of drugs and not in the know. Now that is what I am talking about. Understand?) And, to this end, they have been working toward achieving (with the help of gutless cohort cowards who would not stand up to them or stop them) for countless years; and I have to admit that they are **this** close to attaining their goals – which is the reason I wrote this book! We must act to prevent this – and NOW before we lose our chance for ever more! A photo of the heads of the two families:

Here is some more info on these wonderful families and people:

The Queen of England (the current English royal family is actually German in origin, did you know that? From the House of Hesse and it is claimed they, the UK Royal Family are Freemasons and members of the Illuminati [or definitely connected to them]. I have no clear direct proof of this but it does make one wonder what is really going on?) and the rest or most of the European and World's Royalty and Aristocracy, are well in with them, doing their shadowy shady dealings and investments and looking after **THEIR OWN** interests, not ours I might add – but theirs! They and the Governments of Earth borrow money from THEM for this and that (wars, etc.) and then, WE, the stupid slave/working taxpayers, have to pay it back to THEM (with interest, increased taxes and of course, what always happens from this: INFLATION! Oh, this is so nice for us all – NOT!)

And can I interject here that I am pretty certain that Blair, Bush, Clinton, Obama, etc. all know each other and their families have links and ties. A lot of them have gone to the same schools/universities and are in the same social scene/network. For example – David Cameron - according to an article by The Guardian: David Cameron's family fortune: the Jersey, Panama and Geneva connection Offshore venture in tax haven – named after family home in Aberdeenshire – valued at £25m, Friday 20 April 2012 22.00 BST: 'The family's banking history goes back even further, to the 1860s, when Sir Ewen Cameron joined the industry. He later helped the Rothschild banking dynasty sell war bonds during the Russo-Japanese war...'

Some or most of the top companies in the world are owned or partly owned (or financed) by them (and thus controlled by them). And so are the top banks in the world (and most, if not all of the other banks too). I give a very detailed rundown and history of them here:

SOURCE: http://english.pravda.ru/business/finance/18-10-2011/119355-The_Large_
Families_that_rule_the_world-0/

The Large Families that rule the world

Some people have started realizing that there are large financial groups that dominate the world. Forget the political intrigues, conflicts, revolutions and wars. It is not pure chance. Everything has been planned for a long time. Some call it "conspiracy theories" or New World Order. Anyway, the key to understanding the current political and economic events is a restricted core of families who have accumulated more wealth and power.

We are speaking of 6, 8 or maybe 12 families who truly dominate the world. Know that it is a mystery difficult to unravel. We will not be far from the truth by citing Goldman Sachs, Rockefellers, Loebs Kuh and Lehmans in New York, the Rothschilds of Paris and London, the Warburgs of Hamburg, Paris and Lazards Israel Moses Seifs Rome.

The world's largest companies are now: Bank of America, JP Morgan, Citigroup, Wells Fargo, Goldman Sachs and Morgan Stanley. Let us now review who their shareholders are.

Bank of America:

State Street Corporation, Vanguard Group, BlackRock, FMR (Fidelity), Paulson, JP Morgan, T. Rowe, Capital World Investors, AXA, Bank of NY, Mellon.

JP Morgan:

State Street Corp., Vanguard Group, FMR, BlackRock, T. Rowe, AXA, Capital World Investor, Capital Research Global Investor, Northern Trust Corp. and Bank of Mellon.
Citigroup:

State Street Corporation, Vanguard Group, BlackRock, Paulson, FMR, Capital World Investor, JP Morgan, Northern Trust Corporation, Fairhome Capital Mgmt and Bank of NY Mellon.

Wells Fargo:

Berkshire Hathaway, FMR, State Street, Vanguard Group, Capital World Investors, BlackRock, Wellington Mgmt, AXA, T. Rowe and Davis Selected Advisers.

We can see that now there appears to be a nucleus present in all banks: State Street Corporation, Vanguard Group, BlackRock and FMR (Fidelity). To avoid repeating them, we will now call them the "big four"

The eight largest U.S. financial companies (JP Morgan, Wells Fargo, Bank of America, Citigroup, Goldman Sachs, U.S. Bancorp, Bank of New York Mellon and Morgan Stanley) are 100% controlled by ten shareholders and we have four companies always present in all decisions: BlackRock, State Street, Vanguard and Fidelity.

In addition, the Federal Reserve is comprised of 12 banks, represented by a board of seven people, which comprises representatives of the "big four," which in turn are present in all other entities.

In short, the Federal Reserve is controlled by four large private companies: BlackRock, State Street, Vanguard and Fidelity. These companies control U.S. monetary policy (and world) without any control or "democratic" choice. These companies launched and participated in the current worldwide economic crisis and managed to become even more enriched.

In addition, all these people run the large financial institutions, such as the IMF, the European Central Bank or the World Bank, and were "trained" and remain "employees" of the "big four" that formed them.

The names of the families that control the "big four", never appear.

Translated from the Portuguese version by: Lisa Karpova & Pravda.Ru

http://english.pravda.ru/business/finance/18-10-2011/119355-The_Large_Families_that_rule_the_world-0/
I would personally like to thank Dean for giving me permission to include parts of his book in mine. Plus I like how Dean writes and what he has to say! And, just so you know, I included many other writers and articles in this book so you can see the validity and truth of what I say and that I am not writing empty words or talking out my a**:

The Federal Reserve Cartel: The Eight Families

By Dean Henderson
Global Research, June 01, 2011
1 June 2011
Region: USA
Theme: Global Economy, Oil and Energy

(Part one of a four-part series)

The Four Horsemen of Banking (Bank of America, JP Morgan Chase, Citigroup and Wells Fargo) own the Four Horsemen of Oil (Exxon Mobil, Royal Dutch/Shell, BP and Chevron Texaco); in tandem with Deutsche Bank, BNP, Barclays and other European old money behemoths. But their monopoly over the global economy does not end at the edge of the oil patch.

According to company 10K filings to the SEC, the Four Horsemen of Banking are among the top ten stock holders of virtually every

Fortune 500 corporation.[1]

So who then are the stockholders in these money center banks?

This information is guarded much more closely. My queries to bank regulatory agencies regarding stock ownership in the top 25 US bank holding companies were given Freedom of Information Act status, before being denied on "national security" grounds. This is rather ironic, since many of the bank's stockholders reside in Europe.

One important repository for the wealth of the global oligarchy that owns these bank holding companies is US Trust Corporation – founded in 1853 and now owned by Bank of America. A recent US Trust Corporate Director and Honorary Trustee was Walter Rothschild. Other directors included Daniel Davison of JP Morgan Chase, Richard Tucker of Exxon Mobil, Daniel Roberts of Citigroup and Marshall Schwartz of Morgan Stanley. [2]

J. W. McCallister, an oil industry insider with House of Saud connections, wrote in The Grim Reaper that information he acquired from Saudi bankers cited 80% ownership of the New York Federal Reserve Bank- by far the most powerful Fed branch- by just eight families, four of which reside in the US. They are the Goldman Sachs, Rockefellers, Lehmans and Kuhn Loebs of New York; the Rothschilds of Paris and London; the Warburgs of Hamburg; the Lazards of Paris; and the Israel Moses Seifs of Rome.

CPA Thomas D. Schauf corroborates McCallister's claims, adding that ten banks control all twelve Federal Reserve Bank branches. He names N.M. Rothschild of London, Rothschild Bank of Berlin, Warburg Bank of Hamburg, Warburg Bank of Amsterdam, Lehman Brothers of New York, Lazard Brothers of Paris, Kuhn Loeb Bank of New York, Israel Moses Seif Bank of Italy, Goldman Sachs of New York and JP Morgan Chase Bank of New York. Schauf lists William Rockefeller, Paul Warburg, Jacob Schiff and James Stillman as individuals who own large shares of the Fed. [3] The Schiffs are insiders at Kuhn Loeb. The Stillmans are Citigroup insiders, who married into the Rockefeller clan at the turn of the century.

Eustace Mullins came to the same conclusions in his book The Secrets of the Federal Reserve, in which he displays charts connecting the Fed and its member banks to the families of Rothschild, Warburg, Rockefeller and the others. [4]

The control that these banking families exert over the global economy cannot be overstated and is quite intentionally shrouded in secrecy. Their corporate media arm is quick to discredit any information exposing this private central banking cartel as "conspiracy theory". Yet the facts remain.

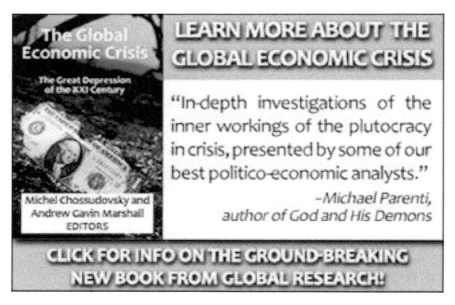

The House of Morgan

The Federal Reserve Bank was born in 1913, the same year US banking scion J. Pierpont Morgan died and the Rockefeller Foundation was formed. The House of Morgan presided over American finance from the corner of Wall Street and Broad, acting as quasi-US central bank since 1838, when George Peabody founded it in London.

In 1937 Interior Secretary Harold Ickes warned of the influence of "America's 60 Families". Historian Ferdinand Lundberg later penned a book of the exact same title. Supreme Court Justice William O. Douglas decried, "Morgan influence…the most pernicious one in industry and finance today."

Jack Morgan responded by nudging the US towards WWII. Morgan had close relations with the Iwasaki and Dan families – Japan's two wealthiest clans – who have owned Mitsubishi and Mitsui, respectively, since the companies emerged from 17th Century shogunates. When Japan invaded Manchuria, slaughtering Chinese peasants at Nanking, Morgan downplayed the incident. Morgan also had close relations with Italian fascist Benito Mussolini, while German Nazi Dr. Hjalmer Schacht was a Morgan Bank liaison during WWII. After the war Morgan representatives met with Schacht at the Bank of International Settlements (BIS) in Basel, Switzerland. [13]

The House of Rockefeller

BIS is the most powerful bank in the world, a global central bank for the Eight Families who control the private central banks of almost all Western and developing nations. The first President of BIS was Rockefeller banker Gates McGarrah- an official at Chase Manhattan and the Federal Reserve. McGarrah was the grandfather of former CIA director Richard Helms. The Rockefellers- like the Morgans- had close ties to London. David Icke writes in Children of the Matrix, that the Rockefellers and Morgans were just "gofers" for the European Rothschilds. [14]

BIS is owned by the Federal Reserve, Bank of England, Bank of Italy, Bank of Canada, Swiss National Bank, Nederlandsche Bank, Bundesbank and Bank of France.

John D. Rockefeller used his oil wealth to acquire Equitable Trust, which had gobbled up several large banks and corporations by the 1920's. The Great Depression helped consolidate Rockefeller's power. His Chase Bank merged with Kuhn Loeb's Manhattan Bank to form Chase Manhattan, cementing a long-time family relationship. The Kuhn-Loeb's had financed – along with Rothschilds – Rockefeller's quest to become king of the oil patch. National City Bank of Cleveland provided John D. with the money needed to embark upon his monopolization of the US oil industry. The bank was identified in Congressional hearings as being one of three Rothschild-owned banks in the US during the 1870's, when Rockefeller first incorporated as Standard Oil of Ohio. [17]

373

One Rockefeller Standard Oil partner was Edward Harkness, whose family came to control Chemical Bank. Another was James Stillman, whose family controlled Manufacturers Hanover Trust. Both banks have merged under the JP Morgan Chase umbrella. Two of James Stillman's daughters married two of William Rockefeller's sons. The two families control a big chunk of Citigroup as well. [18]

In the insurance business, the Rockefellers control Metropolitan Life, Equitable Life, Prudential and New York Life. Rockefeller banks control 25% of all assets of the 50 largest US commercial banks and 30% of all assets of the 50 largest insurance companies. [19] Insurance companies- the first in the US was launched by Freemasons through their Woodman's of America- play a key role in the Bermuda drug money shuffle.

Companies under Rockefeller control include Exxon Mobil, Chevron Texaco, BP Amoco, Marathon Oil, Freeport McMoran, Quaker Oats, ASARCO, United, Delta, Northwest, ITT, International Harvester, Xerox, Boeing, Westinghouse, Hewlett-Packard, Honeywell, International Paper, Pfizer, Motorola, Monsanto, Union Carbide and General Foods.

The Rockefeller Foundation has close financial ties to both Ford and Carnegie Foundations. Other family philanthropic endeavors include Rockefeller Brothers Fund, Rockefeller Institute for Medical Research, General Education Board, Rockefeller University and the University of Chicago- which churns out a steady stream of far right economists as apologists for international capital, including Milton Friedman.

The family owns 30 Rockefeller Plaza, where the national Christmas tree is lighted every year, and Rockefeller Center. David Rockefeller was instrumental in the construction of the World Trade Center towers. The main Rockefeller family home is a hulking complex in upstate New York known as Pocantico Hills. They also own a 32-room 5th Avenue duplex in Manhattan, a mansion in Washington, DC, Monte Sacro Ranch in Venezuela, coffee plantations in Ecuador, several farms in Brazil, an estate at Seal Harbor, Maine and resorts in the Caribbean, Hawaii and Puerto Rico. [20]

Nixon asked him to be Secretary of Treasury, but Rockefeller declined the job, knowing his power was much greater at the helm of the Chase. Author Gary Allen writes in The Rockefeller File that in 1973, "David Rockefeller met with twenty-seven heads of state, including the rulers of Russia and Red China."

Following the 1975 Nugan Hand Bank/CIA coup against Australian Prime Minister Gough Whitlam, his British Crown-appointed successor Malcolm Fraser sped to the US, where he met with President Gerald Ford after conferring with David Rockefeller. [24]

Next Week: Part II: Freemasons & The Bank of the United States

Notes

1   10K Filings of Fortune 500 Corporations to SEC. 3-91
2   10K Filing of US Trust Corporation to SEC. 6-28-95
3   "The Federal Reserve 'Fed Up'. Thomas Schauf. www.davidicke.com 1-02
4   The Secrets of the Federal Reserve. Eustace Mullins. Bankers Research Institute. Staunton, VA. 1983. p.179
5   Ibid. p.53
6   The Triumph of Conservatism. Gabriel Kolko. MacMillan and Company New York. 1963. p.142
7   Rule by Secrecy: The Hidden History that Connects the Trilateral Commission, the Freemasons and the Great Pyramids. Jim Marrs. HarperCollins Publishers. New York. 2000. p.57
8   The House of Morgan. Ron Chernow. Atlantic Monthly Press NewYork 1990
9   Marrs. p.57
10   Democracy for the Few. Michael Parenti. St. Martin's Press. New York. 1977. p.178
11   Chernow
12   The Great Crash of 1929. John Kenneth Galbraith. Houghton, Mifflin Company. Boston. 1979. p.148
13   Chernow
14   Children of the Matrix. David Icke. Bridge of Love. Scottsdale, AZ. 2000
15   The Confidence Game: How Un-Elected Central Bankers are Governing the Changed World Economy. Steven Solomon. Simon & Schuster. New York. 1995. p.112
16   Marrs. p.180
17   Ibid. p.45
18   The Money Lenders: The People and Politics of the World Banking Crisis. Anthony Sampson. Penguin Books. New York. 1981

19   The Rockefeller File. Gary Allen. '76 Press. Seal Beach, CA. 1977

20   Ibid

21   Dope Inc.: The Book That Drove Kissinger Crazy. Editors of Executive Intelligence Review. Washington, DC. 1992

22   Marrs.

23   The Rockefeller Syndrome. Ferdinand Lundberg. Lyle Stuart Inc. Secaucus, NJ. 1975. p.296

24   Marrs. p.53

Dean Henderson is the author of Big Oil & Their Bankers in the Persian Gulf: Four Horsemen, Eight Families & Their Global Intelligence, Narcotics & Terror Network and The Grateful Unrich: Revolution in 50 Countries. His Left Hook blog is at www.deanhenderson.wordpress.com

The Federal Reserve Cartel: Freemasons and The House of Rothschild

By <u>Dean Henderson</u>
Part two of a four-part series

In 1789 Alexander Hamilton became the first Treasury Secretary of the United States. Hamilton was one of many Founding Fathers who were Freemasons. He had close relations with the Rothschild family which owns the Bank of England and leads the European Freemason movement. George Washington, Benjamin Franklin, John Jay, Ethan Allen, Samuel Adams, Patrick Henry, John Brown and Roger Sherman were all Masons.

Andrew Hamilton

Roger Livingston helped Sherman and Franklin write the Declaration of Independence. He gave George Washington his oaths of office while he was Grand Master of the New York Grand Lodge of Freemasons. **Washington himself was Grand Master of the Virginia Lodge.** Of the General Officers in the Revolutionary Army, thirty-three were Masons. This was highly symbolic since 33rd Degree Masons become *Illuminated*. [1]

Populist founding fathers led by John Adams, Thomas Jefferson, James Madison and Thomas Paine- none of whom were Masons- wanted to completely sever ties with the British Crown, but were overruled by the Masonic faction led by Washington, Hamilton and Grand Master of the St. Andrews Lodge in Boston General Joseph Warren, who wanted to "defy Parliament but remain loyal to the Crown". St. Andrews Lodge was the hub of New World Masonry and began issuing Knights Templar Degrees in 1769. [2]

General Joseph Warren

All US Masonic lodges are to this day warranted by the British Crown, whom they serve as a global intelligence and counterrevolutionary subversion network. Their most recent initiative is the Masonic Child Identification Program (CHIP). According to Wikipedia, the CHIP programs allow parents the opportunity to create a kit of identifying materials for their child, free of charge. The kit contains a fingerprint card, a physical description, a video, computer disk, or DVD of the child, a dental imprint, and a DNA sample.

The First Continental Congress convened in Philadelphia in 1774 under the Presidency of Peyton Randolph, who succeeded Washington as Grand Master of the Virginia Lodge. The Second Continental Congress convened in 1775 under the Presidency of Freemason John Hancock. Peyton's brother William succeeded him as Virginia Lodge Grand Master and became the leading proponent of centralization and federalism at the First Constitutional Convention in 1787. The federalism at the heart of the US Constitution is identical to the federalism laid out in the Freemason's *Anderson's Constitutions of 1723*. William Randolph became the nation's first Attorney General and Secretary of State under George Washington. His family returned to

England loyal to the Crown. John Marshall, the nation's first Supreme Court Justice, was also a Mason. [3]

When **Benjamin Franklin** journeyed to France to seek financial help for American revolutionaries, his meetings took place at Rothschild banks. He brokered arms sales *via* German Mason Baron von Steuben. His Committees of Correspondence operated through Freemason channels and paralleled a British spy network. In 1776 Franklin became *de facto* Ambassador to France. In 1779 he became Grand Master of the French *Neuf Soeurs* (Nine Sisters) Lodge, to which John Paul Jones and Voltaire belonged. Franklin was also a member of the more secretive Royal Lodge of Commanders of the Temple West of Carcasonne, whose members included Frederick Prince of Whales. While Franklin preached temperance in the US, he cavorted wildly with his Lodge brothers in Europe. Franklin served as Postmaster General from the 1750's to 1775 – **a role traditionally relegated to British spies.** [4]

Hamilton was only the first in a series of Eight Families cronies to hold the key position of Treasury Secretary. In recent times Kennedy Treasury Secretary Douglas Dillon came from Dillon Read (now part of UBS Warburg). Nixon Treasury Secretaries David Kennedy and William Simon came from Continental Illinois Bank (now part of Bank of America) and Salomon Brothers (now part of Citigroup), respectively. Carter Treasury Secretary Michael Blumenthal came from Goldman Sachs, Reagan Treasury Secretary Donald Regan came from Merrill Lynch (now part of Bank of America), Bush Sr. Treasury Secretary Nicholas Brady came from Dillon Read (UBS Warburg) and both Clinton Treasury Secretary Robert Rubin and Bush Jr. Treasury Secretary Henry Paulson came from Goldman Sachs. Obama Treasury Secretary Tim Geithner worked at Kissinger Associates and the New York Fed.

Thomas Jefferson argued that the United States needed a publicly-owned central bank so that European monarchs and aristocrats could not use the printing of money to control the affairs of the new nation. Jefferson extolled...

But the Rothschild-sponsored Hamilton's arguments for a private US central bank carried the day. In 1791 the Bank of the United States (BUS) was founded, with the Rothschilds as main owners.

Jackson won the election and revoked the bank's charter stating, "The Act seems to be predicated on an erroneous idea that the present shareholders have a prescriptive right to not only the favor, but the bounty of the government... Many of our rich men have not been content with equal protection and equal benefits, but have besought us to make them richer by acts of Congress. I have done my duty to this country."[8]

Populism prevailed and Jackson was re-elected. **In 1835 he was the target of an assassination attempt. The gunman was Richard Lawrence, who confessed that he was, "in touch with the powers in Europe".** [9]

Still, in 1836 Jackson refused to renew the BUS charter. **Under his watch the US national debt went to zero for the first and last time in our nation's history.** This angered the international bankers, whose primary income is derived from interest payments on debt. BUS President Nicholas Biddle cut off funding to the US government in 1842, plunging the US into a depression. Biddle was an agent for the Paris-based Jacob Rothschild. [10]

The Mexican War was simultaneously sprung on Jackson. A few years later the Civil War was unleashed, with London bankers backing the Union and French bankers backing the South. The Lehman family made a fortune smuggling arms to the south and cotton to the north. **By 1861 the US was $100 million in debt.** New President Abraham Lincoln snubbed the Euro-bankers again, issuing Lincoln Greenbacks to pay Union Army bills...

The 1863 National Banking Act reinstated a private US central bank and Chase's war bonds were issued. **Lincoln was re-elected the next year, vowing to repeal the act after he took his January 1865 oaths of office. Before he could act, he was assassinated at the Ford Theatre by John Wilkes Booth. Booth had major connections to the international bankers. His granddaughter wrote *This One Mad Act*, which details Booth's contact with "mysterious Europeans" just**

380

before the Lincoln assassination.

...President John F. Kennedy found himself in the Eight Families' crosshairs. **Kennedy had announced a crackdown on off-shore tax havens and proposed increases in tax rates on large oil and mining companies. He supported eliminating tax loopholes which benefit the super-rich.** His economic policies were publicly attacked by *Fortune* magazine, the *Wall Street Journal* and both David and Nelson Rockefeller. Even Kennedy's own Treasury Secretary Douglas Dillon, who came from the UBS Warburg-controlled Dillon Read investment bank, voiced opposition to the JFK proposals. [13]

Kennedy's fate was sealed in June 1963 when he authorized the issuance of more than $4 billion in United States Notes by his Treasury Department in an attempt to circumvent the high interest rate usury of the private Federal Reserve international banker crowd. The wife of Lee Harvey Oswald, who was conveniently gunned down by Jack Ruby before Ruby himself was shot, told author A. J. Weberman in 1994, "The answer to the Kennedy assassination is with the Federal Reserve Bank. Don't underestimate that. It's wrong to blame it on Angleton and the CIA *per se* only. This is only one finger on the same hand. The people who supply the money are above the CIA". [14]

Fuelled by incoming President Lyndon Johnson's immediate escalation of the Vietnam War, the US sank further into debt. Its citizens were terrorized into silence. If they could kill the President they could kill anyone.

The House of Rothschild

The Dutch House of Orange founded the Bank of Amsterdam in 1609 as the world's first central bank. Prince William of Orange married into the English House of Windsor, taking King James II's daughter Mary as his bride. The Orange Order Brotherhood, which recently fomented Northern Ireland Protestant violence, put William III on the English throne where he ruled both Holland and Britain. In 1694 William III teamed up with the UK aristocracy to launch the private Bank of England.

The Old Lady of Threadneedle Street- as the Bank of England is known- is surrounded by thirty foot walls. Three floors beneath it the third largest stock of gold bullion in the world is stored. [15]

The Rothschilds and their inbred Eight Families partners gradually came to control the Bank of England. The daily London gold "fixing" occurred at the N. M. Rothschild Bank until 2004. As Bank of England Deputy Governor George Blunden put it, "Fear is what makes the bank's powers so acceptable. The bank is able to exert its influence when people are dependent on us and fear losing their privileges or when they are frightened."[16]

Rothschild-controlled Barings bankrolled the Chinese opium and African slave trades. It financed the Louisiana Purchase. When several states defaulted on its loans, Barings bribed Daniel Webster to make speeches stressing the virtues of loan repayment. The states held their ground, so the House of Rothschild cut off the money spigot in 1842, plunging the US into a deep depression. It was often said that the wealth of the Rothschilds depended on the bankruptcy of nations. Mayer Amschel Rothschild once said, "I care not who controls a nation's political affairs, so long as I control her currency".

War didn't hurt the family fortune either. **The House of Rothschild financed the Prussian War, the Crimean War and the British attempt to seize the Suez Canal from the French. Nathan Rothschild made a huge financial bet on Napoleon at the Battle of Waterloo, while also funding the Duke of Wellington's peninsular campaign *against* Napoleon. Both the Mexican War and the Civil War were goldmines for the family.**

Nathan Rothschild

One Rothschild family biography mentions a London meeting where an **"International Banking Syndicate" decided to pit the American North against the South as part of a "divide and conquer" strategy...**

Mayer Rothschild's sons were known as the Frankfurt Five. The eldest – Amschel – ran the family's Frankfurt bank with his father, while Nathan ran London operations. Youngest son Jacob set up shop in Paris, while Salomon ran the Vienna branch and Karl was off to Naples. Author Frederick Morton estimates that by 1850 the Rothschilds were worth over $10 billion. [21] Some researchers believe that their fortune today exceeds $100 trillion.

The Warburgs, Kuhn Loebs, Goldman Sachs, Schiffs and Rothschilds have intermarried into one big happy banking family...

Today the Rothschild's control a far-flung financial empire, which **includes majority stakes in most world central banks.**

Notes

1   *The Temple & the Lodge*. Michael Bagent & Richard Leigh. Arcade Publishing. New York. 1989. p.259
2   Ibid. p.219
3   Ibid. p.253

4   Ibid. p.233
5   *The Robot's Rebellion: The Story of the Spiritual Renaissance.* David Icke. Gateway Books. Bath, UK. 1994. p.156
6   *Democracy for the Few.* Michael Parenti. St. Martin's Press. New York. 1977. p.51
7   *Fourth Reich of the Rich.* Des Griffin. Emissary Publications. Pasadena, CA. 1978. p.171
8   Ibid. p.173
9   *Rule by Secrecy: The Hidden History that Connects the Trilateral Commission, the Freemasons and the Great Pyramids.* Jim Marrs. HarperCollins Publishers. New York. 2000. p.68
10 *The Secrets of the Federal Reserve.* Eustace Mullins. Bankers Research Institute. Staunton, VA. 1983. p.179
11 *Human Race Get Off Your Knees: The Lion Sleeps No More.* David Icke. David Icke Books Ltd. Isle of Wight. UK. 2010. p.92
12 Marrs. p.212
13 Idid. p.139
14 Ibid p.141
15 Icke. *The Robot's Rebellion.* p.114
16 Ibid. p.181
17 *Rothschild: The Wealth and Power of a Dynasty.* Derek Wilson. Charles Schribner's Sons. New York. 1988. p.178
18 *The House of Rothschild.* Niall Ferguson. Viking Press New York 1998 p.28
19 Marrs. p.215
20 Ibid
21 "What You Didn't Know about Taxes and the Crown". Mark Owen. *Paranoia.* #41. Spring 2006. p.66
22 Marrs. p.63
23 "The Coming Fall of the House of Windsor". *The New Federalist.* 1994
24 "The Secret Financial Network Behind 'Wizard' George Soros". William Engdahl. *Executive Intelligence Review.* 11-1-96
25 Marrs. p.86
26 "Murdoch, Rothschild Invest in Israeli Oil Shale". *Jerusalem Post.* November 22, 2010
27 "Sarah Palin hires chief of staff for PAC", Huffington Post. February 2011

Dean Henderson *is the author of* Big Oil & Their Bankers in the Persian Gulf: Four Horsemen, Eight Families & Their Global Intelligence, Narcotics & Terror Network *and* The Grateful Unrich: Revolution in 50 Countries. *His **Left Hook** blog is at <u>www.deanhenderson.wordpress.com</u>*

The Federal Reserve Cartel: The Roundtable &

the Illuminati

Posted on 07/20/2014 | 3 Comments

(Part three of a five-part series excerpted from Chapter 19: The Eight Families: Big Oil & Their Bankers...)

According to former British intelligence agent John Coleman's book, *The Committee of 300*, the Rothschilds exert political control through the secretive Business Roundtable, which they created in 1909 with the help of Lord Alfred Milner and South African industrialist Cecil Rhodes. The Rhodes Scholarship is granted by Cambridge University, out of which oil industry propagandist Cambridge Energy Research Associates operates.

Rhodes founded De Beers and Standard Chartered Bank. According to Gary Allen's expose, *The Rockefeller Files*, Milner financed the Russian Bolsheviks on Rothschild's behalf, with help from Jacob Schiff and Max Warburg.

In 1917 British Foreign Secretary Arthur Balfour penned a letter to Zionist Second Lord Lionel Walter Rothschild in which he expressed support for a Jewish homeland on Palestinian-controlled lands in the Middle East. [1]

The Balfour Declaration justified the brutal seizure of Palestinian

lands for the post-WWII establishment of Israel. Israel would serve, not as some high-minded "Jewish homeland", **but as lynchpin in Rothschild/Eight Families control over the world's oil supply.** Baron Edmond de Rothschild built the first oil pipeline from the Red Sea to the Mediterranean to bring BP Iranian oil to Israel. He founded Israeli General Bank and Paz Oil. He is considered by many the father of modern Israel. [2]

Roundtable inner Circle of Initiates included Lord Milner, Cecil Rhodes, Arthur Balfour, Albert Grey and Lord Nathan Rothschild. The Roundtable takes its name from the legendary knight of King Arthur, whose tale of the Holy Grail is paramount to the *Illuminati* notion of *Sangreal* or holy blood.

John Coleman writes in *The Committee of 300*, "Round Tablers armed with immense wealth from gold, diamond and drug monopolies fanned out throughout the world to take control of fiscal and monetary policies and political leadership in all countries where they operated."

While **Cecil Rhodes** and **the Oppenheimers** went to South Africa, the **Kuhn Loebs** were off to re-colonize America. **Rudyard Kipling** was sent to India. **The Schiffs** and **Warburgs** manhandled Russia. **The Rothschilds, Lazards and Israel Moses Seifs** pushed into the Middle East. In Princeton, New Jersey the Round Table founded the Institute for Advanced Study (IAS) as partner to its All Souls College at Oxford. IAS was funded by the Rockefeller's General Education Board. IAS members Robert Oppenheimer, Neils Bohr and Albert Einstein created the atomic bomb. [3]

In 1919 Rothschild's Business Roundtable spawned the Royal Institute of International Affairs (RIIA) in London. The RIIA soon sponsored sister organizations around the globe, including the US Council on Foreign Relations (CFR), the Asian Institute of Pacific Relations, the Canadian Institute of International Affairs, the Brussels-based *Institute des Relations Internationales*, the Danish Foreign Policy Society, the Indian Council of World Affairs and the Australian Institute of International Affairs. Other affiliates popped up in France, Turkey, Italy, Yugoslavia and Greece. [4]

The RIIA is a registered charity of the Queen and, according to its annual reports, is funded largely by the Four Horsemen. Former British Foreign Secretary and Kissinger Associates co-founder Lord

Carrington was President of both the RIIA and the Bilderbergers. The inner circle at RIIA is dominated by Knights of St. John Jerusalem, Knights of Malta, Knights Templar and 33rd Degree Scottish Rite Freemasons. The Knights of St. John were founded in 1070 and answer directly to the British House of Windsor. Their leading bloodline is the Villiers dynasty, which the Hong Kong Matheson family married into. The Lytton family also married into the Villiers gang. [5]

Colonel Edward Bulwer-Lytton led the English *Rosicrucian* secret society, which Shakespeare opaquely referred to as Rosencranz, while the Freemasons took the role of Guildenstern. Lytton was spiritual father of both the RIIA and Nazi fascism. In 1871 he penned a novel titled, *Vril: The Power of the Coming Race.* Seventy years later the Vril Society received ample mention in Adolf Hitler's *Mein Kampf.* Lytton's son became Viceroy to India in 1876 just before opium production spiked in that country. Lytton's good friend **Rudyard Kipling** worked under Lord Beaverbrook as Propaganda Minister, alongside Sir Charles Hambro of the Hambros banking dynasty. [6]

James Bruce, ancestor to Scottish Rite Freemason founder **Sir Robert the Bruce**, was the 8th Earl of Elgin. He supervised the Caribbean slave trade as Jamaican Governor General from 1842-1846. He was Britain's Ambassador to China during the Second Opium War...

Children of the Roundtable elite are members of a Dionysian cult known as Children of the Sun. Initiates include Aldous Huxley, T. S. Eliot, D. H. Lawrence and H. G. Wells. Wells headed British intelligence during WWI. His books speak of a "one-world brain" and "a police of the mind". **William Butler Yeats**, another Sun member, was a pal of Aleister Crowley. The two formed an Isis Cult based on a Madam Blavatsky manuscript, which **called on the British aristocracy to organize itself into an Isis Aryan priesthood. Most prominent writers of English literature came from the ranks of the Roundtable. All promoted Empire expansion**, however subtly. Blavatsky's Theosophical Society and Bulwer-Lytton's *Rosicrucians* joined forces to form the Thule Society **out of which the Nazis emerged.** [8]

Aleister Crowley formed the British parallel to the Thule Society, the Isis-Urania Hermetic Order of the Golden Dawn. **He tutored LSD guru Aldus Huxley**, who arrived in the US in 1952, the same year **the CIA launched its MK-ULTRA mind control program** with help from the **Warburg-owned** Swiss Sandoz Laboratories and **Rockefeller cousin Allen Dulles**- OSS Station Chief in Berne. Dulles received information from the **Muslim Brotherhood House of Saudi** regarding the **creation of mind-controlled Assassins**. Dulles' assistant was James Warburg. [9]

In 1950 James Warburg, whose elders Max and Paul sat on the board of Nazi business combine IG Farben, testified before the Senate Foreign Relations Committee, **"We shall have world government whether or not you like it- by conquest or consent**

The *Illuminati*

The *Illuminati* **serves as ruling council to all secret societies. Its roots go back to the Guardians of Light in Atlantis, the Brotherhood of the Snake in Sumeria, the Afghan** *Roshaniya*, **the Egyptian Mystery Schools and the Genoese families who bankrolled the Roman Empire. British Prime Minister Benjamin Disraeli, who "handled" mafia-founder and 33rd Degree Mason Guiseppe Mazzini, alluded to the** *Illuminati* **in a speech before the House of Commons in 1856 warning, "There is in Italy a power which we seldom mention. I mean the secret societies. Europe…is covered with a network of secret societies just as the surfaces of the earth are covered with a network of railroads."**[13]

The *Illuminati* is to these secret societies what the Bank of International Settlements is to the Eight Families central bankers. And their constituencies are exactly the same.

The forerunners of the Freemasons -the Knights Templar- founded the concept of banking and created a bond market as a means to control European nobles through war debts. By the 13th century the Templars had used their looted Crusades gold to buy 9,000 castles throughout Europe and ran an empire stretching from Copenhagen to Damascus. They founded modern banking techniques and legitimized usury via interest payments. Templars' bank branches popped up everywhere, backed by their ill-gotten gold. They charged up to 60% interest on loans, launched the concept of trust accounts and introduced a credit card system for Holy Land pilgrims. They acted as tax collectors, though themselves exempted by Roman authorities, and built the great cathedrals of Europe, having also

found instructions regarding secret building techniques alongside the gold they pilfered beneath Solomon's Temple. The stained glass used in the cathedrals resulted from a secret Gothic technique known by few. One who had perfected this art was Omar Khayvam, a good friend of Assassin founder Hasan bin Sabah. [14]

The Templars controlled a huge fleet of ships and their own naval fleet based at the French Atlantic Port of La Rochelle. They were especially cozy with the royals of England. They purchased the island of Cyprus from Richard the Lion Heart, but were later overrun by the Turks. On **Friday October 13, 1307 King Philip IV of France joined forces with Pope Clement V and began rounding up Templars on charges ranging from necromancy to the use of black magic.** Friday the 13th would from that day forward carry negative connotations. "Sion" is believed to be a transliteration of Zion, itself a transliteration for the ancient Hebrew name Jerusalem. **The Priory of Sion came into public view in July 1956. A 1981 notice in the French press listed 121 dignitaries as Priory members. All were bankers, royalty or members of the international political jet set. Pierre Plantard was listed as Grand Master. Plantard is a direct descendent, through King Dagobert II, of the Merovingan Kings. Plantard, who owns property in the Rennes-le-Chateau area of southern France where the Priory of Sion is based, has stated that the order has in its possession lost treasure recovered from beneath Solomon's Temple and that it will be returned to Israel when the time is right.** He also stated that in the near future monarchy would be restored to France and other nations. **The Templars claim to possess secret knowledge that Jesus Christ married Mary Magdalene, fathered children to launch the Merovingan bloodline and was the son of Joseph of Arimathea.** [15]

Joseph was the son of King Solomon. Solomon's Temple is the model for Masonic Temples, which occur without fail in every town of any size in America. It was a place of ill repute where fornicating, drunkenness and human sacrifice were the norm. Accorder to British researcher David Icke, **it's location on Jerusalem's Mount Moriah** may have also been an Anunnaki flight control center. The Annunaki are the reptilian/aliens revealed by the Sumerian clay tablets- the oldest written accounts of humankind known. **The Crusader Knights Templar looted their huge store of gold and numerous sacred artifacts from beneath the Temple. King Solomon was the son of King David- who**

389

during his 1015 BC reign massacred thousands of people.

...The basis of the Sumerian Tables of Destiny which Abraham possessed became known as *Ha Qabala*, Hebrew for "light and knowledge". Those who understood these cryptic secrets, said to be encoded throughout the Old Testament, are referred to deferentially as Ram. The phrase is used in Celtic, Buddhist and Hindu spiritual circles as well. The Knights Templar brought Cabbalistic knowledge to Europe when they returned from their Middle East Crusade adventures. [16]

The Knights created the *Prieure de Sion* on Mt. Zion near Jerusalem in the 11th century to guard such holy relics as the Shroud of Turin, the Ark of the Covenant and the Hapsburg family's Spear of Destiny-which was used to kill Jesus Christ...

The Hapsburgs ran the Holy Roman Empire until its dissolution in 1806, through King Charles V and others. The family traces its roots back to a Swiss estate known as Habichtburg, which was built in 1020. The Hapsburgs are an integral part of the Priory of Sion. **Many researchers believe that Spain's Hapsburg King Philip will be crowned *Sangreal* World King in Jerusalem.** The Hapsburgs are related to the Rothschilds through Holy Roman Emperor Frederick Barbarossa's second son Archibald II.

The Rothschilds- leaders in Cabala, Freemasonry and the Knights Templar- sit at the apex of the *both* the *Illuminati* and the Eight Families banking cartel. The family accumulated its vast wealth issuing war bonds to Black Nobility for centuries, including the British Windsors, the French Bourbons, the German von Thurn und Taxis, the Italian Savoys and the Austrian and Spanish Hapsburgs. The Eight Families have also intermarried with these royals.

Author David Icke believes the Rothschilds represent the head of the Anunnaki Serpent Kings, stating, "They (Rothschilds) had the crown heads of Europe in debt to them and this included the Black Nobility dynasty, the Hapsburgs, who ruled the Holy Roman Empire for 600 years. The Rothschilds also control the Bank of England. If there was a war, the Rothschilds were behind the scenes, creating conflict and funding both sides."[18]

The Rothschilds and the Warburgs are main stockholders of the German *Bundesbank*. Rothschilds control Japan's biggest banking house Nomura Securities *via* a tie-up between Edmund Rothschild

and Tsunao Okumura. The Rothschilds are the richest and most powerful family in the world. They are also inbred. According to several family biographers, over half of the last generation of Rothschild progeny married within the family, presumably to preserve their *Sangreal*. [19]

The 1782 Great Seal of the United States is loaded with *Illuminati* symbolism. So is the reverse side of the US $1 Federal Reserve Note, which was designed by Freemasons. The pyramid on the left side represents those in Egypt- possibly space beacon/energy source to the Anunnaki- whose Pharaohs oversaw the building of the pyramids using slave labor.

...The numbers 3, 9, 13 and 33 are significant to the secret societies. 33rd-degree Freemasons are said to become *Illuminati*. According to the late researcher William Cooper, the Bilderberger Group has a powerful Policy Committee of 13 members. It is one of 3 committees of 13 which answered (until his recent death) to Prince Bernhard- member of the Hapsburg family and leader of the Black Nobility. The Bilderberg Policy Committee answers to a Rothschild Round Table of 9. [22]

1   "The Secret Financial Network Behind 'Wizard' George Soros". William Engdahl. *Executive Intelligence Review.* 11-1-96

2   *Rule by Secrecy: The Hidden History that Connects the Trilateral Commission, the Freemasons and the Great Pyramids.* Jim Marrs. HarperCollins Publishers. New York. 2000. p.83

3   Ibid. p.89

4   *Fourth Reich of the Rich.* Des Griffin. Emissary Publications. Pasadena, CA. 1978. p.77

5   The *Robot's Rebellion: The Story of the Spiritual Renaissance.* David Icke. Gateway Books. Bath, UK. 1994. p.195

6   Ibid

7   *Dope Inc.: The Book that Drove Kissinger Crazy.* The Editors of *Executive Intelligence Review.* Washington, DC. 1992. p.264

8   Ibid. p.538

9   *Dope Inc.*

10   Ibid

11   Ibid

12   Marrs

13   Icke. p.148

14   *Bloodline of the Holy Grail.* Laurence Gardner. Element Books, Inc. Rockport,

MA. 1996

15 *Holy Blood, Holy Grail*. Michael Bagent, Richard Leigh and Henry Lincoln. Dell Publishing Company New York. 1983

16 Icke.

17 *Behold a Pale Horse*. William Cooper. Light Technology Press. Sedona, AZ. 1991. p.79

18 *Children of the Matrix*. David Icke. Bridge of Love Publishing. Scottsdale, AZ. 2000.

19 Marrs. p.71

20 Icke. 1994. p.42

21 Ibid. p.71

22 Cooper

Dean Henderson is the author of five books: <u>Big Oil & Their Bankers in the Persian Gulf: Four Horsemen, Eight Families & Their Global Intelligence, Narcotics & Terror Network</u>, <u>The Grateful Unrich: Revolution in 50 Countries</u>, Das Kartell der Federal Reserve, <u>Stickin' it to the Matrix</u> & <u>The Federal Reserve Cartel</u>. You can subscribe free to his weekly **Left Hook** column @<u>www.hendersonlefthook.wordpress.com</u>

The Federal Reserve Cartel: Part IV: A Financial Parasite

By <u>Dean Henderson</u>

(Excerpted from Chapter 19: <u>Big Oil & Their Bankers</u>...Part four of a five-part series)

United World Federalists founder James Warburg's father was Paul Warburg, who financed Hitler with help from Brown Brothers Harriman partner Prescott Bush. [1] ....

In 1913 the Federal Reserve Bank was born, with Paul Warburg its first Governor. Four years later the US entered World War I, after a secret society known as the Black Hand assassinated Archduke Ferdinand and his Hapsburg wife. The Archduke's friend Count Czerin later said, "A year before the war he informed me that the Masons had resolved upon his death." [5]

That same year, Bolsheviks overthrew the Hohehzollern monarchy in Russia with help from Max Warburg and Jacob Schiff, while the Balfour Declaration leading to the creation of Israel was penned to Zionist Second Lord Rothschild...

The year 1917 also saw the 16th Amendment added to the US Constitution, **levying a national income tax, though it was ratified by only two of the required 36 states. The IRS is a private corporation registered in Delaware.** [8] Four years earlier **the Rockefeller Foundation was launched, to shield family wealth from the new income tax provisions, while steering public...**

Though most Americans think of the Federal Reserve as a government institution, it is privately held by the Eight Families. The Secret Service is employed, not by the Executive Branch, but by the Federal Reserve. [10]

...President Wilson spoke of, "a power so organized, so complete, so pervasive, that they had better not speak above their breaths when they speak in condemnation of it."

The Fed is made up of most every bank in the US, but the New York Federal Reserve Bank controls the Fed by virtue of its enormous capital resources...

In the fifth sub-basement of the 14-story stone hulk lie 10,300 tons of mostly non-US gold, 1/3 of the world's gold reserves and by far the largest gold stock in the world. [14]

"When the president signs this act [the Federal Reserve Act], the invisible government by the money power will be legitimized." Rep. Charles Lindberg (D-NY)

When the Fed was created five New York banks – Citibank, Chase, Chemical Bank, Manufacturers Hanover and Bankers Trust – held a 43% stake in the New York Fed. By 1983 these same five banks owned 53% of the NY Fed. By year 2000, the newly merged Citigroup, JP Morgan Chase and Deutsche Bank combines owned even bigger chunks, as did the European faction of the Eight Families. **Collectively they own majority stock in every Fortune 500 corporation and do the bulk of stock and bond trading. In 1955 the above five banks accounted for 15% of all stock trades. By 1985 they were involved in 85% of all stock transactions.** [15]

Still more powerful are the investment banks which bear the names of many of the Eight Families. In 1982, while Morgan bankers presided over negotiations between Britain and Argentina after the Falklands War, President Reagan pushed through SEC Rule 415, which helped consolidate securities underwriting in the hands of six large investment houses owned by the Eight Families: **Goldman Sachs, Merrill Lynch, Morgan Stanley, Salomon Brothers, First**

Boston and Lehman Brothers. These banks further consolidated their power *via* the merger mania of 1980s and 1990s....

A recent president of the World Bank was James Wolfensohn of Salomon Smith Barney. Merrill Lynch had $435 billion in assets in 1994, before the merger frenzy had really even gotten under way. The biggest commercial bank at the time, Citibank, could claim only $249 billion in assets.

... Following the Lehman Brothers fiasco and the ensuing financial meltdown of 2008, the Four Horsemen of Banking got even bigger... Since the creation of the Federal Reserve, US debt (mostly owed to the Eight Families) has skyrocketed from $1 billion to nearly $14 trillion today. This far surpasses the total of all Third World country debt combined, debt which is mostly owed to these same Eight Families, who own most all the world's central banks.

As Sen. Barry Goldwater (R-AZ) pointed out, "**International bankers make money by extending credit to governments. The greater the debt of the political state, the larger the interest returned to lenders. The national banks of Europe are (also) owned and controlled by private interests. We recognize in a hazy sort of way that the Rothschilds and the Warburgs of Europe and the houses of JP Morgan, Kuhn Loeb & Co., Schiff, Lehman and Rockefeller possess and control vast wealth. How they acquire this vast financial power and employ it is a mystery to most of us.**" [21]

Dean Henderson is the author of _Big Oil & Their Bankers in the Persian Gulf: Four Horsemen, Eight Families & Their Global Intelligence, Narcotics & Terror Network_, _The Grateful Unrich: Revolution in 50 Countries_ and _Das Kartell der Federal Reserve_. Subscriptions to his Left Hook blog are FREE at <u>www.deanhenderson.wordpress.com</u>

Footnotes:

1   *Behold a Pale Horse.* William Cooper. Light Technology Press. Sedona, AZ. 1991. p.81

2   *Dope Inc.: The Book that Drove Kissinger Crazy.* The Editors of *Executive Intelligence Review*. Washington, DC. 1992.

3   *Democracy for the Few.* Michael Parenti. St. Martin's Press. New York. 1977. p.67

4   *Descent into Slavery.* Des Griffin. Emissary Publications. Pasadena 1991

5   The *Robot's Rebellion: The Story of the Spiritual Renaissance.* David Icke. Gateway Books. Bath, UK. 1994. p.158

6   The Editors of *Executive Intelligence Review*. p.504
7   Ibid
8   Ibid
9   Ibid. p.77
10 "Secrets of the Federal Reserve". Discovery Channel. January 2002
11 *The Confidence Game: How Un-Elected Central Bankers are Governing the Changed World Economy*. Steven Solomon. Simon & Schuster. New York. 1995. p.26
12 Icke. p.178
13 Solomon. p.63
14 Ibid. p.27
15 *The Corporate Reapers: The Book of Agribusiness*.A.V. Krebs. Essential Books. Washington, DC. 1992. p.166
16 The Editors of *Executive Intelligence Review*. p.79
17 "Playing the Middle". Anita Raghavan and Bridget O'Brian. *Wall Street Journal*. 10-2-95
18 Securities Data Corporation. 1995
19 CNN Headline News. 1-11-02
20 *The Rockefeller File*. Gary Allen. '76 Press. Seal Beach, CA. 1977. p.156
21 *Rule by Secrecy: The Hidden History that Connects the Trilateral Commission, the Freemasons and the Great Pyramids*. Jim Marrs. HarperCollins Publishers. New York. 2000. p.77

The Federal Reserve Cartel: Part V: The Solution

By <u>Dean Henderson</u>
(Conclusion of a five-part series.)
Thomas Jefferson opined of the Rothschild-led Eight Families central banking cartel which came to control the United States, "Single acts of tyranny may be ascribed to the accidental opinion of the day, but a series of oppressions begun at a distinguished period, unalterable through every change of ministers, too plainly prove a deliberate, systematic plan of reducing us to slavery".
Two centuries and a few decades later this same cabal of trillionaire money changers – mysteriously immune from their own calls for "broad sacrifice" – utilizes the debt lever to ring concessions from the people of Ireland, Greece, Spain, Portugal, Italy and now the United States.
In their never-ending quest to subjugate the planet, the bankers' IMF enforcer – chronic harasser of Third World governments – has

turned its sites on the developed world. To further advance their dizzying concentration of economic power, the whining banksters take a giant wrecking ball to the global middle class as they prepare to eat their young.

No one can argue that the US deficit is not a problem. Much of it accrues paying interest on the $14 trillion debt. Stooped-over Congressional cartel shills with names like Cantor and Boehner argue for slashing entire government departments to satiate the bloodthirsty bond-holders. Liberals argue for higher taxes on the rich and massive Pentagon cuts.

I agree with these latter proposals. **The super-rich paid 90% under Eisenhower and 72% under Nixon. Both were Republicans. They now pay 33%. Most corporations and many elites utilize offshore tax havens and pay nothing.**

It is a myth that most of that $14 trillion debt is owed to the Chinese or other "governments". The vast majority – **around $10 trillion – is owed to the Eight Families Federal Reserve** crowd…

In a June 9, 2011 article for *Marketwatch*, Unicredit's Chief US Economist Harm Bandholz stated that the Federal Reserve is the largest holder of US debt with around 14% of the total. This does not include debt held by Rothschild-controlled central banks of *other*nations – including China, Japan and the GCC oil fiefdoms…

What follows is a ten-step proposal which President Obama and the Congress could enact to lift the $14 trillion debt from the backs of future generations of Americans. These should be done concurrently as part of a single sweeping financial reform bill. Modeled after last week's release of strategic petroleum reserves by twenty-seven nations, this measure should be enacted in tandem with as many willing nations as possible. The same Rothschild-led cabal controls the central banks of most every nation and there is power in numbers. If these measures are enacted separately or by only one nation, the Eight Families cartel will use their financial clout to target and destroy the US:

> **Introduce a Treasury Department-administered infrastructure investment fund,** which workers should be strongly encouraged to opt into using accrued funds from their private 401K plans. This is important because the banker's stock market casino *will*crash due to the next nine steps and workers must be shielded from this event. This fund can be

used to rebuild America's infrastructure, with American workers acting as lenders and receiving a fair rate of interest in return.

The US needs to withdraw from the Bank of International Settlements, the World Trade Organization, the World Bank, the IMF and all Eight Families-controlled multilateral lending facilities. We would save billions funding these banker welfare schemes while freeing ourselves from rules which prevent our financial emancipation.

De-link the dollar from all currency baskets and IMF special drawing rights. Ban trade in dollars on all global exchanges. This will create a demand for dollars and strengthen our badly devalued currency. Impose currency controls by fixing the dollar at 1:1 *euro*, Chinese *yuan*, Canadian dollar and Swiss *franc*; 100:1 Japanese *yen*. During the 1997 Asian financial crisis, Malaysian Prime Minister Mahathir Mohamad fixed the nation's currency – the *ringit*. It was the only currency in the region that did not crash when Rothschild front-man George Soros took aim at the region.

Nationalize the Federal Reserve. According to a London barrister I have been in contact with, under the Federal Reserve Act there is a provision that allows for the US government to buy back the Fed's charter for $4 billion. We should pay this fee, revoke the Fed charter and launch a new US dollar issued by the Treasury Department. With the dollar fixed, the vampires cannot crash it.

Cancel the $10 trillion debt to the *Illuminati* bankers. Debt obligations to foreign governments and small bond-holders should be honored at par.

Arrest the perpetrators. Prosecute to the fullest extent of the law all fraudulent transactions involving the Fed cartel. Send the FBI to the New York Fed. Seize all documents. Confiscate the world's largest gold reserves which are stored there. These were stolen from various governments including from our own Ft. Knox reserves.

Forget just repealing the Bush tax cuts on the rich. The top tax rate on people who make more than $1 million/ year should be raised to 75%. People making more than $500,000/year should pay 50%. All tax brackets below $75,000/year should see tax *cuts*. If you get more from government you need to pay for it, instead of soaking the middle-class and blaming it on the poor.

Slash Pentagon spending. Shut down all US military bases on foreign soil, including those in Europe, Japan and South Korea. Withdraw ALL troops from Iraq and Afghanistan immediately. Use the savings to pay off government and small bond-holders.

Outlaw offshore banking by US citizens and corporations. Bring your money home and pay taxes on it or surrender your US passport/corporate charter. The dramatic increase in tax revenue would be enough to pay off the remaining debt to sovereign governments and small bond-holders, while keeping our obligations to the Social Security trust fund.

Introduce single-payer health care and price controls on prescription drugs. The current corporate for-profit health care bonanza depends upon sickness and ill health for its hefty profits. In 2006 Canada government spent $3,678 per person for free single-payer coverage for all its citizens. The US government spent $6,714 per person covering the insurance, pharmaceutical, hospital and AMA cartels. The savings attained from eliminating insurance/pharmaceutical/hospital chain/doctor-perpetrated Medicare/Medicaid/Social Security fraud will save the US Treasury billions. It is the only solution to skyrocketing and unsustainable health care costs.

Using this methodology the US could wipe out both its deficit and its debt within a year. These measures should be planned in secret and introduced swiftly and in rapid succession. Social security and Medicare will be saved. The middle class will see their tax rates go down, while their retirement fund finances the rebuilding of a 21st Century America. Manufacturing jobs will come home, since the Chinese *yuan* will have seen a dramatic appreciation. Our national security will be enhanced by withdrawing from the role of global policeman.

If we keep thinking inside the banker-manufactured beltway box, our children have no future. They will live in a Third World country which produces nothing, lorded over by debt-collector parasites known as the "financial services industry".

The wealth-destroying Eight Families banker elite are the perpetrators of the US debt crime. **Should a woman who is raped serve the sentence of her rapist? That's absurd. Then why should Americans or any**

other nation pay a fraudulent debt foisted upon them by con-men? It is time for Obama and the Congress to get a backbone and force the criminal Federal Reserve cartel to make the "broad sacrifices".

www.deanhenderson.wordpress.com

Rock on Dean! I love it!!!! I would really like you also to read 'Rule By Secrecy' by Jim Marrs and some of Dean Henderson's other books. And works by other creditable writers out there. Some films and documentaries also exist about these topics too. Why, because they go into a lot more detail than I do on these ruling families and how they got to power. Plus I want you to see that I and what others have been saying for a number of years are **NOT** Conspiracy Theories but true facts which are defacto!

Maybe we do not know every single detail of everything to do with the Rockefellers and the Rothschilds and we never will because a lot of it is well covered up or hidden forever. If someone breaks in to your house or is going to attack you or do you harm, you do not need to do a background check before you defend yourself or retaliate. Legally you are entitled to defend oneself or another. You know who your enemy is now and so you make your choice of what are **YOU** going to do about them and the situation you are in. Well, it may not seem like such a dangerous scenario as this; but I beg to differ because it is even worse than this! The problem with these families and the vast global condition we and this planet are in right now is because they have been doing all their dirty work behind our backs for many years and using their slimy minions high up in Governmental, legal and media spheres; and their many covert agencies (CIA; FBI, NSA, etc.) to cover it all up with lies, empty speeches, rhetoric and false articles to make us think everything is OK (many have been murdered, assassinated, put in prison or sectioned for speaking out or getting in their way or for not doing what they were told. I kid you not!) and they are doing the right thing for us. And they are educated, intelligent people. Leave it all to them because they know best and will look after our interests. What a load of bullshit!

These are just sneaky, dirty, conniving scum, who will stop at nothing to get what they want. And they are very clever, some of them geniuses too. But that makes no difference. They have been covertly and overtly harming and pulling Mankind down for centuries. Even since or before Egyptian times. And we have let them! Isn't it about time we put a stop to them and got back into our own hands the reins of our OWN destiny? Well?

Some others involved are:

JP Morgan Chase (one of the Big Four banks. The other three banks are: Bank of America, Citigroup and Wells Fargo) *The Four Horsemen of Banking (Bank of America, JP Morgan Chase, Citigroup and Wells Fargo) own the Four Horsemen of Oil (Exxon Mobil, Royal Dutch/Shell, BP and Chevron Texaco); in tandem with Deutsche Bank, BNP, Barclays and other European old money behemoths. But their monopoly over the global economy does not end at the edge of the oil patch.*

These banks all work together and with the Federal Reserve and the Bank of England, the IMF, the World Bank and the European Bank and a few others; they control ALL banking and finance on the planet, I kid you not! And they and vice versa are in cahoots with the top 500 companies on the planet.

NOTE: Most (if not all) of what I have written in this book can all be verified in various other books and articles - and most excerpts from other writers and other sources all have quoted their sources or given details on where the data came from; and these can all be checked and verified. Jim Marrs and many other top writers (who are still alive) all have written books about what I say here and have listed their 'source' material: so I and they cannot all be wrong. It has only been with the advent of the internet and the fast world-wide communications systems around the planet, and freedom of speech and the release of various documents under the Official Secrets Act (and some secrets we will NEVER know because they are even above 'Top Secret' or sadly, they have been totally destroyed) and the coming forward of various old or dying or now dead people, who have heavy hearts or want to repent for their sins or whatever the case may be – but thankfully they (using books or other people/writers or Wikileaks, etc.) have revealed their secrets to the world and to us, so we can act before it is too late.

I tell you again, that this is not fiction but FACT. And if we knew the real history of Earth since before Egyptian times up until present and if we knew the 'REAL' history of the history of our countries and in particular Europe and the USA, and what the Aristocracy and the Royal and Ruling Families of the World have been up to with our 'MONEY' and 'RESOURCES' and our 'LIVES', we would not be too happy about it all and we might even – dare I say, would it be possible – we might even take action to rectify matters and put right the evil wrongdoings and suppressive actions that have been occurring on this planet for the last 10,000 years or so and in particular since the times of the Bible and even more so, the more recent 200 years of this planet. I kid you not. But hey, we are all fairly educated now. You check out what I and other writers have said and you decide for yourself and on what course of action to take. But I or anyone else, can NOT do it all alone. NO! Impossible. You will die or you will be stopped or locked up on some false charge or be sectioned in a mental health hospital or be 'brainwashed [or 'mindwashed' really] or 'adjusted' using drugs and deep sleep therapy, etc.(more on this later). Or your reputation, life and family or business will be destroyed. Many have tried to stop or take out the baddies and they have died or committed suicide, etc. I kid you not. I also will not tell you the history that predates Mankind's inhabitance of Earth (before he even came to be on Earth) because you would not believe me anyway and would think I am nuts - and this would be totally against all your religious beliefs. So I'm not even going to go there. Plus, I do not know it all and actually, this is not that important at this time. Neither is the Alien stuff (unless an Alien invasion is coming, in which case it is very important) mentioned very briefly in this book: but that all depends if they are real, what their intentions are and if they are already here, what are they up to and who are they working with, if anyone? But, for now, let's deal with the facts that we **_do_** know and they are in this book. But the BIG question is: what are you going to do with them? The biggest pun and joke of all on all of this 'Alien' stuff which the X-Files made famous, is that we, Mankind could be alien to planet Earth ourselves. Food for thought? I will ask you this and leave it at that: ***What is the worst trap one could be in?***

Answer: ***<u>A trap that one does not even know one is in!</u>***

But I am not taking this and 'aliens' any further than this. We are dealing with what the current state of affairs are right now and what Mankind generally can deal with and handle; and what he can realistically do to sort out those who are ruling, ruining and destroying us and our planet.

Read on for lots more data on the Rockefellers and the Rothschilds. You can research, check out and read all of the books and articles I have included here. I know some of this stuff is VERY hard to believe and some will make you feel sick. However; they use this very fact against us: most people find it hard to face or confront evil and they also use the fact that most people will not 'believe' what they read or hear because it is so far-etched. You do not need to believe all that I have included here below; but you need to believe and understand that these people and families _**ARE**_ controlling and shaping Mankind to what he is today; and their intentions are NOT good but evil even though superficially and in the Media everything seems to be alright and fine – when this is definitely not the case!

I also wanted to show you here what other writers and people have said and discovered so you will not just think I am talking a load of bullshit and rubbish. Source references have been included where possible. This is not easy reading – I know that – but you need to understand who and what we are dealing with – we continue:

The second most powerful family in the world (or at least equal with the Rockefellers):

The Rothschilds

This is a huge banking dynasty that has financed all the major wars in history since the French Revolution; has financed and still does, Kings, Queens, rulers and the super rich; and with its power, has managed to bankroll and lend to most, if not all countries in the world, thus getting them into huge debt to them. And they are in cahoots with the rest of the ruling families (Rockefellers), world leaders and the top 500 companies. This family is fully explained in the other books I have asked you to read. They financed both all sides of World War I & II.

This family and the rest of them are NOT there to help us but to keep us down and slaves to their systems. Please do not make the mistake and this otherwise: they sole purpose in life is make our lives and hell and to destroy the planet!

Hitler's father was the offspring of the Rothschild's secret breeding program which impregnated his grandmother. Hitler was created and groomed for his role, without realizing his heritage at first. My god!!!!

Some other people connected to these families are:

NBC

NBC DIRECTORS	ROTHSCHILD CONNECTIONS
John Brademas	Dir. Rockefeller. Fdtn. chrm

Fed. Reserve Bank of N.Y. which controls
all other Fed.R.Bks. Humanist of the Yr 1978

Cecily B. Selby nat. dir. Girl Scouts (the occult is now
part of the to Girl Scout program),
dir.Avon Products and Loehmann s (dresses).

Husb. James Cole, pres. Bowdoin College
Peter G. Peterson frmr head of Kuhn-Loeb Ex-Sec. of commerce
Robert Cizek dir. First City Bancorp dir. RCA, chairmn Cooper Industries
Thomas O. Paine Pres. of Northrup- large defense contractr.
Dir. of Strategic dir of Inst. of Studies, various
munitions assoc.

Donald Smiley dir. of several Morgan Firms dir. of Ralston- Purina,
Irving Trust, Metro-Life and U.S. Steel and chrm of Macy Co.

David C. Jones Pres. Consolidated Contr., dir. U.S. Steel, Kemper
Insur.

Thornton Bradshaw, dir. Aspen Inst. of Humanistic Studies, Atlantic-Richfield	dir. Rock. Bros. Fund

Oil, Champion Paper Co., chairman of RCA

Brandon Tartikoff	(head of NBC entertainment) Jewish

CBS

Harold Brown, Jewish. ex-Sec. of Air Force and ex-Sec. of Defense.	Ex. dir. Trilat. Com.

Roswell Gilpatric, dir. Fed. Res. Bk.NY.	Kuhn Loeb firm C.S.& M

Henry B. Schnacht, dir. Chase Manhattan, dir AT&T, chnmn Cummins	CFR, Brookings Inst

Engine Co., Committee for Economic Develop

Michel C. Bergerac, chrmn. Revlon	dir. Manufacturers

James D. Wolfensohn	frmr.hd. J. Henry Schröder Bank

Walter Cronkite

Newton D. Minow	dir. Rand Corp

Franklin A. Thomas, head of Ford Found.

Marietta Tree, dir. Winston Churchill Found., dir. Salomon Bro., Foundation & dir., dir. U.S. Trust, granddgtr of fdr. of Groton, hsbd in Br. Intell.,	assoc. w/ Ditchlcy

Hitler was brainwashed and adjusted/modified into the monster he became using Drugs and Deep Sleep Therapy (Monarch Program), etc., all thanks to the Rockefellers/ Rothschilds, their highest followers and with the help of Psychiatry. Hitler was created, not born the way he was and what he become. He **WAS** in fact manufactured. This can all be done because we all have Unconscious Minds and just like Hypnotists work, they can implant their commands and completely erase or alter a person's past, alter/erase their personality and anything else they want to do – and get this – the person or individual will not even suspect or know it. That is evil and has and is being done to many people in the world today. This IS a fact! Hitler was also viewed as the new messiah by these families.

And it is (or was) apparently one of their intentions, to actually get back the British Empire (probably changed by now?) and to further expand it, so it includes the entire world: and there will be one world government and one New World Order: with the Rothschilds, the Rockefellers, The Queen of England and the rest of them running this planet either personally and directly, or through a World President or Leader, who will be financed by and who will only work for them: a bit like how Obama is today; he will have no real power of his own – but just be a automaton puppet – and he (or she) will have to do their dirty work and bidding and we will all bow down and praise them and say 'What great and wonderful leaders they are!' Nice, huh? Well, that is if we allow it to happen, right?

And, as I have said before: America was all planned and manufactured years go, long before it even became the USA? They wanted America to be how it is today and they have been shaping it ever since it began. It is and was their test-bed for the rest of the world. Now, they plan to make the rest of the entire planet in the same blueprint of how the USA is today and join it all together. Fact! This is taking nothing away from the American People, because I really like Americans and there are many talented and friendly people there. But they can be a bit naive at times and very gullible - which could be there downfall. I am just saying, that all this has been happening and going on undetected for centuries, right under the very noses of the good American people, and they didn't (most of them) even know about it. Some Presidents knew what was going on; but they either said nothing, were killed, assassinated, taken out of office or bought off or were just duped. President Kennedy knew or found out and died for it! So have others. Is it not now time that the American People wake up to this fact and the rest of us around the world, and take effective, positive, and revolutionary action to get things changed back to how they should AND to get these families tried in court and imprisoned; and if that is not possible as they own and control most of legal and justice systems and the judges: then, we put pressure on our governments to act and not work with these families. I have other solutions, which I will put to you later.

They have their filthy, thieving and evil paws in almost every activity Mankind is involved in; and it is done in such a manner, that it would probably take a team of experts a year of intensive and covert investigation just to trace and track it all out and BACK to them and their ever-expanding bank accounts and power bases.

Oh, they are not stupid. Far from it. They are very clever and geniuses at what they do. And they recruit, hire, buy or threaten into their service anyone they need to do their evil deeds and work. Most of their employees do not even know who they really work for. It's all a front. I am even certain that they brainwash and hypnotize (using deep sleep therapy, and Psychiatry, etc.) people, without their knowing, to carry out what they want: witness the various assassinations that have occurred over the years (Kennedy, Lennon, Martin Luther King, possibly Michael Jackson and many others you would not even suspect?). Those who get in their way or oppose them are either destroyed by the media, are ruined, sacked or made to resign; suddenly commit suicide; have a mortal accident; are blackmailed/threatened or are just bought off (some will sell their souls and send Mankind down the shoot, just for transient money, power, contracts and titles). They finance and/or decide who the Presidents, Premiers, Prime Ministers and Rulers of the major countries will be, including the USA. And they handpick who the Chairmen/Bosses/ CEOs of their companies and interests will be, and usually get some member of their or a related family or friend. [Can you believe that a Canadian (I have nothing against Canadians!) is now the Governor of the Bank of England – how did that happen?] They are all in with one another and go to all the same schools, Universities, are members of same clubs and go to the same parties and pretty much interbred and intermarry one another, etc. It is a closed club the rest of us – unless they want something from

406

you or you can offer them something.

The top – the GOOD-GUYS - rich, powerful and successful people on this planet know who they are too; or they should do if they do not – for their own sakes (and the BAD GUYS know them too because they usually work with them!) But they know who is running the planet and have been for a long time. And they, and most of the World Leaders and Heads of State and Governments, as well as the owners of the top 500 companies of the planet today: must either be all scarred or they have a lot to gain from having dealings with these two ruling families. How many actually stand up to them? Why have they not been stopped or thwarted them after all this time? Surely, somewhere, there must be enough data and secret files to put them in jail? Surely, with this age of internet, fast world-wide communication and electronics, there is no excuse any more for not taking them out and stopping their nefarious and totally insane plans before it is too late? The top good people of Earth today, will someday, have to answer for not taking action now or before – when they could have but didn't. I can guarantee you that!!!

They are behind all the street drugs being sold around the planet. They are behind all the deaths, rapes and suicides caused directly or as a result of Psychiatry and its brutal and barbaric 'treatment' of us, the low-life's (they think!) and their enemies (yes, to get rid of their enemies in this way too!) using drugs, shock treatment and brain operations. They are behind Psychology and for it being thought in schools and for this idea 'that we are all animals, are not souls and spiritual beings, and everything is caused by our brains, DNA and genes': bollix I say! They are behind the ever-increasing pollution. They are behind all these rates, taxes, interest rates and INFLATIONS and RECESSIONS we have had, and are having. They are behind the fact that there has been little or no real progress in Science and new technologies since the discovery of Nuclear Power and Einstein's $E = MC^2$, which is partially incorrect by the way and has parts missing. They are behind the fact that we have no Perpetual Motion Machines or Free power sources, no free energy (except for Solar Power which is not cheap) or Over Unity devices that can handle Man's energy, fuel and pollution problems and take him cheaply and quickly to the Star's, our own galaxy and our nearest galaxies. They are responsible for and behind all wars that have happened since at least the French Revolution; the finance for them;

the finance for rebuilding the countries, and they are responsible (including those who colluded with them!) for all the deaths and destruction caused by these unnecessary wars. They are behind the dwindling literacy levels and criminal delinquency happening around the world; and they are behind what is being thought in each subject or course in our schools/colleges and Universities: with the intent of making people who are either stupid or made in slaves and robots and who are unable or less able to think for themselves – keep them stupid so we cannot find out about them and be able to solve the problems happening on Earth today, and we can buy and use THEIR Psychiatric drugs and get out Psychology counselling!

What they are not responsible for are the GOOD things and activities being done by good people. And they are not responsible for the fact that WE, the peoples of Earth keep voting in the same assholes who are messing up our countries and planet, and who are working for THEM, not us – even though we pay their wages! They are not responsible for us accepting all these increased taxes, bills, rates, inflation and austerity measures and inequalities between the rich and the working classes and poor and inequalities in sharing the money around so we can all get a good share of it. They are not responsible for us who keep buying diesel and petrol to power our cars and trucks and for their resultant pollution. Why do we accept and put up with these serious factors in our lives? If things are wrong in our countries and on this world as a whole, well I am sorry, but only **WE** can correct them and make them right and the way they should be. Only we can do this because THEY will not and those who work with or for them will not do anything either, because they are too busy counting their money or doing whatever they do in their wonderful, bright and happy lives.

Some contact details of these wonderful, nice families are:

The Rothschild Family: http://www.rothschild.com/contactus (here, you see their addresses and contact details for all the countries they operate in in the world [those which they tell us that is, and jointly together with the Rockefellers, they run pretty much every country on the planet]); They have numerous properties in the UK at (and all over the world):
Ascott House - Ascott, Buckinghamshire

Aston Clinton House - Aston Clinton
Ashton Wold - Northamptonshire
Exbury Estate - Hampshire
Eythrope - Waddesdon
Gunnersbury Park - Ealing
Halton House - Halton, Buckinghamshire
Mentmore Towers - Mentmore
Tring Park - Tring, Hertfordshire
Waddesdon Manor - Waddesdon
Spencer House - St James's, London. A leasehold extending until 2082 was purchased in 1986 from the Spencer family who owns the house. They also have estates and houses in Paris, other parts of France; Frankfurt, Germany; Naples, Vienna, plus all the houses and properties they have in the USA and the rest of the world. Currently, the head of the family is: **Lord Jacob Rothschild, the fourth Baron de Rothschild**
And then we have this article:

The Rothschilds and Rockefellers Join Forces in Multi-Billion Dollar Deal

Jun 7th, 2012 | Category: Latest News | 11267129 comments THE TELEGRAPH
In this article it says:
Mayer Amschel Rothschild stated: *"Give me control of a nation's money and I care not who makes her laws."*
And David Rockefeller stated in his memoirs:
"Some even believe we are part of a secret cabal working against the best interests of the United States, characterizing my family and me as 'internationalists' and of conspiring with others around the world to build a more integrated global political and economic structure – one world, if you will. If that's the charge, I stand guilty, and I am proud of it."
-David Rockefeller, "Memoirs of David Rockefeller" p.405
On the deal, Mr Rockeller said: "Lord Rothschild and I have known each other for five decades. The connection between our two families remains very strong. I am delighted to welcome Jacob and RIT as shareholders."
- Source: The Independent

Right, enough of all that. This was just to give you a very detailed broad picture of who we are dealing with. Nothing more. There is no reason to be scared or in awe of these people: they are probably more scared of us than we are of them; despite all their wealth and power. Trust me. And these guys really are the ones who need help! We now know who our enemies are! They deserve no more attention; just they now need to be handled and stopped. Now let's get down to business and the crunch but before that, I just wanted to mention:

TERRORISM

I had to mention this because we just keep hearing about it in the news almost every week. Very recently we've had the terrorist bombing in Paris (2015). Apparently this was from IS – Islamic State or whatever they call themselves. Before them, we had Bin Laden and his cohorts and all the other so-called terrorist organizations; including the IRA. Even the African gangs, who rape, maim, kill, torture and plunder - get their weapons from somewhere. I do not know about every terrorist group that has ever walked the Earth; but I can tell you that most, if not ALL of these groups have a more covert purpose, agenda and reason for existing. And it is NOT what they (those in the previous chapter) or the media tell you. NO!

These terrorist activities are financed covertly by **them** to cause trouble in any country and region they want; which then allows them to invade or cause a war or depose and get rid of the current ruler or government. It also allows them to threaten and force our countries and leaders to do as they are told: because if they don't some innocent or not so innocent people are going to die or whatever the case may be. They use this man-made 'TERRORISM', which THEY have created to be the excuse to do what they want around the world; and the other world leaders and rulers know this. And then they make so much money selling arms and weapons and giving loans to rebuild the destruction they caused. Like they did in World War I & II.

I know all of this and some of what I have said in this book is hard to believe but that is a trick they use too: because they know most common people will not believe what they read and hear and it can all be hidden under 'CONSPIRACY THEORIES'. And most people cannot handle, deal with and confront pure evil such as this: which would allow millions and millions of people to suffer, be raped, tortured, maimed, drugged, beaten up, killed and imprisoned since at least the wars and terrorism we've had in the last hundred or so years on this planet. All of this has been no accident. I wish you would believe and understand this.

THERE IS A WAR (COVERT) GOING ON THIS PLANET!

And it is a war for your own, and all of Mankind's freedom and future. Make no mistake about this fact: it IS war!

They do it very covertly, very rarely overtly or openly because they know that we, the people on this planet with the real power, would rise up and shoot them down, imprison them or do whatever it would take to stop them.

They have so many sinister and terrible goals:

- Get rid of all churches and religions

- Destroy all of our Constitutions

- Be able to pick up any person anywhere and detain, imprison, kill them or use whatever Psychiatric methods they want on them and/or pain-drug, deep-sleep Hypnosis - no questions would be asked

- Widespread Sexual Immorality

- Any potential future leaders and geniuses, prodigies, etc. will be stunted or stopped in school by widely administering Psychiatric drugs or forcing children to take them: it will be law or they will be intentionally wrongly diagnosed

This is already happening broadly in America and Europe, and many other countries.

Anything that can or will truly help Man (and this planet) and improve his condition or even free him mentally and/or spiritually for real: has been and will be attacked, outlawed or shut down.

THEY claim that what they are doing is 'helping' us and they know best and it is for our own (their) good. What a load of bollix! If the Devil came down, he would say, from his nefarious point of view, that he was helping us by trapping our souls or by putting evil thoughts into our heads or by making us die and suffer endlessly for all eternity in the burning flames of Hell. And he would have the most terrible grin or smirk on this face when he was saying it. Totally callous and cold-blooded. Well, this can be said of those families and people running and guiding this planet to complete slavery and control by them. They think they are doing us good. They are insane. They are not even human to be honest as this implies humility, morales and ethics. Whether they were sent here or are here personally to intentionally enslave Mankind is irrelevant. They exist. They are real, rather hidden (with false public profiles to make us think better of them) and strongly protected and those, with their own vested interests; or by just sheer fear and cowardice – serve them.

It is through terrorism and the laws that are passed to apparently stop it and protect us all; that they strive to take over the world (and via other sinister methods: taxes, finance, oil, etc.) and enslave us all as and make things how they wish. They are and have been shaping the destiny of Mankind since Egyptian times to this end; and they have kept most of us ignorant of it until recently. But luckily there are a very small few among us who are good and who have been trying to do something about it.

They use **misdirection** in this terrorism lark and in other ways to control and keep us down. They direct our attention using the media to something; and you think how terrible it is and that what they are doing is right. They do this on other world issues too or on one individual or country they want to slander or ruin the reputation off. So our attention and thoughts become controlled and directed. And we do not know where this is coming from. The attention is never put on those who <u>REALLY</u> caused and funded the terrorism or whatever the issue may be. And are all so gullible; that we believe what they say, without little or no evidence; because it puts an element of doubt in our minds and then we fill in the blanks or the rest ourselves. We do get the truth. We 'think' terrorists, how could they do that? They should be all shot. Look at this people and children they blew up! Yes, it is terrible; but who gave the orders and who organized it, well? They are masters of this misdirection and thought manipulation and on controlling us and how we think on issues, using the media, which they own, control and finance. Sure we are fed so much crap, even from our parents (who get fed it too), from our schools, colleges, Unis, newspapers, radio and TV; that it is any wonder anyone has a genuine, pure, true thought anywhere. When one has real knowledge and truth; and it is one's own; and one has a means examine and discover more facts, knowledge, truth and if one has the ability to think correctly and sanely and be able to resolve problems correctly and devise good solutions; and when one knows fully and factually who one is and what one can; then, one is not the effect of the above. One can rise above it and also do something about it. But if one is not in this state; then we are all just sheep or animals to be herded around and done with as THEY wish. This is not pie in the sky. This is how it is. And; it would still be the same of one was living on another planet somewhere out there in this vast Universe.

But luckily there are a few among us who are good and who are not just thinking about themselves all the time and who have been trying to do something about it. Thank God for that; otherwise man would have met his demise many centuries ago!

I would like to invite you to join me and be one of them – well? If you want to keep your current house, car, job, money in the bank, investments, holidays, nice food and all the rest, and have nice planet to live on, then it is up to you because a handful of really good-hearted - sometimes overworked - and knightly, saintly people cannot do it alone. There is usually safety and strength, power in numbers – as long as they are organized correctly. So I challenge you to join the team that **IS** doing something to protect and safeguard their own future, that of their friends, family and children; and that of others and of this planet and all life on it. I know it is a huge challenge – but it is one that cannot be ignored or shoved under the carpet. If you say no, you are saying no to your own future happiness, even if you only care about oneself and no-one else. Therefore, it does not take much intellect and analytical thought to consider and answer up to this question; which is more than a question: It is a responsibility and duty that cannot be ignored.

The CIA, FBI, the police, NSA, other various governmental agencies, government leaders and various government departments are all involved in terrorism (and wars and arms/weapons dealing) is some form or another – but they will not admit it of course; they will only say that they are fighting it, which they are not – they are funding, allowing and supporting it. The same with a lot of the wars that have been going on on this planet for the last 100 years or so. The same with illegal drugs, alcohol and Psychiatric drugs. None of this is happening by chance. It is all planned in advance and we and life on this planet; and our children, pay the price.

And, if you think you are going to get off of this planet and that it is the end of you when your body dies – then you have another thing coming. You will just come back and get another body as a spiritual being. No-one that I know off is leaving this planet or going to somewhere like Nirvana or any place else. Sorry to have to tell you that and to maybe ruin your beliefs and hopes. And even if you think you are just a body (which is what they teach us) and when it dies and rots in the ground, that is the end of you – it is not! But regardless of if you believe what I say or not (because I do actually respect peoples beliefs and faiths- better to believe in something than to believe in nothing [which is what they would like us to do.]) I have given you the facts here in this book and you can decide and make up your own mind about what you want to do about them. It cannot be any plainer than that. It's like opening one's window and looking at Sun shining. Sometimes you take it for granted – I mean you see it nearly every day and get used to it being there and, well it is just the same Sun we see all the time and not need to pay much attention to it. But if you really stopped what you were doing and really looked at the Sun; you might be amazed at what you see and what it can do and is doing every second of every day. Well; the facts in this book are kind of like that: we here about them so much and they are over there, not on my doorstep, or the poor and the wars are in another country, not mine. Or that killing or rape did not happen in my neighbourhood but in another part of the country. Well, it is time to shake off the daze you may be in and to pull the wool away from your eyes and to LOOK, I mean really look around at these facts and at one's own life and that of Mankind and this planet. Then you might begin to see the light was what is actually going on?

I know this may be disrelated to what I just said; but in many ways it is not. I have noticed myself while being on holiday in various places and while experiencing life in the place I live – and this is very noticeable – I have observed that most people even though they are from the same country or region, do not talk to each other very much on the street or in the pub or nightclub. If they know you yes or if they need help or need directions or something like this then, yes they will talk to you. But otherwise, they will not. I see no reason for this and why people cannot talk to strangers and be more friendly and helpful to each other? I have done this and most people are friendly and do not bite your head off. OK maybe a few will tell you to *uck off or say: 'Do I know you?' But I have found and you will find that it is OK to talk to people on the street and to those you do not know. I mean how is anyone meant to make friends if people do not want to talk to one another. How is a single man or woman meant to find a lover or partner or get date if people do not talk and communicate? It is OK to talk and communicate to people – so why not do it more and be more in communication with the rest of Mankind, as we all make up and compose this human race. There is no-one else here that we know off. We are all we have got! Maybe it is a bit sad to have to say that, that we are all alone here and pretty much left to our own destiny. So isn't it about time we did something about our destiny, yours, mine and the entire human race?

And, it is coming up to Xmas, as I write this book. I really like Christmas. And how most people feel good and are good to others, and show goodwill to all Mankind. But why can't this Xmas spirit and cheer be all year round? Why can't people be like this to one another all the time, not just at Xmas?

I find it rather strange that this is not occurring?

Right, I move on:

THE TRUTH

http://www.clipartbest.com/clipart-nTBk7rgTA

The Truth – now that is something that Man has been searching for thousands of years. Who am I? What am I? How did I get here? When did I get here? Who or what made me, or did I make myself? What am I made of? Where do I go when I die or what happens to me or *my* spirit (which is a funny question to ask oneself because YOU and WE are all spiritual beings right now – **FACT!**) when I die and all these other perfectly valid questions. I could answer most of these questions; but it would make little difference to how Mankind and Earth is today, and to the URGENT problems and dilemmas he has with the Rockefellers, the Rothschilds, the Banks, the Pollution, our wonderful Governments (who care so much for us – NOT!), the Weather and Climate Change; general job scarcity and low pay; inflation, Capitalism, Monopolies; water and Food shortages: the list goes on and on.

But get this: most, if not all, of these problems can and could be solved, if Mankind realizes who is behind all of the above and why it is happening? I have already told you who is behind all of the above, and each and every one of us has a responsibility for sorting them out or taking them out or putting them way, before we lose forever more the chance to do something about them. ***THEY*** exist to make our lives hell and to make sure we do not ever really and truly discover who we are and what we are capable off both as Humans and as Spiritual Beings.

I will tell you now (as I have done before) that we ARE Immortal Spiritual Beings, with abilities and perceptions far in advance of what they currently are. Ancient Man and Asia knew this eons ago. So did a handful of others down through the Ages. _They_ say we are not meant to be Free as Spiritual Beings; we are not meant to go to the Stars; we are not meant to be happy. The only drawback in all of this, is that we have Unconscious Minds and it is through manipulation of this that Mankind is controlled and kept in chains. We do not need bodies to exist (we may not even need Minds but we have them anyway), although one can have a body and be/exist somewhere else outside the body and still perceive and know what the body is doing. And there are many more tricks and Spiritual activities we can do. But when one has forgotten these and forgotten who and what one is, it is therefore very hard to believe and remember it again. Thus the TRUE KNOWLEDGE OF SELF is lost, then one relies on the so-called _EXPERTS_ and _AUTHORITIES_ to tell us what the truth is. Then one can be hoodwinked and controlled. Then one can be lost, trapped and a slave for ever more – or until someone very special comes along and causes a revolution or discovers the truth again. The Rockefellers, the Rothschilds and the rest of these families (about 10 or 12 of them in all) and their cohorts and minions, which very sadly includes most the Governments of Earth today – they have big evil intentions and purposes; which do not include helping you or I or any of us - except themselves. They say they are helping; but they are not. It is like the Devil: his idea of helping you would be to slowly torture you for a thousand years before eating you alive. And if you asked him; on God's bible, he would swear and fully believe that he was helping you! And they are the same! And we buy and accept almost everything they say via the media, like the good little slaves and sheep we are.

I say: **WAKE THE HELL UP!!!!!! Get rid of this idea that – NOTHING CAN BE DONE ABOUT IT. BOLLIX I SAY!!!!!** Something can always be done about anything or anyone if one really wants too and if one persists. And even if you are a sad, fearful, angry or apathetic person or no matter what kind of person you are: something can be done about it - FACT!!!!!! So the question now is: do we and are we going to do something about the enemies I have mentioned in this book. Yes or no?

I am sorry, but it is as simple as that. I do not actually care what you believe or don't believe right now and you are entitled to believe what you believe and think what you think, and that is very true. However, what I am saying right now is far above and far senior to what any of us believe religiously, otherwise or not. If **WE**, together and united, do not do something about our black-souled enemies right now, today, then we are doomed and your future and that of our children will be just like (if not worse than) that portrayed in George Orwell's book 1984 or the world we would have had if Hitler had of won. But it needs to be done in an organized fashion, and in large numbers and we could bring our countries to a standstill (literally everyone does not go to work and blocks off the roads and motorways with their cars, etc., etc. and this is continued until they give us what we want) to make them listen to us, to change and get rid of some of their stupid and suppressive laws and taxes and to also force them to change their systems for the good of ALL those in every country on planet Earth today. And if we continued this or similar effective actions until we got what we wanted, then we would all win. For **THEY** must not be allowed to win!

I am not kidding here. And somewhere inside yourself, you must know that what I say is true. You have to come up from wherever you are, and realize that SOMETHING CAN be done and it must be done now!!!!!!!!!!!!!

And I am not saying let's have an anarchy planet or let's commit suicide or let's kill all the Governments of Earth or kill the Rothschilds and Rockefellers (but if it comes to us having to defend ourselves from them and we are forced to stop them from destroying Mankind and this planet, then we will have to do and take whatever steps that are necessary to guarantee our and our children's futures. And if that means killing them and their cohorts, then so be it!) No. First we must use peaceful and passive means, within the law, to handle our Governments and their Superiors. But as our legal rights to freedom of speech and to even march and have demonstrations, are being taken away every year; and as we do not even have votes or referendums on important issues anymore; then we may have to resort to violent revolution, just like they did in Libya, Egypt and other countries, and more recently like they did in Brazil - in which they got what they wanted. But we need to do it in very large numbers and on a huge scale. The police and army cannot arrest or kill one million people or more in every country around the planet, can they?

NOTE: I want to say something here about Guns. You may not suspect this; but the Media, for many years now – at least 15 – has been using MAN-GONE-CRAZY-SHOOT-UP massacres in the USA, the UK and around the world to the naive people, to turn them against possession of guns. There is nothing wrong with guns – ever (or other weapons)! It is the person using them always. Just because the person using the gun has gone nuts (or has been made to go nuts) has nothing to do with guns themselves. And these type of people are only about 0.5 (very low percentages) of the entire populations. But the media hypes it up and makes it seem like these mass killings are happening everywhere and families and people feel scared and worried and think they might be next (Unconscious Mind reacting here and the fact that people do not know where these Media stories are coming from and they do not know the truth of the stories themselves – but are given the data or altered facts/truth that **they** want and led to believe what **THEY** want) and they agree with the new legislation or legal changes which are proposed. And there is much more to this. I have not finished on this matter yet. No my friends and human comrades. Why? Because there is a much bigger plot to this scenario and de facto events.

Just like they used the 9/11 TWIN TOWERS disaster in the USA to bring in all over the world (which all countries are ordered to follow) all these crazy, impractical anti-terrorist laws that have been voted on (not by us) and passed and now we have a world which is in constant panic and confusion because there might be a terrorist under their car or bed or something stupid like this. The CIA and other covert groups, actually use these so-called terrorists (they have created, trained and paid for them. And as far as I know Bin Laden, for example, was trained by the CIA) to set a few bombs off here and there or kill a few people with knives or guns and then they can try and bring in anti-gun and anti-knife, anti-weapons laws and bring in more and more anti-terrorist laws (they are pretending there is terrorism everywhere but there isn't. It is ONLY them creating it and making us think it is everywhere, when it is not) which only take more of our freedoms away and any chance we legally have of defending ourselves from then when they move to take over the planet – which they intend to do when the time is right; but they only want to do it when they have used the Media and propaganda to alter and influence Mankind's viewpoint so that he will actually think all of this is a good thing. You see where this is all going and where it is coming from? It is totally and completely nuts and the people who are behind all of this are 1000% nuts anyway and they know it. But now YOU do too, right?!

No, all these gun massacres are covertly intended to make it very hard or almost impossible to buy and own a gun. Why? Because when the Powers-That-Be piss us off to such an extent that we revolt and want to smash our Governments and stop what they are doing (World domination and World Slavery to them: I know this seems cliché and the X-Files and other films and books have covered it all and it is all just Conspiracy Theories and all that. I can say categorically that it **_IS_** true and it has been happening since Biblical and Egyptian times. Definitely since after World War I). What I am saying is that if the populations of the USA, UK and the rest of planet Earth do not have many or any guns to fight them back with when they go to take over big-time (what is happening now around the world is just a starter, a taster – we better be ready my friends because they are coming and it is happening slowly every day that passes. I promise you that!) then we WILL lose and we will be shot down like the dogs or animals they say we are or made into their slaves, after they whittle the population on Mankind down to about 500,000 million or so.

Did you know that nearly (if not all) of those school or town shootings that have occurred over the last 10 to 20 years were ALL pre-planned by them. None happened by accident I assure you that. And most, if not all of those who shot the guns in their schools, offices or homes and then committed suicide, were all on Psychiatric Drugs or so-called Psychiatric treatment or coming off of them. They usually do not print this in the Media. No, they must not harm the wonderful reputation of Psychiatry and Psychology because they do so much good (harm) around the world. I am giving you the facts here. But sadly Mankind believes what he wants to believe – which is another reason why he is in the sorry state he is today. A newspaper prints a story and most people believe it or at least they have an element of doubt about the person, country or company it was written on. The same for Physics, Science, Space Travel and all the rest. The media, PR and Black Propaganda pumps us with so much bullshit which is untrue, half-true, altered or complete lies, that it is unreal. One they sow an element of doubt on their target or their agenda, then they have won and Mankind goes down a peg or two in his knowledge and understanding and he becomes more confused and thinks I should just work and earn as much money as I can, buy a house, have a wife and family and hopefully I will be happy and be allowed to be happy and have a small piece of Planet Earth I can call my own and grow old, retire and die and/or come back or be re-incarnated or something like this. This is sad. But that is the state or condition Mankind is in. And, the leaders. Royal Families, the Power-That-Be and those in the know on Earth know all of this and have been using it on US and Mankind since biblical times and before. They have now perfected the control of humans to almost an art form. They only get attacked or messed up when they go too far in an evil or bad direction or they harm those or a cause that us good. Then the Peoples rise up and say 'NO!' Vietnam is an example of this. So, I wonder if you get what I am saying here - do you? It is important that you do.

There is no reason why we could not bring a country and its government to its knees just by not going to work for a week and parking our cars, trucks, lorries, vans, motorbikes, etc. on the roads and motorways; and getting our placards and flags out, and having a sit-down or sit-in or whatever all over the country, and we do this for as long as it takes (to hell with your mortgages, jobs, money) until we get what we want: which is a change in and how the country and government is run and for some laws and taxes to be cancelled or altered. We are talking FREEDOM here just like in Braveheart; but Wallace made the mistake of trusting his greedy friends, his king and the evil enemy. You cannot do it like he did and win. No. We are not just talking about one country here; we are talking about the entire planet and all the people living on it.

And it needs to be done by millions of people all over the various countries (those with the balls big enough to take the challenge and not give in, no matter what, until the task is completed), and then it needs to spread all over the rest of world.

We are talking about MANKIND'S FREEDOM and FUTURE here!!!!! This is NO JOKE or something to do because we are all bored and have nothing else to do. This is serious business. They mean business and so

MUST we. Not for their sakes and they don't really give a damn about themselves or us anyway. No, we need to take action for OUR sakes.

How much is that worth to you? How much is it worth for our children? How much is it worth for our lovely Planet Earth, and its animals, wildlife, plants, rivers, tress, lakes, beaches and Seas? How much is it worth to those who **ONLY** really care about themselves, even if they say otherwise? Well?

If no-one cares about Mankind and Planet Earth, and is willing – live or die in the attempt (like the knights of old!) – to do whatever it takes, then we will lose and the evil asshole devils will win and that is the end of Mankind as you currently know it. And Earth. For it will be a Hell of immense proportions, with no freedom for anyone or anything. Oblivion. Wipeout. Hitler's plans will be realized and much more than that, dare I say. And we all shall see in real life what he and Germany were very close to achieving. Well, with technology advancing far more than Man's ethics and moral fibre and spiritual awareness and knowledge can cope with; then he does not stand a chance of winning and being truly free. I kid you not. You may think that all those Science Fiction stories and films are all fiction, well anything is possible, and any one of those horrible realities could become a fact on Earth today. Better to act now, while there still is a chance to act, for to wait until later – there will be no later!

Are they going to round us all up and put us in jail or in work camps, or even exterminate us? I don't think so? But it is possible. It is close. They are the ones who should be in jail and **THEY** know it. And they are the truly insane who should be in their own Psychiatric hospitals! Are they going to kill us all for fighting for our rights, for a change in the Governmental Systems and for our Freedom? I say not. Some of us may die; but so what. And if they are going to kill us all (which they would oh so love to do – believe me, except that they would then have no slaves and sheep to rule over and suppress and get to do their dirty work and bidding. Pity that. How sad. Boo-hoo!), then let them do it and get it over with. Better to die fighting than to have not even fought at all! And it may well be better to die and go off to another planet or existence than to stay on this one for the probable future it could have with those who made and created Hitler and started World War I & II (yes they were started by the Rothschilds and the Rockefellers, and our Governments and Royal Families; and the Elite Ruling Classes were all in with them, believe it or not!!!!??????) calling the shots and at the helm, is not even worth contemplating, yet alone experiencing. Believe me on this point. But then again, you are entitled to completely ignore everything I say in this book and just go back to your wonderful or boring or exciting or miserable life – whatever the case may be – and maybe what I have said, will not happen and peace will rule on Earth. Maybe? Maybe not. But, the choice is up to you and all of us right now - at this point in time. For one cannot say or have the excuse that one does not now know that truth and the facts. You can ignore them; but you now know them. And that is the big difference. You now know. And we all now know. The question is: **WHAT ARE YOU GOING TO DO ABOUT THEM? WELL?**

I THANK YOU FOR READING THIS FAR!

I write not for me. I write for YOU!!! I write for planet Earth and all life on this lovely blue planet. I do not say or claim to know everything, and anyone who does is probably a liar but there is always the possibility that someone of this ilk will or already has appeared on Earth. But I would never rule out anything, and maybe a being does exist somewhere, who knows everything – but I have not yet met one.

So, I told you at the beginning of this little novel, that I would hold no punches back. And indeed, some people may have had a big reality adjustment while reading this novelette, because I was maybe talking exclusively about them. Well that's fine. We all have to know where we stand on the various issues I have raised in this book. I am sorry; but the time for playing in the fields, chasing Daisies, cleaning up your house or pottering around in one's garden and waiting to die; or whatever the case may be, are well over. They have to be if WE, together are going to get going on rectifying what is wrong with Mankind and Earth today. Gone also, are the times of just thinking about oneself and how much money one has is the bank (even though none of us take it with us when we die). But even if one only took the actions I have advised in these chapters (and you are perfectly entitled to think up your own positive actions in your own city, village, town, country or whatever the case may be – as different countries have different rules, laws and cultures) just to *only* help oneself, then that is fine too. Just so long as one does something effective to cause the changes necessary to get and keep ALL of Mankind free, happy and successfully living and prospering; and bringing justice and change to those areas, people and fields that need it.

I did not personally make this planet the way it is, and neither did you; but collectively we all did - as did all of our ancestors; and thus we all share and have the same level of responsibility for it and for ourselves: HUMANKIND (and the word 'human' implies that people should be humane to each other?) – as everyone else. Yes we need leaders to help in this and we need funds, etc. too. But if we all, the good people among is, which is the majority thank god, if we all join together and do something to change the fate and destiny of Mankind and Earth, then I am sure you will all agree; despite the hardships, sufferings and even some deaths or even, dare I say wars – it will have been WELL worth it to attain and keep the freedom for us all, and therefore secure a happy future for ourselves, our children, and all life on this planet today. Well?

I cannot do it all myself. Neither can anyone else, even though some try and they usually and mostly fail (and end up dead, are assassinated or strangely and suddenly commit suicide.) Someone once said, 'You have nothing to lose but your chains...' or something to this effect. Well that sounded good at the time but it only allowed Communism to be created (by the Rothschilds of the time), which kept all communists poor and down and in even more chains than before, except that the Commissars and those at the top: who had all the power and money (and it is the same – to varying degrees- all over the other nations and countries of Earth, including China, Brazil, Europe (the EEC), Asia, the USA and all the rest.) And when Russia become Capitalist, those very same few who ruled (or who were high up or working for or connected with the Rothschilds and the Rockefellers and the other high ranking families and individuals) in Communist times, then become the owners of vast Oil, Aluminum and other Business Empires and none of the money was shared out or given to the PEOPLE who were meant to own and share it all. Fuck that!!! Now you know what I am talking about and they now sit on their billions while the common workers in Russia exist on small pay. Nice that. And it is a similar scenario in Brazil, Africa, China, India and other regions.

Capitalism, is just as bad. And so are all the rest. A new system is needed for our countries and for Earth today. An equal, fair and just system, that is not controlled and run by the few – who say they are helping us, when in fact they are not.

Man must change. Governments and ruling systems must be changed. Life must change. Earth must be changed. All the banking, multi-national and big business activities must be changed and the wealth (of which there is enough to go around and be shared among us all). The energy, fuel, power and modes of transport must change. How we grow food and crops; and rear animals for consumption must change. Fertilizers cannot just be allowed to run into the soil, rivers, lakes and the sea and pollute the planet wholesale. And we pay for this? How we dispose of our rubbish and waste must be changed (there is no reason why most of it cannot be recycled or even used to produce clean forms of energy, instead of burying it in the ground or flushing it down the drain and into the sea or pumping it out into the air).

If WE do not act accordingly and effectively **NOW**, then we are doomed. This is the hard and unsavoury TRUTH of the situation, conditions, circumstances and status quo we face, here and now, today. It is not fiction. It is not lies. It is not cover-up or PR bullshit or something I am writing just to scare everyone.

I took the time to write these words for you, because I realized myself that I had to do something about where Mankind is currently headed. And I realized I could not do it by myself. It can only be done by a large good-intentioned worldwide group (or groups or organizations [all legal or if made illegal, then so be it] in every country) and a joint team effort. Even though society today and its various cultures, are being eroded and shaped into slave countries/individuals – which is the effect generated by TV, the internet, our educational systems, newspapers, radio, computers, computer games, mobile phones and all the rest. The family unit and the group and race unit has been and is being, slowly broken down; where money is everything, the body is everything; sex is everything, you only live once and look after No. 1 and fuck everyone else. This is sadly where Mankind is at. Not everyone is in this state; but a large majority are, especially in the Western World. The East and other parts of the world are still strong in religion and Spirituality – but this is also being attacked too, as we speak. And most people still do not even know who they are, what they are, where they are going and how to get there, if there is a 'there' to get to.

The POWERS-THAT-BE have been making and shaping us to be

like this and to be their slaves, to do what we are told and to not think for ourselves or question anyone, anything or any order or command, since at least World War II if not before. And as I said, they use the Media (newspapers and TV), PR companies, Black PR and Propaganda, Psychology, Psychiatry, Drugs (street, Psychiatric and medical), Governments and in particular their leaders and those close to or at the top; Oil and Gas companies, Royal Families, various Rulers & top Leaders, various top Geniuses and Scientists (not all but some), Doctors (they prescribe the drugs), the Rich (I am not saying all rich people are bad, they are not. Plenty of nice rich and super-rich people out there; but some are not good, that is what I am saying. And some just want to make more and more money for themselves, their families, their companies and to hell with everyone else – to the detriment of US!!!!! And of some, you have to ask them: how they made their money?); various particular Technologies, various Electronics and Electronic entertainment, and Pornography.

They also make use of and take advantage of our own stupidity, unconscious minds, false and incorrect data which we believe to be true, and the fact that we do not know the truth about who and what we are, how we got here and why we are here on this planet in the first go off. They also take advantage of the fear, grief and apathy in some of us; and the breakdown of Mankind into controllable individuals: it is very easy to control individuals, much harder to control large groups of people or countries that are good, strong, intelligent, **_really_** educated, and that have strong will, good purposes and determination.

KEEP MAN DOWN is there motto. And **FIND MORE NEW WAYS TO GET AND KEEP HIM DOWN** or dare I say: **WIPE HIM OUT COMPLETELY!** And the sooner we wipe him out, the better. But let's make him suffer first, and make him suffer a for a long time – if not forever more!!!!!!!!!

So now comes the billion dollar question: Are you going to ignore what I have said in this book; or, are you going to decide to take positive action?

Or are you just going to say, 'O well. Nice read. But I've heard it all before. And none of it is true... What can be done about it anyway ...? What's the point...? And I'm just happy and contented to just have my car, my 9-5 job, my house, some money in the bank and retire, hopefully get a pension, grow old, die and then maybe I will get to know the answers to life after death or I will just come back and do it all again, over and over for ever more?'

Well, whatever you decide, I CAN tell you that you WILL be coming back to Earth in some form or another: usually to get a body in the hospital somewhere. And even if you don't, Earth will STILL be in the same state it is in right now or worse. And our children and future generations will have to bear the brunt and suffer the consequences of the actions we take NOW, in this year of 2014. Everything each and everyone one of us does now, everything we decide or ignore, will have an effect on our own future and that of everyone else's on this planet. Why? Because all life (plants, animals, our bodies, cells that grow and are aware, sensing and being alive), all matter (not alive), the entire Physical, Mental and Spiritual Universes - are all part of an almost infinite Super System, with huge sub-systems, within sub-systems and all are interacting with one another (good or bad) in one way or another (this goes from the entire Physical Universe right down to the very smallest atom or particle.) Only a very small percentage of the above are above or not affected by this giant Super System or are outside of it or are undetectable in it. But we are not worried about this small percentage at this time. Right now, we are only concerned with Mankind and planet Earth: as this, right now, is the only planet we have and the only one we can live on and it is the only one that can sustain the current bodies we possess.

Why should we remain blind or, dare I say, be afraid or even ignore what is blatantly going on currently on this planet by a few dozen VERY bad apples at the top – I would not even call them human as this implies they have some 'humanity' left in them (and they don't). They are just sub-human scum, and **THEY** now it. They could actually change if they wanted to but they don't want to change. They have been hiding behind their vast wealth and power now for centuries via their family lines; and have been portraying themselves as do-gooders and philanthropists, when in actual fact this is just cover-up and huge lies.

No. There is only one sane option left. And it is this: we put away or lock them up in a secure but safe environment, where there funds

428

are frozen and shared out amongst the rest of Mankind (in some fair, proportionate way) and all of the debts which other countries owe them are cancelled; and they are rehabilitated 100% (with real evidence of change and betterment) before ever being allowed out again. And all of their corporations, companies, banks and multi-nationals are reformed and made to lower their interest rates, taxes, change their rules of business and operations (plus pay the workers at the bottom better wages) and the shares that the Rockefellers, the Rothschilds and the rest of the families own/have are all sold off or taken away from them and the money goes to fund some GOOD projects that will help all of Mankind (not just a few chosen countries like the USA, the UK and others; or some chosen giant Multi-Nationals).

Then, we have to make or force (by whatever means possible, if needed) all of our nice and wonderful Governments to change how they work for us and their countries and make them reform and change their laws, taxes, systems and all the other rubbish and crap we have had to put up with from them for so many years.

ENOUGH IS ENOUGH!!!!!

However; the **RIGHT** changes must be brought in!!!!! And the **RIGHT** people (good, sane, non-criminal, causative, productive) must be put in power (but not absolute power so they cannot be removed if they don't perform or deliver what WE want and what they promised to deliver or produce) and allowed to make the changes for the good of the entire country and for Mankind and our planet. But also, steps and measures must also be put in place so that the Leader or Prime Minister (or whoever is in power and leading/running the country or the EEC or the USA, etc.) of the country or region, WILL NOT be able to take control of the military and the country and become a despotic dictator or ruler.

And if we, the people, are not happy with a Leader, a Government, a Minister, etc., then, by fair and quick referendum (all legal and above-board) we can vote and get rid of them (before their term of duty has expired) and replace them with someone else who can do the job and who CAN and will serve US, not vested interests or those behind the scenes, who have clout, power, influence, money, titles and all the rest of the bullshit that does be going on.

Then, once the debts and bills of our countries have been gotten under control (or wiped out or cancelled) or paid off, then each country can reform its councils, all its various Governmental Departments; Military and Police Forces; Welfare, Educational and University systems and all the rest: Finance and Banking, can be reformed and improved. Then housing and jobs and fair business (with fair and good wages for all) can be improved and on and on this can go, until Countrywide & Worldwide, we ALL get a nice, sane planet, where criminality is low or non-existent and where we can all have a share of the pie and enjoy a comfortable lifestyle no matter what job or profession or work we do.

I actually have been recently thinking deeply about all these failed Isms: Capitalism, Communism, Colonialism, Imperialism and all the rest. And they have ALL failed to help the majority of mankind but they HAVE (as was the plan) helped those at or near the top of the social strata on this planet. We _ARE_ being (most of us) kept in the class systems and monitorial levels we are currently in, and educational levels (controlled education and therefore controlled people and the knowledge and truth they are allowed to possess, which apparently comes from the so-called 'experts' and 'Authorities' who claim to know everything and they cannot be questioned) so we can be controlled and kept as SLAVES for THEM and their worldwide systems and methodologies. So I have invented a new system. Sadly it still has an ism in it, but as these words sound great with an ism at the end, it would be unwise to change the fad.

The new system for Mankind is called: New Humanism. It is a very simple system whereby all of mankind is owned, run and controlled by and for the real actual benefit and help of ALL mankind – not just the few at or near the top. It is the system that would be in place now in every country around the world IF man was more gooder and more wiser than he is currently and he didn't have (or he knew what to do with the Rockefellers, the Rothschilds and all the rest of those like them, including the Royal Families, Ruling Families and those wonderful illegal, corrupt and criminal politicians, millionaires and billionaires) bad people running, controlling, enslaving us and keeping us down.

New Humanism is where every person and country is responsible for every other person and country and their well-being, happiness, success and stand of living, education, etc. and their talents and abilities, welfare, etc., etc. And it gets rid of this worldwide attitude and way of behaving and thinking: 'Look after No. 1 and fuck everyone else!' and 'It's a dog-eat-dog world!'

It is where everyone takes an active interest in his other fellow human being no matter his race, colour or religious or non-religious beliefs. And the money and wealth of this planet is shared around. Who decides what the minimum wage is or how much people get paid per hour for a particular line of work? Who decides? Well it is other people who decide. Apparently we have no say or vote on this. Who decides who will go to war or what country will have a war or be invaded or taken over by the Military or by some crazy dictator or ruler who does NOT serve his people and country? Who decides these issues? And even if the people of a country get to decide or vote on which party gets in or who the Prime Minister or President is going to be, it is all rigged and set up (even though it appears it isn't and it for the good of us all) so that whoever gets into power WILL serve them – the ones I mentioned in detail above.

New Humanism is where a child can go and play without fear of being raped and/or murdered. Or a young girl or woman can walk safely home and arrive home alive and untouched. It is where truth prevails and it is where politicians and those at the top mean what they say and do what they say they will do and not keep tricking and deceiving us all the time. It is where people and those in school CAN achieve their dreams and goals. It is where natural, kinder remedies are given instead of drugs. It is where Banks and Businesses actually DO help people with their money and with their pay and jobs and actually help them in their lives. It is where people care about one another and are and can be happy and where inventors and geniuses can get their good inventions and technologies safely out to the world. It is where safe, clean and cheap energy and power is available to all. It is where judges and the legal systems ARE fair for EVERYONE and not so heavy-handed.

New Humanism is not just thinking about oneself or just ones immediate family and friends or just one's business and nothing more. And how much money have I got in the bank. Me, me, me and fuck everyone else! No! Others should come in to the equation and be allowed to earn and make good money too and have a good standard of living and be happy and loved as human beings! Hum? When one makes a decision or a major decision, one should consider other people in one's village, town, city, country, other countries, the environment, nature, all life forms and the entire planet we are on. One should, if possible, be kind, respectful and friendly to everyone one meets in life. And if possible smile and give a good genuine handshake, smile or whatever the case may be. People should communicate more and I mean face-to-face. There should be REAL freedom of speech and people should be freely able to have demonstrations or have marches about topics and they should be easily be able to ask for a vote or referendum on important subjects and they definitely should be able to take out of office and power any party, political leader or member of government who is not doing their job well or as they should and who is not serving the people and their country. This should be an easy and fast system. Any sane and demonstrably deserving and talented individual should be able to apply for being elected as a member of parliament or as head of Government. He should not have to be connected and rich or wealthy or have rich and wealthy backers like the Rockefellers and Rothschilds, etc. for whom he or she just becomes and is a puppet.

New Humanism is where Mankind is honest and fair to everyone and this is from the very top to the very bottom. And it is where there are no poor; no homeless and no starving people, unless they want to remain in this state of course. It is also where you do not have a war like that which happened in Yugoslavia or Cambodia, where millions were butchered, murdered and raped and the rest of the world did nothing. It is where there would be no wars, at least not against ourselves but only our real true enemies, who obviously must be stopped. Hitler was created to be the being he was and became. It was no accident. That, and he, did not need to happen and it should not have been allowed to happen. One must always be prepared for war as one never knows fully what might happen and who might be in power (are their intentions good or bad?) But mankind should put in place a worldwide system to prevent wars between or wars within countries. And a fair system that allows for negotiations and settlements and where the truth is given and placed on the table – and the truth is gotten at and investigated. And a system whereby, if a war is imminent – then the other countries of the world - if the war is unfair, evil and unjust – can then put huge pressure on that country or leader or troublemaker and get him to either stop, force him to stop or arrest and try him or whatever actions and steps would be deemed necessary to prevent the war. And then, if the war still cannot be prevented, then the one/s causing it will be fighting the rest of the world (every other country) and they pretty surely would lose, which would be a deterrent in itself.

New Humanism can be further developed and advanced but I think you get the idea I am forwarding. New Humanism is simply the lessons learned from all the past history of mankind and also the past history and lessons learned from all the other previous (now defunct) old 'ISMS' that did not work for us but only worked for the few. New Humanism is reason, morals and ethics and it is founded on the goodness that is in all of us. It is founded on LOVE. You have these, with some intelligence, reason and logic and you have New Humanism. You have New Humanism and you have a good life and a good, sane, successful and prosperous planet for ALL – not just the few at or near the top. That is the big main difference between past ISMS and it. It is for the good of all. And it, in itself, would also address and get reformed those who are evil and doing bad, as deep down there somewhere, there is a soul or being, who wants to do and be good. One cannot have happiness, good money and success for all when one has a world that is mad, not enlightened spiritually, ethically and morally and where people are walking around with unconscious minds which make them do and say crazy or stupid things or agree and go along with it all. And where one has men of evil running the planet. No. New Humanism is not possible then.

One only has a Suppressionism then and that road only leads downwards, not upwards to the stars and the Heavens and beyond. This is the new definition of Humanism, not the current or older one which says from the:

British Humanist Association: **https://humanism.org.uk/ humanism/**

Humanism

Throughout recorded history there have been non-religious people who have believed that this life is the only life we have, that the universe is a natural phenomenon with no supernatural side, and that we can live ethical and fulfilling lives on the basis of reason and humanity. They have trusted to the scientific method, evidence, and reason to discover truths about the universe and have placed human welfare and happiness at the centre of their ethical decision making.

Defining 'Humanism'

> Roughly speaking, the word humanist has come to mean someone who: trusts to the scientific method when it comes to understanding how the universe works and rejects the idea of the supernatural (and is therefore an atheist or agnostic) makes their ethical decisions based on reason, empathy, and a concern for human beings and other sentient animalsbelieves that, in the absence of an afterlife and any discernible purpose to the universe, human beings can act to give their own lives meaning by seeking happiness in this life and helping others to do the same.

However, definitions abound and there are longer and shorter versions. The fullest definition to have a measure of international agreement is contained in the 2002 Amsterdam Declaration of the International humanist and Ethical Union. Some others include:
…a commitment to the perspective, interests and centrality of human persons; a belief in reason and autonomy as foundational aspects of human existence; a belief that reason, scepticism and the scientific method are the only appropriate instruments for discovering truth and structuring the human community; a belief that the foundations for ethics and society are to be found in autonomy and moral equality…
- *Concise Routledge Encyclopedia of Philosophy*
An appeal to reason in contrast to revelation or religious authority as a means of finding out about the natural world and destiny of man, and also giving a grounding for morality…Humanist ethics is also distinguished by placing the end of moral action in the welfare of humanity rather than in fulfilling the will of God.
- *Oxford Companion to Philosophy*
Believing that it is possible to live confidently without metaphysical or religious certainty and that all opinions are open to revision and correction, [Humanists] see human flourishing as dependent on open

communication, discussion, criticism and unforced consensus.
- *Cambridge Dictionary of Philosophy*
That man should show respect to man, irrespective of class, race or creed is fundamental to the humanist attitude to life. Among the fundamental moral principles, he would count those of freedom, justice, tolerance and happiness…the attitude that people can live an honest, meaningful life without following a formal religious creed.
- *Pears Cyclopaedia, 87th edition, 1978*
Rejection of religion in favour of the advancement of humanity by its own efforts.
- *Collins Concise Dictionary*
A non-religious philosophy, based on liberal human values.
- *Little Oxford Dictionary*
We can either broaden the current definition of Humanism or form a new Humanism called New Humanism (as above: better idea actually so they do not get conflicted or confused!!!) to bring it all up to date with our current society and the current state of affairs of this planet we live on. It is your choice?

New Humanism could evolve and be a worldwide Organization existing freely in every country in the world, where people can be members and where they can get help and advice and more importantly, where we can join together to start the changes that need to happen to make this planet a better place for all. And it can also be used to maintain freedom and to keep these changes in worldwide. So, to create a more better, more fairer and more equal world we need a New Humanism, a revolution (try peaceful at first if not then violent as no other choice or a BIG War for Freedom) and a change of all current bad current systems (all worldwide systems and those in individual countries and in banks, Business, etc.), adjustment of worldwide pay (far higher minimum wages globally) in every country so it enables a much better and higher standard of living for all and more importantly - right now at this point in time, the year being 2013, we need to either get the Rockefellers, the Rothschilds and all the other bad and nefarious ruling people and families of this planet to stop doing what they are doing and reform their ways – or we will have to stop them and imprison them if need be or we go to war: whatever it takes and that needs to be the attitude we all need to have to get done what has to be done! Banks, Governments, Businesses, the Media, the Share system (stocks, bonds and shares), the Oil, Gas, Energy and Motor industries all need to reform too and be overhauled, as do the educational, science and nuclear power industries. As do the Drug companies and OPEC. These are the main changes that need to happen but I am sure there are many more.

But FIRST comes YOUR decision, right here, right now, to do something about what I have written in this book and to NOT GIVE UP until there is REAL, TRUE, HONEST and FAIR Treatment and Freedom for ALL Mankind, on all levels and strata. Not just for those at or near the top – right? Got it? And those at or near the top have to be given the same choice: to change their one-sided ways or be made too. I would prefer if those at the top would, all by themselves, would change their ways for the better and good of all mankind and the rest of us. Why? Because they would actually feel much better an happier themselves. There IS joy and happiness in doing REAL good for others and not just thinking of just oneself or ones immediate friends and family (and some think [they are sick by the way] that killing, harming, ruining, making slaves of and controlling others in a bad fashion or making people suffer is _helping_ them) and if those at the top could see and try this, I think they might actually enjoy BEING GOOD and DOING GOOD for all and they can still have power and lots of money except that they would be sharing it around and really and actually be helping others AND themselves – as they need spiritual and mental help too and they – deep down inside – know it too – right? Get it?

This decision has to come first BEFORE anything effective can ever be done. It is not something one does for a day or a week – have a few demonstrations – and that is the end of it or support a few charities and that's it, I've done my bit.

NOOOOOOOOOOOOOO!!!!!!!!!!!!!!!!

That will not work my friend. And it will take as long as it takes to get the job done.

The job can be done quickly if the right effective actions are taken and everyone is organized into worldwide groups and organizations that co-ordinate the actions and activities together and support and help one another, and effectively plan their actions to get done or changed what has to be done or changed.

WE, the people, do and always have had the power. Rome new that. But how many times has it ever been effectively used?

Well, this pattern has to change, right here and right now. Being a Mob and burning down buildings and stealing from shops, etc. achieves very little and gives everyone a bad name.

So, the steps are:

YOU, by yourself right now, make the decision to do something effective about this planet and about those who are running it into the ground and into total slavery.

Then, organize a worldwide legal group or groups (or if they are banned then illegal groups as then one has no other option) to enable those who want to help be able to do so and have safety in numbers. (Something like the 'Occupy Wall Street' group (see later in this chapter for more info on this group) would be a good example or a good one to join or some other new group could be formed for either one's own country only or one's Continent or it could be a worldwide group or organization that anyone could join, with maybe a small membership fee.)

Put effective pressure on our Governments and Businesses to change things in our favour, not theirs and for them to put pressure on the Rockefellers and Rothschilds (and the rest of the Ruling Families and Individuals and those Royal Families involved) to stop them from continuing to interfere in Man's affairs (our affairs, lives, governments, countries and existence) as they have been doing for at least a hundred years.

If peaceful means are prevented or not effective; then we need to go to violent means; and if needed: war – but only as a very last resort and only to defend/protect ourselves and to get what we want; as not many people like wars; the dying and hurting others.

One can also think of other effective ways or actions to cause or bring in the changes that are required to make Earth a safe and good place for all to live and have a good standard of education and living.

If we win, then great, we can get all the changes in place and begin rebuilding this planet as it should be. And Mankind can live in peace without criminals destroying everything and making our lives hell with all their stupid laws and taxes. Then Mankind will have another second Golden Age: The Age of Freedom, where love, success, hard and good work that is fairly and justly rewarded; and happiness can prevail and our children can look forward to a good future and all life can survive; with plenty of good paid jobs for all and with good natural, healthy food to eat at low to medium cost and with good affordable accommodation (houses and apartments), transport and energy available for all. And where Mankind can rise up to the heights he only dreams about and where he can get closer to TRUE SELF and closer to God and beyond!

The other choice is a living HELL on Earth with no freedom, where those at the top control YOU, ME and everything else but not to help us but to make US slaves to them for ever more (until someone appears or comes up from no-where to free Mankind again – but that may not ever happen either, there is no guarantees and we do not know how long that may take) or no Earth any more, total wipe-out of all life on Earth. Nuclear Radiation is king. Pollution is rampant.

Well, my friend (or enemy) I have given you the facts both from myself and from others. I have given you my point of view. I have given you many other points of view. I have given you the options. I have given you the choices. I have also given you the truth and any can check out and verify any and all data, statistics, etc. that I have mentioned in this book and those of others, then YOU decide for yourself what you are going to do about it, if anything????????

YOU and the rest of us can continue with our lives and maybe we will make it to a good future. Or maybe we won't. But if we do not make it, there will not be a second chance. I promise you that! The chance is now. The time is now. This window of opportunity for real Freedom and happiness for all who want it (those who do not it, can be kept away from others for our protection and theirs and they can be treated well in a safe environment, until such day as a mental technology can handle the sick and evil minds they have. Or they can reform themselves right now, by themselves. It has happened before) will not be open and available for very long.

So if you want to pay more and more taxes and obey more and more stupid and suppressive laws; and earn less and less money and pay more and more bills. And if you want to have George Orwell's 1984 future or dare I say even worse than his depiction, then go ahead and do nothing. And we will all end up with nano super chips implanted in to our brains at birth, which my even monitor our thoughts or inflict pain on us for not obeying our orders and leaders. And our breeding will be controlled. Our children and ourselves will be given Mental Shock Treatment and Psychiatric drugs every day as needed to keep us - the sheep - the robots, the slaves, under control and doing what we are ordered. Where freedom of thought and speech are gone. It would actually be the future Hitler and his Creators actually wanted and nearly got. And it would be FAR worse than what Communism did to its peoples on this Earth. I do not think you could imagine the real dark evil suffering future we could have on this lovely planet. Can you? Try to for a moment. I **do** want you to actually think about it; but I rather don't like it myself. No-one does except them; but then this is why I wrote this book. To wake you up a bit; to raise your confront and responsibility and to get you to see what has been going on behind the scenes and de facto for many years. It is up to YOU and all of us now to decide what we are going to do. And the choice is rather a simple one: do nothing or do something?

I prefer a better, more loving and happy future for one and all on this wonderful blue and green planet, that, at this moment in time, is still teeming (just and not as much as it once was) with life. One where an honest smile, a kind handshake; and truth, honesty, love and justice can and do prevail and where, the Arts can and do flourish and prosper; and technology is used in good ways. And the food and crops we eat and grow are not all contaminated and full of pollution and chemicals. And where the air we breathe and the water we drink is clean and pure – not like it is now. And where a good days work, gets a good days pay in proportion with being able to have a good standard of living for oneself and one's family. And people (parents) do not have to do 2, 3 or 4 jobs just to barely make ends meet. And where children *really* get educated; not just in what *they* want us educated in and how they want us educated. And where Governments and Leaders do do a very good job for us all and they do SERVE **US**, the peoples of Earth and not just a few small few who own and control everything at the expense of the rest of us.

Below (Occupy Wall Street) is a good example of a group that is doing some good work in the USA. Greenpeace is another (http://www.

greenpeace.org/international). These groups could be enhanced, co-ordinated and developed worldwide with other groups and made more effective. These could then be the blueprint to be followed by other groups, if they prove to be effective and if they can bring about the necessary worldwide changes that are needed. Or another new worldwide group could be formed, say it could be called 'The Humanitarian League' or some such name, that has a paid membership and/or voluntary donations, with legal representation for people and members and other member benefits; but basically it would handle the issues I have brought up in this book and also handle all other relevant humanitarian, social and planet Earth issues as they arise. Some people like in Brazil and other countries seem to be fighting back too but it is just temporary and not organized very well, with a good plan and agenda. The actions for good change and revolution need to be CONTINUOUS until the desired results are attained and then once attained, they have to be maintained and not lost again. It won't be done in a day; but gradually, with strong support from all the right sides and from the right people, the huge but not impossible task can be accomplished fairly quickly, say maximum 6 months, then another 6 months for things to settle down again. If we have to go to war, who knows how long it could take. But either way, the job has to be done – live or die in the attempt!!!

Well my friends, and enemies (bad and evil people *CAN* change their ways too, if they really want to!?) I have now finished writing this book and I thank you for reading it. I wrote this book for you, for Mankind; and for all that is on planet Earth. This is the only planet we have right now. The question now is: What are you going to do about what I have said in this book and about the current situation we have here on Earth? Your destiny, and that of Mankind, are in YOUR hands now, not just mine. I hope you do not ignore what I have said and I trust you will make the right decision? This is EVERYONE'S RESPONSI-BILITY!!!!!! No just mine or a handful of people. I thank you for any good work you have already done in relevance to the topics covered in this book, and, I thank you in advance for any good work you will do in the future! Thank you and goodbye for now!

And finally, just to illustrate a point, take a look at this:

WEAPONS & MILITARY SPENDING WORLDWIDE

Just in case you are wondering where all the taxpayers money has gone to and why money is sometimes not available for other more important issues like developing new non-pollutive technology, new engines to fully replace petrol and diesel vehicles worldwide (Oh no, they can't do that because governments make so much money from taxes on fuel?); and new power, light and heat sources and many other sorely needed technologies, like new foods and bio-degradable plastics, etc.; more affordable and cheaper housing and higher minimum wages, etc. Here is a look at what WE, the good law-abiding slave taxpayers are paying for, and this is just on the Military – nothing else:

SOURCE: STATISTA

In 2017, the following countries, in descending order, spend the following - in billions of US dollars - on arms and weapons (this is just for ONE YEAR!):

USA 610, China 228, Saudi Arabia 96.4, Russia 66.3, India 63.9 (meant to be a poor country with millions of starving people?), France 57.8, UK 47.2, 45.4, Germany 44.3, South Korea 39.2, Brazil 29.3 (has lots of poor and unemployed people?), Italy 29.2, Australia 27.5, Canada 20.6, Turkey 18.2.

In 2017 alone, total Global Military Expenditure was 1.7 Trillion! My God, can you believe this? And from 2001 until 2017, the total amount spend worldwide was: 25 Trillion, 574 billion!!!

And people are starving, poor or on low-income jobs; pollution is increasing and inflation and the cost of living is going up and up. And this does not include the total amount spend on weapons and defence since the beginning of World War II until now. No wonder global debt is so high in tandem to higher and additional taxes. And don't forget that it is you and I, and our children that are paying for all this – directly or indirectly - and all of the other debt and running and investment expenses our countries have/incur. Nice huh? And who do you think most, if not all of this world debt is owed to? Who do you think owns or runs all the Arms and weapon's manufacturing companies or are on the board of directors?

Anyone who wants some more answers or who wants to help or to be pointed in the right direction, spiritually or otherwise, can contact me at: PaulThor@writeme.com

Thank you!

Paul Thor

PS: I have put together some more miscellaneous material below, some more food for thought:

Check out 'Occupy Wall Street', this growing movement to change the USA and the world.

Here is an interesting article on them; but you can google these and everything else in this book to find out more data on them or to verify what I have said:

Occupy Wall Street

From Wikipedia, the free encyclopedia

http://en.wikipedia.org/wiki/Occupy_Wall_Street

This article is about the protests in New York City. For wider movement, see Occupy movement.

| | It has been suggested that The People's Library be merged into this article. (Discuss)Proposed since August 2013. |

http://en.wikipedia.org/wiki/File:Wall-Street-1.jpg

	Adbusters poster advertising the original protest
	September 17, 2011
Location	New York City 40°42'33.79"N 74°0'40.76"W
Causes	Wealth inequality, political corruption,[1] corporate influence of government, inter alia.

Methods	Occupation Civil disobedience Picketing Demonstrations Internet activism
Number	
	Zuccotti Park Other activity in NYC: 2,000+ marchers (march on police headquarters, October 2, 2011)[2] 700+ marchers arrested (crossing Brooklyn Bridge, October 3, 2011)[3] 15,000+ marchers (Lower Manhattan solidarity march, October 5, 2011)[4] 6,000+ marchers (Times Square recruitment center march, October 15, 2011)[5] 50,000–100,000 marchers (2012 May Day march on Wall St.)[6]

Occupy Wall Street (OWS) is the name given to a protest movement that began on September 17, 2011, in Zuccotti Park, located in New York City's Wall Street financial district. This date may be disputed with a likely trigger event as early as August 1, 2011, as a nude[citation needed] artist performance "Occupation: Wall Street" followed by arrests on Wall Street occurred while protesting American financial institutions.[7][8]

The Canadian, anti-consumerist, pro-environment group/magazine, Adbusters initiated the call for a protest. The ensuing series of events helped lead to media awareness that inspired Occupy protests and movements around the world. In awarding Workhouse its Platinum Award, industry publication PR News noted "The results, obviously, have been spectacular. There's hardly a newspaper, Internet or broadcast media outlet that hasn't covered OWS."[9]

The main issues raised by Occupy Wall Street were social and economic inequality, greed, corruption and the perceived undue influence of corporations on government—particularly from the financial services sector. The OWS slogan, *We are the 99%*, refers to income inequality and wealth distribution in the U.S. between the wealthiest 1% and the rest of the population. To achieve their goals, protesters acted on consensus-based decisions made in general assemblieswhich emphasized direct action over petitioning authorities for redress.[10][nb 1].....

Protesters were forced out of Zuccotti Park on November 15, 2011. After several unsuccessful attempts to re-occupy the original location, protesters turned their focus to occupying banks, corporate headquarters, board meetings, college and university campuses.

On December 29, 2012, Naomi Wolf of *The Guardian* newspaper provided U.S. government documents which revealed that the FBI and DHS had monitored Occupy Wall Street through its Joint Terrorism Task Force, despite labelling it a peaceful movement.[11]

Origins[edit]

...Pulitzer prize winning journalist Chris Hedges, a supporter of the movement, argues that OWS had popular support and "articulated the concerns of the majority of citizens."

Writer: I found this interesting obscure article below while researching this book. It makes one wonder what type of people we are really dealing with and how they all seem to be connected or related or are friends (I have been unable to verify if this data is factual or not but it does appear to make sense!):

SOURCE: AANGIRFAN HTTP://AANGIRFAN.BLOGSPOT.CO.UK/2012/12/MARC-RICH-JEWISH-MAFIA.HTML

(WRITER: IF YOU VISIT THE WEBSITE ABOVE YOU CAN VIEW THE FULL ARTICLE WITH IMAGES!)

DISCLAIMER: THE POSTING OF STORIES, COMMENTARIES, REPORTS, DOCUMENTS AND LINKS (EMBEDDED OR OTHERWISE) ON THIS SITE DOES NOT IN ANY WAY, SHAPE OR FORM, IMPLIED OR OTHERWISE, NECESSARILY EXPRESS OR SUGGEST ENDORSEMENT OR SUPPORT OF ANY OF SUCH POSTED MATERIAL OR PARTS THEREIN.

WEDNESDAY, DECEMBER 26, 2012

MARC RICH; JEWISH MAFIA

Marcell Reich, who calls himself Marc Rich, was born into a Jewish family in Belgium.

Allegedly, Marc Rich is an asset of the CIA, Mossad and the Russian Jewish Mafia.

According to Newsmax, Saturday, March 31, 2001:

"Mark Rich was a key figure in the .... creation of an underground government that survived the break-up of the Soviet Union and still rules Russia today behind the scenes."

Mark Rich Helped KGB Create Hidden Government

Former Israel Prime Minister Ehud Barak mentioned Rich's contributions to Israel's "national security" in phone calls to Clinton, according to statements from Barak's spokesman, Gadi Baltiansky.

A letter from former Mossad chief Shabtai Shavit to Clinton confirmed that Rich had given "assistance" to Mossad.

http://www.7days.ae/2006/04/25/conspiracy-theory.html

Denise Rich (Denise Eisenberg), formerly married to Marc Rich.

Website for this image

"Lewis Libby's real claim to fame is his 18-year collaboration with Russian Mafiya 'godfather' Marc Rich...

"Libby was the personal attorney for Rich from 1985, shortly after Rich fled the United States to avoid criminal prosecution for tax evasion and "trading with the enemy" - for illegal oil dealings with the Khomeini regime in Iran, while they were holding American hostages.

"Rich set up in Zug, Switzerland, and became one of the most important figures in busting the oil embargoes against apartheid South Africa, Iran, and, later, Iraq.

"All the while, Libby toiled as Rich's legal flack in America, presenting the swindler and Mossad bankroller as a victim of overzealous prosecutors."

LaRouche Points to Marc Rich's White House Mole: Lewis Libby

Ayatollah Khomeini, friend of Marc Rich and the CIA.

In 1974, Rich created Glencore, the world's largest commodity trader.

One of the places where Glencore makes money is Zambia, which has copper mines. In 1964, Zambia nationalised its mines, but, the IMF and World Bank forced Zambia to privatise them.

Thus, Switzerland now makes more money from Zambia's copper than Zambia itself.

Rich was wanted by the US justice system for having traded with Iran and for tax evasion.
Rich had a special relationship with the CIA-MI6 assetAyatollah Khomeini.
In 2001, Rich received a presidential pardon from Bill Clinton.
Rich has lived in Switzerland since 1983.
After spending several years in Zug, a place loved by Margaret Thatcher, Rich moved to Meggen, a city in the German speaking Canton of Lucerne.
Rich owns property in the ski resort of St. Moritz, Switzerland, and in Marbella, Spain.

marc rich home.

According to an article at: rense.com/general26/rich.htm
"Marc Rich, the commodity bandit and 'spook' was so interwoven with the White House of George Bush The Elder and later, Bill Clinton, you could not hardly tell whether the White House dirty tricks department was in Washington or Zug, Switzerland, one of Rich's outpposts...

"U.S. Attorney for the Southern District of New York, Rudolph W. Giuliani (later N.Y. city Mayor), wanted to put Rich in jail.

"A Bush Family confidant, Giuliani nevertheless found out too late that Marc Rich was the American CIA's laundry man and was immune."
....

...... Winston Churchill wrote that: "in the Soviet institutions the predominance of Jews is astonishing.
"And the prominent, if not indeed, the principal, part in the system of terrorism applied by the Extraordinary Commissions for Combating Counter-Revolution has been taken by Jews, and in some notable cases by Jewesses...

"The fact that in many cases Jewish interests and Jewish places of worship are excepted by the Bolsheviks from their universal hostility has tended more and more to associate the Jewish race in Russia with villainies which are now being perpetrated..."

Interesting articles below about US debt. Good read!

SOURCE: **MAIL online**

http://www.dailymail.co.uk/news/article-2465544/Surprise-Debt-ceiling-deal-gives-Obama-blank-check-loophole-allow-government-spend-WITHOUT-LIMIT-February.html#ixzz2jVK3tIBy
Follow us: @MailOnline on Twitter | DailyMail on Facebook

Surprise! Debt-ceiling deal gives Obama a blank check: Loophole will allow government to spend WITHOUT LIMIT until February

SOURCE: **MAIL online** Saturday, Nov 02 2013

http://www.dailymail.co.uk/news/article-2442363/Obama-warns-world-markets-guarantee-U-S-avoid-defaulting-debts.html#ixzz2jVHUNOEl
Follow us: @MailOnline on Twitter | DailyMail on Facebook

'You should be concerned': Obama warns world markets there is no guarantee U.S. will avoid defaulting on its debts

SOURCE: Sci/Tech October 30, 2013
Frank Jordans and Geir Moulson contributed reporting from Berlin.
Follow Juergen Baetz on Twitter at http://www.twitter.com/jbaetz

EU spying backlash threatens billions in US trade

BRUSSELS (AP) — The backlash in Europe over U.S. spying is threatening an agreement that generates tens of billions of dollars in trans-Atlantic business every year — and negotiations on another pact worth many times more.

And:

SOURCE: Sci/Tech September 06, 2013
Associated Press writer Stephen Braun contributed to this report.
Follow Jack Gillum on Twitter: http://twitter.com/jackgillum

Report: NSA cracked most online encryption

WASHINGTON (AP) — The National Security Agency, working

with the British government, has secretly been unravelling encryption technology that billions of Internet users rely upon to keep their electronic messages and confidential data safe from prying eyes, according to published reports based on internal U.S. government documents.

SOURCE: Sci/Tech July 02, 2013
http://phys.org/news/2013-07-golden-age-surveillance-big-edge.html

In worldwide surveillance age, US has big edge

In this article, former CIA employee goes into detail about the USA's surveillance of the world and pretty much any country, company or person they want.

SOURCE: UK September 19, 2013
http://www.joplinglobe.com/news/jpmorgan-pays-m-admits-fault-in-trading-loss/article_c39e2006-b102-5668-b864-5d268d8b441e.html

JPMorgan pays $920M, admits fault in trading loss

WASHINGTON (AP) — JPMorgan Chase & Co. will pay $920 million and has admitted that it failed to oversee trading that led to a $6 billion loss and renewed worries about serious risk-taking by major banks.

This fine was one of the biggest ever given against a financial institution.

I wonder how many other types of inside trading and financial irregularities have transpired over the years from such banks and companies and within governments, including the Bank of England and the Federal Reserve in the USA?

Lots. Just they get away with it, cover it up or pay people off. Criminals the lot of them. One set of laws for them and another set for the common people, who must not break the law. No. And if you have money then you can buy you own law and legal judgement.

We live on a very fair and just planet!

WRITER: More odds and ends below:

http://www.breitbart.com/sports/2013/05/30/russian-critic-wide-corruption-at-sochi-games/

Russian critic: Wide corruption at Sochi games

In this article, they say that about $30 billion was stolen on the run-up to the Olympic games. It was estimated to cost $12 billion but that then went up to $51 billion.

Do you know of any country or government without some form of corruption, whether we know about it or not as we only know about it when it is exposed. Most of it is covered up or labelled top secret or will NEVER be known about ever.

I would say NO. We allow criminals to run our countries and to start wars and then pillage, kill, rape and steal when they go to war.

And not long ago we had many troubles, corruptions and questions about FIFA and *FIFA* President Sepp Blatter. And we also had the phoning taping in the UK and Rupert Murdock. And how many other scandals and cover-ups have we had high up in Governments and multi-million pound Organizations and Businesses over the years? Many. Some we will never even hear or find out about. And most of them get away or just get a fine or something or it is lost in some big expensive investigation for years and then when a report is made of its findings and recommendations – you have to ask: what was the point of the investigation in the first go-off and how could the cost of it be justified. Let's just face the fact that those high up usually have friends in high places or up even higher than themselves (and they have plenty of money), and they look after them and one another, and that includes judges, Ministers, etc. And sadly, a lot of these people are two-faced mother fuckers: they smile and seem very friendly to ones face and to and in public; but when our backs are turned, they knife you or us in the back or shaft us openly or covertly up the ass. This is some of the kind of people, high up, who we are dealing with. Most will stop at nothing to get what they want, even murder and an odd rape here and there or some prostitutes on the side or some nice gay boys. Or those, like the late Jimmy Saville in the UK (which seems to be a child sex paedophile ring going high up, how high we will probably never know as those high up will keep it that way) And of course, these type of people use plenty of street drugs and have plenty of parties and orgies, where the deals and private talks occur. And only those who are connected and have ties and relations with them, will get invited. It is the old-boy-network except it is now the modern-boy-network.

EEC says further unification is the solution; why does the world and stock markets react when the World Bank and IMF says things look bad on coming out of the recession (they do this to cause the recession to worsen): why not say we are getting OUT of the recession and put confidence in the world markets and in consumers? The newspapers all get their stories same stories from the same central sources, except for a few local stories added in. The newspapers and media says: 'The World Economy is bad and there is a bad recession and depression on.' And nearly everyone believes it. Then, recently, the newspapers and media say: 'The US and European economies are improving and we are coming out of this recession,' and we believe them.

What real power does the UN and NATO actually have? Where was the US, the UK, NATO, the UN; G8, G20 when human rights were being violated in Cambodia and many other countries that had wars in them: Yugoslavia for example? And recently Syria (2014). No, they only get involved if it helps them and THEIR vested interests (oil, gas, gold, arts, diamonds, political motives, world-wide domination motives and dare I say, even alien technology.) And either way, they make vasts amount of money from selling their weapons.

If the people in Brazil could get organized and work out a plan to free themselves from poverty and the in-equality they have there: then they could be a great example to the rest of the world and then maybe India, China and Russia might follow. Brazilians and other countries have most probably had enough. Riots are fine but if they just got more organized and kept it going to get the changes they want, then they could do it and the Brazilians would be free and have better lives, better wages and less crime, drugs and prostitution. Brazil, are you going to do it? That is my challenge to you? China, are you going to do it? Russia? India? Well? The power is still with the people if they would just use it, get organized and not pillage, loot and destroy things. But be civil, intelligent and logical about it. Get some plans, rules and policies done and weapons organized but only use them if one is forced too. If the army and police get involved or become too extreme and violent, then there is no other option but to fight and if it turns to all-out war, then so be it. That is what I mean by getting organized. And to bring in the new changes and order to one's country, one has to be prepared to do whatever it takes and to continue and persist for however long it takes. But one also has to be careful who one enlists, employs, uses and who one trusts, as the enemy can easily penetrate most groups, get their plans and then one could fail. That is why the amount of people involved has to be in the millions in each country that wants change and improvements.

SOURCE: HealthJuly 12, 2013

Spread of DNA databases sparks ethical concerns

You can ditch your computer and leave your cellphone at home, but you can't escape your DNA.
Article by Jill Lawless can be reached at http://Twitter.com/ JillLawless
You know where all this DNA database stuff is going to go. Don't mind what those at the top say. They will keep at it until we all have to give our DNA, because there is potential terrorism in everyone so it's for everyone's good. Isn't it?
And then they will say we all have to be chipped so we can be tracked and all of our personal data can be scanned without our knowing, at any time. And then if you misbehave, you will be taken in for 'mental programming' or deep sleep therapy using drugs, to adjust you in to a more better and controllable human being. Or they will just throw you in prison or just take you away and dispose of you, in a humane way of course.
This is where all this bullshit is going and it will be worse than this. But they will cause things to happen and mass publicize them in the media they control, so we will all support these new laws and changes – just like they did with 9/11 and other so-called terrorist mishaps. This is how they work. Then we all say how terrible it all is and oh yes, we support them 100% because they are helping us and protecting us and our society!
Wake up I say to you. And I say bollix to them at the top who want to bring in these changes!
Many countries around the world are now using DNA databases.

Interpol says 54 nations are now using them, which includes the USA and UK. Brazil and India are going to join them, and United Arab Emirates plans to DNA their entire population. Nice!

SOURCE: **The Independent**

Brazil riots latest: Protests continue at Confederations Cup matches despite Rio and Sao Paulo leaders agreeing to reverse public transport fare hikes

Riot police use gas bombs and pepper spray to quell protesters in the northern city of Fortaleza

STEVE ANDERSON THURSDAY 20 JUNE 2013

Writer: At least Brazil is doing something to get changes in their country but it needs to more organised and it needs to continue until they force their government to make fairer changes so everyone in their country gets a better life and gets the help they need, not just the few and the rich!!!????

The people in France too are also very active when they want something changed or are not happy with some new tax or law that their government brings in. They literally bring the country or its roads to a standstill and this includes the farmers.

Rock on!

SPEND OUR FOREIGN AID ON BRITISH VICTIMS OF FLOODING

ZoomBookmarkSharePrintListenTranslate

As crisis deepens, MPS tell Cameron ... *'Ask Abyssinia for some cash'*

http://www.dailymail.co.uk/news/article-2554324/Spend-foreign-aid-British-victims-flooding-MPs-impassioned-call-crisis-deepens.html

In the above article it says £11 billion is sent overseas every year in Foerign Aid. The Prime Minsiter plans to increase this to about £12 billion by 2015.

What does the UK get in return for this aid? It must get cheap products and produce from poorer countries and it retains control of these countries and some extent, their leaders. But do you think the rich Western World wants to really help the Third world and poorer countries? I don't think so!

Nigel Farage says in this article:

'Anyone with an ounce of common sense knows that a government's primary duty is to the well-being of its own citizens. Charity begins at home and it is not mean-spirited to say that, it is just basic common sense.'

APPENDIX 1

'MONARCH PROGRAM'
(**Warning**: not for children or the fainthearted**!!! You are warned!**)

This source you can look up and view yourself. Here is the link. It gives full graphic details of this program so please be warned! Ultimately most of this so-called conditioning and control of people for various nefarious reasons was started in ancient times (thousands of years ago) by Muslims and in some Arab countries to create assassins using drugs, pleasure, etc. It was further developed by the Germans in WW I & II and later by the CIA and other covert groups. They are still is use today as you will see below; and you may even be one or a victim and NOT even know it!

SOURCE: http://vigilantcitizen.com/hidden-knowledge/origins-and-techniques-of-monarch-mind-control/
The Monarch Program began after Project MK Ultra.

But To SUMMARISE: The Monarch Programming is a method of mind control used by numerous organizations for covert purposes. It is a continuation of project MK-ULTRA, a mind-control program developed by the CIA, and tested on the military and civilians. The methods are astonishingly sadistic (its entire purpose is to traumatize the victim) and the expected results are horrifying: The creation of a mind-controlled slave who can be triggered at anytime to perform any action required by the handler. While mass media ignores this issue, over 2 million Americans have gone through the horrors of this program. This article looks at the origins of Monarch programming and some of its methods and symbolism.

The other link is just below and I have fully included the details of this here. You are welcome to further investigate and research this yourself, if you want; but you will find it is sick stuff; done by sick, sub-human people!

https://en.wikipedia.org/wiki/Project_MKUltra

And check the US Senate investigation of this: https://archive.org/details/1977MkultraSenateInvestigationProjectMkultra_201604

Project MKUltra—sometimes referred to as the **CIA's mind control program**—was the code name given to an illegal program of experiments on human subjects, designed and undertaken by the United States Central Intelligence Agency (CIA). Experiments on humans were intended to identify and develop drugs and procedures to be used in interrogations and torture, in order to weaken the individual to force confessions through mind control. Organized through the Scientific Intelligence Division of the CIA, the project coordinated with the Special Operations Division of the U.S. Army's Chemical Corps.[1] The program began in the early 1950s, was officially sanctioned in 1953, was reduced in scope in 1964, further curtailed in 1967 and officially halted in 1973.[2] The program engaged in many illegal activities;[3][4][5] in particular it used unwitting U.S. and Canadian citizens as its test subjects, which led to controversy regarding its legitimacy.[3](p74)[6][7][8] MKUltra used numerous methodologies to manipulate people's mental states and alter brain functions, including the surreptitious administration of drugs (especially LSD) and other chemicals, hypnosis,[9] sensory deprivation, isolation, verbal and sexual abuse, as well as various forms of torture. [*not verified in body*]

The scope of Project MKUltra was broad, with research undertaken at 80 institutions, including 44 colleges and universities, as well as hospitals, prisons, and pharmaceutical companies.[10] The CIA operated through these institutions using front organizations, although sometimes top officials at these institutions were aware of the CIA's involvement.[11] As the US Supreme Court later noted, MKULTRA was:

concerned with "the research and development of chemical, biological, and radiological materials capable of employment in clandestine operations to control human behavior." The program consisted of some 149 subprojects which the Agency contracted out to various universities, research foundations, and similar institutions. At least 80 institutions and 185 private researchers participated. Because the Agency funded MKULTRA indirectly, many of the participating individuals were unaware that they were dealing with the Agency.[12] Project MKUltra was first brought to public attention in 1975 by the Church Committee of the U.S. Congress, and a Gerald Ford commission to investigate CIA activities within the United States. Investigative efforts were hampered by the fact that CIA Director Richard Helms ordered all MKUltra files destroyed in 1973; the Church Committee and Rockefeller Commission investigations relied on the sworn testimony of direct participants and on the relatively small number of documents that survived Helms' destruction order.[13] In 1977, a Freedom of Information Act request uncovered a cache of 20,000 documents relating to project MKUltra, which led to Senate hearings later that same year.[3][14] In July 2001, some surviving information regarding MKUltra was officially declassified.

Background

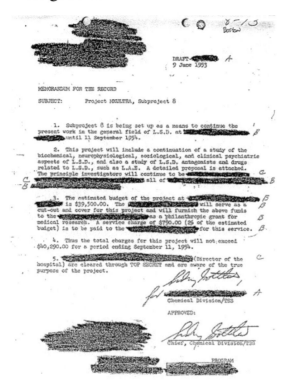

https://en.wikipedia.org/wiki/Project_MKUltra#/media/File:Mkultra-lsd-doc.jpg PUBLIC DOMAIN Dr. Sidney Gottlieb approved of an MKUltra subproject on LSD in this June 9, 1953 letter.

Precursor experiments

In 1945 the Joint Intelligence Objectives Agency was established and given direct responsibility for Operation Paperclip. The program recruited former Nazi scientists,[15] some of whom had been identified and prosecuted as war criminals during the Nuremberg Trials.[16] Several secret U.S. government projects grew out of Operation Paperclip.[citation needed] These projects included Project CHATTER (established 1947), and Project BLUEBIRD (established 1950), which was renamed Project ARTICHOKE in 1951. Their purpose was to study mind control, interrogation, behavior modification and related topics.

MKUltra

The project's intentionally oblique CIA cryptonym is made up of the digraph *MK*, meaning that the project was sponsored by the agency's <u>Technical Services Staff</u>, followed by the word <u>Ultra</u> (which had previously been used to designate the most secret classification of <u>World War II</u> intelligence). Other related cryptonyms include <u>Project MKNAOMI</u> and <u>Project MKDELTA</u>.

Headed by <u>Sidney Gottlieb</u>, the MKUltra project was started on the order of CIA director <u>Allen Welsh Dulles</u> on April 13, 1953.[17] Its aim was to develop mind-controlling drugs for use against the Soviet bloc, largely in response to alleged <u>Soviet</u>, <u>Chinese</u>, and <u>North Korean</u> use of mind control techniques on U.S. <u>prisoners of war</u> in Korea.[18] The CIA wanted to use similar methods on their own captives. The CIA was also interested in being able to manipulate foreign leaders with such techniques,[19] and would later invent several schemes to drug <u>Fidel Castro</u>. Experiments were often conducted without the subjects' knowledge or consent.[20] In some cases, academic researchers being funded through grants from CIA front organizations were unaware that their work was being used for these purposes.[21]

In 1964, the project was renamed MKSEARCH. The project attempted to produce a perfect <u>truth drug</u> for use in interrogating suspected Soviet spies during the <u>Cold War</u>, and generally to explore any other possibilities of mind control. Another MKUltra effort, Subproject 54, was the Navy's top secret "Perfect Concussion" program, which was supposed to use sub-aural frequency blasts to erase memory. However, the program was never carried out.[22]

Because most MKUltra records were deliberately destroyed in 1973 by order of then CIA director <u>Richard Helms</u>, it has been difficult, if not impossible, for investigators to gain a complete understanding of the more than 150 individually funded research sub-projects sponsored by MKUltra and related CIA programs.[23]

The project began during a period of what Rupert Cornwell described as "paranoia" at the CIA, when America had lost its nuclear monopoly, and fear of Communism was at its height.[24] <u>James Jesus Angleton</u>, head of CIA counter-intelligence, believed that the organization had been penetrated by a mole at the highest levels.[24]

Goals

The Agency poured millions of dollars into studies examining methods of influencing and controlling the mind, and of enhancing their ability to extract information from resistant subjects during interrogation.[25][26]

Some historians have asserted that creating a "Manchurian Candidate" subject through "mind control" techniques was a goal of MKUltra and related CIA projects.[27] Alfred McCoy has claimed that the CIA attempted to focus media attention on these sorts of "ridiculous" programs, so that the public would not look at the primary goal of the research, which was developing effective methods of torture and interrogation. Such authors cite as one example that the CIA's KUBARK interrogation manual refers to "studies at McGill University", and that most of the techniques recommended in KUBARK are exactly those that researcher Donald Ewen Cameron used on his test subjects (sensory deprivation, drugs, isolation, etc.).[25]

One 1955 MKUltra document gives an indication of the size and range of the effort; this document refers to the study of an assortment of mind-altering substances described as follows:[28]

> Substances which will promote illogical thinking and impulsiveness to the point where the recipient would be discredited in public.
> Substances which increase the efficiency of mentation and perception.
> Materials which will cause the victim to age faster/slower in maturity.
> Materials which will promote the intoxicating effect of alcohol.
> Materials which will produce the signs and symptoms of recognized diseases in a reversible way so that they may be used for malingering, etc.
> Materials which will cause temporary/permanent brain damage and loss of memory.
> Substances which will enhance the ability of individuals to withstand privation, torture and coercion during interrogation and so-called "brain-washing".
> Materials and physical methods which will produce amnesia for events preceding and during their use.
> Physical methods of producing shock and confusion over extended periods of time and capable of surreptitious use.
> Substances which produce physical disablement such as paralysis of the legs, acute anemia, etc.
> Substances which will produce a chemical that can cause blisters.
> Substances which alter personality structure in such a way that the tendency of the recipient to become dependent upon another

person is enhanced.

A material which will cause mental confusion of such a type that the individual under its influence will find it difficult to maintain a fabrication under questioning.

Substances which will lower the ambition and general working efficiency of men when administered in undetectable amounts.

Substances which promote weakness or distortion of the eyesight or hearing faculties, preferably without permanent effects.

A knockout pill which can surreptitiously be administered in drinks, food, cigarettes, as an aerosol, etc., which will be safe to use, provide a maximum of amnesia, and be suitable for use by agent types on an ad hoc basis.

A material which can be surreptitiously administered by the above routes and which in very small amounts will make it impossible for a person to perform physical activity.

Experiments

CIA documents suggest that "chemical, biological and radiological" means were investigated for the purpose of mind control as part of MKUltra.[29] A secret memorandum granted the MKUltra director up to six percent of the CIA research budget in fiscal year 1953, without oversight or accounting.[30] An estimated $10 million USD (roughly $87.5 million adjusted for inflation) or more was spent.[31]

Drugs

LSD

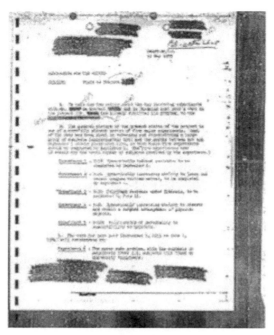

https://en.wikipedia.org/wiki/Project_MKUltra#/media/File:Mkultra-lsd-doc.jpg   PUBLIC DOMAIN

1953 experiment record
Early CIA efforts focused on LSD, which later came to dominate many of MKUltra's programs. Technical Services Staff officials understood that LSD distorted a person's sense of reality, and they felt compelled to learn whether it could alter someone's basic loyalties.[32] The CIA wanted to know if they could make Russian spies defect against their will and whether the Russians could do the same to their own operatives.[32]
Once Project MKUltra officially got underway in April, 1953, experiments included administering LSD to mental patients, prisoners, drug addicts and prostitutes, "people who could not fight back," as one agency officer put it.[33] In one case LSD was administered to a mental patient in Kentucky for 174 days.[33] LSD was also administered to CIA employees, military personnel, doctors, other government agents, and members of the general public in order to study their reactions. LSD and other drugs were usually administered without the subject's knowledge or informed consent, a violation of the Nuremberg Code that the U.S. agreed to follow after World War II. The aim of this was to

find drugs which would irresistibly bring out deep confessions or wipe a subject's mind clean and program him or her as "a robot agent."[34] In Operation Midnight Climax, the CIA set up several brothels in San Francisco, California to obtain a selection of men who would be too embarrassed to talk about the events. The men were dosed with LSD, the brothels were equipped with one-way mirrors, and the sessions were filmed for later viewing and study.[35] In other experiments where people were given LSD without their knowledge, they were interrogated under bright lights with doctors in the background taking notes. The subjects were told that their "trips" would be extended indefinitely if they refused to reveal their secrets. The people being interrogated this way were CIA employees, U.S. military personnel, and agents suspected of working for the other side in the Cold War. Long-term debilitation and several deaths resulted from this.[34] Heroin addicts were bribed into taking LSD with offers of more heroin.[11]

The Office of Security used LSD in interrogations but Dr. Sidney Gottlieb, the chemist who directed MKUltra, had other ideas: he thought it could be used in covert operations. Since its effects were temporary, he believed it could be given to high officials and in this way affect the course of important meetings, speeches etc. Since he realized there was a difference in testing the drug in a laboratory and using it in clandestine operations, he initiated a series of experiments where LSD was given to people in "normal" settings without warning. At first, everyone in Technical Services tried it; a typical experiment involved two people in a room where they observed each other for hours and took notes. As the experimentation progressed, a point was reached where outsiders were drugged with no explanation whatsoever and surprise acid trips became something of an occupational hazard among CIA operatives. Adverse reactions often occurred, for example an operative who had received the drug in his morning coffee, became psychotic and ran across Washington, seeing a monster in every car that passed him. The experiments continued even after Dr. Frank Olson, an Army scientist who had not taken LSD before, went into deep depression after a surprise trip and later fell from a thirteenth story window (it is unclear whether he committed suicide or was murdered).[36]

Some subjects' participation was consensual, and in these cases they appeared to be singled out for even more extreme experiments. In one case, seven volunteers in <u>Kentucky</u> were given LSD for 77 consecutive days.[37]

LSD was eventually dismissed by MKUltra's researchers as too unpredictable in its results.[38] They had given up on the notion that LSD was "the secret that was going to unlock the universe," but it still had a place in the cloak-and-dagger arsenal. However, by 1962 the CIA and the army had developed a series of <u>superhallucinogens</u> such as the highly touted <u>BZ</u>, which was thought to hold greater promise as a mind control weapon. This resulted in the withdrawal of support by many academics and private researchers, and LSD research became less of a priority altogether.[36]

Other drugs

Another technique investigated was connecting a <u>barbiturate</u> <u>IV</u> into one arm and an <u>amphetamine</u> IV into the other.[39] The barbiturates were released into the person first, and as soon as the person began to fall asleep, the amphetamines were released. The person would then begin babbling incoherently, and it was sometimes possible to ask questions and get useful answers.

Other experiments involved <u>heroin</u>, <u>morphine</u>, <u>temazepam</u> (used under code name MKSEARCH), <u>mescaline</u>, <u>psilocybin</u>, <u>scopolamine</u>, <u>marijuana</u>, <u>alcohol</u>, and <u>sodium pentothal</u>.[40]

Electronics

At least one subproject of the MK Ultra project was about the electronic control of human behaviour (subproject 119). Subproject 119 had the purpose to provide funds for a study to make a critical review of the literature and scientific developments related to the recording, analysis and interpretation of bio-electric signals from the human organism, and activation of the human behaviour by remote means. The survey encompassed five main areas: techniques of activation of the human organism by remote electronic means, bio-electric sensors, recording, analysis and standardization of data.[citation needed]

Hypnosis

Declassified MKUltra documents indicate <u>hypnosis</u> was studied in the early 1950s. Experimental goals included: the creation of "hypnotically induced <u>anxieties</u>," "hypnotically increasing ability to learn and recall complex written matter," studying hypnosis and <u>polygraph</u> examinations, "hypnotically increasing ability to observe and recall complex arrangements of physical objects," and studying "relationship of personality to susceptibility to hypnosis."[41] Experiments were conducted with drug induced hypnosis and with <u>anterograde</u> and <u>retrograde amnesia</u> while under the influence of such drugs.

Canadian experiments

https://en.wikipedia.org/wiki/Project_MKUltra#/media/File:Mkultra-lsd-doc.jpg   PUBLIC DOMAIN

Donald Ewen Cameron c.1967
The experiments were exported to Canada when the CIA recruited Scottish psychiatrist <u>Donald Ewen Cameron</u>, creator of the "<u>psychic driving</u>" concept, which the CIA found particularly interesting. Cameron had been hoping to correct schizophrenia by erasing existing memories and reprogramming the psyche. He commuted from <u>Albany, New York</u>, to <u>Montreal</u> every week to work at the <u>Allan Memorial Institute</u> of <u>McGill University</u> and was paid $69,000 from 1957 to 1964 to carry out MKUltra experiments there. These research funds were sent to Dr. Cameron by a CIA front organization, the Society for the Investigation of Human Ecology, and as shown in internal CIA documents, Dr. Cameron did not know that the money originated from the CIA.[42] In addition to LSD, Cameron also experimented with various paralytic drugs as well as <u>electroconvulsive therapy</u> at thirty to forty times the normal power. His "driving" experiments consisted

of putting subjects into drug-induced coma for weeks at a time (up to three months in one case) while playing tape loops of noise or simple repetitive statements. His experiments were typically carried out on patients who had entered the institute for minor problems such as anxiety disorders and postpartum depression, many of whom suffered permanently from his actions.[43] His treatments resulted in victims' incontinence, amnesia, forgetting how to talk, forgetting their parents, and thinking their interrogators were their parents.[44] His work was inspired and paralleled by the British psychiatrist William Sargant at St Thomas' Hospital, London, and Belmont Hospital, Surrey, who was also involved in the Intelligence Services and who experimented extensively on his patients without their consent, causing similar long-term damage.[45]

It was during this era that Cameron became known worldwide as the first chairman of the World Psychiatric Association as well as president of the American and Canadian psychiatric associations. Cameron had also been a member of the Nuremberg medical tribunal in 1946–47.[46] Naomi Klein argues in her book *The Shock Doctrine* that Cameron's research and his contribution to the MKUltra project was actually not about mind control and brainwashing, but about designing "a scientifically based system for extracting information from 'resistant sources.' In other words, torture."[47] Alfred W. McCoy writes that "Stripped of its bizarre excesses, Dr. Cameron's experiments, building upon Donald O. Hebb's earlier breakthrough, laid the scientific foundation for the CIA's two-stage psychological torture method," which refers to first creating a state of disorientation in the subject, and then second creating a situation of "self-inflicted" discomfort in which the disoriented subject can alleviate their pain by capitulating. [48]

Revelation

https://en.wikipedia.org/wiki/Project_MKUltra#/media/File:Mkultra-lsd-doc.jpg   PUBLIC DOMAIN

Frank Church headed the Church Committee, an investigation into the practices of the US intelligence agencies.
In 1973, with the government-wide panic caused by Watergate, the CIA Director Richard Helms ordered all MKUltra files destroyed.[49] Pursuant to this order, most CIA documents regarding the project were destroyed, making a full investigation of MKUltra impossible. A cache of some 20,000 documents survived Helms' purge, as they had been incorrectly stored in a financial records building and were discovered following a FOIA request in 1977. These documents were fully investigated during the Senate Hearings of 1977.[3]
In December 1974, *The New York Times* alleged that the CIA had conducted illegal domestic activities, including experiments on U.S. citizens, during the 1960s. That report prompted investigations by the U.S. Congress, in the form of the Church Committee, and by a presidential commission known as the Rockefeller Commission that looked into domestic activities of the CIA, the FBI, and intelligence-related agencies of the military.
In the summer of 1975, congressional Church Committee reports and the presidential Rockefeller Commission report revealed to the public for the first time that the CIA and the Department of Defense

had conducted experiments on both unwitting and cognizant human subjects as part of an extensive program to influence and control human behavior through the use of psychoactive drugs such as LSD and mescaline and other chemical, biological, and psychological means. They also revealed that at least one subject had died after administration of LSD. Much of what the Church Committee and the Rockefeller Commission learned about MKUltra was contained in a report, prepared by the Inspector General's office in 1963, that had survived the destruction of records ordered in 1973.[50] However, it contained little detail. Sidney Gottlieb, who had retired from the CIA two years previously, was interviewed by the committee but claimed to have very little recollection of the activities of MKUltra.[10]

The congressional committee investigating the CIA research, chaired by Senator Frank Church, concluded that "[p]rior consent was obviously not obtained from any of the subjects". The committee noted that the "experiments sponsored by these researchers ... call into question the decision by the agencies not to fix guidelines for experiments."

Following the recommendations of the Church Committee, President Gerald Ford in 1976 issued the first Executive Order on Intelligence Activities which, among other things, prohibited "experimentation with drugs on human subjects, except with the informed consent, in writing and witnessed by a disinterested party, of each such human subject" and in accordance with the guidelines issued by the National Commission. Subsequent orders by Presidents Carter and Reagan expanded the directive to apply to any human experimentation.

https://en.wikipedia.org/wiki/Project_MKUltra#/media/File:Mkultra-lsd-doc.jpg PUBLIC DOMAIN

1977 United States Senate report on MKUltra

In 1977, during a hearing held by the Senate Select Committee on Intelligence, to look further into MKUltra, Admiral Stansfield Turner, then Director of Central Intelligence, revealed that the CIA had found a set of records, consisting of about 20,000 pages,[citation needed] that had survived the 1973 destruction orders because they had been stored at a records center not usually used for such documents.[50] These files dealt with the financing of MKUltra projects and contained few project details, however much more was learned from them than from the Inspector General's 1963 report.

On the Senate floor in 1977, Senator Ted Kennedy said:

The Deputy Director of the CIA revealed that over thirty universities and institutions were involved in an "extensive testing and experimentation" program which included covert drug tests on unwitting citizens "at all social levels, high and low, native Americans and foreign." Several of these tests involved the administration of LSD to "unwitting subjects in social situations." At least one death, that of Dr. Olson, resulted from these activities. The Agency itself acknowledged that these tests made little scientific sense. The agents doing the monitoring were not qualified scientific observers.[51]

In Canada, the issue took much longer to surface, becoming widely known in 1984 on a CBC news show, *The Fifth Estate*. It was learned that not only had the CIA funded Dr. Cameron's efforts, but perhaps even more shockingly, the Canadian government was fully aware of this, and had later provided another $500,000 in funding to continue the experiments. This revelation largely derailed efforts by the victims to sue the CIA as their U.S. counterparts had, and the Canadian government eventually settled out of court for $100,000 to each of the 127 victims. None of Dr. Cameron's personal records of his involvement with MKUltra survived, since his family destroyed them after his death from a heart attack while mountain climbing in 1967.
[52][*not in citation given*]

1984 U.S. General Accounting Office report

The U.S. General Accounting Office issued a report on September 28, 1984, which stated that between 1940 and 1974, DOD and other national security agencies studied thousands of human subjects in tests and experiments involving hazardous substances.

The quote from the study:[53]

Working with the CIA, the Department of Defense gave hallucinogenic drugs to thousands of "volunteer" soldiers in the 1950s and 1960s. In addition to LSD, the Army also tested quinuclidinyl benzilate, a hallucinogen code-named BZ. (Note 37) Many of these tests were conducted under the so-called MKULTRA program, established to counter perceived Soviet and Chinese advances in brainwashing techniques. Between 1953 and 1964, the program consisted of 149 projects involving drug testing and other studies on unwitting human subjects

Deaths

Given the CIA's purposeful destruction of most records, its failure to follow informed consent protocols with thousands of participants, the uncontrolled nature of the experiments, and the lack of follow-up data, the full impact of MKUltra experiments, including deaths, will never be known.[23][28][53][54]

Several known deaths have been associated with Project MKUltra, most notably that of <u>Frank Olson</u>. Olson, a <u>United States Army</u> biochemist and <u>biological weapons</u> researcher, was given LSD without his knowledge or consent in November, 1953, as part of a CIA experiment and died under suspicious circumstances a week later. A CIA doctor assigned to monitor Olson claimed to have been asleep in another bed in a New York City hotel room when Olson exited the window and fell thirteen stories to his death. In 1953, Olson's death was described as a suicide that had occurred during a severe psychotic episode. The CIA's own internal investigation concluded that the head of MK ULTRA, CIA chemist Sidney Gottlieb, had conducted the LSD experiment with Olson's prior knowledge, although neither Olson nor the other men taking part in the experiment were informed as to the exact nature of the drug until some 20 minutes after its ingestion. The report further suggested that Gottlieb was nonetheless due a reprimand, as he had failed to take into account Olson's already-diagnosed suicidal tendencies, which might have been exacerbated by the LSD.[55]

The Olson family disputes the official version of events. They maintain that Frank Olson was murdered because, especially in the aftermath of his LSD experience, he had become a security risk who might divulge state secrets associated with highly classified CIA programs, about many of which he had direct personal knowledge.[56] A few days before his death, Frank Olson quit his position as acting chief of the Special Operations Division at Detrick, Maryland (later Fort Detrick) because of a severe moral crisis concerning the nature of his biological weapons research. Among Olson's concerns were the development of assassination materials used by the CIA, the CIA's use of biological warfare materials in covert operations, experimentation with biological weapons in populated areas, collaboration with former Nazi scientists under <u>Operation Paperclip</u>, LSD mind-control research, and the use of psychoactive drugs during "terminal" interrogations under a program code-named <u>Project ARTICHOKE</u>.[57] Later forensic evidence conflicted with the official version of events; when Olson's body was exhumed in 1994, cranial injuries indicated that Olson had been knocked unconscious before he exited the window. [55] The medical examiner termed Olson's death a "homicide".[58] In 1975, Olson's family received a $750,000 settlement from the U.S.

government and formal apologies from President Gerald Ford and CIA Director William Colby, though their apologies were limited to informed consent issues concerning Olson's ingestion of LSD.[54][59] On 28 November 2012, the Olson family filed suit against the U.S. federal government for the wrongful death of Frank Olson.[60]

In his 2009 book, *A Terrible Mistake*, researcher H. P. Albarelli Jr. concurs with the Olson family and concludes that Frank Olson was murdered because a personal crisis of conscience made it likely he would divulge state secrets concerning several CIA programs, chief among them Project ARTICHOKE and an MKDELTA project code-named Project SPAN. Albarelli theorizes that Project SPAN involved the contamination of food supplies and the aerosolized spraying of a potent LSD mixture in the village of Pont-Saint-Esprit, France in August, 1951. The 1951 Pont-Saint-Esprit mass poisoning resulted in mass psychosis, 32 commitments to mental institutions, and at least seven deaths. Albarelli writes that Olson was involved in the development of aerosolized delivery systems and had been present at Pont-Saint-Esprit in August, 1951. According to Albarelli, several months before resigning his position Olsen had witnessed a terminal interrogation conducted in Germany under Project ARTICHOKE. While most academic sources accept ergot poisoning, poisoning by mercury, mycotoxins, or nitrogen trichloride, as the cause of the Pont-Saint-Esprit epidemic,[61][62][63][64][65] others like paranormal author John Grant Fuller in *The Day of Saint Anthony's Fire* have reached conclusions similar to Albarelli's.[54][66]

On April 26, 1976, the Church Committee of the United States Senate issued a report, "Final Report of the Select Committee to Study Governmental Operation with Respect to Intelligence Activities".[67] In Book I, Chapter XVII, p 389 this report states:

> LSD was one of the materials tested in the MKUltra program. The final phase of LSD testing involved surreptitious administration to unwitting non-volunteer subjects in normal life settings by undercover officers of the Bureau of Narcotics acting for the CIA.

> A special procedure, designated MKDELTA, was established to govern the use of MKUltra materials abroad. Such materials were used on a number of occasions. Because MKUltra records were

destroyed, it is impossible to reconstruct the operational use of MKUltra materials by the CIA overseas; it has been determined that the use of these materials abroad began in 1953, and possibly as early as 1950.[68][69][70][71][72]

Drugs were used primarily as an aid to interrogations, but MKUltra/MKDelta materials were also used for harassment, discrediting, or disabling purposes.[68][69][70][71][72]

Legal issues involving informed consent

The revelations about the CIA and the Army prompted a number of subjects or their survivors to file lawsuits against the federal government for conducting experiments without informed consent. Although the government aggressively, and sometimes successfully, sought to avoid legal liability, several plaintiffs did receive compensation through court order, out-of-court settlement, or acts of Congress. Frank Olson's family received $750,000 by a special act of Congress, and both President Ford and CIA director William Colby met with Olson's family to apologize publicly.

Previously, the CIA and the Army had actively and successfully sought to withhold incriminating information, even as they secretly provided compensation to the families. One subject of Army drug experimentation, James Stanley, an Army sergeant, brought an important, albeit unsuccessful, suit. The government argued that Stanley was barred from suing under a legal doctrine—known as the Feres doctrine, after a 1950 Supreme Court case, _Feres v. United States_—that prohibits members of the Armed Forces from suing the government for any harms that were inflicted "incident to service."

In 1987, the Supreme Court affirmed this defense in a 5–4 decision that dismissed Stanley's case: _United States v. Stanley_.[73] The majority argued that "a test for liability that depends on the extent to which particular suits would call into question military discipline and decision making would itself require judicial inquiry into, and hence intrusion upon, military matters." In dissent, Justice William Brennan argued that the need to preserve military discipline should not protect the government from liability and punishment for serious violations of constitutional rights:

The medical trials at Nuremberg in 1947 deeply impressed upon the world that experimentation with unknowing human subjects is morally and legally unacceptable. The United States Military Tribunal established the Nuremberg Code as a standard against which to judge German scientists who experimented with human subjects... [I]n defiance of this principle, military intelligence officials ... began surreptitiously testing chemical and biological materials, including LSD.

Justice Sandra Day O'Connor, writing a separate dissent, stated:

No judicially crafted rule should insulate from liability the involuntary and unknowing human experimentation alleged to have occurred in this case. Indeed, as Justice Brennan observes, the United States played an instrumental role in the criminal prosecution of Nazi officials who experimented with human subjects during the Second World War, and the standards that the Nuremberg Military Tribunals developed to judge the behavior of the defendants stated that the 'voluntary consent of the human subject is absolutely essential ... to satisfy moral, ethical, and legal concepts.' If this principle is violated, the very least that society can do is to see that the victims are compensated, as best they can be, by the perpetrators.

In another lawsuit, Wayne Ritchie, a former United States Marshal, after hearing about the project's existence in 1990, alleged the CIA laced his food or drink with LSD at a 1957 Christmas party which resulted in his attempting to commit a robbery at a bar and his subsequent arrest. While the government admitted it was, at that time, drugging people without their consent, U.S. District Judge Marilyn Hall Patel found Ritchie could not prove he was one of the victims of MKUltra or that LSD caused his robbery attempt and dismissed the case in 2007.[74]

Extent of participation

Forty-four American colleges or universities, 15 research foundations or chemical or pharmaceutical companies including Sandoz (now Novartis) and Eli Lilly and Company, 12 hospitals or clinics (in addition to those associated with universities), and three prisons are known to have participated in MKUltra.[75][76]

Scientists involved

Harris Isbell [14]
Donald Ewen Cameron
Harold Alexander Abramson
Louis Jolyon West
Henry Murray

Notable subjects

Merry Prankster Ken Kesey, author of *One Flew Over the Cuckoo's Nest*, volunteered for MKUltra experiments involving LSD and other psychedelic drugs at the Veterans Administration Hospital in Menlo Park while he was a student at nearby Stanford University. Kesey's experiences while under the influence of LSD inspired him to promote the drug outside the context of the MKUltra experiments, which influenced the early development of hippie culture.[77][78]

Robert Hunter is an American lyricist, singer-songwriter, translator, and poet, best known for his association with Jerry Garcia and the Grateful Dead. Along with Ken Kesey, Hunter was an early volunteer MKUltra test subject at Stanford University. Stanford test subjects were paid to take LSD, psilocybin, and mescaline, then report on their experiences. These experiences were creatively formative for Hunter:

> Sit back picture yourself swooping up a shell of purple with foam crests of crystal drops soft nigh they fall unto the sea of morning creep-very-softly mist... and then sort of cascade tinkley-bell-like (must I take you by the hand, every so slowly type) and then conglomerate suddenly into a peal of silver vibrant uncomprehendingly, blood singingly, joyously resounding bells... By my faith if this be insanity, then for the love of God permit me to remain insane.[79]

Cathy O'Brien, author, claims to have been subjected to the program since childhood. She names several prominent government participants in her book *Trance Formation of America*

Candy Jones, American fashion model and radio host, claimed to have been a victim of mind control in the 1960s.[80]

Boston mobster James "Whitey" Bulger volunteered for testing while in prison at USP Leavenworth in 1963.[81]

Ted Kaczynski, Unabomber. From late 1959 to early 1962, Harvard psychologist Henry Murray was responsible for the ethically questionable, CIA-sponsored MK ULTRA experiments in which twenty-two Harvard undergraduates were used as research subjects.[82][83] Among other purposes, Murray's experiments focused on measuring people's reactions under extreme stress. The unwitting undergraduates were submitted to what Murray himself called "vehement, sweeping and personally abusive" attacks. Assaults to their egos, cherished ideas and beliefs were the vehicle used to cause high levels of stress and distress. Among them was 17-year-old Ted Kaczynski, who went on to become the Unabomber, a serial killer targeting academics and technologists. [84] Alston Chase's book Harvard and the Unabomber: The Education of an American Terrorist connects Kaczynski's abusive experiences under Murray to his later criminal career.

Conspiracy theories

MKUltra plays a part in many conspiracy theories due to its nature and the destruction of most records.[85]

Lawrence Teeter, attorney for convicted assassin Sirhan Sirhan, believed Sirhan was under the influence of hypnosis when he fired his weapon at Robert F. Kennedy in 1968. Teeter linked the CIA's MKUltra program to mind control techniques that he claimed were used to control Sirhan.[86][87][not in citation given]

Aftermath

At his retirement in 1972, Gottlieb dismissed his entire effort for the CIA's MKUltra program as useless.[24][88]

Although the CIA insists that MKUltra-type experiments have been abandoned, some CIA observers say there is little reason to believe it does not continue today under a different set of acronyms.[49] Victor Marchetti, author and 14-year CIA veteran, stated in various interviews that the CIA routinely conducted disinformation campaigns and that CIA mind control research continued. In a 1977 interview, Marchetti specifically called the CIA claim that MKUltra was abandoned a "cover story."[89][90]

In popular culture

Books

Bzrk, written by Michael Grant. Described in an artifact, an email, as, "Recent evidence suggests that MK-ULTRA also experimented with early versions of nanotechnology. When those efforts were frustrated by congressional budget cuts, the research was handed off to the Armstrong Fancy Gifts Corporation and their weapons division. All records of AFGC's involvement have been expunged. A number of individuals involved have died under suspicious circumstances."[91]

Film

Conspiracy Theory: A man obsessed with conspiracy theories becomes a target after one of his theories turns out to be true. Unfortunately, in order to save himself, he has to figure out which theory it is.

The Banshee Chapter: Anne investigates the links between her friend's disappearance, a secret government chemical and an odd radio broadcast with an unknown origin.

The Killing Room: Four individuals sign up for a psychological research study only to discover that they are now subjects of a brutal, classified government program.

"The Men Who Stare at Goats"

American Ultra: A stoner—who is in fact a mind-altered "sleeper" government operative—is marked as a liability and targeted for extermination. But he's too well-trained and too high for them to handle.

See also

 United States portal

International

Human experimentation in North Korea
Human radiation experiments
Nazi human experimentation
Poison laboratory of the Soviet secret services
Unethical human experimentation in the United States
Unit 731
Operations

Category:Central Intelligence Agency operations
COINTELPRO
Project MKCHICKWIT
Project MKOFTEN
Other

Harold Blauer

References

See weblink above

APPENDIX 2

WRITER: I had to add in this brave speech by Ex-Iranian President Mahmoud Ahmadinejad. I really admire him. The only world leader who I know of in modern times, who spoke out about what has been happening on this planet. But like all previous people who have spoken out about the Powers-that-be or who defied or went against them: they either failed or ended up dead or out of office. It is my wish that this book, and you the people reading it, will join together effectively to form the groups that can make the necessary changes that are needed around the world by putting the required amount of pressure on our governments, leaders and those high up. It MUST be a group action effort: self-funded groups working together. And of course, good, genuine people or leaders (independent of any vested interest or secret cause) can lead these groups and people to success and victory. These groups should also try and protect themselves from being infiltrated by the enemy or by being controlled or jailed or killed by the police or armies of those governments who serve the enemy. But eventually - reason, goodness, righteousness, good organization, love and plenty of luck and clever hard work will prevail and Man **_WILL_** be free again and he will remain free to develop and progress as he wishes: which should be upward in all spheres of life, spirituality, the mind, ethics and existence. This is my goal for writing this book for you, and, I hope it is yours too?

Ex-Iranian President Mahmoud Ahmadinejad's full speech to the UN:

All Praise Belongs to Allah, the Lord of the Worlds, and May Peace and Blessings be upon the Greatest and Trustworthy Prophet and His Pure Progeny, His Chosen

Companions, and upon all Divine Messengers.

Oh, God, Hasten the Emergence of Your Chosen Beloved, Grant Him Good

Health and Victory, Make us His Best Companions, and all those who attest to His

Rightfulness.

Mr. President,

Excellencies,

Ladies and Gentlemen,

I thank the Almighty God for having once more the chance to participate in this meeting. We have gathered here to ponder and work together for building a better life for the entire human community and for our nations.

Coming from Iran, the land of glory and beauty, the land of knowledge, culture, wisdom and morality, the cradle of philosophy and mysticism, the land of compassion and light, the land of scientists, scholars, philosophers,

masters of literature, and writers, the land of Avicenna, Ferdowsi, Hafiz, Maulana, Attar, Khayyam, and Shariar, I represent a great and proud nation that is a founder of human civilization and an inheritor of respected universal values. I represent a conscious nation which is dedicated to the cause of freedom, peace and compassion, a nation that has experienced the agony and bitter times of aggressions and imposed wars, and profoundly values the blessings of peace and stability. I am now here for the eighth time in the eighth year of my service to my noble people in this august assembly of sisters and brothers from across the world, to show to the world that my noble nation like its brilliant past, has a global vision and welcomes any effort intended to provide and promote peace, stability and tranquillity which can be only realized through harmony, cooperation and joint management of the world.

I am here to voice the divine and humanitarian message of learned men and women of my country to you and to the whole world; a message that Iran's great orator and poet, presented to humanity in his eternal two-line poetry:

Human beings are members of a whole,

In creation of one essence and soul,

If one member is afflicted with pain

Other members uneasy will remain,

I have talked in the past seven years about the current challenges, solutions and prospects of the future world. Today I want to raise and discuss such issues from a different perspective.

Thousands of years has passed since children of Adam (peace be upon Him)

started to settle down in various parts of Earth.

Peoples of different colors, tastes, languages, customs and traditions pursued persistently to fulfill their aspirations to build a noble society for a more beautiful life blessed with lasting peace, security and happiness.

Despite all efforts made by righteous people and justice seekers, and the sufferings and pains endured by masses of people in the quest to achieve happiness and victory, the history of mankind, except in rare cases, is marked with unfulfilled dreams and failures.

Imagine for a moment:

-Had there been no egoism, distrust, malicious behaviors, and dictatorships with no one violating the rights of others;

- Had humanitarian values been viewed as the criterion for social dignity in place of affluence and consumerism,

- Had humanity not experienced the dark age of medieval periods, and centers of power not hindered the flourishing of knowledge and constructive thoughts,

- Had the wars of Crusade and the ensuing periods of slavery and colonialism not happened, and had the inheritors of these dark periods followed a course on the premises of humanitarians principles,

- Had the first and second World Wars in Europe, the wars in Korea, Vietnam, Africa, Latin America, and in the Balkans not happened, and if instead of the occupation of Palestine and imposition of a fake government, displacement and genocide of millions of people around the globe, the truth behind these wars had been revealed based on justice,

- Had Saddam Hussein not invaded Iran, and had the big powers supported the rights of Iranian people instead of siding with Saddam,

- If the tragic incident of September 11, and the military actions against Afghanistan and Iraq that left millions killed and homeless had not happened, and if, instead of killing and throwing the culprit into the sea without trial or without informing the world and people of America, an independent fact-finding team had been formed to make the general public aware of the truth behind the incident, and prepare for bringing to justice the perpetrators,

- Had extremism or terrorism not been used to secure political goals,

- Had the arms been turned into pens, and military expenditures been used to

promote well-being and amity among nations,

- Had the drum of ethnic, religious or racial conflicts not been beaten, and if differences had not been used for the purpose of advancing political agendas,

- Had the right to criticize the hegemonic policies and actions of the world Zionism been recognized to allow the world media to freely report and shed light on the realities, instead of taking deceitful gestures of backing freedom bent on offending the sanctities and most sacred beliefs of human beings and divine messengers, who as the purest and most compassionate human beings are the gift of the Almighty to humanity,

- Had the Security Council not been under the domination of a limited number of governments, thus disabling the United Nations to carry out its responsibilities on a just and equitable basis,

- If the international economic institutions had not been under pressure and were allowed to perform their duties and functions by using their expertise based on fairness and justice,

Had the world capitalists not weakened or victimized the economies of nations in order to make up for their own mistakes,

482

- If integrity and honesty had prevailed on the international relations, and all nations and governments were treated equally and justly in the global efforts to build and expand happiness for the entire mankind,

- And if tens of other unfavorable situations had not occurred in human life,

- Imagine how beautiful and pleasant our lives and how lovely the history of mankind would have been.

- Let us take a look at the world situation today.

a): The Economic Situation

-Poverty is on the rise and the gap is widening between the rich and the poor.

-Total foreign debt of 18 industrial countries has exceeded 60 trillion dollars, whilst the repayment of half of this amount is sufficient to eradicate poverty in the world.

-Economies dependent on consumerism and exploitation of people only serve the interests of a limited number of countries.

-Creation of worthless paper assets by using influence and control over the world's economic centers constitutes the greatest abuse of history, and is considered a major contributor to global economic crisis.

-It has been reported that only 32 trillions of paper assets were printed by one government alone.

-Development planning based on capitalist economy that runs in a vicious circle, triggers unhealthy and devastating competitions and is a failed practice.

b) The Cultural Situation:

From the standpoint of the politicians who control the world power centers, concepts such as moral principles, purity, honesty, integrity, compassion and self-sacrifice are rejected as defunct and outdated notions, and an impediment to the accomplishment of their goals. They openly talk about their disbelief in the relevance of ethics to the political and social affairs.

Pure and indigenous cultures as the product of centuries - old efforts of nations, the common denominator reflecting human profound feeling and love towards beauties, and the force which breeds diversity, cultural vividness, and social dynamism, are under constant attacks, and susceptible to extinction.

A specific life style devoid of individual or social identity is being imposed on nations by organized and systematic destruction and humiliation of identities.

Family as the noblest institution of societies and a center emanating love and humanity has been seriously weakened and its constructive role is on the decline.

Woman's sublime role and personality, as a heavenly being, a manifestation of divine image and beauty, and the main pillar of every society, has been damaged and abused by the powerful and the wealthy.

Human soul has become frustrated and the essence of humankind humiliated and suppressed.

c): Political and Security.Situation

Unilateralism, application of double standards, and imposition of wars, instability and occupations to ensure economic interests, and expand dominance over sensitive centers of the world have turned to be the order of the day.

Arms race and intimidation by nuclear weapons and weapons of mass-destruction by the hegemonic powers have become prevalent: Testing new generations of ultra-modern weaponry and the pledge to disclose these armaments on due time is now being used as a new language of threat against nations to coerce them into accepting a new era of hegemony. Continued threat by the uncivilized Zionists to resort to military action against our great nation is a clear example of this bitter reality.

-A state of mistrust has cast its shadow on the international relations, whilst there is no trusted or just authority to help resolve world conflicts.

- No one feels secure or safe even those who have stockpiled thousands of atomic bombs and other arms in their arsenals.

d): The Environmental Situation

-The environment as a common wealth and heritage of the entire humankind and a constant guarantor of man's survival has been seriously damaged and devastated as a result of irresponsible and excessive use of resources particularly by capitalists across the world, a situation that has caused massive drought, flood, and pollutions inflicting irreparable damage and jeopardizing seriously human life on Earth.

Dear Colleagues,

Despite advances in scientific knowledge and technology, the aspirations of Adam's children have not yet been fulfilled.

Does anybody believe that continuation of the current order is capable of bringing happiness for human society.'?

Today everyone is discontent and disappointed with the current international order.

Dear Colleagues,

Human beings do not deserve to be under continued sufferings of the present situation. God of wisdom and compassion who loves all human beings has not

ordained such a destiny for mankind. He has ordered human, as the Supreme Creature, to make the best and most beautiful life on Earth along with justice, and dignity. We must, therefore, think of a solution.

Who is responsible for all these sufferings and failures?

Some people try to justify that everything is normal and a reflection of divine will, putting the blame on nations as responsible for all prevalent vices and evils.

They are of the opinion that:

-It is the nations that succumb to discrimination and tyranny;

-It is the nations that surrender to dictatorship and greed;

-It is the nations that accept the hegemony of Arrogant and expansionist powers;

-It is the nations that are influenced by the propaganda tactics of powers, and most all vices in our world are the result of their passive attitudes with the inclination to live under the supremacy of the world powers.

-These are the arguments raised by those who tend to blame nations for the unfavorable conditions prevailing in the world, with the intention to justify the attitudes and destructive behaviors of the ruling minority.

-These claims, supposedly authentic, cannot in any way justify continuation of the present oppressive international order. Indeed, Poverty is imposed on nations, and powers' ambitions and goals are pursued either through deceits or resort to force.

-To justify their inhuman actions, they propagate the theory based on 'the Survival of the fittest'.

-While in principle, most governments and nations of justice-seeking people are humble and submissive in the face of Right, and are after fostering dignity, prosperity and constructive interactions.

-Masses of people never want to expand their territories, nor do they seek to obtain legendary wealth. They have no disputes among themselves in principles and have never played any role in the creation of any disastrous events in the course of history.

-I do not believe that Muslims, Christians, Jews, Hindus, Buddhists, and others have any problems, or are hostile against each other. They get along together comfortably and live together in an atmosphere of peace and amity.

They are all devoted to the cause of justice, purity and love.

-The general tendency of nations has always been to accomplish positive common aspirations reflecting exalted divine and human beauties and nobilities.

-The current abysmal situation of the world and the bitter incidents of history are due mainly to the wrong management of the world and the self-proclaimed centers of power who have entrusted themselves to the Devil.

-The order that is rooted in the anti-human thoughts of slavery and the old and new colonialism are responsible for poverty, corruption, ignorance, oppression and discrimination in every corner of the world.

The current world order has certain characteristics, some of which are as follows:

- It is founded on materialism, and that is why it is in no way bound to moral values.

It has been shaped according to selfishness, deception, hatred and animosity.

3- It believes in classification of human beings, humiliation of other nations, trampling upon the rights of others and their domination.

_ It seeks to expand its domination by spreading discord and conflicts amongst ethnic groups and nations.

It aims to monopolize power, wealth, science and technology.

Policies of the world's main centers of power are based on the principles of domination and the conquering of others. These centers only seek supremacy, and are not in favor of peace and definitely not at the service of their nations.

-Are we to believe that those who spend hundreds of millions of dollars on election campaigns have the interests of the people of the world at their hearts?

-Despite what big political parties claim in the capitalistic countries, the money that goes into election campaigns is usually nothing but an investment.

-In such countries, people have to vote for parties that only represent a small number of people.

-The will and the views of the masses have the least impact and influence on the big decisions especially those made about the major domestic and foreign policies. Their voices are not heard even if they constitute 99% of their societies.

-Human and ethical values are sacrificed in order to win votes and the willingness to listen to the demands of the people has become only a tool at the time of election.

7- The current world order is discriminatory and based on injustice.

Distinguished Friends and Colleagues,

What should be done and what is the way out of the current situation?

There is no doubt that the world is in need of a new order and a fresh way of thinking:

1- An order in which man is recognized as God's Supreme Creature, enjoying material and spiritual qualities and possessing a pure and divine nature filled with a desire to seek justice and truth.

2- An order that aims to revive human dignity and believes in universal happiness and perfection.

_ An order which is after peace, lasting security and welfare for all walks of life around the globe.

An order that is founded upon trust and kindness and brings thoughts, hearts and hands closer to each other. Rulers must love people.

A just and fair order in which everybody is equal before law and in which there is no double standard.

Leaders of the world must regard themselves as committed servants of their people, not their superiors.

Authority is a sacred gift from people to their rulers, not a chance to amass power and wealth.

Mr. President, Ladies and Gentlemen,

Is it possible to have such an order without having everybody's contribution to the way the world is run?

It is abundantly evident that when all the people and governments start to think and commit themselves to the above-mentioned principles and become sensitive to the internationally important issues and participate in decision makings, their wishes find a chance to be materialized.

By raising collective awareness, the seeking of a joint global management becomes more vivid with the chances of its implementation increased.

Therefore, Together We Need to:

1-Place our trust in God Almighty and stand against the acquisitive minority with all our might, so that they become isolated, and can no longer decide the destiny of other nations.

2-Believe in the God's bounty of blessing and mercy and seek it in the integration and unity of human societies. Governments emerging from the free will of nations must believe in their own ceaseless capabilities and know that they can achieve victory if they vigorously fight the unjust order and defend human rights.

3-Pave the ground for the joint global management by insisting upon justice in all its aspects, strengthen unity, friendship and expand economic, social, cultural and political interactions in independent and specialized organizations.

4-Care about the interests of all the people of the world and join hands to reform the current structures of the UN with our joint efforts and coordination. It is necessary to note that the UN belongs to nations. Thus, the existence of discrimination amongst the members is a great insult to all. The existence of discrimination and monopoly in the UN is in no way acceptable.

5-Have more coordinated efforts to generate and propagate and firmly establish the language needed for designing the required structures of the joint global management filled with justice, love and freedom. Participation in global management is the basis of lasting peace. The Non-Aligned Movement as the second largest trans-regional group after the UN, held its 16th summit in Tehran with the motto of "Joint Global Management", cognizant of the importance of this issue and the shortcomings of the current mismanagement in the emergence of crises and problems afflicting the world today. During the Summit, participating Heads of State and representatives of more than 120 countries underscored the necessity of a more serious and effective participation of all nations in the global management.

-Fortunately, we are now at a historic juncture. On one hand, Marxism is no longer around and is practically eliminated from the management systems, and on the other, capitalism is bogged down in a self-made quagmire. It has indeed reached a deadlock and does not seem to be able to come up with any noteworthy solution to the various economic, political, security and cultural problems of the world. NAM is proud to once again emphasize the rightfulness of its historic decision to reject the poles of power and the unbridled hegemony ruling the world. On behalf of the members of NAM, I would like to invite all countries of the world to play a more active role in making it possible for everybody to contribute to the global decision-making processes. The need to remove the structural barriers and encourage the process of universal participation in global management has never been greater before.

The UN lacks the efficiency to bring about the required changes. If this inefficiency persists, nations will lose hope in the global structures to defend their rights. If the UN is not restructured, international interactions and the spirit of collective global cooperation will be tarnished and the standing of the UN will be damaged.

The UN that has been created with the purpose of expanding justice and reinstitution of the universal rights has in practice been engulfed by discrimination preparing a supportive ground for the domination of a few powerful countries.

Consequently, UN's inefficiency has been on the rise. Moreover, the existence of the veto right and monopolization of power in the Security Council have made it nearly impossible to defend the rights of the nations.

The issue of UN re-structuring is very vital and is a need that has been emphasized time and again by the representatives of nations, a goal that has not yet been accomplished.

I would like to urge the honorable members of the United Nations and H.E.. the Secretary General and his colleagues to place this issue high on their agenda and devise an appropriate mechanism to make it happen.

NAM stands ready to aid the UN in this essential endeavor.

Mr. President, Friends and Dear Colleagues,

Creating peace and lasting security with decent life for all, although a great and a historic mission can be accomplished. The Almighty God has not left us alone in this mission and has said that it will surely happen. If it doesn't, then it will be contradictory to his wisdom.

-God Almighty has promised us a man of kindness, a man who loves people and loves absolute justice, a man who is a perfect human being and is named Imam Al-Mahdi, a man who will come in the company of Jesus Christ (PBUH) and the righteous. By using the inherent potential of all the worthy men and women of all nations and I repeat, the inherent potential of "all the worthy men and women of all nations" he will lead humanity into achieving its glorious and eternal ideals.

-The arrival of the Ultimate Savior will mark a new beginning, a rebirth and a resurrection. It will be the beginning of peace, lasting security and genuine life.

-His arrival will be the end of oppression, immorality, poverty, discrimination and the beginning of justice, love and empathy.

-He will come and he will cut through ignorance, superstition, prejudice by opening the gates of science and knowledge. He will establish a world brimful of prudence and he will prepare the ground for the collective, active and constructive participation of all in the global management.

-He will come to grant kindness, hope, freedom and dignity to all humanity as a girl.

-He will come so mankind will taste the pleasure of being human and being in the company of other humans.

-He will come so that hands will be joined, hearts will be filled with love and thoughts will be purified to be at service of security, welfare and happiness for all.

-He will come to return all children of Adam irrespective of their skin colors to their innate origin after a long history of separation and division linking them to eternal happiness.

-The arrival of the Ultimate Savior, Jesus Christ and the Righteous will bring about an eternally bright future for mankind, not by force or waging wars but through thought awakening and developing kindness in everyone. Their arrival will breathe a new life in the cold and frozen body of the world. He will bless humanity with a spring that puts an end to our winter of ignorance, poverty and war with the tidings of a season of blooming.

-Now we can sense the sweet scent and the soulful breeze of the spring, a spring that has just begun and doesn't belong to a specific race, ethnicity, nation or a region, a spring that will soon reach all the territories in Asia, Europe, Africa and the US.

-He will be the spring of all the justice-seekers, freedom-lovers and the followers of heavenly prophets. He will be the spring of humanity and the greenery of all ages.

-Let us join hands and clear the way for his eventual arrival with empathy and cooperation, in harmony and unity. Let us march on this path to salvation for the thirsty souls of humanity to taste immortal joy and grace.

Long live this spring, long live this spring and long live this spring.

Thank you

CPSIA information can be obtained
at www.ICGtesting.com
Printed in the USA
LVHW051907020320
648718LV00001B/52